The
Visually Handicapped
Child in School

The
Visually Handicapped
Child in School

Edited by
BERTHOLD LOWENFELD

JOHN DAY BOOKS IN
SE
SPECIAL EDUCATION

THE JOHN DAY COMPANY *New York*
An Intext Publisher

Library of Congress Cataloging in Publication Data

Lowenfeld, Berthold.
  The visually handicapped child in school.

  (John Day books in special education)
  Includes bibliographies.
  1. Visually handicapped children—Addresses, essays, lectures. 2. Blind—Education—Addresses, essays, lectures. I. Title. [DNLM: 1. Education, Special. 2. Vision disorders—In infancy and childhood. 3. Vision disorders—Rehabilitation. HV 1626 L917v 1973]
  HB1626.L75   371.9'11   72-12303
  ISBN 0-381-97097-3

The John Day Company, 257 Park Avenue South, New York N.Y. 10010

Published on the same day in Canada by Longman Canada Limited.

Printed in the United States of America

Text design by Chris Simon

Contents

Chapter 2   **Psychological Considerations**   27

Berthold Lowenfeld

Chapter 3   **Understanding and Meeting Development Needs**   61

Geraldine T. Scholl

Chapter 6   **Educational Programs**   155

Josephine L. Taylor

Chapter 7   **Communication Skills**   185

Freda Henderson

Contents

Chapter 8 **Special Subject Adjustments and Skills** 221

Grace D. Napier

Chapter 9   **Life Adjustment**   279

Stanley Suterko

Contributing Authors

Natalie C. Barraga, Ed.D., is Professor and Coordinator, Program for Visually Handicapped, Department of Special Education, The University of Texas at Austin. She is Editor of *Education of the Visually Handicapped,* a member of Association for Education of the Visually Handicapped, Council for Exceptional Children, and a Fellow, American Academy of Optometry. Among other professional assignments, she is Consultant to the Divisions of Training and of Research, Bureau of Education for the Handicapped, U.S. Office of Education. Dr. Barraga is the author of *Increased Visual Behavior in Low Vision* Children and numerous articles.

Mary K. Bauman is Director of the Personnel Research Center in Philadelphia, Pennsylvania. She holds an M.S. degree from the University of Pennsylvania and is a Diplomate in Counseling and Guidance, American Board of Examiners in Professional Psychology, a Fellow of the American Psychological Association, a Certified Public School Psychologist, Commonwealth of Pennsylvania. Governor William Scranton appointed her to the State Board of Vocational Rehabilitation and to the Chairmanship of the Policy and Planning Board for Comprehensive Statewide Planning for Vocational Rehabilitation. She is a Past President of the Pennsylvania Rehabilitation Association and serves as Executive Secretary of the Association for Education of the Visually Handicapped. She is the author of *Adjustment to Blindness,* 1954; and co-author of a *Manual for the Psychological Examination of the Adult Blind,* of *Adjustment to Blindness—Re-viewed,* and of *Placing the Blind and Visually Handicapped in Professional Occupations.*

Philip H. Hatlen, M.A., is Associate Professor of Education, Department of Special Education, San Francisco State College. He has been a teacher of visually handicapped children, an administrator in a school for blind children, and is involved in various community activities on behalf of visually handicapped children. He has served as a consultant and panel participant to the Office of Education, Bureau of Education for the Handicapped. He is a consultant to various school districts in the San Francisco Bay Area and is a co-author of the book, *Blind Children Learn to Read.*

Freda Henderson holds her Ed.S. from George Peabody College for Teachers in Nashville, Tennessee. She is Elementary Supervisor at the Tennessee School for the Blind and a part-time instructor at George Peabody College in Nashville. In addition to her work with the visually handicapped, she has a background of experience teaching sighted children throughout the elementary and junior high school years. Miss Henderson is co-author of *Programmed Instruction in Braille.* She is currently serving as a member of the AEVH-AAWB Braille Authority; as a member of the AEVH Committee on Teacher Certification; and as a member of the Committee on Reading for the Blind for IRA.

Berthold Lowenfeld holds a Ph.D. degree from the University of Vienna in his native country of Austria. He began teaching blind children in the early 1920s and came to the United States in 1938. From 1939 to 1949 he was Director of Educational Research for the American Foundation for the Blind and served as Special Education Instructor at Teachers College, Columbia University and as Professor at many university summer sessions. From 1949 to 1964 he was the Superintendent of the California School for the Blind. Dr. Lowenfeld is a Fellow of the American Psychological Association and member of many professional organizations. He received the two highest awards in the United States for outstanding services to the blind: The Shotwell Memorial Award of the AAWB in 1965 and the Migel Medal of the American Foundation for the Blind in 1968. He is the author of many books and publications, among them *Our Blind Children—Growing and Learning with Them,* "Psychological Problems of Children with Impaired Vision" in *Psychology of Exceptional Children and Youth,* and is co-author of *Blind Children Learn to Read.*

Grace D. Napier, Ed.D., is Associate Professor of Special Education, University of Northern Colorado, Greeley. She has been instructor on the summer faculty, Department of Special Education and Rehabilitation, Syracuse University. She was formerly an itinerant Educational Counselor with the Department of Educational Services, New Jersey State Commission for the Blind, and teacher-houseparent at Royer-Greaves School for the Blind. Her professional affiliations include Teacher Education Division and Division for the Visually Handicapped of the Council for Exceptional Children, Association for Education of the Visually Handicapped, National Braille Association, and International Communications Society.

Ferne Root Roberts, M.A., is Assistant Professor, Program in Special Education, Hunter College of the City University of New York. She was formerly in the Special Education Department at Syracuse University, Associate in Education of the Visually Handicapped in the New York State Education Department, Director of the Program Development Division at the American Foundation for the Blind, and Director of The Teaching Resource Center of the Division of Teacher Education of the City University of New York. She is Second Vice-President of the Association for Education of the Visually Handicapped and a member of the Early Childhood Education Committee of the Council for Exceptional Children.

Geraldine T. Scholl is Professor of Education, School of Education, the University of Michigan. She holds a B.Mus. degree from Marygrove College, an M.Ed. from Wayne State University, and a Ph.D. from the University of Michigan. She also completed the Perkins-Harvard course for teachers of the blind. She was a braille class teacher in Grand Rapids, Michigan; a teacher of the emotionally disturbed at Hawthorn Center, Northville, Michigan; and elementary supervisor at the Michigan School for the Blind. She has served as Lecturer in the Department of Education at Sheffield (England) University and as Chief, Handicapped Children and Youth Section, U.S. Office of Education. She is a member of many professional organizations, among them the American Psychological Association.

Stanley Suterko, M.A., is Assistant Professor of Education, School of Education and Assistant Director, Institute of Blind Rehabilitation, Western Michigan University. He is consultant to the Veterans Administration and has served as consultant to agency and school programs for the visually handicapped. Mr. Suterko has conducted courses and workshops on orientation and mobility throughout the United States and international workshops in England and France. He established the Midlands Mobility Center at Birmingham, England while a faculty member of Nottingham University, Nottingham, England. He is past Chairman of the American Association of Workers for the Blind Mobility Interest Group and presently Chairman of the Orientation and Mobility Instructors Certification Committee.

Josephine L. Taylor, M.A., is Coordinator of the units on the visually handicapped, multihandicapped, and interrelated areas in the Division of Training Programs, Bureau of Education for the Handicapped, Office of Education, U.S. Department of Health, Education, and Welfare. She was formerly Director of Educational Services with the New Jersey Commission for the Blind, a teacher at Perkins School for the Blind, and a preschool counselor. Miss Taylor has also taught at Teachers College, Columbia University, San Francisco State College, and Jersey City State College. She has served as President of the National Braille Association, President of the New Jersey Conference on the Handicapped, member of the Board of Directors of the American Association of Instructors of the Blind, and various other professional organizations.

Foreword

Readers of this book will enjoy an adventure in shared experience because the knowledge of scholars who have devoted most of their lives to teaching visually handicapped youngsters has been made available in this one compact volume.

If one were to name the most outstanding thinkers and doers in special education for the visually handicapped in the United States, it is probable that the resultant list would include the authors of the eleven contributions selected and edited by Dr. Lowenfeld. Others may have made contributions of equal significance, but the authors chosen are representative of the best philosophies and techniques which have been evolved to date. Indeed, conception of this book itself was made possible by the significant changes brought about in the field by just such dedicated specialists.

In April, 1966 the Council for Exceptional Children's publication *Professional Standards for Personnel in the Education of Handicapped Children* used the term "visually handicapped" to designate the total range of visual loss. The acceptance of this term was long in coming and was the result of many committee sessions with leaders from the fields of the blind and the partially sighted. That hammering-out process laid the foundation for several important developments and attitudinal changes which are increasingly reflected in educational programs. One of the immediate effects was the much closer working relationship of personnel in the two formerly distinct areas of specialization. This resulted in new standards for the preparation of educational personnel, equipped to teach children within the entire range of visual handicap, from total blindness to high degrees of useful residual vision.

With this move to unified teacher training and school program planning, the long-felt need for a college level textbook became acute. The Education Committee of the National Society for the Prevention of Blindness and an ad hoc committee appointed by the American Foundation for the Blind met jointly to formulate the rationale for the book and to draw up a preliminary outline and time-table. As conceived by these two committees and subsequent leaders who participated in the planning, the book was designed to fill the need for an introductory text for university training programs in special education, rehabilitation counseling, social work, nursing, and parent education.

In a very real sense the chapters of this book are a distillation of career-long experiences with visually handicapped children and with educational program planning. Thus, this book fills a training need and at the same time provides historical perspective for a field which has witnessed disastrous events as well as profound and rapid changes in the past three decades: the advent and wane of retrolental fibroplasia; the outbreak of a major rubella epidemic; the development of local day school programs; the emergence of emphasis on full use of residual vision for reading and all other educational activities; the creation of special diagnostic and training programs for multiply handicapped children; the organization of unique teacher-training programs; the increase in materials and equipment resulting from the technology explosion.

This writer, being personally acquainted with all of the authors in this volume, knows them to be quite unaware of the esteem accorded them by their peers. On behalf of the American Foundation for the Blind he extends to them the deep appreciation of the organization itself and of the field in general for their participation. The Foundation especially salutes Dr. Berthold Lowenfeld for his eminently thorough job of selection, coordination, and editing. This major publication in the field of special education in one sense had its inception in the clear-headed and precise enunciations of this man, made over a period of many years.

To those readers then about to share the experiences described herein, we wish as truly satisfying a professional career as the authors seem to have enjoyed; for these readers in turn will become the leaders of tomorrow to the everlasting benefit of visually handicapped children.

M. Robert Barnett
EXECUTIVE DIRECTOR
AMERICAN FOUNDATION FOR THE BLIND, INC.

CHAPTER 1

History of the Education of Visually Handicapped Children

Berthold Lowenfeld

INTRODUCTION

Organized efforts to educate blind children are of comparatively recent date. It was not until 1784 that the first school for blind children was established. This, however, was the result of changes in living conditions of the blind and in societal attitudes toward them which occurred and developed over hundreds, and indeed, thousands of years. Before going into the history of the education of visually handicapped children as such, we will review the four distinct phases in the evolution of the status of the blind in society: separation; ward status; self-emancipation; and integration.

Separation

In tribal life and in primitive societies, individuals who could not provide for themselves or take care of their own defense were generally considered a liability to the tribe or group. They were separated from their group and this separation took two forms: annihilation and veneration. In such centers of

1

early Western civilization as Sparta, Athens, and Rome, blind children and children with other defects were put to death in various ways. This practice was generally accepted, legally sanctioned, and theoretically approved by such philosophers as Plato, Aristotle, and Seneca. On the other hand, there were some blind people in ancient times who were venerated by their contemporaries, as in the case of Homer and the prophets Tiresias and Phineus. This veneration was the benevolent form of separation, though it, too, removed the blind individual from his normal place in society.

Ward Status

The advent and rise of the monotheistic religions led into the second phase, in which the blind were protected and regarded as wards of society. The Old Testament has many protective precepts and the early Christian communities considered children (particularly orphans), the aged, and the blind as special wards of the Church. (These three groups are still singled out as special categories in modern social welfare legislation.) Under the auspices of the Church, asylums and hospitals were founded, such as the one by St. Basil in Caesarea-in-Cappadocia (369 A.D.) to which the blind were also admitted. However, most of the blind were left to a beggar's lot and depended on alms from the Church. During the Middle Ages, a number of hospices were founded exclusively for the blind, among them the Quinze-Vingts, which was opened in 1254 by St. Louis, reportedly for blind Crusaders. In these institutions, the blind were organized in quasi-brotherhoods. Such brotherhoods also existed in Italy, Spain, Germany, and Scandinavia under the patronage of various saints.

Self-Emancipation

Under the protection of this ward status, some blind individuals became well known as bards, singers, and musicians. From the beginning of the eighteenth century, there appeared throughout the Western world blind individuals who by their own efforts not only acquired an education but also became outstanding in various fields of endeavor. Some of them had understanding and imaginative tutors during their youth who assisted them in adapting the tools of learning to their needs. Among these blind self-emancipators were such illustrious persons as the mathematician, Nicholas Saunderson (1682–1739), a Yorkshire man who became Lucasian Professor of Mathematics at Cambridge; John Metcalf (1717–1810), an English road engineer and bridge builder; Thomas Blacklock (1721–1791), a Scotch poet and minister; François

Huber (1750–1831), a Swiss naturalist who specialized in the life of bees; and Maria Theresia von Paradis (1759–1824), a famous Viennese singer and pianist. Many of these self-emancipators devised various ways of writing, doing arithmetic and even higher mathematics, corresponding with each other, and making embossed maps and other appliances individually needed by them.

As we shall see, their achievements and other factors, such as the Enlightenment (i.e., the influence of Diderot, Rousseau, and the other Encyclopedists), created the preconditions for the founding of organized educational facilities for blind children. This ultimately led to the fourth phase, that of integration, for which we are still striving.

Integration

Before dealing more extensively with the developments leading to and affecting the education of blind children, some important changes in the field of work for the adult blind will be discussed that are significant for the trend toward integration. Foremost among them is the great change which has taken place in vocational rehabilitation and its underlying philosophy. In the past, it was generally assumed that "the blind" could do only certain types of work, for which they were prepared in schools and workshops for the blind. Thus, they were occupationally segregated. Our present-day approach is to determine where the individual blind person's aptitudes and interests lie, to provide training in the kind of work for which he is best suited—no matter whether any blind person has done it before, and then to assist him in being placed in the field for which he has been successfully trained. This approach has brought about an influx of blind people into industry, private enterprise, and the professions, resulting in increased occupational integration.

About half a century ago, most agencies for the blind conducted, as an essential part of their services, homes for the blind—sometimes two, one for men and one for women. Now we find that most of these institutions have ceased to operate and that more blind people than ever before live with their families as members of their communities.

Mobility instruction did not come about by chance during the past decades. When the life circle of most blind people was confined to a narrow environment such as the school, the workshop, and a home for the blind, mobility was of no great importance. Now that blind individuals are expected to move about in the normal environment of men, mobility is essential. In the course of the rehabilitation of war-blinded personnel, mobility training techniques were developed, making use of the long Hoover cane, which functions as a probe and a bumper (Hoover, 1950). These techniques have been refined and systemized so that they now constitute a specialized field of instruction for which training facilities are available at the college level. Mobility training is offered by an increasing number of agencies and schools as the most important technique for restoring to blind persons a measure of mobility freedom. It is an indispensable element in increasing the independence of the blind individual, thus promoting his integration into the normal stream of life. (See the discussion of orientation and mobility in Chapter 9.)

College education has become much more common since World War II and the number of blind students attending regular colleges and universities has also greatly increased. Fortunately, the United States has never provided a segregated college for the blind, but has always adhered to the policy of providing higher education for blind students in regular colleges and universities.

Blind people themselves have assumed an increasing role in organizations promoting the interests of the blind. Also, professionalization in work for the blind has made noticeable progress, moving efforts on behalf of the blind away from the beneficiary–philanthropic era toward that of social responsibility.

Last but not least, changes in social welfare and other legislation have occurred which promote integration. Jacobus tenBroek (1966), the noted blind scholar and leader, summed it up by saying

> It is abundantly clear that integration of the disabled is the policy of the nation. This policy has been expressed by Congress and by the state legislatures, not once, but many times, and not merely with respect to a single, narrow area of human endeavor, but with respect to the whole broad range of social, economic, and educational activity backed up with numerous specially created agencies and instrumentalities of government, with affirmative assistance and negative prohibitions, and with vast expenditures of money amounting to hundreds of millions of dollars each year [p. 847].

Integration is not yet an established fact and many individual and societal acts toward the blind and toward blind individuals are the result of previous but not extinct stages and attitudes. From the sequence historically outlined, we can gain a criterion for what is desirable and undesirable in work for the blind:

> Institutions and services for blind individuals, unimpeded by further handicaps, which separate the blind and keep them separated, are regressive. Even though they may be temporarily beneficial to a blind individual, they are undesirable and inimical to the interest of the blind. Institutions and services which aim at the integration of the blind and instill in them the spirit of independence and strengthen those qualities and skills which will enable them to take their rightful place as members of their society are progressive, desirable and in the best interest of the blind [Lowenfeld, 1950, pp. 19–20].

EARLY EDUCATIONAL INSTITUTIONS

Sporadic efforts to educate individual blind persons from their childhood on can be traced back over many centuries. French (1932) reports

> The first important instance of the education of a blind person is that of Didymus of Alexandria, who lived during the fourth century of the Christian era. Didymus won some reputation both as a theologian and as a teacher [p. 66].

We have already mentioned a number of self-emancipators, some of whom undoubtedly had the assistance of teachers and tutors in acquiring an education. By the end of the eighteenth century, the forces of enlightenment had created an intellectual atmosphere and a moral and social consciousness providing the soil in which the seed of organized education for blind children could grow.

Haüy and the First School for the Blind in Europe

Valentin Haüy (1745–1822), pronounced Aw-ee, completed his education in Paris, where he was exposed to the intellectual and social forces which resulted in the French Revolution. He became early aware of the contrast between poverty and wealth. Inspired by the efforts of Abbé de L'Epée in the education of the deaf, he resolved, when only 26 years old, to devote himself to the improvement of conditions for the blind. A personal experience with the degrading and cruel treatment of blind beggars by a Parisian mob, and his acquaintance with Maria Theresia von Paradis, who enchanted French society, supplied the immediate motivation for Haüy's resolution to provide education for blind children. He tutored his first pupil, François Lesueur, but the difference between Haüy and others who had in the past assisted individual blind students was that he did so in order to develop a school for blind children. His efforts were successful and in 1784 he established, with 14 pupils, the first school for the blind, L'Institution Nationale des Jeunes Aveugles, in Paris. Its significance was well described in a report to the Academy of Sciences as having opened "for them, if one may be permitted so to speak, the entrée to the society of other men" (French, 1932, p. 84). Haüy's efforts were guided by his conviction that the education of blind children should be patterned after that of seeing children. Thus, instruction at the Institute followed closely the methods and curriculum of French schools in general. Haüy must also be credited with the invention of embossed printing. After he had observed that his pupil François could recognize printed letters by touch by feeling their embossed negative on the back of the pages, he developed negative typecasts which produced embossed characters. After that he experimented with the simplification of these characters to make them more legible by touch. However, they were "talking to the fingers the language of the eye" (Villey, 1930, p. 39), and it remained for a blind man, Louis Braille, to devise a touch-adequate system of reading and writing for the blind.

In his *Essai sur l'Education des Aveugles* (1786), Haüy (1967) discussed the methods by which he taught writing, arithmetic, geography, music, and handicrafts for occupational purposes. In most of these areas, experiences and achievements of blind people were known, particularly those of Maria Theresia von Paradis, Saunderson, and Weissenburg, an inventive blind German student. Haüy discounted them because he wanted to preserve "the strictest analogy possible between the means of educating the blind and those who see" (p. 189). So far as industrial arts are concerned, spinning, weaving, knitting, sewing, basketry, chair-caning, bookbinding, and printing were among those taught at the school in Paris as future vocational pursuits. Thus, Haüy set the example which influenced teaching and vocational training in residential schools for many decades to come, and in some countries it is followed even at the present time.

Haüy fell into disfavor with Napoleon and left Paris in 1806. He assisted August Zeune in the opening of a school for the blind in Berlin; he also went to Russia, where Emperor Alexander I asked him to assist in the planning of a school for the blind in St. Petersburg. In 1817, he returned to Paris to join his brother René, a famous mineralogist, and died there, almost completely forgotten, in 1822.

Following the example set by Haüy in Paris, schools for the blind were established in 1791 in Liverpool, in 1793 in Bristol and Edinburgh, and in 1804 in Vienna, where Johann Wilhelm Klein (1765–1848) founded the famous Imperial School for the Education of Blind Children. Klein was also productive as a writer and published the first extensive textbook on the instruction of the blind in 1819. Subsequently, schools for the blind came into existence in many larger European cities.

The Founding of Residential Schools for the Blind in the United States

It took a comparatively long time until the example of the first European schools for the blind was followed in the United States. The three great Eastern private schools for the blind were founded at almost the same time. The New England Asylum for the Blind (soon to be named Perkins Institution and Massachusetts Asylum for the Blind) was incorporated in 1829 and opened in July 1832 in Boston; the New York Institution for the Blind was incorporated in 1831 and opened in March 1832 in New York City; and the Pennsylvania Institution for the Instruction of the Blind was founded and opened in 1833 in Philadelphia and moved in 1899 to Overbrook.

The men who were instrumental in the movement that led to the establishment of these three schools were Samuel Gridley Howe, the first director of what is now Perkins School for the Blind; John D. Russ, the first superintendent of the present New York Institute for the Education of the Blind; and Julius R. Friedlander, the first principal of what became the Overbrook School for the Blind. Of these three "founding fathers," Samuel Gridley Howe was undoubtedly the most important, influential, innovative, and adventurous.

Samuel Gridley Howe (1801–1876), brought up in a Boston family, attended Brown University and began medical studies at Harvard Medical School. Before entering practice he decided to go to Greece and to take part in its struggle for independence. On his return to Boston in 1831, he was engaged by the corporation of the New-England Asylum for the Blind as the man best suited to start its work "to educate sightless persons." Howe went to Europe in order to become acquainted with some of the outstanding schools for the blind that were already in existence and in this task showed remarkable discrimination, summing up his impressions that in general the schools there can serve as "beacons to warn rather than lights to guide." At the same time he showed tendencies which would continue all his life, and which in a lesser man would have been ruinous. Becoming deeply concerned over Polish refugees interned in Prussia, he impetuously visited that country in their behalf, was imprisoned as a dangerous radical, and was only extricated from this situation by the aging Lafayette, who tactfully suggested that he come back to America and look after liberty here.

The positive results of his visits to European schools have been summed up as follows.

1. That each blind child must be considered as an individual and be trained in accordance with his personal ability and opportunity to use the training in his community.
2. That the curriculum of a school for the blind should be well rounded and conform insofar as possible to that of the common schools, but that more music and crafts should be provided.
3. That the main objective must be to train blind youth to be able to take their places in the social and economic life of their home communities as contributing members [Farrell, 1956, p. 45].

Like Haüy, Howe began his educational adventure on a limited scale—with two blind girls, Abby and Sophia Carter, who proved to be bright and curious pupils. From these small beginnings, the Asylum grew into a school that served increasing numbers of blind children. Howe issued annual reports of the school which contained some of his most enlightened observations. He recognized early that helping blind children to grow into productive adults relieves the public from supporting them by taxation of the community; that physical education is an important part of blind children's upbringing because of their natural tendency to physical inactivity; that even neglect is better than excessive attention and coddling, since it does not stunt the blind child's inquisitiveness.

Besides forming a new approach to the education of blind children at his own school, Howe's activities in the field of education of the blind branched out in two other directions. He became a promoter of schools for blind children in other states by demonstrating to their legislators the achievements of blind children brought up at his own school. This resulted in the founding of the first state-supported school for blind children in Ohio in 1837, followed by others in Kentucky, South Carolina, and other states. Howe also became the first educator in America to devote himself to the education of a deaf and blind child, Laura Bridgman, who came to his school in 1837. His extensive and perceptive reports about her development and education are an invaluable source of knowledge as well as inspiration for the education of deaf–blind children.

As Howe continued to develop Perkins, he also evolved his progressive conception of the education of blind children. One of his most memorable documents was the address he delivered at the laying of the cornerstone of the New York State Institution for the Blind at Batavia in 1866 (Howe, 1965). The following quotation from this address is characteristic of Howe's basic attitude toward residential school living.

> All great establishments in the nature of boarding schools, where the sexes must be separated; where there must be boarding in common, and sleeping in congregate dormitories; where there must be routine, and formality, and restraint, and repression of individuality; where the charms and refining influences of the true family relation cannot be had,—all such institutions are unnatural, undesirable, and very liable to abuse. We should have as few of them as is possible, and those few should be kept as small as possible [p. 182].

Besides his activities connected with the education of blind and deaf–blind children, which included the invention of the Boston Line Type (discussed in the following section), Howe involved himself in many civil activities, such as the teaching of articulation for deaf mutes, resulting in the establishment of the Clarke Institution for the Deaf at Northampton, Massachusetts; the promotion of public school education for all children; the Abolitionist movement; the improvement of provisions for the insane; and, while serving in the Massachusetts Legislature, the investigation and improvement of prison facilities. It can well be said that no other man in the field of the education of the blind has contributed so much and so widely as Samuel Gridley Howe.

At the time of Howe's death, more than 20 schools for blind children had been established. By now practically every state has at least one residential school for blind children. One could ask why the education of blind children began to be available in the form of residential school facilities. Two main reasons might be given as an explanation. First, the task of educating blind children appeared to be such a massive undertaking that only a completely blind-oriented school seemed to promise success. Second, public schools were not as common as they are today, nor did they have teachers trained to relate to blind children and provide solutions to their educational problems. In fact, residential schools proved effective and remained much attended as the only medium for educating blind children for more than 100 years.

READING AND WRITING

Before turning to the development of public school facilities, we must discuss one of the preconditions to make any education of blind children comparable to that of the seeing—a workable system of reading and writing. "Prehistoric" efforts to enable blind persons to read or to communicate with others date back over many hundreds of years. Writing on wax tablets, having a blind person follow the shape of letters carved in wood, forming letters with wire, using knots of varying thicknesses and at different distances on a thread, and pinpricking letters tangible in relief into felt or paper are some of the ways used for reading in the past. Even a system of movable lead type producing raised letters was tried as early as 1640 (Ross, 1951). As already mentioned, Haüy used letters cast in reverse for embossed letter printing and he had his students use a metal pen with a rounded tip to write raised letters in reverse form on the back of heavy paper. Haüy modified certain letters of the alphabet and used a system of abbreviations by putting either a line above the letter or a dot below it. Howe also developed an embossed letter type, the Boston Line Type, which is an angular modification of Roman letters. Books in this type were printed at Perkins from 1853 on by the first American printing press for the blind. Boston Line Type remained dominant in the United States for five decades. The only surviving embossed line system is that of Dr. William Moon, a blind man from Kent, England. Except for eight unaltered letters, Moon Type characters either have some letter parts left out or are new simple forms of the conventional letters. It was printed with one line running from left to right and the following line from right to left, so that no effort was lost on return sweeps.

Louis Braille and His System

Louis Braille (1809–1852) grew up in the small village of Coupvray near Paris in the family of a harness maker. When he was three years old, he hurt one of his eyes while playing with one of his father's knives and soon afterward he lost his sight completely in both eyes. He received his first education in his local school and it is reported that his father made embossed letters for him with upholsterer's nails driven into a board (Roblin, Illustration 22). When he was 10 years old, he entered the Institution Royale des Jeunes Aveugles in Paris as a pupil and remained there, as a teacher, until he died of tuberculosis. Since 1952, Louis Braille's body has rested in the Pantheon in Paris among the immortals of France.

As with many inventions, Braille's system was based on the concept of another contemporary, the Frenchman Charles Barbier, an officer in the French army. Barbier wanted to find a means by which messages could be read in the dark of night. For this purpose, he conceived the use of embossed dots to be read by touch. His "Ecriture Nocturne" consisted of 12 dots, six vertical dots in two rows, and it was a phonetic system. For the purpose of writing it, he devised a slate and a stylus in essentially the form in which they are still used for writing braille. Louis Braille knew Barbier's system because it was demonstrated and experimented with at the Institution in Paris. He must have recognized that the vertical six-dot arrangement of the Barbier cell was too high to be covered by the fingertips. It was a stroke of genius that he reduced the cell to three dots in a two-row arrangement and designed an alphabet within this basic six-dot cell. Later experiments provided evidence that this arrangement is the one most suitable for touch reading. By 1834, Braille had worked out his system of reading, as well as that of musical notation. It became officially accepted at the French school only in 1854, two years after Braille's death, and as time passed it was adapted to most other languages.

The Missouri School for the Blind in St. Louis was the first American school to adopt braille, in or about 1869, after Dr. Simon Pollak, a Board member, had introduced it. The final adoption and codification of the system did not occur until 1932, when an agreement was signed between the British and the Americans to adopt Standard English Braille as the uniform type. The adoption was delayed for so long by what has been called the Battle of the Dots and the Battle of Contractions.

The Battle of the Dots aligned those who were in favor of braille, a logically designed system which did not take letter frequency into account, against New York Point and American Braille. New York Point used a cell of only two vertical dots, but extending horizontally to a maximum of four dots (known as a "variable base"). Its letter symbols were assigned so that the more frequently occurring letters had the least number of dots. New York Point was sponsored primarily by William Bell Wait, the Superintendent of the New York Institute for the Blind. American Braille kept the braille cell but assigned its combinations of dots on the basis of frequency of letter occurrence. It provided for capitalization by an easily legible dot prefix.

Howe was guilty of a great man's great error in absolutely rejecting braille,

Braille, as officially approved, comprises two grades.*   Grade 1 Braille is in full spelling and consists of the letters of the alphabet, punctuation, numbers, and a number of composition signs which are special to braille.   Grade 2 Braille consists of Grade 1 and 189 contractions and short-form words, and should be known as "English Braille." However, uncontracted braille should be designated as "English Braille Grade 1."   Below is a complete chart of the braille characters and their meanings:

ALPHABET AND NUMBERS

1	2	3	4	5	6	7	8	9	0
a	b	c	d	e	f	g	h	i	j

k	l	m	n	o	p	q	r	s	t

u	v	w	x	y	z

PUNCTUATION AND COMPOSITION SIGNS

Sign	Meaning	Sign	Meaning
,	comma	'	opening single quotation mark
;	semicolon	*	asterisk
:	colon	"	closing double quotation mark
.	period	'	closing single quotation mark
!	exclamation	/	bar; oblique stroke; fraction-line sign
( )	opening and closing parentheses	#	number sign
[	opening bracket	'	apostrophe
]	closing bracket	. . .	ellipsis
" ?	opening double quotation; question mark	-	hyphen
—	dash		letter sign
——	long dash		capital sign
	accent sign		double capital sign
	italic sign; decimal point		termination sign
	double italic sign		

*For other grades of braille, see Appendix C.

which he branded "Choctaw"; he opposed its adoption at the Perkins School right up until his death in 1876. Michael Anagnos, his son-in-law and successor at Perkins School for the Blind, though continuing the use of Howe's Boston Line Type, approved Joel W. Smith's experiments with American Braille. Books in Boston Line Type only began to disappear after 1900, and almost equal numbers of American schools for blind children used either New York Point or American Braille.

The Battle of Contractions arose because the Americans and the British had worked out different grades of braille—Grade 1 fully spelled out, Grade 1½ with a limited number of contractions, Grade 2 moderately contracted, and Grade 3 highly contracted. Grade 1½ was an American invention based on the assumption that the more contracted Grade 2 was too difficult to learn and needed an intermediate form. Finally, after long and acrimonious struggles Louis Braille's alphabet and Grade 2 (Standard English Braille) prevailed.

While the Battle of the Dots was raging, Frank H. Hall (1841–1911), superintendent of the Illinois School for the Blind, completed a mechanical braillewriter in 1892, using features of the first commercial typewriter. Hall's machine had a moving carriage, and braille letters were embossed by pressing down those of the six keys which were required for the dot combinations particular to the various letters. The machine had, therefore, a simple keyboard consisting of three keys on the left and three keys on the right, representing the six dots of the cell, with a spacebar in between. Hall also developed a braille stereotype machine which embossed braille on metal plates and made possible the printing of braille. Since then, the printing of braille has undergone many changes. In the 1920s, the American Foundation for the Blind developed machinery for interpoint printings of braille in order to print on both sides of a page. This reduced cost by 40% and made for less bulky braille publications. The latest development is the printing of braille by computers.

Although many types of mechanical braillewriters are available in different parts of the world, the Perkins Brailler developed in 1950 by the Howe Press of the Perkins School for the Blind is generally recognized as the best-designed and easiest to operate mechanical braillewriter presently available. By 1969, 50,000 Perkins Braillers had been produced.

The slate and stylus are still widely used by the blind as equivalent to the pencil–paper notetaking of the seeing. Slates are available in various sizes and designs to meet various requirements.

American Printing House for the Blind

Founded in 1858 as the oldest national agency for the blind in the United States, the American Printing House for the Blind provides books and educational materials on a quota basis for blind children and youth being educated in either local or residential schools in the United States. Largely through the efforts of the American Association of Instructors for the Blind (now the Association for Education of the Visually Handicapped), Congress passed in 1879 the act "To Promote the Education of the Blind" and provided a grant of $10,000 per year to the American Printing House for the Blind for the previously mentioned purposes. The present annual appropriation is more than 100 times that of the original one. The American Printing House for the Blind annually registers all eligible blind children enrolled in public educational facilities and determines on the basis of the appropriation from Congress an annually current per capita quota for each student. Educational facilities are assigned a multiple of that quota corresponding to their enrollment and can order books and materials according to their needs. Three administrative committees guide its activities: the Publications Committee, the Tangible Aids Committee, and the Committee on Educational Research. Besides its official obligations, the American Printing House for the Blind is engaged in various private printing and production activities. It also has available and keeps up to date a Central Catalog of Volunteer-Transcribed Textbooks. (See American Foundation for the Blind: *Sources of Reading Material for the Visually Handicapped.*)

Library of Congress

The Library of Congress, Division for the Blind and Physically Handicapped, has received since 1931 an annual appropriation from Congress to provide free reading materials to the blind. The Division selects and orders embossed and recorded books and directs their distribution to regional libraries serving blind and physically handicapped people in the United States, its Territories, and its insular possessions. These libraries function as distributing centers. The Division keeps an up-to-date *Union Catalog of Volunteer-Produced Non-Textbook Materials* for the blind and lists general literature in the *Braille Book Review* and *Talking Book Topics.* (See American Foundation for the Blind: *Sources of Reading Materials for the Visually Handicapped.*)

PUBLIC SCHOOL EDUCATION FOR
VISUALLY HANDICAPPED CHILDREN

Provisions for Blind Children

Of the three great men who founded residential schools for the blind—Haüy, Klein, and Howe—the two last-mentioned envisioned and seriously considered the education of blind children in regular schools.

As early as 1810, Johann Wilhelm Klein advocated that places be reserved for blind children in the local schools for the seeing. When complaints were voiced that no guidance was available for teachers on how to teach these children, Klein wrote in 1819 his previously mentioned *Textbook for the Education of the Blind.* One of his later publications is entitled *Guide to Provide for Blind Children the Necessary Education in the Schools of Their Home Communities and in the Circle of Their Families* (1836; revised edition, 1845). He reported the following decree by the government of Lower Austria, dated December 30, 1842, which undoubtedly was influenced, if not written, by him as the highest official concerned with the education of blind children.

> According to experiences the existing institutions for the blind are insufficient to accept all the blind who are in need of education. Those who are accepted must as a rule be removed from their home conditions and be transferred into an environment strange to them until then. There they become acquainted with desires and habits of a kind which they cannot satisfy in their future lives. Therefore, the need is obvious that education of blind children according to their needs be provided in their parental home and in the school of their community, and that education of the blind be whenever possible incorporated into the regular institutions for the people's education, the public schools [Klein, 1845, p. 26, translation by author].

Johann Wilhelm Klein discussed in some detail the question of teacher training and considered cooperation between schools for the blind and teacher training institutions the most desirable solution to this problem. He also discussed possibilities for special teacher education if the school for the blind and the teacher training institutions were not in the same community or if one or the other was not available.

Klein's efforts on behalf of public school education for blind children did not meet with lasting success, though the residential school which he founded in Vienna became one of the most famous in the world.

Samuel Gridley Howe's attitude toward residential schools has already been cited. A further quotation from his 1866 Batavia address indicates that he was positively in favor of public school education:

> In deciding upon who are to be received as pupils, you should first ascertain how many of the applicants are really blind, and then, instead of imitating the example of ordinary institutions, and getting as many into the school as possible, you should receive as few as possible; that is, you should reject every one who can be taught in common schools. And here, it should be remarked, that it is much easier to have children who are partially blind, and even those totally blind, received and taught in common schools than it was formerly, because the existence of Institutions for the Blind during the third of a century has familiarized people with the fact that sight is not essential for instruction in the common

branches. A great many persons have become acquainted with the methods used in the Institutions, and with the use of books in raised letters. I am constantly applied to by teachers to know how to proceed with a blind child; and I always encourage them to keep it at home, and let it go to the common school as long as possible [Howe, 1866, p. 185].

Howe's admonitions, like Klein's, went unheeded. It took other influences to bring about the placement of blind children in regular educational facilities.

While some European countries experimented with the placement of blind pupils in public schools, primarily in Scotland and London, pragmatic American education began to develop a system of braille classes for blind children in the public schools, the first of which opened in 1900 in Chicago. It is significant that its inception was due largely to the efforts of three men, two of whom were blind, John B. Curtis and Edward J. Nolan. The third man responsible for the Chicago braille class was the superintendent of the Illinois School for the Blind, Frank H. Hall, who had supported braille against New York Point and had invented the first mechanical braillewriter and the first stereotype machine.

There were three main factors which favored the establishment of braille classes in public schools: (1) the increasing integration of the blind into society; (2) the American high regard for public school education; and (3) growing recognition of the importance of family life for the individual child (Lowenfeld, 1956).

The first factor, integration of the blind into society, has already been discussed. Public school education is perhaps nowhere as universally a fundamental instrument of education as in the United States. Parochial and private schools follow essentially the same methods and procedures which have over the years become characteristic of American public school education. While boarding schools are an accepted fact in some European countries, they have never received general approval in the United States, where public school education prevails almost exclusively.

The vital role of family life has always been recognized in a rather general way. The more specific values of family living for the individual have been brought to attention only in the more immediate past. This is particularly true of the role which the maternal relationship plays in the life of the young child and of the detrimental effects caused by early separation from the mother. Children in later childhood are considered less vulnerable, though length of separation, preparation of the child for the separation, and the love and understanding provided by those who are in charge of the child are potent influences throughout childhood and early adolescence.

The example of the Chicago public school braille classes was followed in 1905 by Cincinnati, and by 1910 eight cities in the United States had public school provisions for blind children. After a period of initial growth, the number of public school classes and the number of children attending them reached a plateau which lasted until about 1948. During the years preceding 1948, about 500 to 600 pupils, or less than 10% of all blind children educated in the United States, attended public school classes, which were then available in about 20 to 25 communities. From 1949 on—the year when the first retro-lental fibroplasia cases reached school age—the total number of blind children in the United States began to increase, but public school classes and their population have grown much faster than residential schools. Many parents of retrolental fibroplasia children, particularly those whose children were capa-ble, insisted that their local school systems had a responsibility to provide for the education of their blind children also. At present, about 60% of all blind children educated in the United States attend schools in their home communi-ties, whereas about 40% receive their education in residential schools.

Provisions for Partially Seeing Children

The placement of partially seeing children in schools for the blind was viewed with doubt by educators in England as well as in the United States at the turn of the century. In 1902 N. Bishop Harman, a London ophthalmolo-gist, found many children with a high degree myopia in schools for the blind and reported this discovery to Dr. James Kerr, the medical director of the London School Board. Dr. Kerr took action, as a result of which the first separate school for partially seeing children was established in 1908 at Cam-berwell in South London. It was located on the playground of a large elemen-tary school. Harman named it "Myope School." The children worked together with their sighted peers and did oral work almost exclusively. Hathaway (1959) reported that there was an inscription over the door, "Reading and Writing Shall Not Enter Here!" (p. 4), but gradually large-letter reading became accepted. The limitation of including only children with high myopia in special classes was recognized early in Strassburg, Germany, where they began to admit children with all kinds of eye difficulties. Subsequently, similar classes were opened in other German cities and later on in other European countries.

Edward E. Allen, after Howe and Anagnos the third director of Perkins School for the Blind, had voiced as early as 1892 his objection to the presence of partially seeing children in schools for the blind. He had observed that partially seeing children can do their work and many other things better than the blind, and that the blind often became dependent on them (Hathaway, 1959). To this must be added that partially seeing children who are forced into learning braille use all kinds of subterfuge to read print or read braille with their eyes. More fundamentally, the partially seeing child whose visual capabil-ity is neither recognized nor used is liable to become a frustrated and disturbed individual, causing problems for himself and for the school in which he is placed.

When Dr. Allen visited London in 1909, he became acquainted with the schools for myopes and returned to the United States with plans for similar classes in Boston. He did not think it was sound to limit these classes to children who were partially seeing because of high myopia, but wanted all children with severe visual problems included. He secured support for his idea and as a result of it the first class for partially seeing children in America was opened in 1913 by the Boston School Committee at Roxbury. Just as in Europe the British example was followed by school systems in other cities and countries, so in the United States other cities followed the Boston example. The second class for partially seeing children became established in Cleveland, Ohio in the same year. There, Robert B. Irwin, who later became the highly influential executive director of the American Foundation for the Blind, was in charge of special classes for blind children and had introduced a cooperative plan by which blind children attended as many classes as possible with their seeing fellow students. He applied the same principle when the partially seeing children were separated from the blind children in a special class. The Boston system of a segregated class for partially seeing children and the Cleveland system of a cooperative program by which partially seeing children went from their special classroom to regular classes for certain subjects and activities were followed for many years as provisions for partially seeing children in public schools spread in the United States. The Boston classes were called "classes for conservation of eyesight," and those in Cleveland, "conservation of vision classes." Later on, the term "sight-saving classes" became more widely accepted, although it ultimately turned out to be a misnomer.

CHANGES AND CURRENT TRENDS

Residential Schools

The three factors mentioned as influential in the establishment of braille classes in public schools—increasing integration of the blind into society, high regard for public school education, and recognition of the importance of family life—also influenced the policies and practices of residential schools. Not all such institutions have reacted in an equally responsive way to these forces. Some have remained quite traditional, with policies and attitudes dating back to the days of segregation. Others are more progressive and more responsive to positive social changes.

Bledsoe (1971) discerns three types of present-day residential school patterns:

The *Classic Type* is the school which in most of its modifications has kept rather strictly to its original purpose of educating blind children and youth. It may have many modern ways of doing this; it may tailor its program to meet individual needs, and it may have certain special departments such as a program for the deaf–blind. But basically it is still a school for blind children from kindergarten through high school.

The *Center Type* is the school which has modified this original pattern a great deal to become a kind of center with special services for blind children and youth, but is zealous, even aggressive, in propelling pupils into every learning experience possible outside the residential in schools with sighted children, going extra miles to promote community relations.

The *Hospital Type* is the school which makes such a specialty of serving multiply handicapped children, that it is on its way to being a hospital school and it is interesting that of the four schools founded in the past 50 years, two, the Hope School and the Royer-Greaves School, were established exclusively for blind children with additional handicaps [p. 31].

That these three patterns have evolved from a single one in response to the impact of newly arising needs is a credit to the adaptability of many schools. It shows that they, along with public school provisions, have been responsive to the demands of emergency situations, such as retrolental fibroplasia and rubella epidemics.

Administrators and educational personnel in residential schools are aware that blind children must be brought up to assume as adults their rightful places in society with the privileges and responsibilities of all citizens. Some schools believe they can do this best by retaining their pupils completely in an environment which prepares them for their future life but does not expose them to it. Many other schools seek every opportunity to give their pupils experiences which they would have were they growing up in their home communities. They have turned from more or less "closed" schools into more or less "open" ones. They open their doors for community influences to enter and for their children to go out into the community. Their teachers live in the community and bring its events to the school to be shared. The children take part in community organizations and events; they attend churches of their denominations, Sunday school, and church activities individually, and not as a group of blind children; they are familiarized with the recreational facilities of the community and use them according to their suitability; membership in the Boy Scouts or Girl Scouts, or in similar organizations, is arranged on an individual basis rather than in the form of a "blind Scout troop." This may not always be possible for all children of a residential school, but the ones who are ready to join the neighborhood Scout troop are assisted to do so. Children have as close and continuing a contact as possible with their families, returning home for weekends, holidays, vacations, and other occasions. The families in turn are welcome at the school and their interest in the child is maintained by all possible means.

Residential schools should transfer pupils to the local public schools whenever they are ready for it or when a public school facility for blind children becomes available in the student's home community. Some residential schools have their high school students attend the public high school of the community in which the residential school is located, while the residential school serves as a boarding place and resource facility providing reader service, guidance, tutoring in subjects which the blind student might find difficult to master without help, and mobility training. Under such an arrangement, the blind student has an opportunity to become a fully participating member of a high school community of seeing students, while he can still be assisted and guided by a residential school staff familiar with the problems of blindness. Residential schools have only a small enrollment in each high school class and, therefore, can offer only a very limited number of courses. What James B. Conant (1959) has said about small high schools in general is even more true of those in residential schools for the blind:

> The enrollment of many American public high schools is too small to allow a diversified curriculum except at exorbitant expense. The prevalence of such high schools—those with graduating classes of less than one hundred students—constitutes one of the serious obstacles to good secondary education throughout most of the United States. I believe such schools are not in a position to provide a satisfactory education for any group of their students—the academically talented, the vocationally oriented, or the slow reader. The instructional program is neither sufficiently broad nor sufficiently challenging. A small high school cannot by its very nature offer a comprehensive curriculum [p. 77].

At the time of their inception, residential schools for blind children were placed administratively in various departments, such as those of Institutions and Asylums, Public Welfare, Boards of Control, and other controlling bodies. It is now considered most appropriate for residential schools to be administered by Departments of Education so that they function as integral parts of a state's school system.

It should also be noted that teacher education programs originated in residential schools, such as Perkins School for the Blind and the New York Institute for the Education of the Blind, because residential schools were predominantly in need of specially trained teachers for blind children and had the necessary know-how. Teacher education programs are now a part of many colleges and universities where either Departments of Special Education or Departments of Education are responsible for their administration.

Public Schools

The first public school classes for blind children were called "braille classes." Frank H. Hall had urged at their inception that the blind children should be permitted to take part in the regular classes to the fullest extent possible. John B. Curtis, who was a graduate of the Illinois School for the Blind, became the first supervisor of the Chicago classes. Blind children were placed in homerooms located in various school buildings of different school districts, and special teachers assisted them in gaining those skills and in learning those subjects which they could not acquire in the regular classrooms. When in 1905 Cincinnati became the second city in the United States to place blind children in public schools, the blind students were segregated in a special building. Fortunately, other cities, like Milwaukee and Racine in Wisconsin, Cleveland, and New York, followed the Chicago example of sending blind pupils from homerooms to the regular classrooms for most of their work. In 1913, Cincinnati also changed to this plan. In 1917, Los Angeles started classes for blind children but soon afterward consolidated them in a special day school for blind children which has remained a segregated school up to the present.

Robert B. Irwin, who was put in charge of the Cleveland public school classes, became their most active and vocal advocate. He recognized that the day school plan for blind children needed supplementation, and accordingly made special arrangements for music instruction, manual training, acquisition of social skills, and home economics.

As the cooperative arrangement between homeroom and regular classroom proved successful, the accent in pupil placement gradually shifted. Instead of placing the child in the homeroom, the administration placed him in the regular classroom where he, like his fellow pupils, was the responsibility of the regular classroom teacher. The homeroom teacher became a resource teacher, ready and with equipment at his disposal to assist the blind student as well as his classroom teacher whenever any special assistance was needed. Naturally, the young blind child must in general spend more time than the older student in the resource room, since only the special teacher can give him basic instruction in the tool subjects. As he grows older, he spends more and more time in the regular classroom and makes fewer demands on the resource teacher.

Resource facilities in public schools appeared to be feasible only in communities where a sufficient number of blind children was located. Some of these communities were so large that it did not seem reasonable to transport the children to a centrally located school facility having a resource room. This led to a new arrangement of providing public school education for blind children —the itinerant teacher provision. Under this arrangement, the blind child is in full attendance in the regular classroom and the itinerant teacher assists only by giving advice to the regular teacher whenever any special problem arises. The itinerant teacher works only occasionally with the child himself. For blind children on the elementary level, the itinerant teacher program can only be successful if the teacher can spend a considerable amount of time working directly with the individual young pupil. Therefore, the itinerant teacher can be assigned only a very small number of students. No doubt individual pupils who receive understanding help at home can get along well with itinerant teacher services. As a matter of fact, some pupils at all times have been successful even without special teachers, except perhaps for the teaching of braille reading and writing.

For the success of all types of public school provisions, effective supervision by an experienced educator-administrator is of greatest importance. The school principal cannot be expected to be sufficiently familiar with the education of blind children to judge the effectiveness of the work of the special teacher for blind children. This supervision must be provided on either the city, county, or state level, depending on the number of classes and the size of the area served.

Partially Seeing Children

For a long time, visual acuity was the main characteristic used in determining the placement of a visually handicapped child. Children with a visual acuity of 20/200 or less (Snellen distance measurement) were considered "blind," whereas those who had a visual acuity better than 20/200 up to and including 20/70 were considered partially seeing. The 20/200 division also determined whether a child should be taught to read braille or print, frequently large type. With this arrangement, many children with borderline vision and even those having considerably less than 20/200 would either read braille with their eyes or read regular print—often against the rules of the school and behind the backs of the teachers. The idea of "saving sight" was responsible for the insistence of the school personnel on enforcing the division between braille and print readers.

As ophthalmologists began to question the concept of "saving" sight by limiting its use, and ultimately concluded that normal use of the eye, even of a defective one, in most cases does no harm, the artificial dividing line between braille and print readers began to be disregarded. The common dictum that reading matter must be held at a certain distance from the eye, which deprived many children with defective vision of the use of sight for reading, also became obsolete. Children are now encouraged to use magnifiers if they aid them in their reading and to hold the reading matter as close to their eye as is best for their reading. In addition, many more large-print books have become available.

When sight-saving classes were the favored way of providing education for partially seeing children, the physical classroom environment was arranged according to their special needs. The illumination of the rooms, control of daylight and electrical lighting, choice of wall color, and reflectance of walls, ceilings, woodwork, and floors had to follow certain specifications. The same was true for blackboards (dull grey-green was the preferred color), chalk, writing paper, etc. Most of these specifications, required in the past for sight-saving rooms only, are now general standards for all classrooms.

As a consequence of all these changes, many partially seeing children are able to attend regular classes and some who do not can be served by either resource rooms or itinerant teachers. This has led to a decrease in the number of classes for partially seeing children on the one hand, and on the other hand to the need for teachers of blind children to become teachers of the broad range of visually handicapped children. Teacher preparation is now geared to the task of making teachers competent to serve all visually handicapped children, though it does not overlook the differences which exist between children who are totally blind and those who have varying amounts of sight.

As an indication of this change, the National Society for the Prevention of Blindness, which under the leadership of Mrs. Winifred Hathaway was concerned with the promotion of special educational provisions for partially seeing children, has withdrawn from this area and turned over its responsibilities to the American Foundation for the Blind, which now promotes the interest of all visually handicapped children.

A LOOK INTO THE FUTURE

The consensus of educators of the visually handicapped and of organizations devoted to the interests of visually handicapped children is that public school provisions, in the form of resource rooms and itinerant teachers, and residential schools will continue to serve as special educational facilities. In order to foresee possible changes, it is necessary to consider the types of visually handicapped children who in the future will be in need of education.

The years beginning with the 1950s were characterized by a decisive increase in the number of visually handicapped children with additional handicapping conditions. This was due at first to retrolental fibroplasia, a cause of blindness due to oxygen therapy of prematurely born babies, and later to the effects of maternal rubella (German measles) epidemics. The percentage of multihandicapped blind children has increased almost catastrophically, so that a 1965 investigation of multihandicapped blind children in residential schools gave a prevalence rate of 25 mentally retarded children per 100 blind children (Wolf, 1967). In another study in 1968 limited to one state (California), 45% of visually handicapped children in educational facilities were found to be multihandicapped, that is, having another additional "marked" handicapping condition (Lowenfeld, 1969). Though one could argue about case-finding methods, definitions used, and inconsistencies found, there is no denying the seriousness of the increase and its resulting need for action. Lowenfeld recommended intensive preschool services, diagnostic centers, training and adjustment centers, psychotherapy, and guidance and counseling services for parents and children as essential elements of a program for these children.

The question arises whether, after reasonable control of retrolental fibroplasia and maternal rubella, the educational capacity of visually handicapped children will revert to the previous fairly normal distribution of intelligence among this group of children. Since the effects of the most recent epidemic of maternal rubella in the middle of the 1960s will affect the visually handicapped school-age population until about the middle of the 1980s, any improvement could occur only by that time. Whether the rubella epidemic expected for the early 1970s will be curtailed by the newly found vaccine remains to be seen.

Assuming that retrolental fibroplasia and maternal rubella will be reasonably controlled, another factor is expected to exert its influence. During the past decades, a change in the causes of blindness has taken place. Prenatal causes of blindness, many of which not only affect the eye but may also cause additional abnormalities, have increased; and such other causes as infectious diseases and accidents, many of which affect only the eye and leave the child's other sensory, intellectual, and physical capabilities intact, have decreased. This change contributes to the increase in multihandicapped blind children and to the decrease in blind children with no other handicaps. This trend will most likely continue in the foreseeable future.

So far as responsibilities of residential schools and public school facilities for the education of visually handicapped children are concerned, it stands to reason that residential schools will tend to serve visually handicapped children who have additional handicaps. Public school facilities will most likely accept a larger percentage of "normal" visually handicapped children, though their special education provisions will also include some multihandicapped children with visual handicaps.

Research on technical appliances has so far not produced any special instruments useful to the blind. Talking books and tape recordings are results of already available inventions, as are some other special tools useful to the blind and used in the education of the blind. Whether the near future has some special instruments in store, such as a reading machine which can make regular print readable to the blind or a mechanical guidance device which will essentially improve a blind person's mobility, is a matter of speculation.

Certain, however, is that our national conscience is increasingly aware of the public responsibility for providing a suitable education for every child and that handicapped children will benefit from this movement. Such provisions as the Research and Demonstration Centers, research grants from various agencies, research dissemination programs, and the intensification in broadness and depth of teacher education programs are bound to have a profound effect on the education of visually handicapped children.

SUMMARY

Four historical phases in the status and treatment of the blind in Western society are described: separation, ward, emancipation, and integration. Each phase is discussed and facts are cited which support the thesis that we are now in the age of integration of the blind into society, though this is by no means an actuality but rather an ideal for which to strive.

During the ward status, some blind individuals convincingly demonstrated their own educability and this led to the establishment of the first schools for the blind, which took the form of residential institutions. Valentin Haüy in France, Samuel Gridley Howe in the United States, and Johann William Klein in Austria were the great founder personalities. Education of blind children paralleling that of seeing children became possible through Louis Braille, a blind teacher, who invented a system of embossed dot symbols which bears his name.

Residential schools for the blind remained practically the only educational provision in America for blind children until about 1900. From then on, public schools began to provide education for visually handicapped children. This was first arranged in Chicago, whence it spread to other cities, in the beginning largely in the midwest. Public school classes first were conducted as segregated classes and gradually changed to cooperative classes. At present, most blind children receive their education in public schools, through either resource programs or itinerant teacher arrangements. More than 60% of the visually handicapped children registered with the American Printing House for the Blind attend public schools, whereas 40% are placed in residential schools.

Residential schools have also undergone considerable change, turning from "closed schools" to "open schools" which stress community cooperation, parent involvement, and provide for exchange of students with public schools as the student's readiness and the available facilities permit.

The retrolental fibroplasia wave caused many parents of visually handicapped children to demand local education for them so that they would not need to be separated from their families and thus gave impetus to the growth of public school programs for visually handicapped children. The maternal rubella epidemic made those responsible for the education of blind children more aware of the pressing educational needs of multihandicapped blind and deaf–blind children and is stimulating the growth of programs geared to their needs.

REFERENCES

American Foundation for the Blind. *Sources of reading material for the visually handicapped*: New York, 1969.

Bledsoe, C. W. The family of residential schools. *Blindness 1971*. Washington, D. C.: American Association of Workers for the Blind. Pp. 19–73.

Conant, J. B. *The American high school today*. New York: McGraw-Hill, 1959.

Farrell, G. *The story of blindness*. Cambridge, Mass.: Harvard University Press, 1956.

French, R. S. *From Homer to Helen Keller*. New York: American Foundation for the Blind, 1932.

Hathaway, W. *Education and health of the partially seeing child* (4th ed.). New York: Columbia University Press, 1959.

Haüy, V. *An essay on the education of the blind*. Leicester: Tompkin & Shardlow, 1889. (Republished: *Blindness 1967*. Washington, D.C.: American Association of Workers for the Blind. Pp. 179–199.)

Hoover, R. E. The cane as a travel aid. In P. A. Zahl (Ed.), *Blindness*. Princeton: Princeton University Press, 1950. Pp. 353–365.

Howe, S. G. Address, delivered at the ceremony of laying the corner-stone of the New York Institution for the Blind at Batavia, September 6, 1866. (Republished: *Blindness 1965*. Washington, D.C.: American Association of Workers for the Blind. Pp. 165–188.)

Klein, J. W. *Anleitung blinden Kindern die nöthige Bildung in den Schulen ihres Wohnortes und in dem Kreise ihrer Familien zu verschaffen*. Wien: K. K. Blinden-Institute, 1836. (Rev. ed: 1845.)

Lowenfeld, B. Cooperation in work for the blind, here and abroad. *Proceedings of the 24th Convention of the American Association of Workers for the Blind*, 1950. Pp. 17–20.

Lowenfeld, B. History and development of specialized education for the blind. *Exceptional Children*, 1956, **23**, 53–57, 90.

Lowenfeld, B. Multihandicapped blind and deaf–blind children in California. *Research Bulletin No. 19*. New York: American Foundation for the Blind, June 1969. Pp. 1–72.

Roblin, J. *Louis Braille*. London: Royal National Institute for the Blind, n.d.

Ross, I. *Journey into light*. New York: Appleton, 1951.

tenBroek, J. The right to live in the world: The disabled in the law of torts. *California Law Review*, 1966, **54**, 841–919.

Villey, P. *The world of the blind: A psychological study*. New York: Macmillan, 1930.

Wolf, J. M. *The blind child with concomitant disabilities*. New York: American Foundation for the Blind, 1967.

CHAPTER 2

Psychological Considerations

Berthold Lowenfeld

Education must aim at giving the blind child a knowledge of the realities around him, the confidence to cope with these realities, and the feeling that he is recognized and accepted as an individual in his own right.

A severe impairment like total blindness or serious loss of vision is bound to have psychological effects on an individual. These effects are either the direct intrinsic results produced by the visual impairment as such or the indirect extrinsic results stemming from the reactions of the social environment to the impairment. The former as well as the latter affect the visually handicapped child in various ways and degrees during his development.

Before discussing the direct and indirect effects of visual impairments we must treat some factors which will help us to a better understanding of the meaning and influence of a visual handicap for the individual child and of some issues directly related to it.

INDIVIDUAL CONSIDERATIONS

Every teacher who deals with a visually handicapped child must be aware of certain characteristics of or related to the child's visual impairment. If he wants to individualize his approach, as he should, anything that will help him to a better recognition of a child's individual needs should be known to him. There are some variables caused by the visual impairment which must be added to those characteristics (such as sex, age, intelligence, aptitudes, family status, and economic conditions) to be considered for any child. These variables are the cause of the visual impairment, degree of the visual impairment, age at onset of the visual impairment, present condition of the eyes and required eye care, and home environment.

Since some of the variables caused by blindness are the concern of medical or allied professional experts, a description of their responsibilities is given so that their functions may be better understood and proper referrals can be made.

An *ophthalmologist* or *oculist* is a physician—an M.D.—who specializes in diagnosis and treatment of defects and diseases of the eye, performing surgery when necessary or prescribing other types of treatment, including glasses.

An *optometrist,* a licensed, nonmedical practitioner, measures refractive errors—that is, irregularities in the size or shape of the eyeball or surface of the cornea—and eye muscle disturbances. In his treatment the optometrist uses glasses, prisms, and exercises only.

An *optician* grinds lenses, fits them into frames, and adjusts the frames to the wearer. (Definitions are from the United States Department of Health, Education, & Welfare.)

Cause of Visual Impairment

There are many causes of visual impairments, such as anomalies and diseases of the eyeball, cornea, lens, retina, optic nerve, and uveal tract. Some of them will be discussed in greater detail in Chapter 5. It would not serve any practical purpose to give the latest available figures on causes of blindness among school children because they date back to a survey made during the school year 1958–1959. In addition, current statistics on the causes of blindness would be heavily distorted by two pathological factors: retrolental fibroplasia (RLF) and maternal rubella. RLF, an eye disease which was diagnosed in 1942, was rampant in the United States and elsewhere between 1949 and 1954. In the latter year medical research ascertained that the major cause of this disease was the administration of high concentrations of oxygen over prolonged periods of time to prematurely born infants. As a consequence of this finding, the epidemic character of RLF is now controlled. Rubella (German measles) contracted by women during their first trimester of pregnancy produces blindness in many children, as well as concomitant cardiac and other abnormalities such as deafness and mental retardation. Rubella epidemics occur in 6- to 7-year cycles; the last one, between 1964 and 1966, resulted in an estimated 30,000 cases of defective children. A vaccine for German measles is already available and it can be hoped that it will be effectively applied to prevent any future epidemic and its sorrowful results.

In 1958–1959, the largest single cause of blindness among children, almost 50%, was classified as "prenatal influence." This shows that our medical knowledge, and as a result our preventive measures, are still greatly in need of improvement. With RLF virtually controlled and maternal rubella beginning to come under control, the percentage of visual impairments caused by prenatal influence will almost certainly rise.

It is important for the teacher to know the cause of the visual impairment of each child because in some cases this awareness will indicate whether the anomaly is confined only to the eye or is a systemic one, as for instance in cataracts caused by diabetes. In cases of albinism, the teacher will know that she must often expect the child to show photophobia (fear of light) because of eye discomfort in bright light. Therefore, the child should be placed in the shady area of the classroom and needs to wear dark glasses in bright light. Also, the cause of blindness may be the key to the understanding of certain parental attitudes, such as guilt feelings, if the parents believe—rightly or wrongly—that they are responsible for their child's visual handicap.

Degree of Visual Impairment

The integrity of vision can be impaired essentially in three ways: (1) Visual acuity may be reduced; (2) the field of vision may be restricted; and (3) color vision may be defective. Extrinsic or external muscle imbalances may also produce visual impairment, as for instance in amblyopia ex anopsia, a dimming of vision from disuse of the eye as a result of strabismus.

In measuring visual acuity, the Snellen chart is used. It consists of lines of letters, numbers, or symbols of graduated sizes which must be read at a distance of 20 feet. Each size corresponds to the standard distance at which a person with normal vision can distinguish it. Thus, if the 20-foot-size letter or symbol can be read at a distance of 20 feet, the eye has a visual acuity of 20/20, which is normal. When a person can read only the large 200-foot size at a distance of 20 feet, he has 20/200 vision. In other words, an object that the normal eye can discern 200 feet away must be brought close to 20 feet away in order to be distinguished by a person who has 20/200 visual acuity. In visual acuities lower than 20/200, the numerator varies, since the 200-foot letter or symbol is usually read at distances closer than 20 feet. Thus, 5/200 means that an object which can be distinguished by the normal eye at a distance of 200 feet must be brought as close as 5 feet in order to be recognized.

The most widely used definition of blindness, applied largely for legal purposes, describes a person as blind if he has "central visual acuity of 20/200 or less in the better eye, with correcting glasses; or central visual acuity of more than 20/200 if there is a field defect in which the peripheral field has contracted to such an extent that the widest diameter of visual field subtends an angular distance no greater than 20 degrees." This definition does not cover the important factor of near or reading vision.

In a report of the Section on Ophthalmology of the American Medical Association (1955), "visual efficiency" includes visual acuity at a distance and near vision, as well as such factors as visual fields, ocular motility, binocular vision, adaptation to light and dark, color vision, and accommodation. The relationship between Snellen measurements of visual acuity for distance and the percentage of visual efficiency is shown in Table 1.

TABLE 1
Central Visual Acuity for Distance and Corresponding
Percentage of Visual Efficiency

Snellen measure of central visual acuity	Percent of visual efficiency
20/20	100
20/40	85
20/50	75
20/80	60
20/100	50
20/200	20

The ophthalmology section of the American Medical Association also interpreted the measurement of near vision in terms of visual efficiency. Near vision is measured by a special Snellen chart designed to be read at a distance of 14 inches. Also available is a Jaeger chart, which presents lines of type of different sizes which are numbered. In addition, near vision can be measured by the point size of the type a person is able to read. Table 2 correlates all these measurements.

TABLE 2
Central Visual Acuity for Near Vision and Corresponding
Percentage of Visual Efficiency

Snellen measure	Jaeger	Point	Percent of visual efficiency
14/14	1	3	100
14/18	2	4	100
14/28	3	6	90
14/35	6	8	50
14/56	8	12	20
14/70	11	14	15
14/122	14	22	5
14/140	—	—	2

The ophthalmologically defined visual acuity and efficiency is only a part of what could be called functional visual efficiency, which is determined by such additional factors as environmental influences and their effects, attitude of the individual toward his visual impairment, and motivation. For the teacher who works with visually handicapped children, this functional visual efficiency is the most important factor to be considered.

The ophthalmological–legal definition of blindness also includes a severe restriction in the field of vision. The field of vision is determined by the use of the perimeter, which maps out on a chart the field limitations in the various directions. If peripheral vision is reduced to an angle of 20 degrees or less, it becomes equivalent to blindness. This kind of visual defect is well described as "gun barrel'" or "tunnel" vision. In some eyes, central vision may be lost as the result of a scotoma (a blind or partially blind area on the retina) in or near the center of the visual field. In these cases, peripheral vision (which, however, is not as distinct as central vision) must be used.

Hathaway (1959) classified partially seeing children as follows.

1. Children having a visual acuity of 20/70 or less in the better eye after all necessary medical or surgical treatment has been given and compensating lenses provided when the need for them is indicated. Such children must, however, have a residue of sight that makes it possible to use this as the chief avenue of approach to the brain.
2. Children with a visual deviation from the normal who, in the opinion of the eye specialist, can benefit from the special educational facilities provided for the partially seeing [p. 16].

During the past decades, educators have recognized that the functional visual efficiency, the way in which a child utilizes his vision, is more important than his measured visual acuity. Therefore, a functional definition of blindness, rather than the ophthalmological one given above, is being sought. Since Chapter 5 elaborates on this and other points, only general comments need to be made here.

If a child is totally blind or has only light perception, he needs to be given opportunities to observe with *his* sensory equipment and to learn the skills of self-care and social living, of mobility and communication, by the use of his nonvisual senses. Children who have some sight will experience the world and themselves more like seeing children. They should use their visual potential to the fullest and teachers must encourage this, since ophthalmologists agree that use of the eyes under normal conditions is in no way harmful. For instance, a child may bring his reading matter as close to his eyes, or his one eye, as he finds most comfortable. Needless to say, everything must be done to provide the best optical correction for the impaired eye, including those magnifying devices which are found to be most suitable for the individual child for a given purpose, such as reading or getting about.

Onset of Visual Impairment

Two factors connected with the onset of the visual impairment are of importance: the age at which it occurred and the way in which it occurred. It is now generally accepted, and confirmed by such studies as those of Schlaegel (1953) and Blank (1958), that children who lost their sight before they were 5 to 7 years of age do not retain a useful visual imagery nor most likely any color ideas. They rely completely upon their nonvisual senses and must be educated by methods adapted accordingly. Children who lose their sight later in life may retain visual imagery and color ideas of which they make use in their learning processes. However, they are not able to make any current visual observations.

The visual impairment may have a sudden onset, as in case of an accident; or it may develop gradually, as it does in many cases of retinitis pigmentosa. A sudden onset may result in shock and possibly withdrawal, with the psychological effects decreasing in time. A gradual onset may disturb a child profoundly for longer periods of time, since it causes acute fear and anxiety for the future. The teacher must be sensitive to the individual reactions of children who have become blind in the more recent past.

If a child has become visually impaired after school entrance, the teacher must also consider his past school experiences, because he may have attended school as a seeing child and would need assistance in adjusting to a different school and learning situation.

Eye Condition and Required Eye Care

In most visually handicapped children, the condition of their eyes is static and needs attention only if an acute problem should occur. In some chldren's eyes, however, pathological processes may still be active and require more or less frequent medical examinations and continued treatment. This can cause acute discomfort and increased feelings of insecurity. Prolonged treatment and instability of the eye condition and the capacity to see are likely to produce great anxiety about the final outcome of the eye disorder. The teacher should not only be aware of this and assist the parents in providing the necessary treatment but must also understand the child's emotional reactions to his condition.

There are many children who must wear glasses, sometimes rather heavy ones, and the teacher can assist in securing the child's cooperation in the wearing and care of these glasses. It must be expected that glasses as well as frames will be broken, damaged, or mislaid and lost occasionally. If the frames are damaged, the glasses may in certain cases do more harm than good and must be adjusted or replaced. Some children must wear artificial eyes, in one or both sockets. These need to be cleaned as recommended by the ophthalmologist and checked from time to time to avoid discomfort or inadequate fitting because of the child's growth. Having the children's optimum sight restored, preserved, and used should be one of the primary concerns of the teacher.

In some instances, the eye defect may result in facial disfiguration, which can often be corrected or improved by wearing dark glasses or by cosmetic surgery. Though it cannot be the teacher's task to arrange the latter, she, as a more objective person, can give advice to the parents. They may not be aware of the adverse impression their child's eye or eyes make on others, or may be emotionally too involved to recognize it.

Home Environment

The home environment is in most cases the strongest continuous force affecting any child's development. If this is mentioned as a special factor to be considered for visually handicapped children, there is good reason for it. Parents of visually handicapped children are more likely to have emotional difficulties and conflicts as a consequence of their child's handicap. As a result, more problems are liable to interfere with providing a wholesome environment for their blind child's development. Their own difficulties arise from their disappointment at having a child who does not appear to fulfill the wish, common to all parents, for a healthy and normal offspring. They are also in most cases experiencing feelings of guilt, since they often hold themselves responsible for the fact that their child has a serious visual handicap. Whether such self-accusations are justified or not makes little difference; they are certainly supported by the deep-rooted common belief, based on religious convictions and on superstition, that parental sins or mistakes are responsible for a child's handicap. Thus, it becomes emotionally more difficult for the parents of a visually handicapped child to provide for him a healthy environment which will give him the additional opportunities he needs in order to make up for his visual impairment. Many visually handicapped children come to school without having had an experiential background comparable to that of their seeing peers, without having learned the routines of daily living according to their age, and without the ego strengths which can help them in their adjustment to a strange, and for many children frightening, new school situation. Chapter 3 elaborates on these points.

The teacher who finds at the beginning of a school year that a blind child is a member of his class will certainly benefit from becoming acquainted with the child's parents and knowing the background which his home provides. He will then be better able to understand certain facets of the child's behavior and will be better prepared to assist the child himself.

EFFECTS ON THE COGNITIVE FUNCTIONS

Most educational provisions for visually handicapped children now serve children ranging from those who are totally blind to those who are partially seeing. This does not imply, however, that there are no important and even basic psychological differences between children with various degrees of visual impairments, particularly in the area of cognitive functions. It is obvious that a child who was born totally blind experiences the world around him in a different way than the child who is partially seeing. The former must make use of his nonvisual senses while the latter can gain a knowledge of the world by the use of his vision as well as of his other senses. Since vision plays such a dominant role in cognition, the blind child's position and needs in this area will show specific differences as compared with other children. There is no question that the blind child can gain a knowledge of the realities around him, but he gains it in a different way and the knowledge itself is in some respects of a different nature. From experience and research it can be stated that only in the areas of cognitive functions and mobility does blindness create problems *sui generis.*

The following discussion of cognitive functions will largely concern itself with the child who is totally blind or has only light perception and either was born with or acquired this condition early in life. Partially seeing children either approximate or are equal in their cognitive functions to children who have no visual impairment.

As this author has stated (Lowenfeld, 1950), blindness imposes, as a direct result of the loss of vision, three basic limitations on an individual: (1) in the range and variety of his experiences; (2) in his ability to get about; (3) in his interaction with the environment.

Range and Variety of Experiences

In developing his conception of the world, the totally blind person must rely upon the use of his remaining senses. Touch and kinesthetic experiences, as well as audition, are the most important sensory avenues used for this purpose. Audition gives clues of distance and direction—provided the object makes any sound, but it does not assist in gaining concrete ideas of objects as such. The song of a bird that a blind child hears does not give him any concrete idea of the bird itself. He may know in which direction the bird is located and approximately how far away he is, provided he has learned this through past experiences and associations, which play a great role in the utilization of audition. The same is true of olfactory impressions, which give important clues to the presence, distance, and quality of objects. Vision and hearing are the two main distance senses, and olfaction also has some functions in this respect. Whereas vision gives details of form, size, color, and spatial relationship of objects, audition gives only clues. The importance of audition is in the area of verbal communication.

A blind person can gain a knowledge of the spatial qualities of objects only by touch observations, in which kinesthetic experiences play an important part. In order to perform any touch observation, direct contact must be had with the object to be observed. Herein lies the strength and the weakness of touch. Its strength, because the touch senses convey not only spatial form, but also surface quality, texture, resilience, temperature, weight, and pliability, thus going in many ways far beyond impressions resulting from visual observations. Also, touch functions independently of light. Its weakness, because many things are inaccessible (the sun, heavenly bodies—now with the exception of the moon, the horizon), many are too large (mountains, large buildings), too small (a fly or an ant), or too fragile (a butterfly, snowflakes) to be observed by touch. Also, objects in certain conditions, for example, moving (airplanes), burning, or boiling, and objects which have no shape of their own and must be kept in containers (mercury in a thermometer) cannot be directly observed tactually.

Although the physical process of seeing and optical laws can be explained to blind students, there are some visual phenomena which are very difficult to explain, for instance, mirror reflection and perspective. Comparisons with sound echoes for the former and with the diminution of sound with increasing distance for the latter offer some analogies.

One aspect of vision, color perception, cannot be performed by any other sensory organ, since it is a function of the retina. Therefore, any totally blind person cannot have the actual experience, nor consequently any real concept, of color. Since color words are widely used in our world of the seeing, blind individuals build up associations with certain colors which can be verbal, sensory, and emotional. The color "white" may for instance be associated with snow, and whiteness may become identified with coldness, crispness, and cleanness. These color associations vary from person to person as well as from time to time. Blind children need to be conversant with the most common visual color associations, since they will live in the world of the seeing, but nobody should assume that color has any primary meaning for them. It should be mentioned here that in talking with a blind person, one should not hesitate to use the regular vocabulary, including such expressions as "you see" or "look here"—the blind person knows the meaning of such phrases and makes his own applications of them and other visual terms.

Since touch requires direct contact with the object to be observed, blind children often gain only a partial knowledge of objects which they either cannot or do not have time to observe *in toto.* Also, the sense of touch generally functions only if it is actively employed for the purpose of cognition, whereas vision is active as long as the eyes are open and hearing functions continually unless its organ is obstructed. Therefore, blind children must frequently be encouraged to apply touch for the purpose of cognition. In our society where something like a "touch taboo" prevails from infancy on, encouragement to apply touch is often prevented by a need to avoid social disapproval felt by parents and sometimes by educators.

Vision has a most important function in serving as a unifying and structuring sense (Witkin, Birnbaum, Lomonaco, Lehr, & Herman, 1968). There is some evidence that the lack of vision as an organizer and integrator puts blind children at some disadvantage in certain auditory and tactual activities (Axelrod, 1959; Omwake & Solnit, 1961; Rubin, 1964).

For a long time it was believed that the blind are automatically compensated for the loss of one sense by increased effectiveness of their other senses. Scientific investigations of comparative sensory thresholds did not confirm this assumption (Hayes, 1941). It may have been accepted because of a wishful supposition that nature is just, which would relieve the individual's feelings of guilt and social responsibility. There is, however, no doubt that blind people who must rely on nonvisual sensory data learn to make better use of their other senses. The same refining by usage and need occurs with some seeing people who are engaged in special occupations—the cardiologist who listens to the heartbeat, the surgeon who performs delicate operative procedures, the tea taster, etc.

> Any higher efficiency of the blind in interpreting the sensory data perceived, must be the result of attention, practice, adaptation, and increased use of the remaining faculties [Lowenfeld, 1971, p. 221].

As already mentioned, hearing has its main function as a medium of verbal communication. Since much knowledge is communicated through language, blindness does not put the individual at a disadvantage in this respect. This fact may produce a tendency to "verbalism" in blind children (which will be discussed later) and sometimes in their teachers as well.

Practically all investigators of how the blind dream agree that hearing plays the dominant sensory role in their dreams, with tactile–kinesthetic components next. Blank (1958) concludes from a study of dreams of the blind that there are no fundamental phenomenological differences between the dreams of the blind and those of the seeing which would require any revision of the psychoanalytic theory of dreams.

It can be seen from our discussion of the blind child's sensory activities that he is limited in the range and variety of his experiences and that educational measures are necessary to overcome this limitation so far as it is possible.

Ability to Get About (Mobility)

Totally blind individuals are from early childhood on severely handicapped in their ability to move around by themselves. Even a small amount of vision can be used functionally in mobility. Total loss of sight makes the person dependent on his other senses, which even at best results in increased difficulties and deceleration in getting about. Many regard this restriction as the most severe single effect of blindness, even though great strides have been made in devising special methods and tools for mobility instruction (as discussed in Chapter 9).

The limitation in mobility has results which affect the blind person in two different spheres of his life: his opportunities for experiences and his social relations. The person who cannot move about on his own and thus expose himself to new experiences is deprived of an important avenue of acquiring knowledge and stimulation. He is limited in following his spontaneous decision to engage in or follow up on various pursuits of knowledge and happiness. In the social area, a blind person, even with high mobility skills, is somewhat dependent on the assistance of others, which, as Cutsforth (1933) has forcefully pointed out, affects his social attitudes:

> Since the blind live in a world of the seeing, it is necessary to procure visual aid and information. Whether this be volunteered or solicited, it represents a curtailment of self-expression and is registered emotionally as such. Thus, the act of asking a stranger the name of an approaching streetcar is an admission of inferiority for which there must be compensation. And the thoughtful, kind-hearted guide through a traffic jam must be pleasantly thanked for his assistance —society demands it—while the emotions demand that he be cursed or struck down with the cane [p. 73].

Rather than ask for and accept assistance, a blind person may decide to forego participation in an activity or, in the extreme case, he may fall into a pattern of withdrawal. Thus, it must be recognized that a blind individual, besides being restricted in his cognitive activities, is also from early infancy on limited in his ability to expose himself to experiences and opportunities. To be concrete about this, the blind child cannot just at will go out on the street for the many reasons which seeing children find attractive: to walk down the main thoroughfare and observe the window displays or the variety of people and objects moving by; nor can he run down to the brook or river or go exploring into fields and woods. Even if he does, being taken along by his friends, the comparable amount of knowledge which he gains through tactual and other sensory observations is far less than that of the other children.

As this author has pointed out (Lowenfeld, 1948), mobility, the capacity or facility of movement, consists of two components: physical locomotion and mental orientation. Both are essential for mobility and though they can be distinguished, they are not separate functions but are coordinated in the actual process of getting about. *Locomotion* has been defined as "the movement of an organism from place to place by means of its organic mechanism," and *mental orientation* as the "ability of an individual to recognize his surroundings and their temporal or spatial relations to himself" (Warren, 1934). These two functions work together in the actual process of getting about. For instance, if a blind student wants to leave his dormitory in order to go to the cafeteria, he must have a mental map outlining to him the path he will have to follow. As he moves, he uses certain clues from his environment, for instance the noise peculiar to a street crossing; the odor of a drugstore at a corner where he must turn left; the changes in the surfacing of his path where he must cross the campus mall; and the passing of an open area when he feels the point at which the walls of buildings end and where they begin again and where he knows the cafeteria is located. He also uses his muscular memory and his time sense in determining his position as he approaches his goal. He does not count steps or seconds, but as he travels his route frequently, he becomes more and more familiar with it and selective in using his clues. Thus he is able to follow a definite path according to his mental orientation.

This path must also be safe, because if he should be unable to execute the step-by-step locomotion effectively he will not reach his goal. In this process of locomotion, he makes use of all the clues he can get from the changing environment as he moves ahead, and can also use either a cane or a dog guide. The cane will indicate to him whether his foot (including the lower part of his body) can step into an obstacle-free space. The dog guide will lead him on only if his whole body can move into an obstacle-free space. In this process of mobility, the blind person makes use of practically all of his senses. He observes by hearing all kinds of sounds, including echoes; he notices temperature changes and air currents affecting his exposed skin; he feels with his feet the nature of the ground; and he interprets odors from whatever familiar source they come. All these impressions he uses inseparably for the purpose of locomotion as well as of orientation, and thereby achieves mobility.*

Although research evidence on the total problem of mobility is scant, one aspect of it has for a long time occupied scientists: the ability of blind individuals to perceive obstacles in their path before they have any direct contact with the object. A research team (Supa, Cotzin, & Dallenbach, 1944) at Cornell University proved convincingly that aural stimulation by reflected high-frequency sound waves is responsible for this phenomenon. (For a complete

*The author is aware that the field of mobility instruction uses a somewhat different nomenclature (which, however, is in flux). He believes that his distinction of locomotion and orientation as components of mobility is of value and hopes that ultimately a nomenclature consistent with it will prevail.

review see Lowenfeld, 1971.) "Obstacle perception" is most useful when the blind person moves about indoors. Outdoors it can only apply if conditions are favorable, that is, when no drowning-out noises, like heavy traffic, rain, or winds, are present, or when no sound deadening occurs, such as happens with snow on the ground. It has been demonstrated that seeing individuals can also acquire this ability.

Since even low degrees of vision are important for mobility, Barraga's (1964) study should be mentioned here; in it she concluded:

> The data of this experiment strongly suggest that blind children with remaining vision could improve their visual efficiency to the degree that they would be able to use their low vision more effectively for educational purposes if a planned sequence of visual stimulation were available to them in their early school years [p. 71].

It must be hoped that planned visual stimulation lessons as used in her experiments will be further tested and, if successful, generally used in order to improve the visual discrimination of all low-vision children.

Interaction with the Environment

Visual experiences have a long-distance object quality which is unique among the human senses. This permits a control of the environment and of the self in relation to it far more effective than that achieved by the other senses, either singly or in combination. Thus, lack of sight causes a detachment from the physical and to some extent from the social environment. The blind person cannot inform himself at a glance of his situation within a given environment as the seeing person can. He may hear a loud crash or he may smell something burning, but he cannot immediately, that is, just by looking around, inform himself about the cause of these impressions, nor can he gear his actions in response to them. This may not only keep him in a state of curiosity but it also causes him anxiety until he is able to gain information from a seeing person.

The detachment from the environment has many effects on children; these effects differ at various stages of the child's development (see Chapter 3). For instance, the fact that blind children are not visually stimulated to reach out and search for the source of a sound has been found to affect the ego development of blind infants (Fraiberg, Siegel, & Gibson, 1966). It also causes a tendency to immobility in young blind children which is in contrast to the spontaneous active behavior of seeing children. Burlingham (1964) claims that this immobilization is displaced from the motor area to other ego functions and thus has rather far-reaching effects. Sandler and Wills (1965) observed that in role-playing situations blind children copy adult activities mostly on the verbal and not on the active physical level as seeing children do. This they consider the cause of problems which become apparent only in the later adjustment of blind individuals.

Sandler (1963) makes the lack of visual sensory continuity responsible for the blind child's retardation in the process of turning from the self to the outer world. Being to a large extent deprived of the satisfactions of external stimulation, the blind infant turns to repetitive self-stimulating behavior. She concludes that this must have a profound effect on later stages of development. These psychoanalytic interpreters of the effects of blindness on children consider the detachment caused by lack of vision as a source of possible emotional difficulties in later life.

Many of the daily activities which children must learn are mastered on the basis of visual imitation. This imitative behavior plays an important role in learning to walk, talk, and play; acquiring and maintaining good posture (Siegel, 1966); learning expressive movements; and performing many other actions. Only one of these many areas will be discussed here, that of eating. Eating a meal properly is a much more strenuous and time-consuming activity for a person who cannot control the process by sight than for a sighted person. From the simple mechanics of picking up the food to the conforming with eating patterns acceptable to and expected by society, the blind person must cope with greatly increased difficulties and frequent frustrations. This can also be said for many other activities, such as getting dressed, shopping in a store, and doing many of the household tasks which boys, girls, men, and women generally must perform.

In the social aspects of an individual's life, blindness does not essentially interfere with communication but it does affect expressive movements, whether facial expressions or gestural behavior, because most of them are acquired by visual imitation. Learning them by other means demands special efforts and the results often may appear somewhat artificial. The blind person himself cannot observe the expressive reactions of his partner but he learns to interpret subtle changes in a person's voice as indications of verbally hidden reactions. Blind people are greatly influenced by the quality of voices, just as seeing people are by outward appearances, but they are not better able to judge a person by his voice than are other people.

The limitation in interaction with the environment shows itself also in the blind person's inability to determine whether he is observed at any given time by others. Thus, blind children, and adults for that matter, are often apprehensive and even fearful of being watched and feel that they must control themselves in situations where others can relax.

In discussing cognitive functions and mobility, we have naturally had to stress negative aspects and handicapping effects, since blindness is certainly a major sensory impairment. However, I do not want to conclude this discussion without a definite positive comment: In spite of all difficulties, most blind children who are free of additional handicaps learn to cope with their problems and their intellectual, social, and often their economic achievements compare well with those of their seeing peers.

PRINCIPLES OF SPECIAL METHODS

It will now be our task to deduce from the observations we have made in the two preceding sections certain principles which need to be applied in the education of blind children. Ever since formal education of blind children began, enlightened teachers of the blind have practiced such principles, mostly without being theoretically aware of them. To what extent they can be applied in the actual process of teaching depends somewhat on whether visually handicapped children receive their education as a group in an environment geared to their needs, as residential schools are, or as single individuals in public school facilities where they may have an understanding general classroom teacher and should have a resource or itinerant teacher who is aware of and knows how to meet their special needs.

Need for Concrete Experiences

In order to give the blind child a knowledge of the realities around him, the teacher must aim at providing him with a wide variety of concrete experiences, thus making up to a certain extent for the limitation in the range and variety of his experiences. For the blind child it is not important to learn concretely about exotic things; his primary need is to learn about his environment. To make this explicit the following is quoted from an older British survey (*Education of the Blind,* 1936) which has not lost current validity.

> The young seeing child is familiar with a multitude of characters and scenes of domestic and social life; he knows the postman, the policeman, the "bus driver"; the contents of the kitchen and bedroom; the wares of the confectioner's, the greengrocer's and butcher's shops; the scenes and incidents of street-life or the farmyard and countryside; he knows the birds, the domestic animals, trees, bushes and flowers, and vaguely or definitely a thousand things besides. Every common noun that he uses, whether cloud or chimney or looking-glass, represents a host of experiences that he has discriminated and classified and summed up in the word. Experiences of such things as these, and of their observed relationships, are the very stuff of the child's mind, and on them the teacher draws daily for the purposes of his art. . . . The deepest and most fundamental needs of blind children are a rich and intimate experience of common things, and a direct acquaintance with the many characters that move across the scenes of daily life, and the activities in which these characters engage. For these no verbal

substitutes will serve; the children must learn to know persons and things in terms of their own sensory powers, and to meet the situations in which they occur on an independent footing. Without this direct contact with the world, all subsequent formalizations of knowledge may be riddled with errors and misunderstandings, and all evaluations of what is good and worthy in life may be shattered by encounter with reality [pp. 45–47].

The need of totally blind children for concrete experiences with objects and situations has been confirmed in a number of studies, particularly those by Nagera and Colonna (1965), Rubin (1964), and Zweibelson and Barg (1967). Cutsforth (1932) called attention to blind children's inclination to verbalism and refers to this as "verbal unreality" or naming things without any real experience or idea of them. Nolan (1960) repeated Cutsforth's experiments and found significantly lower percentages of verbalisms, which brought him to the conclusion "that 'verbal unreality' is not a significant problem for the group studied" (p. 102). Harley (1963) also studied verbalisms and found them to be higher in the areas of food, farm, and nature than in the areas of home, clothing, and community. He emphasized "that blind children need a unique program in order to help them learn simple concepts that sighted children have developed through incidental learning" (p. 53).

Concreteness in teaching can be achieved in essentially two ways: by having the children observe the object or situation itself, or by providing them with a model of the object. In all cases if there is any possibility, reality is to be preferred. Of course, children must be given sufficient time for the observation and in many cases, it is good practice to leave the object available for informal observation after class. In such situations visually handicapped children can learn much from each other or from their sighted peers. Study excursions and field trips can familiarize children with many situations which otherwise would remain abstract for them. The value of such field trips depends to a large extent upon their preparation and follow-up.

If an object cannot be observed in reality by blind children, for reasons which have already been discussed, a model or replica of it can give them an opportunity to observe certain of its characteristic features. A model or replica can only be a substitute and will always in some ways be incomplete or distorted. For instance, stuffed and mounted animals are usually true to size, shape, and to a certain extent texture, but they cannot give the feeling of warmth, life, and motion (nor can they make any noise) that live animals do. If a replica of the animal is used, the only characteristic preserved for touch observation is shape, while size and texture are missing. Very often the size is so different from reality that children may acquire distorted notions about the relative size of animals unless the teacher is careful and persistent in making the students fully aware of size and other distortions. Sometimes stuffed animals may be used to supplement the actual experience of the child with the real animal, which may not hold still long enough to have details of his body observed.

The use of embossed pictures to give blind children an equivalent of visual illustrations has often been tried but never had any lasting success. Embossed outlined representations of essentially two-dimension objects, such as leaves, a fork, or a butterfly, may be identified by blind children, and even a man's figure will be understood because the child will relate the body parts to his own bodily experiences. Merry and Merry (1933) concluded a study of the tactual recognition of embossed pictures by blind children as follows.

> It may be of value to make use of embossed designs of a bi-dimensional type in the education of blind children, but it is very doubtful if embossed pictures of tri-dimensional objects, wherein perspective is involved, possess any real meaning for children without sight even after systematic instruction [p. 163].

From experience it is known that such embossed pictures can even result in wrong ideas, as for instance when a four-legged animal is shown with only three legs, since the fourth one is visually hidden. Besides this, the legs are shown in a plane and not "at the four corners of the body," as a child remarked. Of course, diagrams and embossed maps are most valuable from the early school years on in developing spatial concepts and basic relationships needed for orientation and other purposes.

Giving blind children a knowledge of the realities around them is not a question of enriching the child's vocabulary, but of giving him a sense of reality about his environment. It will prevent him from falling into a pattern of unreality toward which he may be inclined for other reasons. (These disposing factors may be in his family relationships or in some personal disappointments which everyone must face from time to time, but blind children more frequently than their sighted peers.) It will also be valuable to him in his social life, because in conversations he will not feel left out by lack of concrete knowledge but will be able to take an active part as the result of experiences which he has in common with others.

Need for Unifying Experiences

It has already been stressed that blind children are at a serious disadvantage in experiencing things and situations in their totality. Touch permits simultaneous observation only of objects that can be embraced by either the hands or the body. Larger objects must be observed by consecutive touch motions and in many instances, only parts of them are observed in this way. Vision permits a unification of observations and it structures and organizes discrete impressions received by other sensory organs. The lack of unifying integrative experiences, of gestalt formation, must be counteracted by teachers who give blind children opportunities to experience situations in their totality and to unify part-experiences into meaningful wholes. The teaching by study units is an important means of achieving this end. By this method blind children will not only learn the facts of a given topic as seeing children do, but will also recognize how the different parts combine into a total object, situation, or topic.

This author has attempted to describe the experiences of a blind child who is taken along by his mother on a shopping trip to the grocery store (Lowenfeld, 1950).

> Johnny enters the store; a wave of mixed odor sensations accompanies his entrance. If he has previously been in a grocery store, he probably identifies the place on the basis of former odor associations. He holds his mother's hand and walks with her until she stops in front of the counter. If Johnny is an alert blind child who has been encouraged to explore, his free hand probably reaches out while he is walking and may touch one or the other object. He cannot identify any of them because the contacts are too fleeting. If he is less alert or active, he will just cling to his mother, making no attempt to explore. Now he stands in front of the counter listening to the orders given to the clerk, hearing him walk behind the counter and placing things upon it. His hands may reach out and get hold of some objects, perhaps some wrapped packages (he doesn't know that bread is in them), some bottles (he doesn't know what they contain), or some boxes (he may identify them as containing candy of which he is quite fond). When mother has finished her shopping which Johnny had tried to interrupt with questions that she had no time to answer satisfactorily, they leave the store [p. 92].

In comparing this child's experiences with those of seeing children, the teacher will recognize how much a study unit on the grocery store can contribute to the blind child's concept of it. Many of the objects will have to be presented concretely. A visit to the store, prearranged at a time when shoppers are not crowding it, and a follow-up by arranging such a store in the classroom will help in giving the blind child new experiences as well as in organizing and unifying them. Such a study unit offers opportunities for applying various skills, including reading, writing, spelling, number work, nature study, geography, etc., for seeing as well as blind children. As was mentioned already in the discussion of concrete experiences, study units needed for blind children should not deal with exotic topics but with those of everyday importance, such as means of transportation, the post office, workshops and factories, the farm, the woods, and what we drink and eat.

Need for Learning by Doing

As a result of their blindness and because of the environmental reactions to this handicap, blind children have in general significantly less opportunities for self-activity. Therefore, special attention must be given at home and in school to encouraging blind children to do as many things for themselves as are desirable and compatible with a well-conceived time economy. That blind children from an early age on are not visually stimulated by their environment to imitate activities of others, combined with the tendency of many parents to be content with just satisfying their child's bodily needs, causes a tendency toward inertia in many blind children. They need to learn many of the routine daily activities by having them shown to them in their way, and this takes effort, time, and patience. Undoubtedly, there is a point of diminishing returns, at which it becomes more economical and even in the child's interest to do something for or with him rather than to let him go through the process of learning to do it by himself. The general approach, however, should be to encourage blind children to learn to do things themselves with as little assistance as possible. This should begin with the child's first attempts in prehension, in getting about, and in such broad areas as eating, dressing, playing, and meeting people. The blind child should be encouraged to become independent and successful at these endeavors. The more situations he has learned to master, the stronger will be his feelings of security and the more positive his self-concept. This does not mean that the blind child should be shielded from negative experiences and disappointments, since like other children he must learn what his limitations are. But these experiences occur by necessity in a blind child's normal life, whereas the positive ones need to be increased and reinforced.

It is recognized that a child's feelings of security or insecurity are largely a result of his acceptance by his family during the early formative years. The degree of his acceptance determines to a large extent whether he will be given opportunities for self-activities or not, at least during his early years while he is at home. When he goes to school the teacher's attitudes will have a similar influence. A teacher who is reasonably secure herself and derives pleasure and satisfaction from her work can give blind children the opportunities for self-activities which they need. The teacher as well as the parent will need to distinguish between tasks and skills that are essential for the child to perform at a given stage of his development and those which must be left for later or need not be mastered at all. They will need to assist him in his learning by finding a progression toward accomplishment by which each step is within the child's capability and still poses a challenge to him. This requires sensitivity and identification on the part of the educator and inserts an art element into teaching which is challenging to pursue and satisfying in its results.

As regards the creative activities of blind children, educators should not impose their "seeing taste" on blind children, but should let them create things according to their own concepts and emotions. The visual aspects of a piece of clay modeling are irrelevant for the blind child, who works by touch and expresses through his sculpture his touch concepts of things and events. Thus, the result may be a product which in no way resembles the visually perceived object, but truly expresses what the blind child knows and feels. It is the process that counts and not the product. As Viktor Lowenfeld (1957) said,

> It is time to realize that the most primitive creative work, born in the mind of a blind person and produced with his own hands, is of greater value than the most effective imitation [p. 446].

From all that has been said about individual considerations and about the special educational needs of blind children, it is obvious that the teacher can fulfill her role only if the number of children in her group is small. This is true for classes in residential schools as well as for facilities in local schools, with either resource room or itinerant teachers. The actual number of children will depend on such factors as grade level, age and grade spread, subject matter (in the upper grades), and geographic location (for itinerant teachers). In general, between five and ten children can normally be assigned to one teacher. If special conditions exist, such as an itinerant teacher serving blind children in primary grades, or if the children are multihandicapped, a much smaller teacher–pupil ratio, sometimes one to one, may be essential for success.

EMOTIONAL AND SOCIAL EFFECTS

While blindness causes specific and unique effects in the area of cognitive functions and mobility, the emotional and social effects of visual handicaps are nonspecific. The emotional and social reactions of visually handicapped children are the same that can be found in other children, though in the latter they may be caused by different factors. For instance, if a visually handicapped child feels rejected by his playmates because he is less successful in a competitive game than they expect him to be, other children may feel rejected by their peers because of different characteristics, such as race, religion, or physical characteristics (being too small, too tall, or even redheaded).

Environmental Attitudes

There is no doubt that environmental attitudes play a primary role in the personality formation of visually handicapped children.

Wright (1960) described the stereotype of a person with a disability as "one who has suffered a great misfortune and whose life is consequently disturbed, distorted, and damaged forever" (p. 17). Blindness is generally considered the most severe handicap, and the stereotype of the blind individual is loaded with negative characteristics and connotations, such as helplessness, dependency, incapacity, and unhappiness. As a result of this stereotyping, blindness evokes pity and "represents an unusual stimulus to uninitiated others, a stimulus which may arouse feelings of threat, conflict, and fundamental impotence" (Gowman, 1957, p. xv). The uninitiated will also tend to focus their attention on the visual handicap, and it will take some time and reorientation until they will be able to look at the child rather than at his visual handicap. Therefore, stereotypical reactions must be overcome as a precondition for readiness to assist and teach blind children. Specifically, teachers will need to dissociate themselves from a tendency to ascribe all difficulties of the child to his visual handicap; to consider any achievement of such a child as "remarkable" or "wonderful"; to think that the visually handicapped child is in need of special consideration in every aspect of his school life; and to believe that things must be done or arranged for him rather than by or with him.

There are some people who, because of their own personal experiences (which are unconscious and may date back to such childhood practices as peeping, exhibitionism, and sex exploration), cannot approach blind persons without undue feelings of guilt, pity, or oversolicitation. Such people should not consider going into the profession of teaching visually handicapped children or into work with the visually handicapped in general, unless they have received successful psychotherapeutic intervention. Blank (1954) discussed in detail the unconscious conflicts about blindness and their effects in interfering with the professional worker's efforts in helping blind individuals.

It is interesting that teaching blind children has been found to rank high in prestige as compared with other special education groups. (Special education teaching in general carries a higher prestige than regular classroom teaching.) The most likely explanation for this high prestige is the recognition that teaching blind children demands, besides special knowledge, a high degree of insight, sensitivity, and devotion (Jones & Gotfried, 1966; Sharples & Thomas, 1969).

Related to the question of prestige is that of the acceptance of visually handicapped children by other children—do they choose them as friends, playmates, and workmates? It appears, from a study (Jones, Gottfried, & Owens, 1966) in which high school students were used as subjects, that blind children hold, in general, a position in the middle of the acceptance continuum. Children with comparatively mild handicaps, for instance the partially seeing, generally rank higher. There is no research available for younger visually handicapped children.

From experience it can be stated that young children usually accept visually handicapped schoolmates quite readily, sometimes after an initial phase of curiosity. They soon learn that the blind child cannot see with his eyes but does so with his hands; that they must be more specific in talking to the blind child, by not using "here" and "there" but by showing him the place and object meant so that he can touch it. Of course, seeing children will soon sense any apprehensions or reservations that their teacher may harbor about accepting a visually handicapped child in her classroom; but if they are left to themselves, they will in a natural way adjust to the presence of the visually handicapped child and accept him as one of the group. In stating this we have in mind a visually handicapped child who is himself normally developed. Any additional handicaps or behavior difficulties are liable to evoke different reactions from at least some of the seeing children.

Teachers have observed that attitude changes for the better occur in seeing children as they become more closely acquainted with a blind child. Bateman (1962) has examined this question and has found that subjects who had known blind children judged their abilities more positively, and that these judgments became even more favorable as the number of blind children known increased. She found a particular increase in Grades 3 through 6, though some increases occurred throughout all grade levels. Children in urban communities were more positive in their attitudes than those in rural communities. Thus, the dictum that "blind children are their own best salesmen" has received some research support.

In which way blindness is experienced by the blind child himself and how it affects his self-concept depends on two factors which are interacting. The growing blind child learns in various ways about the direct effects of blindness, as the differences in sensory usage between himself and others in his environment become apparent to him. He cannot pick up a toy he has dropped or catch the ball that is thrown to him in the same way as others do and he cannot move about as easily and quickly as they. When he goes to school he learns to read and write braille, which is different from the reading and writing of other children, and he learns to perform many tasks by using different skills and tools than his seeing peers. In many situations it is more difficult for him to gain the satisfaction of success, but when success comes, it can be a greater and stronger force in the development of a positive self-concept.

The second factor is the reactions of his environment to his visual handicap. If the people around him show anxieties and tenseness in reacting to his visual handicap, the blind child, like other children in similar circumstances, will reflect these attitudes in his own actions. He may become timid and develop a tendency toward withdrawal and daydreaming. On the other hand, an environment which stimulates the blind child and makes demands upon him which he can fulfill or which challenge him because they are at the fringe of his capabilities enables the blind child to develop a healthy self-concept and confidence in his own abilities.

At certain times of a growing youngster's life, the visual handicap, particularly total lack of sight, creates specific problems in our culture. The blind adolescent has greater difficulties in satisfying his sex curiosity than his seeing peers, who acquire most of their information about the physical sex differences in a visual way. Acceptable modes of acquiring such information by the blind adolescent must be by direct contact, as in dancing, but even at best they are far less informative than visual means. This problem was discussed by 't Hooft and Heslinga (1968), who recommend, among other sex education measures, the use of realistic teaching models of male and female nudes. The visually handicapped adolescent also has more difficulties in dating and if he is blind, he has far less freedom in choosing and approaching his partner. In addition, he may have the experience of meeting parents who are reluctant to have their child go out with a blind partner. There are frequently all-consuming interest spheres in the lives of seeing adolescents, such as bicycling, motorcycling, and later automobile driving, in which the visually handicapped youngster cannot compete with his seeing peers. Also, it is only natural that the visually handicapped adolescent experiences more intense anxiety about his economic and personal future (Lowenfeld, 1959; Miller, 1970): Will he be able to get a job and earn a living? Will he find a partner for marriage and marital happiness? Will his offspring be free of his visual handicap?

Many blind adolescents have coped with all of these problems because their ego strength had been built up by past experiences so that they could withstand occasional disappointments. An adult person in whom they have developed confidence and who neither sugarcoats nor exaggerates their problems can be of immense help to the growing young person (Abel, 1961).

Steinzor (1966) concluded a study on attitudes of visually handicapped children toward their blindness as follows.

> The ability to recognize their handicaps and to accept them, their aspirations to find a place in a world based on sight, their ability to identify themselves as persons rather than as blind, and the strength not to gloss over differences between sightedness and blindness seemed to be the main theme expressed by this group of young handicapped people. Their awareness of being blind was paralleled by their recognition of the necessity of adjusting to the sighted, their standards and their ways [p. 311].

There is one special problem which needs to be mentioned. Many blind children exhibit, particularly when they are young, certain behavior patterns which have been called "blindisms," such as turning the head rapidly, rocking back and forth, and eye-poking. Cutsforth (1933) considers them "acts of automatic self-stimulation" to compensate for the lack of stimulation from the outside world. In this he is supported by Sandler (1963), as already mentioned. It has been found that these reactions of blind children are the same as have been observed in seeing children as a result of similar deprivations and life situations (Smith, Chethik, & Adelson, 1969). However, with blind children these mannerisms are often looked upon with apprehension by parents and teachers because of fear of social disapproval and because they are interpreted as signs of maladjustment or retardation. In young blind children, the appearance of such behavior patterns seems almost unavoidable because they cannot gain stimulation by outside impressions comparable to what seeing children can gain by themselves. When the blind child grows older, blindisms usually decrease and tend to disappear as he becomes more interested in other pursuits and capable of occupying his energies more constructively.

It has also been suggested (Morse, 1965) that anxiety and frustrations are the cause of these mannerisms, since similar behavior occurs in others when they are in states of anxiety or frustration. Rewarding personal relationships were recommended as substitutes for these expressions. Cutsforth (1950), in a later article, came close to this point of view when he said that blindisms

> are only the responses of the individual reacting to his own physical awareness, in an attempt to resolve the tension and gain the satisfaction denied by his non-aggressiveness [p. 181].

It is to be expected that blind children with additional handicaps, particularly those who are retarded, will continue to exhibit these behavior patterns much longer and sometimes into adulthood.

Family

As has been stressed in our earlier discussions of the home environment and environmental attitudes, the attitudes of parents are the most important factor in a child's environment. Parents, as well as other important persons around the child, for instance teachers, are a part of the general public. Their attitudes, at least initially, are the same as those generally prevailing.

While the parents struggle with their inner conflicts, the blind infant grows and reacts, and his daily needs must be met. In most cases, the natural feelings of parents for their child are strong enough to make them seek advice and learn to do what is best for the child as he is.

Parental attitudes have been critically examined in a few studies. Sommers (1944) distinguished five reaction patterns: acceptance of the child and his handicap; denial of the effects of the handicap; overprotectiveness; disguised rejection; and overt rejection. Only the denial reaction needs some further explanation. It corresponds to the parental attitude category which Kanner (1957) classified as "perfectionism." Parents who have the attitude that the visual handicap has no limiting effects are liable to expect from the child more than is realistic. Thus, they may adversely affect the growing child's self-concept because he may not be able to meet their expectations. On the other hand, such parents often make self-sacrificing efforts for their child, just in order to prove that the visual handicap is no obstacle.

The adjustive mechanisms of the children to the five parental reaction patterns were found to be compensatory reactions; denial reactions; defensive reactions (rationalization, projection); withdrawal reactions; and nonadjustive behavior reactions. Sommers (1944) considers only the last two reactions maladjustments, because they lead either to resignation and avoidance of social contacts or to inability to deal with life problems. In a sense, withdrawal reactions may be considered as adjustive behavior, though this form of personal adjustment may not be socially approved.

Attitudes may change from time to time and even from situation to situation, but one or the other usually dominates and is characteristic of the total parental response. Sommers considers acceptance of the child and denial reaction as positive influences since they permit the child to develop, use opportunities, and participate in activities. Overprotection and disguised and overt rejection are negative attitudes because they interfere with the child's growth and development and deprive him of opportunities. She also stated, concerning the cause of the differences in parental attitudes:

> The meaning the child's handicap held for his parents, especially his mother, the intensity of her emotional reactions, and the kind of adjustment she was able to make seemed to depend largely on the psychological makeup of the individual parent, her marital relationships, and her own personal and social adjustment to life [Sommers, 1944, p. 105].

It is a truism that parental love and its manifestations are the most important factors influencing the child's growth and development and his future personality formation. If this love leads the parents, particularly the mother, to an understanding of the blind child, so that they can foresee his actions and reactions, the child's chances for a healthy personality development are greatly enhanced (Cowen, Underberg, Verillo, & Benham, 1961).

There is no question that the presence of a visually handicapped child in a family makes additional demands on, and offers unusual challenges to, primarily the mother but also the other members of the family. This is particularly the case as long as the child is young and must acquire skills in self-care and be given opportunities for new experiences. Reid (1958) stressed the need of parents for personal self-fulfillment and states:

> Professional persons must accept the task of lightening the load for such parents and giving them a chance to be free—free of guilt, remorse, and resentment and free of a 24-hour-a-day schedule of child care and therapy [p. 16].

Teachers assume an important role in helping parents, not only by taking care of the child for a part of the day, but also by understanding sympathetically the parents' needs and problems, and on this basis giving them advice and guidance.

There is no research available on the attitudes of siblings toward their blind brother or sister. Steinzor's 1967 study, the only exception so far, deals with multihandicapped blind children. Some observations on this aspect of the blind child's family can be made. Siblings of a blind child, particularly if they are older than he is, will tend to show their helpfulness to the blind child. If this is done spontaneously—most likely influenced by the example of the mother —it is desirable unless it interferes with the blind child's need for self-activity. There is, however, some danger that the siblings will be expected to do too much. For instance, it may appear natural and convenient for the older brother or sister to take the blind child to school. If doing so deprives the sibling of the companionship of his classmates in going to and coming from school, he may become resentful of this task. These feelings may not be expressed because of fear of disapproval, but they can turn into hostility toward the blind child which may find various kinds of expression. It is, therefore, necessary for parents to be sensitive also to the needs of their other children and to find acceptable limits of making siblings responsible for their blind brother or sister. That the blind child naturally receives somewhat more attention tends to make his siblings jealous and envious in many situations. Therefore, parents must be careful not to give their blind child too much praise or to single him out too often at the expense of the other children. What has been said here about parents does have some application also to teachers who have a blind child in their class.

Personality

Personality is the psychophysical organization of the individual as modified by his life experiences, and thus is influenced by heredity as well as by environment. The effects which blindness may have on personality are reflected in two statements indicating the extreme positions which blind people themselves take on this question. Cutsforth (1933) believes that "blindness changes and utterly reorganizes the entire mental life of the individual. The earlier this frustration occurs, the greater the reorganization that it demands . . ." (p. 2). Others assert that blindness is a mere inconvenience which does not have anything to do with the personality of an individual. The most distinguished sociological representative of the "inconvenience group," tenBroek, wrote,

> In simple terms, the thesis is that the blind as a group are mentally competent, psychologically stable, and socially adaptable; and that their needs are therefore those of ordinary people, of normal men and women, caught at a physical and social disadvantage [tenBroek & Matson, 1959, p. 1].

In fact, the proponents of both points of view are not so far apart as it may appear. If the reorganization which Cutsforth postulates is successful, blind individuals make "the joyous discovery that the condition of blindness is the least important thing about themselves and that it is of no importance at all to others" (Cutsforth, 1950, p. 180).

What are the results of psychological research in answering some of the questions concerning the influence of the visual handicap on personality? (Personality development is elaborated on in Chapter 3.) Many authors have stressed that increased anxiety is a personality characteristic of visually handicapped persons. Research on this problem was hampered by a general recognition that tests for the personality assessment of the seeing are not adequate when used with the blind (Sommers, 1944; Barker, Wright, Meyerson, & gonick, 1953). An Anxiety Scale for the Blind (Hardy, 1968) was given only to residential school students and its results are, therefore, not applicable to blind children in general.

Bauman (1964) developed, specifically for use with blind adolescents, the Adolescent Emotional Factors Inventory and applied it to matched groups of students of residential and public school classes. Among her results were that partially seeing students showed significantly higher anxiety and insecurity than the blind; the residential school group showed more anxiety and insecurity, more difficulties in relating to the home and parents, and more problems of social and emotional adjustment than the public school group; attitudes of depression and withdrawal were more evident in the residential school students than in the nonresidential group. Bauman questions whether the differences between residential and public school students are due to the direct effects of the residential school environment, the separation from the family, or socioeconomic differences between children who go to residential schools and those who go to public schools. She stressed the need for further research.

There is one major study, *Adjustment to Visual Disability in Adolescence* (Cowen et al., 1961), in which a number of specially developed instruments were used for the measurement of child adjustment, parental attitudes, and parental understanding. Visually handicapped adolescents attending public school facilities, others attending residential school facilities, and a control group of sighted adolescents, matched in essential characteristics, were compared. For all three groups, it was found that parental understanding is highly and consistently correlated with good adjustment of the adolescent. No systematic or consistent differences were found in personality characteristics or adjustment among the three groups. The authors stated that the core of their "findings is well summarized in the statement that visually disabled subjects are remarkably comparable to their sighted peers with respect to the adequacy of their psychological adjustment" (p. 127).

Studies that were made by using the self-concept in comparing visually handicapped and seeing adolescents (Jervis, 1959; Zunich & Ledwith, 1965) showed no essential and consistent differences between visually handicapped and sighted children. Both studies noticed that blind subjects tended to a larger extent than sighted subjects to use extremes, such as either highly positive or highly negative attitudes toward themselves and others, or exclusive statements.

One of the few studies of congenitally blind children (McGuire & Meyers, 1971) came to the conclusion that behavior disturbances shown by these children have a psychogenic base and are "a high risk of, but not inevitable to, congenital blindness" (p. 142). They ascribe these behavior problems to the first-year self-preoccupation that is an inevitable result of lack of vision and to the limitations in the control of their physical and social environment which have already been discussed in this chapter.

Thus, the results of these studies confirm our initially stated observation that there is no inevitable link between blindness and specific personality patterns or maladjustment in the individual. In other words, there is no such thing as a "blind personality."

Facial expressions are important as manifestations of personality from which seeing people often derive important conclusions. If blind people—and here we are talking of those who are congenitally and totally blind—showed no differences in the intensity and frequency of their facial expressions, as compared with the seeing, it would not be necessary to mention them. However, blind children are from early infancy on severely disadvantaged in the interaction between themselves and others so far as facial expressions and gestural patterns are concerned. Blind babies show facial expressions of emotions, such as laughing, smiling, discomfort, and crying, in essentially the same form as seeing infants do, though in a more fleeting and facially less active way (Freedman, 1964; Fulcher, 1942; Thompson, 1941). As children mature, facial activity and expressiveness decrease with the blind, while they increase with the seeing. This is most likely the result of the difference between the two groups in observing and reacting to the facial expressions of others.

Many have observed the "silent faces" of the blind and interpreted them as disinterest or boredom. It is, therefore, the parent's and teacher's task to actively encourage facial expression in blind children. This can be done by making the child aware that his face does not really express what he feels in a given situation. If blind children are consistently encouraged from an early age to show by their facial expressions when they are pleased, happy, amused, or sad, and to move their heads in the direction of the person with whom they are talking so that he can see their facial expression (and hear them better), they will become used to doing so and thus remove an obstacle to interpersonal relationships.

Partially seeing children are placed in a marginal position where their functions and roles overlap with those of the seeing and those of the blind (Meyerson, 1971). There are certain activities in which they cannot share or if they do, their achievement will be inferior. For instance, in playing ball the partially seeing child cannot see the ball approaching him as well as his seeing peers and he will soon lose out in any competitive playing or be the least-valued player on any team. In an environment geared to the blind child's needs, he will not be given opportunities to make full use of his vision, which, though defective, he considers his greatest sensory asset. If he is frustrated in his visual functioning, he will be dissatisfied and become an outsider or hostile to his environment. The experience of many teachers as well as the results of some studies (Cowen et al., 1961; Cowen & Bobgrove, 1966; Greenberg & Jordan, 1957) give some indication that partially seeing children tend to be less well-adjusted than either the blind or the seeing.

Barker et al. concluded a 1953 review of then available studies on the social behavior and personality of the blind with a comment that is still valid:

> Probably the most impressive fact yet discovered about the psychology of the blind is the relatively small amount of personality disturbance that accompanies it. How persons can accommodate to so radical a shift in psychological living conditions without greater changes in behavior would seem to have important implications for students of personality as well as for those concerned with the adjustment of the blind [p. 290].

SUMMARY

People with visual handicaps are often referred to as the blind, the visually handicapped, or the partially seeing, with the underlying assumption that they are a homogeneous group. In fact, they are no more homogeneous than any equal group of seeing individuals would be, but even show some additional individual characteristics that are caused by their visual impairment. The following five of these variables have been discussed: cause of the visual impairment; degree of the visual impairment; onset of the visual impairment; eye condition and required eye care; and home environment.

The main points stressed were that (1) among the causes of blindness, retrolental fibroplasia and maternal rubella were particularly important during the past two or three decades, but the largest single cause of blindness is still prenatal influence of undetermined etiology. (2) The measurable degree of visual acuity has become less important, whereas functional visual efficiency has assumed increased relevance because unlimited use of the eyes under normal environmental conditions has become ophthalmologically approved. (3) The onset of the visual impairment and its duration have importance for retaining visual imagery and color ideas. The emotional consequences of the kind of onset, whether it is sudden or gradual, must be recognized. (4) The conditions of a child's eyes as well as the care they require affect him not only physically but also emotionally. Glasses as well as artificial eyes may cause discomfort and need special care. (5) The visually handicapped child, particularly the blind child, depends to a far greater extent than seeing children on the opportunities for experiences and learning which the home environment must provide during his preschool years.

Visual impairment, particularly total blindness that is congenital, has unique effects only in the area of cognitive functions. Blind children are limited in the range and variety of their experiences since they must apply touch for the purpose of cognition and this cannot be done with all objects nor in all situations. Though touch has some unique advantages, vision functions as a unifying and structuring sense and in this it cannot be replaced by any or all of the remaining senses.

Blindness also interferes seriously, from early childhood on, with the ability to get about. Even the most efficient use of the cane, the dog guide, and human guidance cannot eliminate difficulties and deceleration. Physical locomotion and mental orientation are discussed as the two essential and interacting components of mobility.

Lack of sight also causes some detachment from the physical and to a lesser degree from the social world. This affects the ego development of blind infants and plays an important role in other skills which children must acquire, such as walking, maintaining good posture, playing, learning expressive movements, and in all other performances where imitation is involved. Blindness, however, does not interfere with verbal communication.

In spite of these difficulties, the achievements of most blind children who have no additional impairments compare well with those of their seeing peers.

The effects of blindness on cognitive functions demand the application of certain principles of special methods in the education of visually handicapped children. They need concrete experiences in order to make up for the wealth of knowledge which vision allows seeing children to gain in a casual way. They need unifying and structuring experiences in order to learn about objects and situations in their totality. They need increased opportunities for learning by doing in order to compensate for reduced environmental stimulation and its resulting inertia. Self-activity and opportunities for creative expression strengthen the child's feelings of self-confidence, and successful management of skills and of situations contributes to a positive self-concept.

It is stressed that the emotional and social reactions of visually handicapped children are nonspecific: They are the same as can be found in other children, though caused by different factors.

Environmental attitudes, which are important in determining the child's reactions to his visual handicap, are stereotypical and determined by the fact that blindness evokes such feelings as guilt, pity, and oversolicitation. Early childhood experiences are considered determinants for these attitudes.

Attitudes of the family, particularly the mother, are of utmost importance in their influence on the growing child. Various reaction patterns of parents are reported and it is stressed that teachers have an obligation to assist the parents. There is no doubt that siblings are affected by the presence of a visually handicapped child in the family, though practically no research on this problem is available.

The attitudes of teachers and school peers have been the topic of some investigations. Blind children were found to rank in the middle of the acceptance continuum. Attitude changes for the better come with closer acquaintance with blind children.

Blind people themselves appear to take different views of the effects of their impairment on personality. Research has found some personality differences between blind and seeing adolescents, but in general results show that visually handicapped students are remarkably comparable to their sighted peers. However, the marginal position of partially seeing students manifests itself in their increased anxiety and insecurity as compared with the blind and the seeing.

Blind adolescents have special difficulties in satisfying their sex curiosity and often in establishing relationships with the opposite sex.

As a result of the decreased feedback in the interaction of facial expressions, blind individuals show less facial expressiveness. For the same reason they also show a decrease in gestural patterns. This may, at least initially, affect social contact formation.

The self-concepts of visually handicapped and seeing adolescents appear to be essentially similar and, in general, it can be said that there is no typical "blind personality."

REFERENCES

Abel, G. L. The blind adolescent and his needs. *Exceptional Children,* 1961, **27,** 309–310, 331–334.

A.M.A. Committee Report. *Estimation of loss of visual efficiency.* A.M.A. Archives of Industrial Health, October 1955.

Axelrod, S. *Effects of early blindness: Performance of blind and sighted children on tactile and auditory tasks.* New York: American Foundation for the Blind, 1959.

Barker, R. B., Wright, B. A., Meyerson, L., & Gonick, M. R. *Adjustment to physical handicap and illness: A survey of the social psychology of physique and disability* (Rev. ed.). New York: Social Science Research Council, 1953.

Barraga, N. *Increased visual behavior in low vision children.* New York: American Foundation for the Blind, 1964.

Bateman, B. Sighted children's perceptions of blind children's abilities. *Exceptional Children,* 1962, **29,** 42–46.

Bauman, M. K. Group differences disclosed by inventory items. *International Journal for the Education of the Blind,* 1964, **13,** 101–106.

Blank, H. R. Countertransference problems in the professional worker. *Outlook for the Blind,* 1954, **48,** 185–188.

Blank, H. R. Dreams of the blind. *The Psychoanalytic Quarterly,* 1958, **27,** 158–174.

Burlingham, D. Hearing and its role in the development of the blind. *The Psychoanalytic Study of the Child,* 1964, **19,** 95–112.

Cowen, E. L., & Bobgrove, P. H. Marginality of disability and adjustment. *Perceptual and Motor Skills,* 1966, **23,** 869–870.

Cowen, E. L., Underberg, R. P., Verillo, R. T., & Benham, F. G. *Adjustment to visual disability in adolescence.* New York: American Foundation for the Blind, 1961.

Cutsforth, T. D. The unreality of words to the blind. *The Teacher's Forum,* 1932, **4,** 86–89.

Cutsforth, T. D. *The blind in school and society.* New York: Appleton, 1933. (Rev. ed.). New York: American Foundation for the Blind, 1951.

Cutsforth, T. D. Personality and social adjustment among the blind. In P. A. Zahl (Ed.), *Blindness.* Princeton: Princeton University Press, 1950. Pp. 174–187.

Education of the blind: A survey. London: Arnold, 1936.

Fraiberg, S., Siegel, B. L., & Gibson, R. The role of sound in the search behavior of a blind infant. *The Psychoanalytic Study of the Child,* 1966, **21,** 327–357.

Freedman, D. Smiling in blind infants and the issue of innate vs. acquired. *Journal of Child Psychology and Psychiatry,* 1964, **5,** 171–184. Reprinted in *Outlook for the Blind,* 1967, **61,** 156–163; 194–201.

Fulcher, J. S. *"Voluntary" facial expression in blind and seeing children.* New York: Archives of Psychology, **272,** 1942.

Gowman, A. G. *The war blind in American social structure.* New York: American Foundation for the Blind, 1957.

Greenberg, H., & Jordan, S. Differential effects of total blindness and partial sight. *Exceptional Children,* 1957, **24,** 123–124.

Hardy, R. E. A study of manifest anxiety among blind residential school students. *Outlook for the Blind,* 1968, **62,** 173–180.

Harley, R. K., Jr. *Verbalism among blind children.* New York: American Foundation for the Blind, 1963.

Hathaway, W. *Education and health of the partially seeing child* (4th ed.). New York: Columbia University Press, 1959.

Hayes, S. P. *Contributions to a psychology of blindness.* New York: American Foundation for the Blind, 1941.

't Hooft, F., & Heslinga, K. Sex education of blind-born babies. *Outlook for the Blind,* 1968, **62,** 15–21.

Jervis, F. M. A comparison of self-concepts of blind and sighted children. In C. J. Davis (Ed.), *Guidance programs for blind children.* Watertown, Mass.: Perkins Institution for the Blind, 1959. Pp. 19–25.

Jones, R. L., & Gottfried, N. W. The prestige of special education teaching. *Exceptional Children,* 1966, **32,** 465–468.

Jones, R. L., Gottfried, N. W., & Owens, A. The social distance of the exceptional: A study at the high school level. *Exceptional Children,* 1966, **32,** 551–557.

Kanner, L. *Child Psychiatry* (3rd ed.). Springfield, Ill.: Charles C Thomas, 1957.

Lowenfeld, B. Effects of blindness on the cognitive functions of children. *The Nervous Child,* 1948, **7,** 45–54.

Lowenfeld, B. Psychological foundation of special methods in teaching blind children. In P. A. Zahl (Ed.), *Blindness.* Princeton: Princeton University Press, 1950. Pp. 89–108.

Lowenfeld, B. The blind adolescent in a seeing world. *Exceptional Children,* 1959, **25,** 310–315.

Lowenfeld, B. Psychological problems of children with impaired vision. In W. M. Cruickshank (Ed.), *Psychology of exceptional children and youth* (3rd ed.). Englewood Cliffs, N. J.: Prentice-Hall, 1971. Pp. 211–307.

Lowenfeld, B. *Our blind children: Growing and learning with them* (3rd ed.). Springfield, Ill.: Charles C Thomas, 1971.

Lowenfeld, V. *Creative and mental growth* (3rd ed.). New York: Macmillan, 1957.

McGuire, L.L., & Meyers, C.E. Early personality in the congenitally blind child. *Outlook for the Blind,* 1971, **65**, 137–143.

Merry, R. V., & Merry, F. K. The tactual recognition of embossed pictures by blind children. *Journal of Applied Psychology,* 1933, **17**, 148–164.

Meyerson, L. Somatopsychology of physical disability. In W.M. Cruickshank (Ed.), *Psychology of exceptional children and youth* (3rd. ed.). Englewood Cliffs, N.J.: Prentice-Hall, 1971. Pp. 1–74.

Miller, W.H. Manifest anxiety in visually impaired adolescents. *Education of the Visually Handicapped,* 1970, **2**, 91–95.

Morse, J.L. Mannerisms, not blindisms: Causation and treatment. *International Journal for the Education of the Blind,* 1965, **15**, 12–16.

Nagera, H., & Colonna, A. Aspects of the contributions of sight to ego and drive development: A comparison of the development of some blind and sighted children. *The Psychoanalytic Study of the Child,* 1965, **20**, 267–287.

Nolan, C. Y. On the unreality of words to the blind. *Outlook for the Blind,* 1960, **54**, 100–102.

Omwake, E. G., & Solnit, A. J. It isn't fair: The treatment of a blind child. *The Psychoanalytic Study of the Child,* 1961, **16**, 352–404.

Reid, E. S. Helping parents of handicapped children. *Children,* 1958, **5**, 15–19.

Rubin, E. J. *Abstract functioning in the blind.* New York: American Foundation for the Blind, 1964.

Sandler, A. M. Aspects of passivity and ego development in the blind infant. *The Psychoanalytic Study of the Child,* 1963, **18**, 343–360.

Sandler, A. M., & Willis, D. M. Preliminary notes on play and mastery in the blind child. *Journal of Child Psychotherapy,* 1965, **1**, 7–19.

Schlaegel, T. F., Jr. The dominant method of imagery in blind as compared to sighted adolescents. *Journal of Genetic Psychology,* 1953, **83**, 265–277.

Sharples, D., & Thomas, D. J. The perceived prestige of normal and special education teachers. *Exceptional Children,* 1969, **35**, 473–479.

Siegel, I. M. *Posture in the blind.* New York: American Foundation for the Blind, 1966.

Smith, M., Chethik, M., & Adelson, E. Differential assessments of "blindisms." *American Journal of Orthopsychiatry,* 1969, **39**, 807–817.

Sommers, V. S. *The influence of parental attitudes and social environment on the personality development of the adolescent blind.* New York: American Foundation for the Blind, 1944.

Steinzor, L. V. Visually handicapped children: Their attitudes toward blindness. *Outlook for the Blind,* 1966, **60**, 307–311.

Steinzor, L. V. Siblings of visually handicapped children. *Outlook for the Blind,* 1967, **61**, 48–52.

Supa, M., Cotzin, M., & Dallenbach, K. M. "Facial vision": The perception of obstacles by the blind. *American Journal of Psychology,* 1944, **57**, 133–183.

tenBroek, J., & Matson, F. W. *Hope deferred.* Berkeley: University of California Press, 1959.

Thompson, J. *Development of facial expression of emotion in blind and seeing children.* New York: Archives of Psychology, **264,** 1941.

Warren, H. C. (Ed.). *Dictionary of psychology.* Boston: Houghton Mifflin, 1934.

Witkin, H. A., Birnbaum, J., Lomonaco, S., Lehr, S., & Herman, J.L. Cognitive patterning in congenitally totally blind children. *Child Development,* 1968, **39,** 767–786.

Wright, B. A. *Physical disability—A psychological approach.* New York: Harper, 1960.

Zunich, M., & Ledwith, B. E. Self-concepts of visually handicapped and sighted children. *Perceptual and Motor Skills,* 1965, **21,** 771–774.

Zweibelson, I., & Barg, C. F. Concept development of blind children. *Outlook for the Blind,* 1967, **61,** 218–222.

CHAPTER 3

Understanding and Meeting Developmental Needs

Geraldine T. Scholl

*School of Education
The University of Michigan*

INTRODUCTION

The process of growth and development for any individual child is at the same time similar to and different from that for any other child. It is similar because growth is sequential, with identifiable stages through which all children progress; it is different because each child progresses at his own unique rate as a result of his own individual needs. This principle applies to visually handicapped children as well, and in general their similarities *to* are greater than their differences *from* sighted children.

The variations that are observed in the growth and development of visually handicapped compared with sighted children are more often than not variations in the rate of growth that result from direct or indirect influences of the impairment. Wright (1960) refers to these influences as *handicaps*. In this chapter, a distinction will be made between those influences or handicaps which are direct and those which are indirect. The direct impose limitations or restrictions on the child for which he must receive compensatory experiences; the indirect are culturally or environmentally determined and in general are alleviated by programs directed toward modifying certain forces outside the child himself. While there is some overlap, the distinction may help the student of special education identify those areas for which compensatory experiences through special education are appropriate and those areas where environmental manipulation, such as through programs of prevention, is necessary.

Direct influences are those which result immediately from the visual impairment in a cause–effect relationship and which generally have a handicapping or disabling effect on the development of the individual. The impact of the visual impairment on cognitive development, which was discussed in Chapter 2, illustrates a direct influence. In general, the present state of knowledge, particularly in psychological and medical fields, precludes instituting effective remedial measures to counteract direct influences of total blindness. It is possible, however, that future research to test present theoretical positions on the substitution of one sensory system for another (Tanner, 1963) may change or modify to a degree the now inevitable handicapping effect of certain direct influences.

The indirect influences are more difficult to define but often have a greater impact in the developmental process. Indirect influences are those environmental forces which restrict and deprive individuals of opportunities and experiences because of such factors as attitudes toward and lack of knowledge about the nature of the impairment. They tend to impose serious limitations on the individual when he reaches adulthood. These indirect influences occur most often in the social and emotional areas of development, as described in Chapter 2. Indirect influences often give rise to a slower rate of growth, which may result in an appearance of mental retardation in the visually handicapped child. It is necessary, therefore, that the educator be aware of the potential impact of the indirect influences on the developmental process and work to reduce the effects of such influences.

There is little definitive research on the relative handicapping effects of either direct or indirect influences on the growth and development of the visually handicapped. Case studies and other descriptive research often do not take into account variations which may result from such factors as degree of vision and age of onset of visual impairment. Ideally, to control for these variables, a population of congenitally blind children should be identified. Such a population is difficult to locate. Therefore, the content for this chapter is drawn from available studies of the visually handicapped, from research on other handicapped and disadvantaged groups, and from the author's observations and experiences with the visually handicapped. These resources form the basis for drawing comparisons between the growth and development of the sighted and the visually handicapped.

The focus in this chapter is on the direct and indirect influences of the visual impairment on growth and development. The various aspects of growth and development, namely, physical, mental, social, and emotional, are discussed as though they can be isolated. In reality, no one aspect can be singled out as occurring in isolation; rather all are interrelated and exert mutual influence upon each other. Additionally, this chapter considers the growth and development of the congenitally blind child with no vision, within the normal range of intelligence, and with no additional marked impairments. Variations in developmental needs will occur as a result of the visual factors described in Chapter 2 as well as the incidence of other disabilities as outlined in later chapters.

GENERAL CHARACTERISTICS OF GROWTH
AND DEVELOPMENT

From studies of the so-called normal, some general characteristics of growth and development can be identified. These include the role of heredity and environment, the sequential nature of development, and the stability of the organism as it proceeds through the stages of growth and development.

Each human being is endowed at birth with an inherited potential; the degree to which this potential is achieved is dependent on the environment and the opportunities it provides (Hunt, 1961). The theoretical question whether all human beings are endowed equally at conception can probably never be answered because the exact impact, particularly of prenatal factors, cannot be determined. Efforts to attribute intellectual differences to heredity are questioned (Jensen, 1969; Kagan et al., 1969) partly because the concept that "all men are created equal" is deeply rooted in the American culture. In addition, the best measure of intellectual potential at the present time is the test of intelligence, which has lmited applicability to groups other than white middle-class Americans. It is probably safe to assume, however, that no one achieves his maximum potential for a variety of reasons. The direct influences of a visual impairment on certain aspects of cognitive development make it theoretically impossible for the visually handicapped child to achieve the maximum potential in certain areas that can be achieved by the normal child. However, experiences provided by his environment can compensate to a degree for certain of his deficiencies.

Although the existence of equal hereditary potential for all may not be known, variations in the environment are recognized and a "perfect" environment remains an illusive ideal. Amounts of environmental stimulation exist on a continuum and some deprivation is present to a degree for all. Fortunately for most children, an enriched environment can compensate considerably for the inevitable "mistakes" in handling, deprivations in experience, and restricted opportunities for developmental stimulation. When environmental deficiencies are excessive and occur at an early age, however, certain difficulties may arise in achieving maximum potential (Bloom, 1964). Remedial measures for reducing the deprivation caused by direct and indirect influences of the visual impairment on growth and development need to be provided in order that the visually handicapped child may achieve his individual maximum potential.

In most aspects, the developmental process occurs in a sequence with definable stages through which all children pass. Knowledge and understanding of this sequential nature of growth and development are particularly essential for parents and teachers of visually handicapped children. Enriched experiences are often necessary to help the child master the particular skills or tasks of one stage in order for him to move on to the next stage. Further, the mastery of a particular skill cannot be expected until its antecedent steps in the sequence have been mastered. For example, attempts to teach reading will fail unless the child has sufficient skill in understanding and using oral language to express his thoughts. The acquisition of oral language precedes written language in the developmental sequence; teachers must know how to evaluate skill in oral language to determine when it is appropriate to introduce reading, and how to provide opportunities for meaningful expression orally if the child lacks such skill. Readiness for any aspect of learning can be most readily assessed when the stages in the developmental process are recognized and experiences provided at the optimal time. This process is sometimes referred to as *pacing* (Olson, 1959).

The attempts of the organism to maintain its stability are recognized by developmental psychologists. Spurts in growth tend to be followed by periods when gains are consolidated. Temporary regression, particularly in emotional development, will often appear prior to movement to a higher integrative level. Parents and teachers need to recognize that the growth process may not always be smooth and that temporary periods of disorganization or disequilibrium are to be expected. Patience and understanding will go a long way toward helping both the child and the parents over such rough periods.

PHYSICAL AND MOTOR DEVELOPMENT

The visual impairment in and of itself does not retard physical and motor development; however, there are important indirect influences which may and often do retard development. These influences include the etiology of the visual impairment, which may also contribute to the presence of concomitant physical disabilities; lack of opportunity because of parental overprotection, neglect, and misunderstanding of needs; inability to acquire skills naturally because of deficient imitative learning; delayed development because of lack of the visual stimulation that may be necessary to learn certain skills. In addition, the way the impairment limits the ability to get about and to control the environment, may affect optimal physical and motor development. Potential hazards to development due to these influences and special needs in the physical and motor areas are discussed in this section.

Hazards to Physical and Motor Development

Structuring an enriched environment in which the blind child can develop fully his physical and motor skills presents a challenge to the teacher and parent. A brief observation of the activities of the normal infant leads to an appreciation of the role that vision plays in stimulating his physical growth and development. The visual stimulus of a desired toy often provides the necessary motivation to reach and grasp, thereby developing muscles and body control. Parents and teachers must provide opportunities to compensate for the lack of such visual stimulation in the blind child's environment.

An understanding of normal growth and development is necessary in order to know at what point and how these compensating opportunities may be introduced. For convenience, early physical and motor development will be discussed in 2 stages: prewalking and walking.

Prewalking Stage

Physical growth and development proceeds in a head-to-foot direction, sometimes called cephalocaudal sequence (Olson, 1959). The infant progresses to the walking stage through this sequence: holds up his head; sits up; stands; and finally walks. Creeping and crawling may also be a part of this sequence for some infants. Further, he gains control of his arms before he controls his legs. The physical development of the blind infant proceeds through the same sequential pattern but his rate is usually retarded because he lacks the visual stimulation which motivates the normal child throughout this stage, particularly at the beginning. Two areas in development may be retarded by the visual impairment: good hand coordination and skill in using the body.

At 16 weeks of age, the normal infant will follow a moving object with his eyes and may even attempt to reach for it (Ilg & Ames, 1955). This early visual tracking of an object marks the beginning of learning to control arms, hands, and finally fingers. Good hand coordination thus evolves from early experiences and experiments with eye–hand movement. Because he cannot see an object and therefore lacks the stimulation for this visual tracking, the blind infant is truly handicapped as he enters this developmental sequence.

Retardation in learning to control fingers and in the efficient use of hands is often observed by teachers of young blind children. Experiences with activities that are directed toward improving hand and finger coordination are often necessary before reading and writing can be introduced. The manipulation of blocks, the identification of textures by touch, and various craft and handwork activities are illustrative of the kind of experiences that should be provided. Such remedial measures may come too late, as evidenced by observation of some congenitally blind adults. A weak handshake and awkwardness in such activities as lighting a cigarette attest to a lack of opportunity to develop good hand coordination at an early age. It becomes important, therefore, for parents and teachers working with blind infants to provide the necessary experiences as early as 16 weeks of age that will ensure as near normal development of hand coordination as possible.

An important guideline for providing substitutes for visual tracking should be noted. For the blind child, knowledge of the object world comes primarily through tactile and only secondarily through auditory channels. Consequently, the blind infant must first know and recognize a sound toy by touch before that toy can be used for auditory tracking and/or motivation for reaching and grasping. Attempts to use an auditory stimulus to attract the attention of the young blind child will not be effective unless the child recognizes the sound as coming from an object he knows and wants (Fraiberg, Smith, & Adelson, 1969). Further, talking to the infant as new toys and experiences are introduced helps develop concept formation as well as interest in the world outside himself.

Specific suggestions regarding substitute experiences for increasing the efficiency of other sensory channels may be found in Chapter 5.

The second sequence which may be affected by the visual impairment is that leading to walking. The normal infant at 16 weeks of age has, to a degree, gained considerable control of his head. He enjoys looking at his world from the eyes-front position and although he cannot as yet sit by himself, he does like to be held in a sitting position (Ilg & Ames, 1955). Holding up his head to look at his world provides the exercise necessary to gain muscular control of neck and upper trunk muscles; support in a sitting postion helps to strengthen those muscles. Each is a step in the sequence of learning to walk.

The blind infant at 16 weeks of age has little motivation for holding up his head. The world of objects beyond the reach of his arms is unknown to him and his ability to explore within arms' reach is often restricted by his poor muscular control. If by chance he discovers some object within arms' reach, he often encounters difficulty finding it again, should he lose it. The world of sounds soon becomes meaningless until he can attach significance to an auditory stimulus. The sound of his mother's voice becomes relevant when he knows he will soon be picked up, fed, or otherwise attended. The object world provides stimulation for the normal infant to hold his head erect, to gaze at it, and later grasp by creeping to get it. There can be no such motivation for the blind infant unless efforts of the parents are directed toward providing substitute experiences. Sound toys that are made desirable objects for the infant can be used for motivating him to grasp when they are held within his reach. Later, the name of the toy may be used for motivating him to reach or creep or walk toward it.

When compensatory experiences are provided for the blind child during these early stages of physical and motor development, he has a better chance to enter the second year of his life more or less equal to his sighted peers.

Walking Stage

By 15 months of age the sighted child is walking and exploring his world on his own (Ilg & Ames, 1955). Once he is comfortable in an upright position and achieves balance to propel himself forward, he is soon running and jumping, and by the time he is 6 years of age, skipping. Often the blind child enters this stage of his development at a disadvantage. He may walk at a later age because he lacks the motivation to propel himself by taking his first steps from a standing position in order to obtain some desired object. The ever-present unseen dangers in his environment prevent him running freely and with abandon. Jumping and skipping must usually be taught, since he cannot learn these skills by imitation.

The effects of this retarded physical development are noted by the teacher and later the mobility instructor when the child enters school. The opportunities provided by the school to compensate for the student's poor use of his body are often too late to enable him to walk easily, freely, and gracefully.

Meeting Developmental Needs

The role of parent and teacher in the developmental process is to reduce the impact of potentially retarding indirect influences. Early intervention is essential if the child is to develop as near normally as possible. The contribution of parent education programs and nursery school experiences cannot be underestimated as important ingredients in this process. Delays in the acquisition of skills beyond the stage of readiness may result in irreversible retardation or below-average performance of that skill. Kindergarten may be too late to initiate intervention; hence, it is essential that early work with parents be an integral part of the educational process.

There are additional needs in physical and motor areas which must be satisfied if near-normal development is to be achieved. These include motility and mobility; skills of daily living; and relaxation.

Motility and Mobility

Motility may be defined as having the power of spontaneous motion; mobility, as the state of being in motion with freedom and ease. Due to lack of experience, the congenitally blind child may be deficient in one or both. All children have a basic need for movement, a "hunger for sheer activity" (Olson,

1959, p. 98). The normal child is stimulated to move spontaneously in order to obtain a better grasp of his environment. The preschool child is in constant motion, as parents and nursery school teachers can attest. Teachers of elementary-school-age children plan their programs to channel the need for activity into acceptable forms and provide opportunities for satisfying this basic need for movement. Educational programs for adolescents include activities designed to drain off their excess physical energy. Opportunities to satisfy the basic need for movement from earliest infancy lead to increased ability to control one's body in space, to learn the place of one's body relative to persons and objects in the environment, and finally, to differentiate the self from the nonself. The development of the self-concept, discussed later on, is based on the perception of one's body relative to one's environment.

The lack of vision tends to make the blind child seek to satisfy this basic need for movement within himself rather than outside himself. He lacks the visual input to make the nonself desirable to grasp and to reach toward. His motility or power of spontaneous motion is therefore restricted. The satisfaction of his basic need for movement may then come from seemingly aimless physical activities which are sometimes referred to as blindisms.

Whereas the environment itself usually provides the child with stimulation to satisfy his basic need for motion, the environment of the blind child must often be structured to help him meet that need. Sensory stimulation through channels other than vision helps make the world outside himself more interesting. Such sensory stimulation, however, must be meaningful. Where possible, objects should be attached to the sounds they make; constant playing of radio or TV should be avoided. Unless meaning or significance is attached to a stimulus, it will tend to be ignored. The environment, therefore, should be structured with stimuli that are meaningful and can be utilized by the blind child to learn about that environment.

In addition to adequate sensory stimulation, the direct teaching of motor skills will provide outlets to satisfy the child's basic need for movement. Physical and motor activities are usually learned through imitation, and the child perfects his skills through watching others and attempting to model his movements on theirs. Parents and teachers should observe the activities of the blind child's peers and make a conscious effort to teach him the same activities. Peers can often be used as "instructors" for teaching skills and sometimes may be more effective than adults in helping the blind child learn. Through teaching, the blind child can acquire proficiency in many motor skills at approximately the "norm" for all children. In addition, a play area should be identified where the blind child can engage safely in free and unrestricted movement, such as running. The awareness of the danger of running into obstacles often inhibits the child; but if he knows that a certain area is free of obstacles, he can experiment safely with various forms of physical and motor activities.

The knowledge of how one's body moves in space helps the child orient himself in relation to his environment. The young blind child can derive a great deal of benefit from formal instruction in movement education. Movement exploration is directed toward helping the child understand and control the many ways his body may move (Halsey & Porter, 1963). He learns about his body by making himself as large or small as possible, using a variety of ways to go under or over an object, and coordinating his movement with that of another person. Later, he learns how various parts of his body can be used to express feelings; he develops an awareness of his body in space; and he learns how his body can be moved into various positions for specific purposes. Movement exploration lays the groundwork for subsequent experiences in physical education, including dance, which are an essential part of the curriculum for visually handicapped children.

Play provides further outlets for expending physical energy and opportunities to learn and practice physical and motor skills, as well as to acquire social skills. Again, since much of the young child's play is imitative in nature, the blind child often needs help in learning how to play and how to participate in the play activities of his sighted peers. Encouragement to participate and the direct teaching of skills utilized in particular play activities may often be necessary. Frequently, sighted peers are helpful and their cooperation must be enlisted to involve the blind child in play activities.

The child's environment both at home and at school should also encourage the development of fine muscle coordination. The normal toddler brings his mother small bits from the floor, thus learning to use his thumb and index finger. His daily play activities are directed toward developing fine muscle coordination and use of the hands. The blind child lacks such natural opportunities. Toys which require use of thumb and forefinger for manipulation may help, and finger plays may also be useful and provide experience necessary to develop good hand coordination.

Parents and teachers should provide experiences early in the child's life that will increase his skills in orientation, body coordination, and ability to get about easily and efficiently in his environment. The blind child should be provided with opportunities that will enable him to develop to his maximum potential in this area. The later work of the orientation and mobility instructor discussed in Chapter 9 will be more effective when early opportunities to develop motor skills have been provided.

Skills of Daily Living

The foundation for the acquisition of skills of daily living is laid during infancy. The degree to which the congenitally blind adult can and does care for his physical needs is probably related to the degree to which this was expected of him as a child. Again, it should be noted that expecting too much can be as dangerous as expecting too little; both parents and teachers must be sensitive to the child's readiness for assuming responsibility for self-care.

Feeding and toilet training should present no greater difficulty for the blind child than for the sighted child, provided a few guidelines are followed. For both these activities, a state of readiness or "set" must be established. This can be done in several ways. Verbal communication between parent and child can make the experience pleasant and one the child anticipates eagerly. An unhurried atmosphere will also help make the experience pleasant. New things must be introduced slowly, with plenty of opportunity to explore through the sense of touch. For example, in introducing the potty or potty-chair, the parent should allow the child many chances to explore it tactilely, and should explain it verbally, before placing him on it. After successful use, the child should, if he is interested, be permitted to explore his "accomplishment." The mother's acceptance and understanding of the need to satisfy the child's natural curiosity regarding this normal physiological function will help to prevent subsequent problems in toilet training as well as in the area of sex.

Similar opportunities to explore new foods tactilely should be provided during the feeding process, even though the results may be messy for mother. In addition, table utensils need explanation and exploration about their use as they are introduced. Again, because the lack of vision prevents imitative learning, direct teaching may often be necessary, particularly for acceptable table manners. The standards expected of the seeing child can and should be expected of the blind child as he matures.

The beginning process of dressing should present no difficulties. Exploring his clothing by touch, experimenting with taking off and putting on each item of clothing, and finally dressing himself can be expected at about the same age as for the sighted child, provided a set has been established and he shows a readiness for it. Again verbal explanations from the mother help the child learn the name of each item and where it belongs. Talking about colors of his clothing, even though he cannot experience the concept of color, may help to stimulate his interest in color combinations that will be useful to him as an adult.

Although dressing himself may present no problems, habits of good grooming may. The ability to see oneself as others see one begins in the sighted child with the mirror play of the preschool years and continues into adolescence, when time is spent in long and critical evaluation of one's face, body, and general appearance. The mirror provides stimulation and motivation for good grooming. The blind child lacks this motivation and unless parents and teachers become his "mirror," he may have little interest in his personal appearance and in how he presents himself to others. The educational procedures for the development of daily living skills are described in Chapter 9.

Relaxation

Although there is little research evidence, discussions with and observations of blind adults support the notion that a state of tension is almost inevitable, particularly when moving about. The environment beyond the blind person's fingertips consists of unknown dangers. Familiar surroundings are subject to frequent though slight changes, thus depriving the individual of free movement even within his own home. The constant facing of the unknown with the ever-present potential of danger contributes to a state of tension. The blind adult has two alternatives: he may either remain inactive or learn to deal with his tensions.

Little attention is directed in our educational programs to helping the blind child meet and cope with tension so that he will not resort to inactivity as a defense. Opportunities for relaxing experiences as well as direct instruction in relaxation exercises would be helpful. The inclusion of this aspect in the educational program may help prevent extraneous movements, tics, and other outlets for tension which are frequently noted in the adult blind person.

EMOTIONAL, SOCIAL, AND PERSONALITY DEVELOPMENT

The interrelationship of emotional, social, and personality development makes it difficult to separate these aspects; therefore, they will be considered together in this section. Influences of the visual impairment on development as described in this section are primarily indirect. The existence of any direct influence is debatable, but it is possible in the light of certain difficulties observed in the developmental process of young blind children. These will be discussed as they are related to the aspects presented in the following subsections.

Socialization

Parental Relationships

Socialization begins for the child when he forms his first meaningful relationship with his mother. The process is initiated soon after birth when the mother holds the baby in her arms for the first time. Some blind infants do not have this very early contact with their mothers, and the first close human contact of being held may be delayed for as long as 4 to 5 months. The infant's delicate physical condition immediately after birth sometimes requires time in the sterile isolation of an incubator or isolet where physical needs are met by minimal handling and human contact. The beneficial effect for the mother to regain her strength while her infant is cared for in the hopsital cannot be denied; the handicapping effect on the infant's emotional development may be another matter. The impact of the separation may affect both the infant and his parents. When he is brought home, the infant, unaccustomed to close human contact, may need time to learn to enjoy the comfort of being held; the parents, deprived of immediate close contact, may need time to readjust to his entrance into their lives. It is important that parents receive support and encouragement during this crucial time while infant and parents learn to respond to each other. An understanding social worker may be needed to help parents through this initial adjustment period.

As the sighted infant grows older, his eye contact initiates the development of a relationship with his mother first, and later the rest of the family. Visual contact seems to be an essential element in the process of building relationships (Burlingham, 1964). Lack of eye contact may represent a direct influence of the visual impairment on development that has an impact on early mother–child relationships. The possibility that deviant development may be attributed to the visual impairment has been noted (Fraiberg & Freedman, 1964; Nagera & Colonna, 1965). More research, preferably longitudinal studies of the congenitally blind, is needed to determine the exact role of vision in the formation of early relationships.

The reinforcement that parents usually gain from the response of their infant to them through physical contact and through eye contact may need to be supplied by resources outside the family. When parents react negatively in response to their infant's lack of response, a cycle of reinforcement in an undesirable direction may be initiated. The negative response of the parents may further retard the development of an adequate and meaningful relationship between parent and child. The early study of Sommers (1944) showed the positive relationship of parental attitudes to eventual adjustment of the blind adolescent. More recently, Cholden (1958) and Cowen et al. (1961) have supported the need for developing positive attitudes within the family toward the blind child in order to effect satisfactory adult adjustment. Early parent counseling is needed to facilitate formation of healthy parent–child relationships.

Sibling Relationships

After his parents, the sighted infant expands his world to include other family members, particularly his siblings. The relationship of the blind child to his siblings is largely an unexplored area, although some descriptive observations are available. The position of the child among his siblings, the sex of the child and his siblings, and age differences are undoubtedly important factors. Parents need to encourage acceptance of the blind child by his siblings but should expect the normal problems of sibling rivalry and competition.

Peer Group Relationships

From the security gained through meaningful relationships with the family group, the child moves to others outside the family. Blindness may be a handicap in forming such relationships at certain ages. The blind child lacks the visual stimulus of other children to initiate his first efforts to enlarge his circle of relevant others. The sighted preschooler watches and imitates his peers; their reactions provide him with the feedback necessary to know if and when he is acceptable. Visual contacts thus help the child move into a relationship, usually with one child first, and later with the group. The blind child is handicapped in initiating contacts and in knowing whether and when he is accepted and acceptable. Parents and at times siblings are needed to help in this process.

Sometimes it may be necessary to demonstrate the abilities of the blind child to his peer group; activities planned by the family to include his peers may assist in bridging the gap between the security of the home and the unknown world outside the home. In attempting to participate in group activities with his peers, the blind child may encounter some reality-based difficulties. He may know what he is to perform and how, but his visual impairment may reduce his utility to the group, thereby contributing to rejection. For example, the blind child may know how to throw a ball and hold a bat, but he undoubtedly can never be a sought-after member of the neighborhood baseball team. Assistance in accepting the reality of his limitations is therefore often necessary.

The blind child's inability to learn by imitation requires parents to engage in more structured teaching of skills and acceptable modes of dress and behavior throughout the life of the child from infancy through adolescence. The process of socialization is facilitated when the individual is accepted; acceptance comes from compatibility and correspondence with peer group norms, which must often be taught the blind child. Observation and experience of parents and teachers support the notion that the range of acceptable behavior is probably more narrow for the handicapped than for the normal. Research is needed to determine at what ages and in what circumstances more conforming behavior is required of the handicapped in order to be socially acceptable.

Adolescence presents particular difficulties in the socialization process. The adolescent rejection of those not like themselves may be a reality with which the blind adolescent must learn to cope. His visual impairment restricts his ability to act and look like his peers. The help of parents, siblings, and teachers is needed to identify the deficiencies of the blind adolescent in being like his group and, where possible, to help him overcome such deficiencies. For example, information concerning current fads in dress must be provided for the blind adolescent by the relevant others in his life. Interest in his appearance comes easily during adolescence when parents have stimulated such interest during early childhood and have provided feedback and reinforcement to substitute for a mirror in the life of the normal child.

Prevention of later difficulties in the process of socialization begins in infancy. Attempts to make the blind adolescent acceptable to his peer group will fail unless he has been accepted first within his own family and later in his neighborhood. Further socialization is facilitated when he has experienced the give and take of social behavior from early childhood and has had many and varied social experiences. The sympathetic help of parent, teacher, and counselor should be directed toward helping the blind child feel at ease in various social situations so that those around him will likewise feel at ease.

Meeting Affective Needs

Learning to love and to be loved begins in infancy. The delay in initiating human contact mentioned in the previous subsection may also contribute to hazards relative to meeting affective needs. Every infant needs fondling and cuddling. When this need is satisfied during infancy and early childhood, he learns to accept love and becomes ready to give love. Delays in being fondled for the blind infant may be caused by his extended period in the hospital immediately after birth as well as by difficulties in parental acceptance of the visual impairment and fear of handling the infant because he is not "normal." The risk of not providing adequate cuddling is therefore greater for the blind infant and his need for being held close to another human being may not be met adequately. Again, early parent education and counseling may avoid later problems.

Teachers of young blind children often need to provide more physical contact than is necessary for sighted children. The greater need for being close to an adult may be due to a delay in being handled which can result in some retardation in this area, or it may be a reflection of obtaining security and acceptance that the normal child receives from eye contact. Teachers must be aware of the individual child's needs but must also recognize that there is a point beyond which close contact with another person becomes socially unacceptable. A teacher holding a blind adolescent on her lap to give him security may not be perceived as encouraging appropriate behavior.

The need to be liked by others should also be recognized. Again this is related to socialization, discussed earlier. To be liked implies acceptability by others and the meaning of acceptability must often be taught consciously to the blind child. Such teaching must begin in early childhood in order to promote socially important behaviors.

The Self-Concept

The term *self-concept* will be used in this section to refer to the individual's perception of himself relative to his physical and social environment, or that which is the *not-self.* The development of the self-concept begins in infancy and continues throughout the life-span, undergoing constant modification in response to the environment.

Vision provides the infant with his first experiences in knowing himself as distinct from his environment. As he observes his mother moving away from and toward him, he begins to learn that she is an object separate from him. Additionally, he discovers his fingers and hands, toes and feet, spending hours visually exploring their relationship to him. Gradually he learns they are a real part of him, unlike his toys, which can be separated from his body. The process of developing a body image, an aspect of self-concept, continues through visual exploration of other parts of the body, through mimicry play with parents and siblings, and later through observation and study of himself in a mirror.

The recognition of himself as an individual is facilitated by parents and family and later by teachers. In the home, love and acceptance, opportunities to move from a protected to a semiprotected position outside the family, and expectations of success communicated to him will help the child develop a positive view of himself. The teacher continues the process by encouraging him to meet challenges within the school setting and to recognize his capacities and limitations realistically, and by expecting from him a level of performance consistent with his abilities. The self-concept continues to evolve throughout childhood as the environment provides experiences with success and failure that form the basis for evaluation of oneself and what one can and cannot do. The peer group often provides the feedback and reinforcement necessary to learn about oneself, giving approval or disapproval, encouragement or discouragement to actions and behavior. This give and take is often nonverbal in nature, such as frowns or approving smiles.

During adolescence, the concept of oneself as male or female emerges on the basis of prior experiences in the life-span. These include opportunities for identifying with an appropriate sex model, and imitation of dress, mannerisms, and behavior of that model. A system of values becomes incorporated into the self, based primarily on family and peer relationships and experiences. The acceptance of oneself as a person of worth is the ultimate objective of this process. While the major focus in this chapter is on childhood and adolescence, it should be noted that, unlike certain human characteristics such as physical height, one's self-concept is responsive to the environment throughout the life-span and changes constantly.

The preceding paragraphs represent a brief and somewhat oversimplified description of how the self-concept evolves. For the interested reader, Diggory (1966) and Wylie (1961) are recommended.

The difficulties encountered by the blind child in acquiring an adequate self-concept are evident as the role of vision in the process is recognized. The blind infant can explore the object world only through touch. It takes him longer to discover that hands and feet belong to him, and often this discovery is only made when he succeeds in exploring these appendages with his mouth. His mother's presence is known at first only by touch, and the association of her presence with the sounds she makes comes later than the visual association of the sighted infant. The body image normally acquired through visual obser-

vation and mirror play becomes real to the blind child through tactile exploration and later through verbal communication and feedback when language
becomes meaningful; these avenues are inferior in providing information concerning his body as compared to the bodies of others. Thus the formation of
a body image is delayed.

The more limited range of peers and peer experiences further retards the
blind child in developing an idea of himself. Often, too, parents attempt to
protect him from negative feedback concerning appearance and behavior; this
overprotection may contribute to his developing an unrealistic view of himself.
School experiences sometimes reinforce these feelings when teachers are not
realistic in their expectations and make special concessions and excuses
because of the visual impairment. While in general success experiences are
necessary to develop an adequate self-concept, some experiences with failure
may provide the necessary ingredient for developing a realistic self-concept,
which is essential for successful adult adjustment. A reality-based vocational
aspiration is particularly necessary.

During adolescence vision plays an important role in developing an identity
with one's own sex. In general the blind adolescent lacks the opportunity to
imitate the dress, manners, and behavior of a model, and thus may encounter
problems in adjusting to his sex role identification. The blind boy is at a
particular disadvantage. His experiences tend to be more within the security
of the home under maternal influence rather than in the male-dominated
environment of his peers. Further, the rough play of male adolescents is often
unknown to him and therefore he lacks one opportunity to learn the conventional masculine role. The uncertainty of a secure vocational future, discussed
later, further contributes to feelings of inadequacy.

The adolescent may encounter further difficulties in learning to accept himself as a blind person, with certain capacities and limitations as defined by his
impairment. Cholden (1958) has postulated that the adolescent must first
accept himself as a person before he can accept himself as a blind person. Since
acceptance of one's disability is considered an important step in the adjustment
process (Wright, 1960), it is necessary that the foundation be laid during
childhood and adolescence for an adequate and realistic self-concept, so that
acceptance of oneself as a blind person may evolve.

It becomes obvious that additional help must be provided within the experiential life of the blind child to help him develop an adequate self-concept. The
basic ingredients of love, security, and care must be supplied during early
infancy and continued throughout adolescence. A wide range of experiences
must be provided during preschool years and through high school. Such
experiences should approximate those available more readily and naturally to
sighted children. Finally, experiences should include a balance between success
and failure that will assure the development of realistic self-appraisal. The

importance of the self-concept in successful academic achievement for disadvantaged groups is recognized (Coleman et al., 1966). While research evidence for the visually handicapped is lacking, the principle seems clear that those handicapped who have an adequate self-concept tend to be the most successful (Wright, 1960).

Growing into Independence

One objective in the maturation process is to become independent. Total independence in all areas is neither a desirable nor an attainable goal, however. Everyone does rely on one or more other persons for the complete gratification of his needs. The restrictions imposed by the visual impairment do tend to prolong the period of dependence and make the blind person's degree of independence realistically unattainable when compared with that of the sighted. Therefore, one important element in working with the blind child is to help him know in what circumstances independence is a desirable goal and when dependence must be accepted. The converse of too strong a desire for independence is the potential withdrawal into a state of complete dependence. This too is not desirable and the blind child needs encouragement to become as independent as possible within the limitations of his impairment.

The young sighted child struggles to be free and independent early in his childhood. As soon as he has acquired mobility and can move freely in his environment, he is off and running, expanding his scope of life experiences. He soon attempts feeding and dressing himself, and at about 2½ years of age he asserts his control of his environment by frequent use of the word "No." Throughout the preschool years he grows more independent in all his activities, so that by the time he enters school, he is ready to leave the security of home and move into forces of influence outside the family. The growth toward independence reaches a climax during adolescence as he moves into the adult role.

Parents and teachers of the blind child must be aware of his readiness to assume more independence at each stage of his life. It is often necessary to provide stimulation at the critical times in order to ensure the learning of a particular skill at the appropriate age. Feeding and dressing himself may be used to illustrate this need. The normal child attempts to help himself by seizing the spoon or article of clothing from his mother's hands. He then uses it in imitation of his mother. Unless the blind child is encouraged to feel the feeding utensil or article of clothing and then follow his mother's hand as it is being used, he may not connect the object with its utilitarian purpose. After several years of being fed or being dressed, he loses the incentive to do such things for himself. Providing stimulation and guidance at the appropriate time of readiness will encourage the incentive to be independent. At all ages the objective should be to encourage the maximum degree of independence, approximating the norm to as great an extent as possible.

The struggle for independence can be particularly difficult for the adolescent and for the male. The normal adolescent tries to free himself of parental domination in a variety of ways: earning money to buy his own clothes and entertainment; driving a car; traveling to distant places by himself; making and executing his own plans for his time, his present activities, and his future. Many of these avenues for asserting independence are closed to the blind adolescent. Until his orientation and mobility skills are refined and he can travel safely on his own, he must remain dependent on others, usually his family, to take him where he wants to go. Some frustration in the adolescent drive for independence should be anticipated and can best be handled by patient parents and teachers who understand the dynamics of his frustrations and who help him learn to accept his limitations.

The cultural expectation for the male in American society is an individual who is dominant, independent, and able to rely on his own resources. The blind male can only approximate this ideal and, more often than not, plays a dependent role in certain social situations. For example, the blind male adolescent must rely on his sighted date to take him to their destination and to perform such activities as reading the menu in a restaurant. This inability to play certain aspects of the male role may become a threat to the striving for masculinity. Substitute opportunities to be masculine should be provided in order to help the adolescent learn his sex role.

Throughout the period of childhood and adolescence the blind child must be helped to accept dependence in those areas where independence cannot be achieved because of his impairment. He must be helped and guided to know when he needs assistance, how he can secure the assistance, and how to accept or decline graciously offers of assistance. It may be of help to the blind child and especially the adolescent to recognize independence as occurring on a continuum, where every individual has his needs for dependence and where everyone must learn to cope with the realities of his limitations.

MENTAL DEVELOPMENT

General Effects of the Impairment

Direct Influences

A visual impairment present at birth deprives the child of a vital source of sensory input that has a direct influence on his cognitive development. The preceding chapter describes the handicapping effect of the lack of vision on cognition. Other aspects of mental functioning are also probably affected, but the exact nature and degree of the impact on overall intelligence is difficult to determine. There is probably uneven development across specific intellectual abilities, but research on the cognitive development of the congenitally blind is necessary in order to determine what abilities are affected and to what extent each is affected. Such research is difficult to carry out because the number of children totally blind from birth and intact except for the visual impairment is relatively small. It would appear, however, that the depth of experiences through other sources of sensory input may compensate in part for the lack of breadth across the total sensory base; a rich background of sensory stimulation through other inputs may substitute to a degree for the deficiency in vision.

Indirect Influences

Compensation for the indirect influences of the visual impairment on mental development should be noted, especially since these are more amenable to control and modification by both parent and educator. Bloom (1964) postulates that an enriched environment is more effective in producing positive change in human characteristics when they are in their period of most rapid growth. Further, as much development in intelligence occurs during the first 4 years of life as in the next 13 years (Bloom, 1964). Compensatory educational programs are planned to offset the retardation of disadvantaged children from lack of appropriate experiences and meaningful sensory stimulation during the preschool years (see Crow, Murray, & Smythe, 1966). Such children often enter school having had few experiences outside the home, such as trips to the grocery store, the zoo, or museums; further, their language development is often retarded, thus limiting their ability to communicate their ideas effectively. These descriptions of the kind of experiential background found among disadvantaged children are consistent with observations of teachers concerning backgrounds of many blind children. The necessity for parent education programs and nursery school experiences, especially with sighted children, becomes evident. A rich background of experiences to help the blind child toward more normal mental development must be provided during the preschool years when his growth in intelligence is greatest.

Research with disadvantaged children shows that overstimulation during preschool years may lead to later ignoring of relevant stimuli in the school setting (Kagan & Moss, 1962). The child bombarded by too many stimuli is unable to sort out that which he needs for a particular learning task; his frustration leads to his blocking out all stimuli and giving the appearance of not paying attention. This research finding has implications for teachers and parents of blind children. Often parents provide a variety of stimuli, particularly through auditory channels, that hold no meaning for the blind child. New sensory experiences should be introduced in a setting where meaning or significance can be attached to them and where they can at first be easily distinguished from other stimuli. When presented with too much auditory stimulation that requires insufficient involvement in the process, the blind child can easily slip into his own world where no response is necessary. A good illustration of this is the blind child sitting in a rocking chair with television or radio blaring in his ears; his environment expects nothing of him and he derives satisfaction from his own fantasies while he rocks back and forth.

A Theory of Intellectual Development

The developmental theory of Piaget will form the frame of reference for identifying mental developmental needs. Piaget's stages of intellectual development are outlined very briefly here. (For more details, see Flavell, 1963; Ginsburg & Opper, 1969; and Maier, 1965.)

The first 2 years of life are described as the *sensorimotor stage*. The infant progresses from purely reflex activity to more systematic and organized behavior. He learns that he has some control over the object world and will search for a toy he has lost. He learns that objects are independent of himself. Finally he learns to imitate and to respond to people through imitative behavior.

At approximately 2 years of age the child enters the *symbolic or preconceptual phase*. The imitative behavior of the previous period becomes internal imitation (accommodation) and provides the child with symbols which acquire meaning through assimilation. He will apply his symbols in a playful make-believe fashion to other situations as he tests out their appropriateness. He begins to use language for objects and events that may not be present at the moment.

The child enters the phase of *intuitive thought* at about 4 years of age. This phase and the preceding *preconceptual* phase are sometimes called the *preoperational stage*. Language now becomes repetition, monologue and collective monologue; it is described by Piaget as egocentric, that is, the child is neither concerned with nor interested in what another is saying. By contrast, communication is based on interaction with others and has as a purpose the relaying or sharing of information. During this period, the child employs imitation more or less consciously in a preidentification fashion. Further, he broadens his social horizons and interest in the world about him.

From approximately 7 to 11 years of age the child passes through the stage of *concrete operations*. During these years, the child acquires the ability to order and to relate his experiences into a gestalt, or organized whole. He establishes systems of classification and moves from inductive to deductive thinking. While language is now a tool of communication, he still employs symbolic speech without true understanding of meanings. He looks beyond his family for models to imitate.

At about the age of 12, the child enters the stage of *formal operations*, the final period of intellectual development. During this stage, the adolescent moves from the concrete to the abstract. He enters the world of ideas. He formulates hypotheses concerning the various results of an action and considers what might occur. He utilizes language as a means of communicating thoughts and ideas. He reaches an understanding of his world and where he fits in that world.

It should be remembered that the ages attached to the stages in this outline are approximate, and that development through the stages may not proceed evenly on all fronts.

Development of the Blind Child

The blind child has special needs as he progresses through the stages of intellectual development just outlined. His visual impairment places him at a disadvantage in the areas of sensory stimulation, concept formation, and communication.

Sensory Stimulation

The need for adequate sensory stimulation for the blind infant has been stressed in the previous section. The role of vision in the intellectual development process is evident in the theory of Piaget presented above. Early parent education and nursery school programs are necessary to enable the blind child to progress near the norm intellectually. He needs many concrete experiences, especially during the sensorimotor stage, to enable him to develop knowledge of the object world. While imitative activities must be confined primarily to auditory stimuli, he needs to be taught those activities normally learned by visual imitation.

His entrance into school provides further opportunities for sensory stimulation. In the past, the education of blind children almost wholly neglected the development of maximum utilization of residual vision. The majority of children being educated in residential and day schools today have some useful vision. The educational program should direct efforts toward maximum utilization of remaining vision. Additionally, other sources of sensory input must be exploited to the maximum. The total environment of home and school should be structured so that each sensory experience will be effective for more meaningful learning. All available sensory cues should be utilized in order to make up for the deficiencies caused by the visual impairment.

Suggestions for maximizing the use of residual vision and for utilizing other sources of sensory input may be found in Chapter 5.

Concept Formation

Concepts grow out of the perceptual process and become enriched as the child develops language. The breadth of concept development is dependent in large measure on the breadth of the perceptual experiences. Because the blind child lacks one source of sensory input, his perceptual processes are deficient. He may never grasp some concepts and may need more experience than the sighted child to grasp others.

Abstractions such as a concept of color may never be formed, since the child has no possibility of acquiring a background of sensory input for this concept. His understanding of this group of concepts will of necessity remain on the verbal level and be based on what others have described to him. Thus, his grasp of such concepts will come only through vicarious experiences and cannot truly be his own. In this area, he may have difficulty moving beyond the stage of concrete operations.

The concepts of distance and time illustrate another group which eventually may or may not be grasped, depending on the variety and number of experiences designed to give them meaning. For example, the sighted child may acquire some meaningful concept of distance by visual input, that is, how far he can see, and later through an understanding of relative distances as shown on a map drawn to scale. While the blind child may reach some understanding of distance through his kinesthetic sense, he encounters difficulty in doing so. Walking a specific distance would be the most meaningful procedure, but a walk of sufficient length to give an idea of great distance would not be feasible. Further, his deficiency in grasping what distance is prevents his making maximum use of maps through his tactile sense in order to acquire a concept of relative distance. He needs many concrete experiences through his kinesthetic sense in order to use maps effectively.

Educators need to be aware of potential difficulties in the area of concept formation and particularly should emphasize meaningful concrete experiences in order to maximize concepts that have relevance for the child.

Communication

Each individual communicates his ideas and concepts with others through oral and written communication. The essential ingredients in this process are speech and language. Both speech and language are sequential in their development, beginning in early infancy. The acquisition of speech begins with the cooing of the infant at about 16 weeks; he babbles at about 28 weeks; and by 40 weeks he begins to put sounds together to form words that only his parents can interpret. Certain complicated speech sounds take longer to develop and may not be spoken correctly until the child enters school. Language development proceeds in a similar sequential fashion. At 28 weeks the infant attends to voices; by 40 weeks he responds to simple commands and is on his way to understanding language. By 15 months, he says single words to express his ideas and by 2 years he puts words together to form simple sentences.

The process of acquiring speech and language is the same for the blind child as for the sighted. However, if the blind child is slow in his physical development, he will probably also be slow in his acquisition of speech and language. The number of words acquired during the early years will also be fewer. The sighted child rapidly learns names for the many objects he sees; his visual sensory input provides him with the background of experience necessary for expanding his vocabulary. The lack of visual stimulation results in a slower rate of vocabulary acquisition. In addition, the blind child's vocabulary consists of two types of words: those which do have meaning for him based on his personal experiences, and those which are verbalizations acquired from hearing others but which are meaningless to him (Burlingham, 1965). The latter are necessary for communication with others, but overuse may lead to verbalism, which tends to discourage attaching meaning to other words as well. Opportunities for many and varied experiences as well as increased sensory input through other avenues will tend to offset the retardation and prevent meaningless verbalism (Harley, 1963).

At about 6 years of age the blind child has acquired sufficient facility in speech and language to begin learning the skills of written communication. Reading and writing are normally introduced in the blind child's school experience at about the same age as for the sighted child. Details of teaching and learning this process are presented in Chapter 7.

The use of nonverbal communication by the blind represents an area where little is known. As early as 16 weeks of age the normal infant smiles in response to a smile, a nonverbal response. During his first year, he often expresses his wants nonverbally, as with a frown, and in turn responds to looks of others. As he grows through childhood, he continues to respond to others with various forms of nonverbal communication. Since most nonverbal communication is dependent on visual stimuli, the blind child is unable to utilize it to communicate his thoughts and feelings. Indeed he must be encouraged to smile, scowl, and otherwise express himself through visual rather than oral communication.

There is great variation in the extent to which the tone of voice and other activities, such as the scraping of feet, are utilized by the blind person as a means of nonverbal communication to assess certain social situations. Since various forms of nonverbal communication are utilized more or less extensively in the sighted population, research is necessary to determine what forms can be employed by the blind person, and more important, whether skill in nonverbal communication appropriate to the blind can be learned.

EDUCATIONAL DEVELOPMENT

A visual impairment should not deprive a child of his rightful access to an educational program commensurate with his needs and abilities. Much of the instruction in classrooms today is oral, and the blind child is at no disadvantage in such rooms. Provided with his special materials and instruction in the skills of written communication unique to the blind, the child can often take his place in the classroom beside his normal peers.

There are various types of educational programs available to the blind child, and the one which best meets his needs should be selected. These programs and guidelines on selection for the individual child are described in Chapter 6.

The modifications necessary in presenting the various subject areas are detailed in Chapter 8. The focus of this section will be on general principles and guidelines for attaining optimal educational development of the visually handicapped child and the role of the educator in facilitating that development.

Guidelines

Basically the educational needs of the blind child are similar to those of the sighted one. The curriculum for all children should be directed toward helping each child attain his maximum potential and realize his own personal objectives. Educational systems that function on this philosophical base tend to be pupil oriented rather than subject oriented. In pupil-oriented schools all children, including the child who differs from the norm in any way, have an opportunity of receiving a meaningful education. In such a school setting, the visually handicapped child can readily receive his education with sighted children and have an individualized instructional program that will meet his educational needs. Unfortunately, not all school systems, nor even all schools within a school system, are pupil oriented. In such settings, the visually handicapped child may need special assistance.

In general, the blind child should have the same curricular content as the sighted child. In addition he needs special content areas such as orientation and mobility. His educational program should also include guidance in daily living skills, sex education, and a health education program that gives information concerning those topics of personal concern to him: vision, eye care, and hereditary factors in visual conditions. He also needs an individualized instructional approach; such an approach is appropriate for, and should be available to, all children. He needs access to specialized educational materials that will enable him to learn in the classroom setting as near normally as possible. Finally, the blind child needs experiences with sighted children. The successful vocational rehabilitation of handicapped persons is frequently hampered by an unrealistic appraisal of abilities. Children learn to assess their capacities and limitations by comparing themselves with their peers. Visually handicapped children need to assess themselves against the norm rather than against a handicapped group, because in adulthood they are expected to function in a normal not a handicapped world. Early and continuing experiences with sighted children can prepare the visually handicapped child better for the adult competitive society.

The continuous involvement of parents in the educational process is an essential element in educational programming. Parents should participate in all decisions which affect their child from the first day he enters school. Too often schools encourage parents to abdicate their parental responsibility by omitting them from the decision-making process; parents begin to feel that if the school is making all decisions concerning the child, then the school should assume all responsibility for him. As the child matures, he should also be included as a participant in making decisions that affect him. Knowledge and understanding of available options, and opportunities to participate in decisions regarding the most appropriate one, will help the visually handicapped adolescent become self-directive. Parent and student involvement in the various aspects of the program will help the student to derive more benefit from his school experience.

When the foregoing principles are followed, the educational needs of the visually handicapped child will be adequately met.

The Role of the Teacher

The importance of the teacher to a quality educational program for the visually handicapped cannot be overestimated. It is the teacher who can help the blind child fit into the school program through creative modifications and adaptations. The teacher helps others who have contact with the child to know, understand, and accept the child's capacities and limitations, and guides them in meeting his needs within the school program. Similarly, the teacher helps the child meet and deal with the inevitable frustrations of the school experience and, most of all, helps him learn to cope with failure when necessary. The teacher identifies acceptable behavior and reinforces that behavior which will assist him in his eventual adjustment to a sighted society. The teacher guides the child through the whole of his educational experience and runs interference for him when he needs it. Finally, the teacher helps the child with his peer group relationships: assists him to know and to accept when his needs are secondary to the needs of the group. All these roles are necessary and must be performed by a well-qualified professional. The preparation necessary for teachers of the visually handicapped is described in Chapter 9. However, preparation is meaningless unless a warm accepting teacher is available to the visually handicapped child for helping to meet his educational needs.

ENTERING THE ADULT WORLD

Special problems arise for the blind adolescent as he prepares to enter the adult world. These revolve about his adjustment to a minority status in American culture, assuming an adult role, and selecting an appropriate vocational objective.

The Minority Status

The handicapped share with certain racial and religious groups a minority position in American society (Wright, 1960). The handicapped may, however, encounter greater difficulty in adjusting to that position because they lack a well-defined group with whom to identify and because the wide variance within the handicapped group emphasizes differences rather than similarities. A review of the nature of the "visually handicapped" population will illustrate this situation.

The vast majority of the visually handicapped is found in the older age groups; there are relatively few children and young adults with visual impairments. The total population of persons with visual impairments is small, so that within any one community the visually handicapped person tends to be an oddity. The degrees of visual impairments occur on a continuum from total loss to approaching the norm, and qualitative variations may be more differentiating from the norm than degree of vision. Finally, needs and characteristics of the subgroups, such as the school-age population, vary so much that generalizations, even about a subgroup, are almost impossible. Thus, while he is assigned a minority role by society, the visually handicapped adolescent encounters difficulty in drawing security from any well-defined minority group identification in order to adjust to his role as a minority group member.

Society is ambivalent about its expectations for its minority group citizens. On the one hand, the minority is expected to absorb the cultural values of the majority but when it does, it may not be permitted full acceptance by and membership with the majority. The visually handicapped adolescent, for example, absorbs through his school experience cultural values regarding work, but when he finishes his schooling, he may be denied opportunities to use his skills in productive employment.

A further complication arises from the attitudes of society which are expressed in stereotypes. The "blind beggar" stereotype is hard to combat. The independent, self-supporting visually handicapped person is viewed as an exception and society prefers not to see him in a role inconsistent with the beggar stereotype (Scott, 1969).

Discrimination toward the disabled is a reality which probably will not be eliminated for some time. Until then, and until attitudes of society can be modified, parents and teachers should help the visually handicapped adolescent accept the realities of his minority role. He needs to develop knowledge and understanding about why rejection and discrimination exist and how he can best cope with them. He needs help to face the reality that often he must be better than the sighted in order to attain majority group status in certain areas, especially in the job market. He needs to learn ways he can become accepted as a person of value in his own right despite his disability. Finally, he needs to recognize that through his efforts and his example, he as an individual can do much to help society learn to accept the disabled as potentially contributing members. The degree of acceptance by society depends on the degree to which labels can be discarded. The label "blind" or "visually handicapped" is discarded when the individual finds security and success within his group and ultimately is judged by his behavior rather than by his disability.

The questions arise where and how the visually handicapped adolescent might best learn to accept his minority group status. Can this be accomplished more effectively in a setting with sighted students, where daily he lives his minority role? Or is it better to live in a more or less segregated setting with other visually handicapped in order to learn the "blind" role and thereby be more comfortable with it? In the absence of any research to shed light on these questions, a common sense approach should be adopted. There can be no one answer for all visually handicapped nor for any one individual nor for the entire school experience of any individual. The principle to be adopted is one of striking a balance between spending enough time with other visually handicapped to learn one's identity, but not so long as to reinforce the minority role to the extent that adjustment to a sighted society becomes painful. Parents and teachers should be involved in helping the adolescent with this difficult developmental task and be sensitive to his varying needs at different times during the growing-up process.

The Adult Role

As the adolescent approaches the end of his school career, he is expected to assume the duties and responsibilities of an adult. The visually handicapped adolescent may encounter difficulties in this developmental task, partly because the nature of his disability forces him in some areas into a dependent role from which he realistically cannot escape. Aside from his vocational preparation, which is discussed later, he must find satisfactory social outlets, learn and assume an appropriate sex role, and find meaning in his life as a contributing member of society.

As the time that is required to earn a living decreases for all, including the blind, the need for learning to fill leisure time with productive activities increases. Education programs for the visually handicapped must provide opportunities for such learning experiences. The pursuit of hobbies, the acquisition of skills in a variety of handwork and craft activities, and the development of an avocational interest in music, both listening and performing, should begin in school in order to provide resources for use during adult leisure time. Physical education programs should include assistance in selecting appropriate recreational outlets, through sports, games, and particularly physical activities. In a highly mobile society, adults are often sedentary; the visually handicapped tend to be even more so. Hence, there is a need to stimulate interest in participation in a variety of physical activities. Preparation for participation in a variety of active recreational and leisure time activities may help to reduce the social isolation of blind adults (Josephson, 1968).

Learning an appropriate sex role as a developmental task of the adolescent is described in an earlier section. An evaluation of what constitutes a meaningful and satisfactory relationship with the opposite sex is difficult to determine. The rate of marriage in a population is often used for making such a determination. The rate of marriage among the handicapped is lower than that in the normal population (Wright, 1960). The rate of marriage in the visually handicapped population is also lower than in the sighted population and seems to be related to vocational success (Scholl, Bauman, & Crissey, 1969). Cause and effect cannot be generalized from measures of relationship, but it would seem that those who find productive employment tend to be married and to participate in a greater number of social and community activities. The key to personal and social adjustment for the visually handicapped may lie in their level of economic independence.

Selecting a Vocational Objective

Economic self-sufficiency is probably the most meaningful way the handicapped person can feel productive in society. Work as a right and privilege is often denied the handicapped and the rate of unemployment and underemployment among the handicapped is extremely high (Scholl et al., 1969). While the educator can probably do little to combat job discrimination, he can do much to help the visually handicapped adolescent find a meaningful place in the employment market.

The selection of a realistic vocational goal is the first step in achieving this objective, and the level of aspiration is a vital ingredient in this process. The adolescent's level of aspiration is largely determined by his self-concept and how he feels about his abilities compared to those of his peers.

Two aspects of the self-concept should be noted in particular because of their importance to the adolescent as he moves into the world of work. Parents, with their attitudes toward the adolescent and his disability, their aspirations for him, and their willingness to see him move into independent adult status, are the key figures. Too often, parents really do not want their child to leave them. To counteract this, it becomes essential that parents be involved throughout the process of vocational selection and that they learn to encourage and accept independence in their offspring.

A second aspect is the degree to which the adolescent has been able to assess his own capacities and limitations. This is accomplished through objective as well as subjective procedures. The availability and use of tests in guidance and counseling for the visually handicapped is discussed in Chapter 4. For any assessment to be of value in selecting a vocation, the adolescent must be involved in meaningful discussion of the results with a rehabilitation counselor. The counselor must also be knowledgeable about the present and future job market. In addition, the adolescent should have experiences with his sighted peers in a variety of situations that will enable him to compare his abilities with those of the general population with whom he must compete on the employment market. Through both objective and subjective procedures for assessing his abilities, the visually handicapped adolescent is in a better position to select an appropriate vocational field.

An educational program cannot stop when the vocational objective is selected. Plans for realizing the objective must be made and implemented. If possible, opportunities to work in the setting selected should be provided. Adolescents normally have many chances to try out jobs in a variety of settings through after-school, weekend, and summer employment. Such opportunities are often unavailable to the visually handicapped. Schools can lend a hand in eliminating the barriers of job discrimination so that the blind adolescent can have the chance to prove himself. A close working relationship between schools and vocational rehabilitation agencies will assure that vocational plans are implemented and that job tryouts are available.

It is difficult to prepare the adolescent for the job discrimination he will undoubtedly meet. The best preparation probably lies in developing good work habits and superior job skills, so that these are valued by the prospective employer over the presence of the visual impairment.

Before leaving this topic, it is well to recognize that not all visually handicapped are or can be employable. For those who cannot be, the educational program should include preparation in some socially useful activity in order that the satisfaction of work may be gained even by those who will not become vocationally independent.

SUMMARY

The growth and development of the blind child is more *like* than *unlike* that of the sighted child. In each area his growth and development passes through the same sequence, but his rate may be slower due to direct and indirect influences of his visual impairment. Direct influences are those which result immediately from the impairment; indirect are environmental restrictions imposed on the individual because he is blind.

Rich experiences and opportunities for participating in a variety of physical activities will aid the development of physical and motor skills, which need not be deficient when compared with the sighted. Direct teaching may be necessary to substitute for the imitative learning of physical and motor skills by the child with normal vision.

The blind infant is deprived of vision necessary to initiate his first relationships with persons and objects in his environment. This deficiency may retard his social, emotional, and personality development. Experiences paced according to his current level of development can help overcome most of this delay. The environment must provide positive reinforcing experiences with others, including his family, so that the child will develop a satisfactory relationship with himself and with his world. The adjustment process, particularly during adolescence, can be facilitated by understanding teachers and parents.

The visual impairment deprives the child of an invaluable source of sensory input essential to cognitive development. Early parent education and nursery school experiences will help offset the retarding impact of the impairment during preschool years. The educational program must include opportunities for utilization of residual vision and other sources of sensory input to maximize sensory stimulation. Meaningful experiences and attention to language development will improve concept formation. The life space of the blind child should help him realize his full intellectual potential.

The visually handicapped child has a right to the same educational opportunities as the sighted child. He needs specialized materials and instruction in those areas that will enable him to compensate for his visual impairment. He should receive an education in the setting which best meets his needs. His educational experience should include opportunities to work with normal peers, so that he will be prepared to compete in a sighted world. His education should be under the direction of well-qualified professionals. Finally, his parents should be involved in all aspects of the educational process.

During adolescence, he should have access to objective and subjective measures of his abilities in order to form the base on which he can select an appropriate vocational objective. His educational program should include vocational guidance and counseling as well as opportunities to try out different kinds of jobs.

The process of growth and development is highly individualized. Each child's unique genetic endowment and different environmental influences join to make him the individual he is destined to become. For the visually handicapped, additional variables may further individualize the process. Visual factors (the age at which vision was lost, the degree of loss, the etiology, and the type of onset) will each in its own way affect the optimal satisfaction of developmental needs. The presence of other disabilities will have further influence on the process of growth and development. Principles can be stated and generalizations can be made, but application to all is difficult because each child is different and has his own unique set of needs.

REFERENCES

Bloom, B. S. *Stability and change in human characteristics.* New York: Wiley, 1964.

Burlingham, D. Hearing and its role in the development of the blind. *The Psychoanalytic Study of the Child,* 1964, **19,** 95–112.

Burlingham, D. Some problems of ego development in blind children. *The Psychoanalytic Study of the Child,* 1965, **20,** 194–208.

Cholden, L. S. *A psychiatrist works with blindness.* New York: American Foundation for the Blind, 1958.

Coleman, J. S., Campbell, E. Q., Hobson, C. J., McPartland, J., Mood, A. M., Weinfield, F. D., & York, R. L. *Equality of educational opportunity* (OE-38001.). Washington D.C.: U.S. Government Printing Office, 1966.

Cowen, E. L., Underberg, R. P., Verillo, R. T., & Benham, F. G. *Adjustment to visual disability in adolescence.* New York: American Foundation for the Blind, 1961.

Crow, L. D., Murray, W. I., & Smythe, H. H. *Educating the culturally disadvantaged child.* New York: McKay, 1966.

Diggory, J. C. *Self-evaluation: Concepts and studies.* New York: Wiley, 1966.

Flavell, J. H. *The developmental psychology of Jean Piaget.* New York: Van Nostrand-Reinhold, 1963.

Fraiberg, S., & Freedman, D. Studies in the ego development of the congenitally blind child. *The Psychoanalytic Study of the Child,* 1964, **19,** 113–169.

Fraiberg, S., Smith, M., & Adelson, E. An educational program for blind infants. *Journal of Special Education,* 1969, **3,** 121–139.

Ginsburg, H., & Opper, S. *Piaget's theory of intellectual development.* Englewood Cliffs, N. J.: Prentice-Hall, 1969.

Halsey, E, & Porter, L. *Physical education for children.* New York: Holt, 1963.

Harley, R. K. *Verbalism among blind children.* New York: American Foundation for the Blind, 1963.

Hunt, J. M. *Intelligence and experience.* New York: Ronald Press, 1961.

Ilg, F. L., & Ames, L. B. *Child behavior.* New York: Harper, 1955.

Jensen, A. R. How much can we boost IQ and scholastic achievement? *Harvard Educational Review,* Winter 1969, **39,** 1–123.

Josephson, E. *The social life of blind people.* New York: American Foundation for the Blind, 1968.

Kagan, J., Hunt, J. M., Crow, J. F., Bereiter, C., Elkind, D., Cronbach, L. J., & Brazziel, W. F. How much can we boost IQ and scholastic achievement, a discussion. *Harvard Educational Review,* Spring 1969, **39,** 273–356.

Kagan, J., & Moss, H. A. *Birth to maturity.* New York: Wiley, 1962.

Maier, H. W. *Three theories of child development.* New York: Harper, 1965.

Nagera, H., & Colonna, A. Aspects of the contribution of sight to ego and drive development. *The Psychoanalytic Study of the Child,* 1965, **22,** 267–287.

Olson, W. C. *Child development.* Indianapolis, Indiana: Heath, 1959.

Scholl, G. T., Bauman, M. K., & Crissey, M. S. *A study of the vocational success of groups of the visually handicapped.* SRS Research Grant No. RF–2554–s. Ann Arbor, Mich.: University of Michigan, Project No. 02248–1–f, 1969.

Scott, R. A. *The making of blind men.* New York: Russell Sage Foundation, 1969.

Sommers, V. S. *The influence of parental attitudes and social environment on the personality development of the adolescent blind.* New York: American Foundation for the Blind, 1944.

Tanner, W. P., Jr. The simulation of living systems: On the question of substituting one sensory system for another. In L. L. Clark (Ed.), *International Congress on Technology and Blindness Proceedings,* Vol. 2. New York: American Foundation for the Blind, 1963. Pp. 209–219.

Wright, B. A. *Physical disability—a psychological approach.* New York: Harper, 1960.

Wylie, R. C. *The self-concept.* Lincoln, Nebr.: University of Nebraska Press, 1961.

CHAPTER 4

Psychological and Educational Assessment

Mary K. Bauman

Personnel Research Center, Inc.
Philadelphia, Pennsylvania

EARLY PSYCHOLOGICAL STUDIES OF BLINDNESS

Since the psychologist is much concerned with sensation, perception, learning, and emotional reactions to all kinds of stress, it is natural that a number of early psychologists were attracted to the study of the effects of a severe visual handicap in all these areas.

The sighted world, feeling its own stress in confronting a blind person, often assuages its concern by positing some form of compensation for what is correctly perceived as the disadvantage of blindness. The generally accepted notions that blind people could hear better, get information by taste or smell, or handle problems of sensation and perception through some magic, were tested by G. Stanley Hall (studies of taste and smell) as early as 1879, by Griesbach (studies of hearing and touch) in 1899, and by Seashore (six varied sensory fields) in 1918. A number of other psychologists, including Hayes (1941), who gives a good account of the whole area, have followed with evidence consistently. pointing away from the notion that blind people do anything more than use their remaining senses more effectively—because they must!

However, psychological testing of the visually handicapped in order to help them and their educators, not just to satisfy the curiosity of the psychologist, was pretty much limited to attempts at mental measurement and achievement testing, and even these attempts were on a very small scale until World War II.

The leader in this early testing was unquestionably Dr. Samuel P. Hayes, long associated with Perkins School for the Blind in Watertown, Massachusetts, but acting as psychological advisor to a number of other schools. Through this opportunity to work with a large number of children, directly or through local test administrators, he was enabled both to develop the earlier tests, including his Interim Hayes-Binet, and to determine just what visually handicapped children could most readily learn and do. Although his concept of "a psychology of blindness" included nothing about nonverbal or nonacademic abilities, interest, or personality, it did form a firm foundation upon which other psychologists rapidly built, beginning in the early 1940s and progressing with increasing interest as research and training were supported by the Federal government in the last two decades.

THE ROLE OF THE PSYCHOLOGIST

The role of the psychologist is obviously defined by the situation within which he is working and by the questions he is asked to answer. His work with a specific child should always start with referral information which clearly indicates, for example, whether the child is to be examined for admission to a certain school or class (the requirements and characteristics of which he should know or be given), whether the student is failing in his school work, having trouble with his peers, presenting behavior which troubles those about him (in which case, the nature of this behavior should be given in some detail), or merely because the state requires that a psychological report be filed in order to admit the child to any kind of special instruction. These are, of course, only a few samples of the possible reasons for requesting a psychological evaluation, but the point being made is that the reason or reasons for requesting psychological evaluation should be fully stated, so that the psychologist may use all appropriate tools in his examination and include answers to the presenting questions in his report. A good psychological report starts with good referral information, including the child's physical, social, and school histories.

When the psychologist knows what information he wants to obtain through his examination, he will often find that he would like to be able to use a variety of test instruments, which fall into these categories: (a) tests which have been developed for or have satisfactorily been adapted to use with blind students or adults and which can be used with a high degree of confidence with the

visually handicapped; (b) tests which have been developed and are well established as measures for the seeing, but which have rarely or with limited
satisfaction been used with the visually handicapped; and (c) tests which do
not exist or are not well proven for anyone, with or without a visual handicap.
As illustrations of these three we might name (a) the Wechsler Verbal Scales,
(b) the Thematic Apperception Test (TAT), and (c) a measure of honesty.

This is another way of saying that the total science of psychological evaluation leaves even its most ardent practitioners unsatisfied with the lack of
appropriate and proven tools to answer some kinds of questions, while the
younger and less developed field of evaluation of the visually handicapped is
still struggling with the development of materials and procedures especially
appropriate to both children and adults who have either no or very limited
vision. In these circumstances, the psychologist as a professional worker must
responsibly combine his science with the art of constructing or adapting useful
materials and procedures to achieve his evaluation goals and must apply his
total experience with a wisdom which may rarely be called for when he works
with sighted clients, for whom good normative groups and many reported
applications of satisfactory tests make a diagnosis almost automatic.

Certainly testing the visually handicapped child is never automatic and for
this reason it forms a professional challenge. Let us consider some of the
reasons for this and their implications for the psychologist.

Amount of Vision and Its Effect upon the Testing Process

Although good referral information will always state the child's or adult's
amount of vision, usually taken from an opthalmological report, this gives only
a rough idea of the interplay between vision and testing materials unless, of
course, the individual is totally blind. When any vision remains, the psychologist should determine by questioning whether the individual, if in school,
works with braille, large-print, or regular-print materials. For tests available
in both forms, such as certain personality inventories, it is usually wise to allow
the testee to determine whether he prefers to work with orally or visually
presented materials. Even children who use braille may have enough residual
vision to be quite useful in working with such concrete test materials as
formboards and, as will be noted subsequently, this materially affects the way
in which results of all such tests are interpreted.

Age of Onset of Blindness

Even for the totally blind student, one piece of vision data may be very
important, the age at which the individual became totally blind. If he func-
tioned visually to an age where he had already established concepts such as

shape, color, and visual aspects of the environment like clouds, he can use these concepts in the testing process. For certain tests or items within tests, the scores of a child who did not have vision up to an age where such concepts could be established require different interpretations.

Deprivation and Test Interpretation

When a psychologist purchases a test, he expects to receive with it a manual which, at the minimum, provides instruction for its use and norms for its interpretation. Many test developers go to great lengths to obtain "representative" normative groups which their manuals describe in more or less detail.

The psychologist who works with visually handicapped children must realize that his clients just about never fit into these normative groups. Their life experiences have been limited or changed not only by the obvious effects of poor vision itself, but probably by many other factors, of which the following are only a few examples.

Overprotection. This consideration is especially important in the testing of young children. In very many cases family, friends, and even school staff have, out of genuine concern for the safety of the individual or out of pity or merely out of a wish to be helpful, done so much for the child that he has not had normal learning experiences. He may not have learned to dress himself because his mother has done this for him far beyond the age where she would dress her sighted children. He may have had no experience in helping with chores at home (a great learning opportunity) because the family would not ask a blind child to empty wastebaskets, make a bed, or set a table. In school he may never really have learned what a cafeteria line is because someone always brings his lunch to him.

Exclusion. Within a school or even a college he may have been excluded from certain courses or extracurricular activities which are regarded as important learning opportunities for sighted students. Visually handicapped students are too often excluded from laboratory experiences of any kind, physical education, even typing! This has an effect upon the academic gains presumed to come from such classes, upon the individual's place in the school social structure, and upon his concept of himself and of blindness. The effects are found not only in tests of specific knowledge but in interest and personality measures as well.

Lack of Appropriate Learning Materials. Particularly in the evaluation of achievement, the psychologist needs assurance that the child has had appropriate resources for learning. Have books in large print or recorded form been available—the same books the sighted members of the class were using? Were they ready for him at the beginning of the term, or did he receive them only a month or two before the end of the school year? Does he have a good note-taking system? Were at least some tactual materials provided to parallel picture content in the books of sighted fellow students (such as raised surface maps)?

The psychologist is often in the difficult position of trying to determine whether he is testing the individual or his environment. If there are failures, are they the failures of the child or of the school?

Procedural Problems in Test Administration

The psychologist who is asked to test a blind person is sometimes tempted to say he cannot do this, not because of limitations in his professional knowledge but because he does not know how to guide a blind person, how to explain visual material to him, and generally how to deal with the ways in which blindness changes or may change an interpersonal relationship. The obvious remedy is to learn how to deal with these personal sources of awkwardness so that both he and the client can be at ease. This may be less a concern in dealing with young children, since they are usually brought to the psychologist by their parents, a teacher, or someone else who can bridge this problem, and in many cases the adult can tell the psychologist what help is needed and thus dispel the awkwardness. In short, there is less to worry about than one might think. However, brief illustrated brochures of information on how to guide, orient, and otherwise give needed information to a blind person can usually be obtained from a local agency for the blind, and it is worth getting one of these, if only because it helps to put the psychologist at ease.

With regard to the testing situation as such, a fair guide is to tell the blind person all pertinent information that a seeing person, child or adult, would naturally obtain through sight. Unless the object of the test is to determine whether the individual can, by touch or other means, tell what has been placed before him, the psychologist should simply describe the object, stating, for example, "Here is a board with a lot of holes in it, each one of different shape. Why don't you touch each one until you know just where they are and how they differ?" If the client hesitates, the psychologist may appropriately guide his hands across the entire board, describing each shape and giving ample time for the client to become acquainted with it. As the psychologist decides just how he will present each test to the blind person, he must also decide exactly what he wants to learn from the test itself. He must tell the blind person everything except what the test is testing, so that he eliminates as nearly as he can the possibility of actually testing tactual discrimination when he meant to test speed, or orientation when he meant to test ability to follow instructions.

It is easy to adapt questionnaire types of tests, whether in the field of personality or in other fields, to use with the visually handicapped by reading them aloud, either in person or through tape recording. If the testee is proficient in braille, the tests may also be put into braille, but the psychologist should determine the braille reading ability of each testee before he trusts using much in the way of brailled test material.

If oral reading of a test is done individually with each testee, the answers can be given orally and recorded by the examiner. This can be done quite efficiently where a single decision is involved, as with a personality item to which the testee is to reply "True" or "False." However, in a multiple-choice test, such as the Miller Analogies or certain tests of judgment, the blind person's score is likely to be reduced by the requirement that he keep in mind, very accurately, each of four or five alternative answers. If such tests are frequently used by oral presentation, the possible answers should be put into braille, so that the testee may refer to them as he decides upon his answer. In the case of the Miller Analogies test such supplementary braille forms are available through the Psychological Corporation.

While individual reading and oral answering of a test may be comfortable, it does deprive the testee of the privacy the sighted person has when he reads a test for himself and records his answer by paper and pencil procedures. One way to overcome this disadvantage is to have the testee record his answer by either typing or braille, and this tempts the psychologist to save time by reading to a number of persons at once. This procedure may be particularly attractive to the school psychologist, who could thus test a whole class at one time. However, if he wishes to do this, he should be very careful to choose designations for True and False (or their equivalent, as necessary for the given test) which use either the same number of typing strokes or the same number of braille dots. For example, in writing in braille, four punches of the stylus are necessary to make a T for True, whereas only three are needed to make an F for False; since the use of the stylus is quite audible, the individual totally loses his privacy through such a procedure. If, on the other hand, the psychologist has the class use T for True and N for Not True, the same number of braille dots are needed and no one can tell from the sound which response is being made.

Another procedure which can be used very effectively is having the testee make his reply through the placement of tickets, one for each response, in different piles. These tickets may be small pieces of cardboard which the psychologist has prepared ahead of time by numbering as many as are required for the test to be given and placing them in numerical order in a small box. He then instructs the testee to take them out one at a time (and, of course, in order) and place them to the right for True and to the left for False. Such cards can be used over and over, but have the disadvantage that they must be put back into numerical order after each use.

It is also possible to obtain rather inexpensively strips of tickets which are already numbered. This is the kind of ticket frequently used for selling chances or for admission to various events. A roll of these tickets can easily be prepared so that it contains the correct number of tickets needed for the test to be administered, and each tenth (or other designated) ticket has a hole punched through it. If this procedure is used with a recording of the test, the voice on the recording can state when the next ticket should have a hole punched through it, and the client can be instructed to let the test administrator know if he does not come to such a punched ticket when the voice indicates that he should. Thus, there will be constant checks on whether he is working with the correctly numbered portion of his roll of tickets. Provided with such a prepared roll of response tickets, even clients of rather limited ability can usually respond correctly to a tape-recorded test. Moreover, this method secures the advantages to the client of privacy and to the psychologist of saving his time and avoiding the boredom of personally reading the test.

MEASURES OF LEARNING ABILITY

Individual Verbal Tests

A study by Bauman (1968) showed that the single test most frequently used with blind clients of all ages by psychologists in the United States was some form of the Wechsler test. In a very large number of cases, only the Verbal Scale was used, but many psychologists also used the Performance Scale when the client had useful vision. The Wechsler Intelligence Scale for Children (WISC) or Wechsler Adult Intelligence Scale (WAIS) were most frequently used, but a number of psychologists accustomed to the Wechsler-Bellevue II found it entirely satisfactory. All of these verbal scales can be used with essentially no modification. Where the instructions indicate that the arithmetic items should be read by the testee, these can be provided in braille or large type, but Hayes (1941) suggested that the items be read twice before timing was started, and experience shows that with this adjustment no form of print presentation is necessary. The WAIS, of course, eliminated presenting arithmetic problems in printed form for all testees, so no adjustment whatever is necessary in using it. A few comprehension items may be slightly rephrased because the totally blind child would be unlikely to have this experience. For example, the WISC item "What should you do if you see a train approaching a broken track?" may be rephrased "What should a person do if he sees a train approaching a broken track?" However, experience shows that even if these items are not rephrased, few visually handicapped children are troubled, since they are quite aware that the question is hypothetical (i.e., there seems to be no blocking on the fact that the child could not himself see the train approaching).

Unfortunately, the more recently published WPPSI is less adaptable to the young blind child. Unusually many of the items imply visual learning, and the printed arithmetic items must be duplicated in some concrete form. Also, one does not know just what may be the effect of not interspersing the verbal and performance subtests. It is being used to some extent by psychologists who work with blind preschool children, but although great satisfaction with the other Verbal Scales has been expressed by large numbers of psychologists working with blind clients over the age of six, reservations are expressed about the application of the WPPSI at early age levels..

Interpretation of the Wechsler Verbal Scales must of course be done in the light of the child's or adult's opportunities for learning, but this would be true for sighted children too and most psychologists feel comfortable with this. For example, they realize that when information, arithmetic, and vocabulary subtests are low, while comprehension and digit span are high, this probably means some form of deprivation academically. The source of the deprivation may be different for the blind child, but the implications are the same.

Prior to the publication of the Wechsler Scales, the Interim Hayes-Binet was widely used, and it continues to see some use among psychologists long accustomed to it. This scale was developed by Samuel P. Hayes largely by combining verbal items from Forms L and M of the Stanford Binet. Some of the content is still as useful as it was when Hayes published the form about 30 years ago, but other items seem sadly dated and awkward for use with today's children.

Carl Davis, psychologist of Perkins School for the Blind, has for the past several years been working on a new adaptation of more modern versions of the Binet, to be known as the Perkins Binet. Into this he has built performance as well as verbal items with far better balance, and when this test becomes available in the near future, it should provide an excellent resource for evaluating both types of learning ability.

Individual Performance Tests

For many years, those who worked with the visually handicapped, and more especially those who evaluated many totally blind persons, felt keenly the lack of any source of the kind of information the psychologist is accustomed to obtaining, with sighted persons, through performance scales. With partially seeing clients the Wechsler Performance Scales might be used, as a whole if the residual vision were considerable or in part if only the block design or object assembly subtests seemed feasible. However, if the Performance IQ were low, the psychologist never felt sure that he was not measuring lack of vision rather than lack of mental ability.

An early effort to fill this gap was Bauman's Non-language Learning (NLL) test. This is adapted from the old Dearborn Formboard, and Bauman describes it as a clinical instrument rather than as a test because she varies administration with both the vision and to some extent the intellectual ability of the testee, and because she is more interested in observing how the client reacts and how much he improves from trial to trial than in a numerical score. The NLL has the advantage of being usable with almost all ages, since a very few capable preschool children do it well, whereas it can be a challenge to the totally blind adult. It also has the advantage of enabling the psychologist to watch the reactions of the testee far better than many tests permit. Through changes in the mode of presentation, the same material can be varied somewhat in level of difficulty and be used as a measure of both problem solving and learning. Its disadvantage (if disadvantage it is) lies in the fact that it becomes more and more meaningful the more the psychologist uses it—which implies that the first couple of times he uses it, interpretation may be difficult.

The NLL consists of a formboard containing eight holes, two ovals, two diamonds, two rectangles, and two hexagons. These holes are filled, in some cases by two blocks, in some cases by three blocks, which are interchangeable between holes of the same shape. The board is set up by the test administrator by removing four blocks, one half block of each shape, and so rearranging the blocks within the board that moves which follow certain rules will readily get the removed blocks back in place.

Testees with enough vision to distinguish the shapes of the blocks may be told merely to get the blocks back into the board, with the advice that they remember how they work it out, so that on the next trial they can do it faster. A totally blind client of roughly average ability or less is taught both through verbal presentation of rules and by a step-by-step teaching process just how to get the blocks in, and if he fails to do this independently he is retaught for each of three trials. Between these extremes of no and intense teaching, the clinician may use variations which give the testee more or less help.

Interpretation of the results relates only to a small extent to the speed with which the blocks are actually returned to the board. In addition, valuable information is gained from such factors as ability of the client to apply the rules and to react flexibly when he makes an error, tendency to repeat over and over again the same incorrect move, planfulness versus obvious trial and error, and initiative in departing in a useful way from the procedures originally taught.

With younger children or even with adults whose ability is so limited that they cannot show any real learning through several trials of the NLL, simpler formboards may be useful. These range from mere pegboards through the typical Three Block Formboard which is usually in the test cabinet of every psychologist who works with young children, the Seguin-type board, and the relatively complex Witmer Cylinders. Normative data for visually handicapped children are not available for any of these, but the psychologist experienced in their value with sighted children will, after a little practice, gain helpful insight from their application with the visually handicapped child.

Haptic Intelligence Scale

Although Shurrager and Shurrager (1964) state in the *Manual* that the HIS was not intended as an adaptation of the Wechsler Performance Scale, some subtests were obviously inspired by the WAIS and the blind persons selected by the Shurragers as a normative group follow closely the proportion of various ages, sexes, and geographic patterns in the WAIS normative group. As is true for the WAIS, norms start at age 16. The tests consists of six subtests:

Digit Symbol: This consists of a series of shapes presented in raised form and numbered from one to six by raised dots. The same six forms are then presented in random order, but of course without the raised dots, and the testee associates the proper number with each form. The more quickly he learns to do this and moves correctly and speedily through the naming process, the better his score is.

Block Design: This is an adaptation of the Kohs Block Design Test in tactual form. The testee is asked to copy designs through various placements of four blocks which duplicate the colors of the typical Kohs with variations in texture.

Object Assembly: The parts of four objects, a doll, a block, a hand, and a ball, are presented in succession, and the client's score depends on the speed and accuracy with which he assembles each object from its parts.

Object Completion: Small objects, such as a comb, an animal, a lock, and a telephone, are presented with some important part missing. Obviously, the client must first identify the object and then indicate what part is missing.

Pattern Board: This is a pegboard with a fixed center peg around which designs of increasing difficulty are first set up by the test administrator and then copied from memory by the client.

Bead Arithmetic: The abacus is the basis of this test in which the client is first taught how to identify and read numbers of increasing complexity, then how to set these up himself and how to add.

Much excellent professional effort went into the development of the HIS, and it was hoped that it might truly satisfy the expressed need for a performance scale to be used with the WAIS Verbal Scale just as both verbal and performance scales are almost invariably used with sighted testees. In practice this has not worked out to any large extent for at least some of the following reasons. (a) Administration time can easily run over 1 hour, sometimes even over 2. Frequently it is inappropriate to use this much of the test day on the measurement of mental ability, since there is a high correlation between this and the verbal scale and especially when the psychologist must complete his evaluation within one visit by the client to his office. Interest, personality, and special ability measures may also be an important part of the evaluation and require their fair share of the time abailable. (b) Norms of the HIS do not go below age 16. (c) Norms are based entirely on a group without useful vision. In the practice of most psychologists there are more partially seeing than totally blind individuals. (d) The abacus subtest is invalidated if the client has had prior training or experience with the abacus. (e) Clear research evidence is not yet available to show that the HIS is indeed measuring the same thing the Wechsler Performance Scale measures, and interpretation of the results is clouded by this lack.

Stanford Kohs Block Design Test

Following a lead by Owaki in Japan, Suinn and Dauterman (1966) adapted the general idea of the Kohs Block Design Test by making the blocks larger, rough and smooth rather than varied in color, and varied in the complexity of the pattern to be copied from very simple to unusually complex tasks. Unlike the HIS, where six kinds of mental operations are evaluated, the Kohs adaptation has the disadvantage of using a single kind of material, and a few otherwise very competent blind people simply do not seem able to work with this, hence it proves to be no real measure of their total performance ability. Also, for some totally blind clients the test can be very time consuming and fatiguing. Perhaps its most significant disadvantage is again that no norms are available below age 16. However, it has the advantages of norms for both totally blind and partially seeing; the material itself is not cumbersome; and opportunities to evaluate how the client approaches the task are considerable. There is also some evidence, not yet documented by a formal study, that reactions typical of organic brain damage can be detected, especially when the client loses his concept of squareness, shows reversals, etc.

VISAB and TRP

The Vocational Intelligence Scale for the Adult Blind (VISAB) and the Tactual Reproduction Pegboard (TRP) were developed by Jones and Gruber as part of a complex project at Purdue University under the direction of Tiffin (1960). Persons used to develop the norms of these two tests were also used in other published studies, including that describing The Sound Test (Palacios, 1964), which will be discussed later. The detailed information thus available on this normative group could be an advantage, although this is probably more true in relation to research than in the application of the tests to typical psychological evaluation of individual children. Again, norms begin at age 16, but norms are available for both totally blind and partially sighted. Neither test has had a great deal of acceptance, perhaps because each measures only a single kind of mental operation, and there is limited evidence concerning just what can be predicted, in the practical sense, on the basis of these scores.

SPECIAL ABILITY TESTS

Roughness Discrimination Test

Because of the importance of reading in the educational progress of all students, sighted and blind, but especially because of the difficulty many children experience in learning to read braille, many teachers are greatly concerned with predicting success in braille reading.

Reading readiness tests for sighted children usually consist of various materials which test the child's ability to discriminate differences, first between pictures, then between more abstract symbols; and it is assumed that the more readily the child discriminates rather small differences, the more readily he will discriminate letters and words—although, of course, attaching meaning to those letters and words is also vital.

In braille reading, the required discrimination is tactual in nature, so that the ability to use the tactual receptors and the hands in a coordinated and orderly fashion is a prerequisite to successful braille reading. The Roughness Discrimination Test (RDT) was developed as a measure of the development of these abilities, but particularly as a measure of tactual discrimination.

The test consists of cards on which 2-inch squares of sandpaper are mounted. On each card, three squares are of equal grit size while the fourth is of a different grit size. The child is asked to indicate which is different. The gamelike quality of the task recommends it for the preschooler, although the authors do indicate that the ability of the child to maintain attention may also have a significant bearing on his ability to learn to read. Nolan and Morris (1965) report that for first-grade students tested at the beginning of the school year, the RDT correctly predicted whether the student would be in the upper or lower half of his reading group at the end of the school year 70% of the time when reading errors was the criterion, and 75% of the time when reading speed was the criterion. Prediction was considerably increased when both IQ and RDT scores were used, since IQ pulls into consideration the child's ability to attach meaning, as well as to discriminate tactually.

Language Aptitude Test

Another special area of learning which could have great value for certain blind students is that of learning a foreign language. A few years ago the Federal Rehabilitation Services Administration supported training to develop translators of Russian and some consideration was given to similar projects to develop top ability in other languages.

At that time Gardner (1965) modified the Modern Language Aptitude Test and appeared to have developed a very promising tool for determing which students would profit most by training in modern languages. However, both the learning and, more especially, the application of such aptitude in employment seem to include many elements not reached by a language aptitude test, and this test is now rarely used.

Other Aptitude Tests for Special Abilities

Almost any completely verbal special ability or special aptitude measure can be used with visually handicapped persons of appropriate age and background. All that is necessary is to change the mode of presentation from ink print to braille, large print, or oral means. Ordinarily, the psychologist will need such measures only occasionally, and directly reading the test to the client is likely to be the most feasible procedure. If we are careful to recognize that for the blind (and, indeed, for the sighted) success in selling or in supervision, for example, requires qualities of personality and interpersonal skills in addition to the specific "how to" knowledge usually tapped by the special ability test, prediction on the basis of such test results is no different for the blind than for the sighted.

However, most such tests are in multiple-choice form, and in their application the cautions discussed in the earlier section on procedures in testing must be kept in mind.

GROUP TESTS OF APTITUDE AND ACHIEVEMENT

Scholastic Aptitude Test

Widely used at the junior and senior high school levels, and required for admission to many colleges, the Scholastic Aptitude Test of the College Entrance Examination Board has been put into braille and oral presentation form, with answers to be typed by the student. The tests are distributed by the CEEB under the same control applied for the sighted student, must be administered by approved persons, and must be returned to the CEEB for evaluation. The results are treated as the equivalent of scores resulting from the regular printed version of the test.

Procedures for the administration of this test to blind students are most generous, allowing almost unlimited time and therefore permitting each student to proceed at his own pace. No clear study of the effect this lack of a time limit may have on predictive value has been made.

Stanford Achievement Tests

Achievement was one of the earliest areas of concern in the evaluation of visually handicapped children, and the record of use of various achievement tests goes back to 1918 with adaptations of such materials as the Gray Oral Reading Check Tests, the Metropolitan Achievement Tests, the Myers-Ruch High School Progress Test, and many editions of the Stanford Achievement Tests. Nolan (1962) has excellently described the problems in adapting such standard tests to use with blind children, and any teacher who considers making such an adaptation would be wise to read his discussion.

Much time and effort has been put into the adaptation of Stanford Achievement Tests, Forms X and W, so that there is every reason to suppose that these two forms can be used with confidence. However, the time required for their administration is far greater than the time required for the regular-print versions with normally seeing children.

Other Group Tests

A similar careful and technically complex process was used to adapt the Sequential Tests of Educational Progress (STEP) and the catalog of the American Printing House for the Blind also lists the availability of the Cooperative School and College Ability Tests (SCAT), the Diagnostic Reading Tests, and the Iowa Tests of Basic Skills. The Gray Standardized Oral Reading Paragraph, one of the first tests to be used with visually handicapped children, is also still available. Less frequently used, but helpful in school systems where standards for sighted children are set through them, are many of the California Tests and the Differential Aptitude Tests.

The psychologist or teacher who wishes to use the latter tests with blind children should consider carefully the implications of necessary changes in procedure and timing, and should interpret their results in the light of the very real possibility, discussed earlier in this chapter, that the blind child has not had learning opportunities truly equivalent to those of his sighted fellow students.

MEASURES OF SOCIAL COMPETENCY

Maxfield-Buchholz Scale

Although there is certainly no complete correlation, for those with good vision, between intellectual ability and social competency, there is reason to argue that for the visually handicapped correlation between these two is even lower. That the totally blind child cannot learn social behavior by direct visual observation of what others do, the limitations in his experience already described in this and the Chapters 2 and 3, and the fact that it is often easy for him to let others do things for him, all tend to lower the social competency of those with visual handicaps and particularly those who have been totally blind from birth. Yet, in casual contacts with the public, or even in contacts with fellow students or fellow workers, such skills are often the first, if not the only, qualities observed.

In part for this reason, but also because of the difficulty in using formal tests with very young children, a scale of social development at the preschool level was developed by Maxfield, refined several times, and reached its final form in the Maxfield-Buchholz Scale in 1957.

Items at the 0–1 age level are largely physical, such as balancing the head, rolling over, reaching for objects, pulling self to standing position with help, grasping with thumb and finger. At higher age levels, items concerning dressing, self-care, play, adjustment to group situations, etc., are included. The scale ends at age 6–0 but it has long provided an extremely valuable resource, particularly in view of the unsatisfactory nature of verbal or performance testing materials at the preschool level.

Overbrook Social Competency Scale

Recent work by Bauman has extended the values of a social competency measure to the young adult level through the Overbrook Social Competency Scale. Although present norms are tentative and the author expects both to enlarge the normative group and to develop standards through the superior adult level, this material can now be used to provide supplementary information on those aspects of individual development which are related to independence in daily living, interpersonal skills, mobility, and many aspects of group activity.

For both the Maxfield and Overbrook scales, administration is through an interview, usually not with the subject himself but with a parent, residence supervisor (in a residential school), or similar person who can accurately describe the typical behavior of the child or young adult. Both scales point up areas in which change might be desirable and in which training and/or counseling could be helpful, so that the record form becomes a guide to improvement. An additional advantage, particularly in the evaluation of the very young child, is that results are based on the child's typical behavior, whereas his response to tests may easily be affected by his health and energy on the day of examination, his fright at being taken to an unfamiliar place for testing, the fatigue and excitement of the trip, etc.

MEASURES OF MANUAL DEXTERITY

The psychological evaluation of blind persons in areas other than intelligence and achievement grew largely out of World War II, spurred by both the desire to place blind workers in jobs and the desire to serve men blinded in the war. Since a very large percentage of the jobs then available were factory jobs, evaluation of speed and dexterity in various manual tasks was important.

Today visually handicapped persons find a much wider range of job opportunities available to them and the need to evaluate manipulative skills is reduced. However, dexterity tests can give the psychologist far more information than the mere measure of manual speed.

These tasks provide an opportunity to see the client in action, doing rather than verbalizing. When the client has difficulties, his reactions can be observed and, through repeated assistance and training, his response in a learning situation can be probed. Orientation in a work space, ability to follow patterns of movement, ability to maintain attention and effort at a repetitive task, and sheer motivation (the will to do one's best in any circumstances) are demonstrated. Without these action tests, the psychologist would fail to see quite so complete a picture of his client.

When used for these purposes, dexterity tests may appropriately be given to children at lower age levels, even as young as 9 or 10, though normative data are lacking at these age levels and prediction of success in manual work is scarcely the problem.

Minnesota Rate of Manipulation

This test consists of a long, narrow board into which round holes have been cut, four from top to bottom and 15 from one end of the board to the other. Therefore, the board contains 60 holes into which identical round blocks can fit.

For the procedure known as Displacing, the testee moves the blocks, one by one, in a pattern which is simple, yet for some persons difficult to follow. The ease with which the pattern is learned and the accuracy with which it is followed provide an unusually good measure of orientation in a work space. The operation requires only one hand and may therefore be used with individuals with effective use of only one hand.

The procedure known as Turning requires that each block be turned over with a standard movement sequence which requires both hands and requires working alternately left and right down the length of the board. Although the difficulties in orientation are much less than for Displacing, a need to change hand movement patterns at the end of each row proves difficult for some clients and the inability to perform this procedure, or marked difficulty in mastering it, correlates highly with low IQ.

Some adjustment is made for variations in amount of vision by giving additional training trials to totally blind persons, and norms are available for the totally blind and for those with vision useful in the test situation (i.e., a person who can orient himself visually and does not need touch to identify what is before him).

Penn Bi-Manual Worksample

At each end of the board involved in this test is a pan, one containing bolts and the other nuts. Between the pans are 100 holes, ten rows of ten each, forming a square. The task requires picking up a bolt with one hand, a nut with the other, twisting them together just enough to catch, and placing them into the holes. Whether bolts or nuts are at the right of the testee depends on his handedness. A second part of the task requires picking up, disassembling, and replacing nuts and bolts in the correct pan. The scores are the number of minutes and seconds required to complete each of the two activities.

Of the various dexterity tests, this probably involves the most comprehensive and varied sampling of manual activities and has consistently shown better relationship to success in manipulative jobs. In fact, this is a familiar test for selecting sighted workers for manual jobs. The variation in the task for a blind person lies only in giving much more training time, regularly two complete trials, and in basing prediction as much on the amount of improvement on the second trial as on the actual score.

In addition to the speed score itself, the psychologist may here observe the ability to orient, since some clients are totally unable to follow the rows whereas others do so very effectively; ability to follow instructions, especially in relation to how far the nuts and bolts are twisted together; coordination of the two hands in moderately complex movements; and resistance to boredom on a highly repetitive task.

Adjustment for amount of vision is made by giving extra training time to the totally blind, and norms are available for those with and without useful vision.

Crawford Small Parts Dexterity—Screwdriver

The Crawford test involves two parts. The part requiring use of a tweezer to place pins into holes has not been found useful with blind persons, although it might be relevant to some specific jobs for persons with partial vision. The part involving use of a screwdriver and small screws to be placed into 36 holes (plus a practice row of six holes) has been very effective in evaluating the ability of blind persons to work through use of tools. Again, the score is the number of minutes and seconds required to complete the task, but norms developed by Bauman are based upon timing the first three test rows separately from the last three, so that improvement with practice can be noted. When this is done (for those without useful vision only), the obtained time for the better half is doubled before comparison with the norms. Norms are available for both the totally blind and for persons with vision useful in the test setting.

Other Dexterity Tests

Some work has been done with the Purdue Pegboard, and psychologists familiar with other tests, such as the Bennett Hand Tool Dexterity Test and the O'Connor tests, have found them useful, although norms for visually handicapped persons are not available.

MEASURES OF PERSONALITY

Questionnaires

In the area of personality evaluation, perhaps more than in any other area of psychological testing, the familiarity of the psychologist with his instrument is extremely important. Therefore, many psychologists, quite correctly, use personality measures which they know well because of long use with sighted persons and they use them quite effectively.

This applies particularly to the Minnesota Multiphasic Personality Inventory(MMPI). In Bauman's (1968) study of current usage, the MMPI was mentioned twice as often as any other questionnaire–type measure. Part of the reason for this is that it is frequently used along with at least one other measure, and many psychologists report that they use it only when observation of the client, or his history, suggests problems outside the normal range of adjustment. When interpretation is done with an awareness of some of the special problems of blindness, it is a most effective tool.

Bauman has developed an Emotional Factors Inventory and, more recently, an Adolescent Emotional Factors Inventory(AEFI), in which items are largely based upon adjustment behavior as described by visually handicapped persons. The first step in the development of both tests was a series of meetings of psychologists with small groups of the visually handicapped; in these meetings the emotional problems experienced as a visually handicapped person were discussed. Some of these problems are, of course, the emotional difficulties common to all people, with or without good vision; other problems are, however, especially related to the limitations and frustrations resulting from lack of vision.

It is recommended that these measures be administered either through large print (for the individual who can read this) or through tape recording, as described in the section of this chapter dealing with procedures. This guarantee of privacy in making his response could be important to the blind person and improves the predictive value of the results.

Both tests result in scores on a series of subscales: Sensitivity, or the broad tendency to become emotional; Somatic Symptoms of inner tension; Social Competency; Attitudes of Distrust, or mildly paranoid tendencies; Feelings of Inadequacy, or doubt of one's ability to cope; Depression, or lack of the morale and positive orientation so important to accomplishment; and Attitudes regarding Blindness. The AEFI also includes measures of adjustment specific to family, boy–girl relationships, and school. Both questionnaires include a validation scale.

With children below the teens, it is often difficult to maintain attention for questionnaries, but the short Aspects of Personality appears to have some value—and the interplay between child and psychologist in the process of administering it by direct reading may have even more.

Several short scales have been developed, such as the Jervis (1960) scale for adjustment and the Hardy (1968) scale for anxiety, but they suffer from limited normative groups and lack of enough reported use to place them beyond the experimental stages.

As noted in the first paragraph of this section, the psychologist may be wise to use an instrument with which he is familiar, since interpretation often goes beyond a simple reading of the norms (and should!), but he would also be wise to read through his chosen test for items which could have a very different implication for those with little or no vision. Interpretation must also take this into account.

Nonquestionnaire Personality Evaluation

The psychologist who is most comfortable with projective procedures naturally wishes to apply them with his blind clients, and this seems particularly desirable with the younger child, whose vocabulary and attention span may both be doubtful.

A number of kinds of stimuli have been tried out, with various sound sequences among the most popular. Unfortunately, none of these has had enough study and application to be described as beyond the experimental stages, although The Sound Test (Palacios, 1964) was part of a larger project in the evaluation of blind adults and does have some fairly solid findings as a result. These findings are based on persons over 16 years of age and have a rather heavy loading of those in sheltered employment, but the procedure does show promise.

Various forms of the Sentence Completion Test have had very wide usage and have won considerable approval. With this there seems to be little objection to oral administration, although the task could also easily be handled by having the stems tape-recorded and allowing the testee to type his responses. For clients with useful vision, the Bender Visual Motor Gestalt Test and the House-Tree-Person give generally satisfactory results, although again the psychologist must be concerned with the possible effects of distortion resulting from the visual condition, not the emotional qualities.

MEASURES OF INTEREST

Although the Kuder Preference Record is much the most widely used, the California Occupational Interest Inventory (Lee Thorpe) and the Strong Vocational Interest Blank have wide acceptance among psychologists working with visually handicapped adolescents and adults. None of these are adapted in content, and the mode of administration is usually large type or oral presentation. For the Kuder, Howe Press makes a raised dot answer sheet, and it is also possible to test several students together by having them type their responses. However, because privacy is less important in testing of interest than in personality measurement, probably the most frequent form of administration is direct oral reading with the reader also recording the responses.

Any interest inventory may be used with visually handicapped persons if they are instructed to make their choices on the assumption that they have enough vision to perform all the activities listed. Most visually handicapped persons seem able to do this, but at times choices do seem to reflect "what I can see to do" more that "what I like to do." To cope with this, Bauman has in the experimental stages an inventory based entirely on content of jobs done or hobbies chosen by blind people.

In the area of interest, interpretation of results may be more challenging than problems of administration. There is a marked tendency, among visually handicapped persons, to make many choices in the social service area and, to slightly less extent, in music. The first of these tendencies seems, often, to result from the fact that blindness tends to enforce dependence upon others, and the individual would like to repay this and also might find ego satisfaction in playing the role of the helper. He had admired those who have helped him and would like the experience of being the person to whom others are grateful. The interest in music arises in part from the fact that the blind person, of necessity, turns to sound as a source of pleasure, and perhaps in part from some extra emphasis on music in many schools for the blind.

INTERPRETATION OF TEST RESULTS

For all clients, at all times, good psychological reports go far beyond a simple reporting of test results. Tests are merely the tools of the psychologist. His responsibilities include knowing those tools well and using them accurately and appropriately in terms of the nature of the client and of the problem to be solved. His responsibilities also include evaluating the test results and interpreting them in such a way that the findings can be understood and used with confidence and insight by those to whom the psychological reports go— educators, counselors, rehabilitation workers, medical staff, or parents.

Because of the many ways in which the background of the visually handicapped client may be different from the typical history, the psychologist must, in the interpretation of test scores for visually handicapped subjects, be especially concerned that he understand that background and that he make his interpretation in the light of it. In an earlier section, some of the differences were briefly mentioned. Here it seems necessary only to reiterate how very important it is to consider and tie in every bit of history—family reactions, medical and opthalmolgical history, social history, known results of earlier examinations, reports of special training (such as mobility training), and of course educational history in detail. To do so will usually result in a complete and well-rounded picture of the subject; not to do so may not only fall far short of good psychological reporting but can easily cause the psychologist to say some very foolish things.

The psychologist must also consider to whom the report will go and how it is likely to be used. When the child is young, the most frequent users of psychological reports are school staffs, and it is helpful if the psychologist knows, at least to some degree, what the school has to offer, whether special help from the point of view of vision is available, what remedial help could be obtained, and whether counseling or psychotherapy is part of the school program when needed.

Too often it is said that teachers regard IQs—especially low IQs—as an excuse for allowing a child to sit on the sidelines, making little progress. Especially with the visually handicapped child, it is extremely important that this should not be the attitude of the teacher. As is true for most disadvantaged groups, all evidence points to very large gains in IQ when the child is transferred from an inadequate and unstimulating background to one which offers both appropriate materials from the visual point of view and teachers trained in work with the visually handicapped. At almost any point in life, but certainly in the young child, or in the child just transferring from regular classes to special classes for the visually handicapped, the IQ should be regarded as a baseline against which to measure improvement.

As the child matures, interest becomes increasingly important, both as a possible guide to motivating the child and as a very important guide to choices of elective classes or extracurricular activities. At roughly the age of 16, in most states, the rehabilitation agency becomes involved, or should become involved, in helping the student plan for his future. This does not mean that the school abdicates its responsibility, but education and rehabilitation should work very closely together so that, between them, the maturing student may be offered the greatest and most appropriate opportunities to know his own abilities, job content, and training opportunities, and to know very realistically just what is required for success in the several fields of work in which he may feel some interest. The school carries its total responsibility well only when it recognizes that it is preparing future citizens, individuals who should understand and be ready to carry responsibilities in a home and family, a community, and a job. The good psychological report assists in guidance toward all of these.

SUPPLIERS OF TESTS

Wechsler Intelligence Scales
  Psychological Corporation, 304 E. 45th St., New York, N. Y. 10017
Hayes-Binet
  Perkins School for the Blind, 175 N. Beacon St., Watertown, Mass. 02172
Non-language Learning Test
  Personnel Research Center, 1604 Spruce St., Philadelphia, Pa. 19103
Haptic Intelligence Scale
  Psychology Research, Box 14, Technology Center, Chicago, Ill. 60616
Stanford Kohs Block Design Test
  William L. Dauterman, Casa Calina Hospital, Pomona, Calif.
Vocational Intelligence Scale for the Adult Blind
Tactual Reproduction Pegboard
  Dr. Robert J. Teare, 185 Kings Rd., Athens, Ga. 30601
Roughness Discrimination Test
  American Printing House for the Blind, 1839 Frankfort Ave., Louisville, Ky. 40206
Modern Language Aptitude Test
  Psychological Corporation
Scholastic Aptitude Test
  Educational Testing Service, Princeton, N. J.
Stanford Achievement Test
Sequential Tests of Educational Progress
School and College Ability Tests
  American Printing House for the Blind
Maxfield-Buchholz Scale
  American Foundation for the Blind, 15 W. 16th St., New York, N. Y.
Overbrook Social Competency Scale
  Personnel Research Center
Minnesota Rate of Manipulation

Penn Bi-Manual Worksample
 Educational Testing Bureau, 720 Washington Ave., Minneapolis, Minn.
Crawford Small Parts Dexterity Test
 Psychological Corporation
Minnesota Multiphasic Personality Inventory
 Psychological Corporation
Emotional Factors Inventory
Adolescent Emotional Factors Inventory
 Personnel Research Center
The Sound Test
 Dr. Robert J. Teare, 185 Kings Rd., Athens, Ga. 30601
Kuder Preference Record
 Science Research Associates, 259 E. Erie St., Chicago, Ill. 60611
 (Answer sheets—Howe Press, Perkins School for the Blind)
California Occupational Interest Inventory
 California Test Bureau, Del Monte Research Park, Monterey, Calif. 93940
PRC Interest Inventory
 Personnel Research Center

REFERENCES

Bauman, Mary K. *A report and a reprint: Tests used in the psychological evaluation of blind and visually handicapped persons & A manual of norms for tests used in counseling blind persons.* Washington: American Association of Workers for the Blind, 1968.

Gardner, R. C. A language aptitude test for blind students. *Journal of Applied Psychology,* 1965, **49,** 135–141.

Hardy, R. E. A study of manifest anxiety among blind residential school students. *New Outlook for the Blind,* 1968, **62,** 173–180.

Hayes, S. P. *Contributions to a psychology of blindness.* New York: American Foundation for the Blind, 1941.

Jervis, F. M. A comparison of self-concepts of blind and sighted children. In *Guidance programs for blind children.* Watertown, Mass.: Perkins School Publication, No. 20, 1960.

Nolan, C. Y. Evaluating the scholastic achievement of visually handicapped children. *Exceptional Children,* 1962, **28,** 493–496.

Nolan, C. Y. and Morris, J. E. *Roughness discrimination test manual.* Louisville, Ky.: American Printing House for the Blind, 1965.

Palacios, M. H. *The sound test: An auditory technique.* Marion, Ind.: Author, 1964.

Shurrager, H. C. and Shurrager, P. S. *Manual for the Haptic Intelligence Scale for adult blind.* Chicago: Psychology Research, 1964.

Suinn, R. M. and Dauterman, W. L. *Manual for the Stanford-Kohs block design test for the blind.* Washington: Vocational Rehabilitation Administration, U.S. Dept. of Health, Education, & Welfare, 1966.

Tiffin, J. (Project Director) *An investigation of vocational success with the blind.* Lafayette, Ind.: Purdue Research Foundation, Purdue University, 1960.

CHAPTER 5

Utilization of Sensory-Perceptual Abilities

Natalie C. Barraga

Department of Special Education
The University of Texas at Austin

INTRODUCTION

Many theories regarding the dimensions of development in human beings have been suggested, all of which can contribute to knowledge regarding children's behavioral reactions. Ideas suggested by information theory appear to have greater relevance for an understanding of the difficulties encountered by children who have an information-gathering organ which is useless to them or which is so defective that the limitations in its function restrict the amount and type of information available for learning. Such is the case with children who are totally blind or who have conditions which inhibit the full use of the eye; they are commonly described as visually handicapped children.

As a basis for understanding the sensory-perceptual abilities and limitations of visually handicapped children, some discussion of the process by which all children experience and receive the world seems imperative. With his first breath at the moment of birth an infant has the capacity to become a receiving, participating, interacting human being who enjoys a reciprocally satisfying relationship with his immediate environment, and eventually a fulfilling involvement with an ever-expanding world. The central nervous system of the

117

human organism is so constituted that it experiences a continuing hunger for stimulation through the sense organs in order to establish contact between the body and external surroundings. "The sensory processes are the links that connect all behaving organisms to their external environment and provide information about that environment as well as about the organism's own internal environment" (Corso, 1967, p. 36). Physical energy within the human being or from the outside excites the sensory receptors and acts as a stimulus which upsets the body's state of equilibrium and creates the need for a satisfying "input."

Although the growth, development, and expansion of human beings into the larger world encompasses many dimensions, the present discussion will focus primarily on the interactions and processes which facilitate learning and mental growth through the sense organs. In this context, the eyes, ears, hands, body movements, nose, and mouth will be considered the organs through which information about the self and the world is received; transmitted to the brain for interpretation, processing, and storage; and used as a basis for response and interaction with and upon the environment. The postulation is suggested that "the centers of the central nervous system, including the brain, resonate to information" (Gibson, 1966, p. 367) instead of constructing information from sensory input. "Learning to know" can be continuous as mental development reaches a level from which the mind can generate thoughts and ideas.

Sensation is a function of the sensory organs and the peripheral nervous system, whereas perception (interpretation) and organized responses are mediated through the central nervous system (Merleau-Ponty, 1969). Stimulation of sensory organs may or may not provide information, depending on the receptivity of the transmitting channels, the efficiency of the receptor centers in the brain, the connecting links or pathways among the various sensory channels, and the ability of the coding and processing centers to give meaningful interpretation to the information in order for satisfying responses to be generated through the motor system. The circle of interaction indicative of learning is complete only when the human being receives feedback through expression or additional information (Bateman, 1967). The perceptual systems (receptor and processing centers) are subject to modification and change, whereas the sensory channels themselves are unalterable.

Nerve cells within each sensory organ have variable activation thresholds and require different intensities of external stimulation for information to be transmitted. Furthermore, receptor cells in various organs have affinity or disposition to external stimuli designed specifically for that sense (Buddenbrock, 1953); for example, only cells in the retina of the eye are sensitive to light rays; receptor cells in the inner ear are totally indifferent to light rays, but are acutely sensitive to sound waves, which arouse no activity in retinal cells. An explanation of the receptive abilities of each sensory system, the nature of the information conveyed, and its ultimate value in the total process of learning and concept development may contribute to a clearer understanding of visually handicapped children as they seek to utilize their sensory-perceptual abilities.

Visual Sense

As an outgrowth of the brain, the optic nerve extends to cover the retinal portion of the eye. Retinal images received in the brain provide information no other sense organs can transmit. Led by his eyes to reach out, move about, and maintain contact with his surroundings, the child attends to selective visual sensations as he is attracted by their physical qualities and as his perceptual learning enables him to derive meaning from them. As visual stimulations and experiences increase, the child seeks and attends to those visual stimuli which clarify or relate to his previous impressions. Through the visual sense a greater quantity and more refined quality of information is available than can be acquired through any other one sense. Through the eye the brain receives sensations for the interpretation of color, the dimensional quality of objects, the impression of distance, and the ability to follow an experienced movement while the body remains stationary. Often called the primary sensory channel for extension of the human being beyond his own body, vision is the mediator for other sensory impressions and acts as a stabilizer between man and the external world.

Tactual–Kinesthetic Senses

The receptor systems in "skin senses" and the information available through these channels may be accorded less importance than is deserved. The tactile sense actually has the capacity to respond to a multitude of stimuli, including mechanical, thermal, electrical, and chemical. The human organism may be "acted upon" more readily by the visual and auditory senses, but active involvement with the environment is necessary to seek and acquire information through the skin and by manipulation of body parts.

"The tactile system is activated by the production of tension within the cutaneous tissues containing the receptor cells" (Corso, 1967, p. 142). The nerve receptors in the skin mediate a wide variety of vibratory stimuli to experience distant events. Pain and temperature receptors are numerous all over the body and provide facts about the adjacent world. Hands can grope, grasp, press, rub, and lift to get information; however, the fingertips provide degrees of discrete impressions with accuracy far exceeding that achieved through vision (Fieandt, 1966).

In order for the sense of touch to convey messages to the brain, the skin of a stationary hand must be dented by the stimuli; or the hand must be moving, thus involving muscles; or the hand may grasp or "lay hold of" objects, in which case muscles, tendons, and joints are involved dynamically. With increased body movement in the "search and locate" activities of children, the interaction of each body part with the object world fosters the refining and discriminating of perceptions and leave the child to touch and move for the purpose of clarifying the information he receives. The visual system may be involved in tactual explorations to the extent that it may actually influence the nature of the tactual information (Bartley, 1971). Such possibilities suggest definite intersensory relationships. Increased movements of the whole body enable the child to begin to determine the boundaries of space in relation to his own body as well as to interpret the extensions of space beyond his reach. Through the haptic sense (touch and body movement) impressions about the environment, the body, and the body in relation to the environment are received.

Auditory Sense

Receptor cells in the ear are recessed within the skull and are far less susceptible to activation by sound stimuli, especially at birth, since the nerve endings are surrounded by fluid. With the gradual impinging of vibrations set up by sound waves, the circulation of the fluid activates the nerve fibers and produces the sensation of sound. The fluids in the inner ear provide protection for the delicate nerve fibers but at the same time make them less receptive to ordinary environmental sounds than are the retinal cells to light. Responses to light and visual images and to tactile and movement stimulations seem to precede responses to sounds. With continued exposure to sounds the fluid circulation has the effect of lowering the threshold of sensitivity and the auditory sense then begins to supply information from the environment.

The sound of the human voice is soothing and pleasurable; as the child begins to listen and attend to it, other sounds begin to arouse his curiosity. Through sound the human being is able to specify the direction and locate the source in relation to his body. The richer the stimulation of human voices, the more meaning he is able to derive from the variations in quality; very early in life the child distinguishes bewteen human sounds (those produced by his own vocal system as well as those voiced by others) and object or environmental sounds. The search for additional auditory clarification leads him to engage in vocal play with sounds he produces, and eventually to imitate sounds produced by other human beings. This process of imitation establishes a firm contact between him and the world of sound fostered by the identification with those who "talk" with him. Imitation of vocal and other sounds is essential to future language development because as he imitates, the child internalizes the feelings of pleasure necessary for repetition and clarification of his own sound production (Myklebust, 1960). Information fed to the brain through the auditory sense forms the basis for the development of language and speech through which the ultimate in communication and interaction with the external world is achieved.

Olfactory and Gustatory Senses

Receptors in both the nose and mouth react to the chemical qualities of the environment. Some smells and tastes are soothing to the senses and are experienced as pleasing sensations, while others are irritating and cause unpleasant sensations. The olfactory sense (smell) receives very differentiated information, whereas the gustatory sense (taste) is much less discriminatory; when both senses are operating the messages are mixed and the brain has difficulty in interpreting the information as coming from either one alone (Allport, 1955). In addition to the taste sense, the mouth provides information regarding textural qualities, contour, and size. Receptors on the tip of the tongue are especially sensitive and are useful in providing discrete discriminations of the qualities of objects and even symbols. Persons have been reported to use the tip of the tongue for reading braille.

Summary

Stimulation of the senses through exploration in a rich sensory environment is necessary to develop an adequate model of the external world. Attention to information from the various senses and learning to respond to new stimulations begins the process of perceptual development. The relation of information from one specific sense organ to that from other sensory systems contributes to the "strategy" of perceptual interpretation which culminates in the coding and organizing of information in order to understand the distinguishable features of the total environment in relation to the human body (Gibson, 1966). Only when learning has progressed to this level is the human being capable of using information to think for himself, adapt his responses, and be dynamically involved in formulating a realistic conception of himself within the world.

Little, if any, definitive information exists regarding the existence of or possibility for intermodal transposition of sensory information in human beings. In the case of limited or total lack of input through one channel, as would be the case with visually handicapped children, even less is known. In a study designed to look at the ability structure of visually handicapped persons, Juurmaa (1967, p. 108) hypothesized that "the discriminative sensitivities of vision and audition are interdependent; and, on the other hand, when compensatory tendencies make their appearance, these occur in the tactual sphere." In studies with deaf children, discrimination and perception of verbal materials was enhanced by the combination of the senses of touch and vision (Frisina, 1967). Greater intake of information resulted than had occurred through either sensory channel alone. However, children may well translate sensory information received through one modality into another modality for storage and thinking (Buktenica, 1968). At an early age, perceptions in all sensory modalities are undifferentiated and may be less "organ-bound" than at more advanced stages of development. The suggestion of the possible existence of a primary spatial perceptual factor developed independently of the individual sensory systems (touch, vision, olfaction, etc.) involved has merit (Fieandt, 1966). If such could be verified, the idea of cross-modal transposition could be tested so as to establish the relevance of teaching "perceptual strategies" to sensorially impaired children.

THE VISUAL SENSORY SYSTEM

Introduction

The total visual system encompasses much more than the single organ of the eye, which may be thought of as the mechanism through which information is received. However, in order for the eyes to perform their functions, the muscular system must be developed sufficiently to direct the light rays to the visual receptors on the retina. The coordination of the organ parts and the muscles to work in harmony in two eyes is a most complicated phenomenon.

In addition to the optical aspects, the stimulation of retinal cells and the transmission of information through the optic nerve involves the "neuro-percepto" system as the messages proceed to the brain (occipital lobe) for coding, organization, and interpretation. The act of seeing involves the sciences of physics, physiology, and psychology (Wilman, 1966).

In order to communicate the growth and development of the visual process with clarity, the definition of terminology as used in this discussion may be helpful. *Visual acuity* refers to a measurement of the ability to discriminate clearly the fine details of objects or symbols at a given distance and is indicative only of the reception of visual stimuli by foveal cells connected directly to the visual receptors in the occipital cortex. Knowledge of visual acuity alone may be misleading in regard to the effective use of the total visual system in terms of its information-gathering ability. This fact is succinctly verified by a noted ophthalmologist, Dr. Faye, who says that "even if acuity is poor, the brain receives visual impressions and combines visual, auditory, and other sensory information" (Faye, 1970, p. 137).

A far more encompassing term is *visual perception,* which refers to the neuropsychological factors involved in the processing and meaningful interpretation of all messages received through the visual sense. A more comprehensive explanation will be included in the following section. *Visual efficiency* is the most inclusive term in that it relates the effective control of the optical mechanism, the speed and filtering abilities of the transmitting channels, and the strength and rapidity of the processing capacities in the brain to the expenditure of energy. The discussion of the visual system and the total process of seeing will refer to all of these functions as they contribute to learning.

Physiological Development

Structurally, the eye with all its component parts is complete at birth, although it increases gradually in size until the early teen years, when maximal physical growth is reached. The functioning of the system follows a sequence of developments which are concurrent but not uniform (Gesell, Ilg, & Bullis, 1950). The degree and intensity of light must be at or above the minimum threshold of sensitivity in order for visual receptor cells to be activated; as light rays from the environment strike the eye and stimulate the mechanism, reflexive behaviors of fixation and tracking develop rapidly. Muscular control progresses as the eye (in constant movement) seeks to refine the quality of the information received by focusing upon specific objects and fusing the images into one for transmission to the brain. For example,

> when one looks at an object, the pupil and lens are adjusted for proper display of the visual image on the retinas; the eyeballs are oriented and brought into convergence by the oculomotor muscles, the head and even the entire body is brought into a position that will permit proper regard of the object beheld [Foulke, 1968, p. 78].

Pattern and spatial vision become a more reliable source of information as eye–hand coodination develops and the body serves as an anchor for location of objects. Visual development seems to depend on movement of the eyes, body, and arms to give spatial meaning and appears to be influenced at every point by current and antecedent motor behavior (Buktenica, 1968).

Continued stimulation enhances discriminatory abilities and hastens the development of interpretive unification in the brain itself. Evidence regarding the specific role of sensory and motor functions in visual development has yet to be clarified, but experimental studies indicate a functional relatedness between them. The extent and nature of the relation appears to be dependent, at least to some degree, on the stimulating visual experiences as a concomitant to functional development.

Visual Perceptual Development

Factors Involved

Visual perception involves the examining of an object, distinguishing the essential features, understanding the relationship between the elements, and integrating the information into a meaningful whole. Accomplishment of such abilities moves through a sequence or series of processes for each perceptual act to "pervade, permeate, and most intimately interweave with another so as to compose one single act, the act of perception in the wider sense" (Gurwitsch, 1969, p. 256). Visual perception is an interaction with a sensory stimulus outside a person coordinated with something that happens within the person to enable him to utilize the information (Bartley, 1971).

In infancy, visual perceptions are blurred and unorganized and objects are seen as vague masses with no distinct contour, no shape, and no spatial location. They are somewhat diffused into the surroundings but sufficiently cohesive to resemble blobs and to convey the knowledge that something exists in the visual field. Such visual perceptions are primitive and indistinct and in the sequence of development are often referred to as the undifferentiated stage. As the search for meaning proceeds, a more analytic process develops in which the object becomes located within a spatial field; it stands out from its background; some details are perceivable and it begins to behave in a certain way (object constancy), so that predictions and probabilities may be assigned to the image. Although children tend to overlook or not attend to differences that are insignificant or unimportant for classifying a particular object, some objects may be identified by a fleeting or partial visual impression which is obtained by a scanning process. A more advanced stage of distinct visual perception emerges as the child searches for more categories of visual cues at the same time (Buktenica, 1968). The final process is an integrative one in which separate details are organized and synthesized into a meaningful entity (Vernon, 1954). An object can be said to be fully perceived only to the extent that it can be related to some organized shape which remains constant.

As visual learning continues, the coding processes are refined even more and additional phases of visual perception occur, as outlined by Douglas (1947):

1. A constructional process wherein the sensory qualities are suitably weighed and combined, each in its appropriate degree of importance, into a more or less clearly differentiated formal structure.
2. An assimilative process whereby the present percept is related to the body of past experience—compared, accepted or rejected—and is then referred back to some part of the external environment from which it can assume to have originated.
3. A response tendency, indicating the observer's reaction, overt or implicit, to the full implications of the percept [p. 5].

The efficiency of the described visual perceptual process may be related closely to the interpretative process in learning (Lancaster, 1949; Gibson & Gibson, 1955), which seems to involve the development of

1. Attention, in order to bring the stimuli within visual range;
2. Awareness and recognition of visual form, which involves cortical and emotional factors;
3. Response, as an indication that learning is occurring;
4. Satisfaction, an emotional component which determines the success or failure of the learning process;
5. Repetition, the means by which learning patterns are fully established.

The efficiency of the visual sensory system conceivably may be affected by restriction of or interference with the development of any one of these phases (Barraga, 1964). That visual perceptual development must be considered in connection with the individual's wishes and objectives (emotion and satisfaction) is emphasized by Valvo (1971) in his revelation that "visual memory is not at all a mechanical process or automatic registration of impressions, but rather is conditioned or hindered by affectivity, interest, and inhibition [p. 47]."

Visual discrimination may differentiate the specific characteristics of the objects viewed, but the act of recognition is a higher form of learning; it involves the assignment of a name which places the object as distinct from all other objects or as a member of a categorical group of objects. Visual perceptual ability developed to this level becomes a "decision process which involves the utilization of discriminatory cues dynamically maintained by a continuous frequency variation and adaptability" (Bruner, 1957, p. 127). Previously acquired visual information is absolutely essential for visual recognition, since it is the mind which deduces or infers from the stored knowledge the discrete shape and position in space of an object, and combines these data with information from other senses to build up a recognizable visual world (Valvo, 1971).

Development of Visual Perceptual Abilities

To illustrate the progressive nature of visual perceptual learning, a suggested plan for development of visual perceptual abilities (readiness for visual learning) is presented, followed by suggested activities to establish the relationship and associations necessary for maximum visual efficiency (Barraga, 1964).

1. Form perception—Geometric forms related in size and contour and presented in solid black are most easily discriminated and recognized.
2. Object perception—Single objects of one class, presented first in solid black for contour, next in outline form for shape, and finally as pictures with

limited inner detail, enable the development of object constancy when the perspective varies and hasten the recognition process.
3. Sorting and categorizing—Pictures of everyday objects from the environment presented singly, then in groups, provide the opportunity for differentiating single objects among others, then identifying and organizing them into classes.
4. Symbolic representation—Words and letters (abstract symbols) of different configuration and of similar contour foster the learning of relationships and symbolic representation.
5. Symbolic representation of expressed ideas—Word groups, phrases, and sentences involve the interpretive decisions within the context of continuously changing symbols.

Activities to Stimulate Visual Perceptual Learning

The variety of perceptual learning activities to use with the materials just listed follows a hierarchical sequence which begins with gross learning patterns, progresses to more discrete analyses, and builds up to integrated discriminations prior to the ultimate recognition process.

1. Noting likenesses and differences of forms, objects, and symbols in terms of classes, sizes, spatial positions, and inner details is the basic discriminatory activity.
2. Matching of forms, objects, and symbols of the same class, of different classes and shapes, and of similar classes and shapes continues perceptual discrimination and begins sorting of visual information.
3. Ordering of forms, objects, and symbols in decreasing and increasing sizes and sequence of uses or events introduces the opportunity for learning sequential perceptual progressions.
4. Relating and categorizing forms, objects, and symbols as to their general groups, uses, and specific class relationships stresses the organizing of perceptual units.
5. Discriminating specific missing portions of forms, objects, and symbols with and without the total stimulus visible requires analysis and subsequent integration of individual parts into the whole.
6. Integrating discrete elements of forms, objects, and symbols into unknown wholes strengthens perceptual closure and stability and fosters reduction of predictive probabilities, two critical factors in visual efficiency.

Some environmental conditions and experiences facilitate these visual learning patterns, and many children seem to progress in a logical fashion through incidental exposure to their world. However, under less stimulating and structured conditions, or when defects in the visual or perceptual system, or in both, slow down or stop the flow of sensory data, greater attention needs to be directed to each step in the developmental sequence. Visually handicapped children have a diversity of impairments in the mechanism which may impose a wide range of limitations on their visual abilities. Visual experiences and opportunities for visual stimulation are usually meager, and the child with limited vision has no means to develop a visual frame of reference by which to judge his own visual development. The following section will discuss many of the conditions of the impairment and offer suggestions relative to the degree of disability encountered in the acquisition, processing, and organizing of information for understanding and interpretation through the visual sense.

Impairments in the Visual System

Structural Defects

The varieties of impairments in the structure and function of the optical system of the eye are many. Most of them are correctable by eye specialists if children are examined early in life. Unfortunately, children are seldom taken to vision specialists unless the condition is serious enough to be observable or interferes markedly with movements and behavior. Some rather minor conditions may become uncorrectable if not discovered before the child enters school. Increasing numbers of schools are conducting vision screening programs to detect children who need eye care, whose visual comfort can be improved, or whose achievement progress may be enhanced. State chapters of the National Society for the Prevention of Blindness often initiate preschool vision screening programs which identify large numbers of children at an age when their conditions are more amenable to correction. Although screening procedures detect only problems in distance vision, all such programs for early detection are to be encouraged because they prevent many children from becoming visually handicapped in later years.

Children are very adaptable and flexible in the use of their bodies and sense organs. Having no knowledge of what they should see or how they should see it, they may be totally unaware of limitations in their visual capacities or efficiency in functioning. The minor impairments and their influence on visual functioning and visual perceptual abilities will be discussed prior to those which markedly inhibit learning through the visual sense.

Refractive Errors

Deviations in the shape of the cornea or irregularities in its surface may result in problems that, if not corrected through corrective lenses, may interfere with the development of optimal visual efficiency. The most common error is that of myopia or nearsightedness, which is usually associated with the structural alignment of the eye; either because of increased curvature of the cornea or extended growth of the eyeball, there is an excess of refractive power and the rays of light reach a point in front of the foveal area of the retina when objects are 20 feet or more in the distance. Because of the accommodative power of the eye for near vision, this impairment has little effect on the child's functioning in play or his movements within the home. The world beyond 20 feet, however, may be a blur or even an unknown void. An uncorrected error of this nature limits the range and variety of refined information available for sequential development of visual perceptual ability. Even though the child may search for more distinct characteristics and seek to clarify specific aspects of his spatial world, he is likely to find it more rewarding to restrict his attempts to learn about the distant world. As a consequence of his visual confusion, he confines himself to his immediate environment, in which he is able to achieve the clarity and discriminating cues to satisfy his curiosity.

The primary deficit to the child is in the incidental learning which he misses unknowingly. His frame of reference for sorting, organizing, and relating sensory impressions to construction and assimilation of complete percepts becomes more and more limited in scope.

Another refractive error is that of hyperopia or farsightedness; because of a flattened corneal surface or a too-short eyeball, the refractive power is insufficient and the point of convergence of the rays of light falls beyond the retinal fovea. Although the sharpness and clarity (visual acuity) may be slightly diminished, visual functioning is less affected in the early years than it is in the child who is nearsighted. His greatest difficulty comes with increased near-point activities when he enters school. Because he is constantly working to "remove the blur" (which is greater at near point), he is likely to experience discomfort and tire more easily. If the condition remains uncorrected, he may avoid schoolwork to the degree that he falls further and further behind in academic learning. Unless the problem exists to a marked degree, he may not be identified through a screening program which includes only distance measures; furthermore, unless the child complains of headaches and blurring when reading, his difficulty may be undetected by the eye specialist in a casual examination which does not measure near-point acuity.

Unevenness in the surface of the cornea results in a refractive error referred to as astigmatism. Although this condition usually poses few problems in visual performance during the preschool years, increased discomfort may be experienced as the child progresses in school. The rays of light are refracted unevenly at different planes and fail to converge at one point. Words and letters may blur together or be confused with each other. The condition may occur as an entity in itself or may be found in combination with either myopia or hyperopia (U. S. Department of Health, Education, & Welfare, 1967).

None of the refractive errors is likely to result in a serious handicap to visual learning, but if not detected or if left uncorrected such errors can interfere with optimal visual perceptual development and eventual visual efficiency. The psychological and emotional factors associated with visual discomfort could precipitate avoidance of visual activities and influence the desire for learning.

Muscle Problems

The control and alignment of the eye for coordinating binocular functioning is as important as the refractive mechanism. One or the other of the eyes may turn in or out or up or down to the extent that fusion of the two images is difficult or impossible. Because the brain cannot process two different images, the clearer one will be received and the poorer one rejected. In some instances the deviation is slight, and when the refractive abilities in each eye are equal, and a clear image is received by each, the child may alternate the use of his eyes when he is unable to fuse them to a singular image. However, when the muscular problem is severe, or the image in one eye is better than in the other, he may resort to the use of only one eye. When this occurs in the preschool years and the condition is not alleviated, the sensitivity in the receptor cells in the unused eye is diminished (amblyopia). Information reaching the brain through the visual sense may be limited in quantity and quality with continued disuse. The resultant limitation in visual efficiency may pose problems in reading, participation in outdoor games, and judgment of distance in movement.

Abnormalities in the Lens

Most impairments in the lens of the eye present at birth or which develop in early childhood (cataracts) seriously interfere with the passage of light through the center of the eye; as a consequence, fewer retinal cells receive stimulation. Frequently those cells which do are in the peripheral retina. Visual functioning is inhibited to a marked degree, especially when both lenses are clouded; it is virtually impossible to view any objects with sharpness and clarity, and color discrimination is difficult if not impossible. Distance vision is seriously limited because objects must be very close in order for the rays to be brought to a point of focus on any part of the retina. Cataracts pose severe visual disabilities, restrict development of the use of the mechanism, and interfere with the quantity and quality of sensory information transmitted through the visual channel.

Because of limited visual capacity, children with congenital cataracts often appear as though they were unable to see at all. Unless careful attention is given to bringing objects very close, they may have little opportunity to develop muscular control and motility to fixate and attend to objects. If given the freedom to move about and explore, they will soon learn to use shadows and large moving objects as cues within the environment. As the child with cataracts is led to investigate more of these indistinct things, by bringing them close enough for him to achieve clarity, visual learning begins and sufficient information is transmitted to contribute to visual perceptual development. "The patterns of visual behavior are thought to continue their attempted growth," even though hampered by defects, "and experience and training may act as ameliorating forces in improving visual efficiency" (Barraga, 1964, p. 8).

Other defects in the lens may occur as the result of sharp blows to the head or face which may cause the lens to become dislocated or even displaced. If it cannot be restored to its position, visual functioning in the eye involved will be affected in relation to the degree of dislodgement.

Choroid and Retinal Defects

Impairments in the choroid and retinal tissues of the eye may be associated with genetic factors, developmental deviations *in utero,* or a variety of unknown etiologies. Since the retina lies against the choroid (which is its source of blood and nourishment), any break in the tissue of either coat, or detachment of the retina from the choroid, interferes with the functioning of the receptor cells in the eye and usually creates a severe visual handicap, although not all such conditions result in total lack of vision. The area of the retina which is affected determines in large measure the degree to which visual receptive ability is limited.

Degenerative conditions or colobomas (clefts) in the peripheral areas of the retina restrict the visual field, possibly interfere with spatial discrimination, and inhibit functioning in poor illumination. When the damaged area is within the macular region, central acuity is affected markedly and development of the visual process is extremely slow if not totally inhibited. The stimulation of visual cells in the peripheral retina may produce sufficient excitation for the discrimination of gross forms; however, the visual impulse may be so weak that it limits coordinated motor activities as well as the discrimination of details. In any event, the sensations transmitted are likely to be weak, disorganized (Day, 1957), and difficult for the brain to code and organize into meaningful interpretation.

Experimental evidence suggests the possibility that longer repeated stimulation is necessary in order for transmissions from the retina to the brain to be effective (Barraga, 1964; Renshaw, 1945). Continued exposure of forms, objects, and symbols increases the clarifying possibilities and the brain is able to complete the recognition and interpretive functions of the visual perceptual process on vague and distorted sensory patterns (Ashcroft, Halliday, & Barraga, 1965; Drury, 1933).

In addition to the conditions already discussed, optic nerve damage, through atrophy or other causes, may impede the transmission of visual sensations even when the primary structures of the eye itself are functioning normally. The nerve pathways in the brain leading to the occipital lobe may be affected in numerous ways. To what extent and in what manner these dysfunctions affect visual perceptual development is difficult to determine. The accuracy of assumptions inferred from responses is dependent on many psychological factors unique to individuals. Except for those whom eye specialists can diagnose as having an optic nerve condition, children are rarely considered as being visually handicapped. The present state of knowledge does not permit clear-cut decisions in such cases unless the defect is in the eye itself. However, the information reaching the brain through the visual sense when optic nerve damage exists may be as scanty and disorganized as is the case in retinal conditions.

Regardless of the etiological factors involved or the location of the disruptive sensory patterns, eye specialists and educators alike stress that all children with low vision suffer from lack of spontaneous visual stimulation and may need to be taught to develop their visual perceptual abilities in order to achieve their potential visual efficiency (Bateman, 1967; Bier, 1960; Margach, 1969). The congenitally severely visually impaired child at any age is like a baby, as far as visual development is concerned, unless he is carefully stimulated and taught how to look, to note visual cues, and to learn to make visual comparisons. Complete visual maturity takes about 16 years, and to reach a stage of full visual perceptual integration may take even longer (Valvo, 1971).

Experimental programs designed to alter visual behaviors of children with limited residual vision have been very successful (Ashcroft et al., 1965; Barraga, 1964). These studies indicate that children who had been considered unable to receive and interpret information visually (educationally blind) made significant gains in visual efficiency. The challenge for teachers is an important one—to provide the opportunity for every child (even those who are thought to perceive only light) to be taught to develop his visual perceptual abilities (through the sequence of activities previously suggested) for maximum efficiency in learning. Even though the information acquired may be supplementary to more primary sensory channels, there is every indication that visual sensory data provide greater clarity for organizing perceptions. A teacher's guide for utilization of low vision with activities and suggested materials has been developed specifically for teachers along with a visual efficiency scale which suggests the level of visual functioning in relation to visual learning tasks (Barraga, 1970).

Environmental and Psychological Factors Affecting Visual Efficiency

In addition to the sequential development of visual abilities, many environmental conditions and psychological characteristics appear to have a direct influence on the development and utilization of visual capacities. Lighting conditions suitable for some children are not as desirable for others. Certain degrees of contrast in figure and ground of materials may be effective for some children and useless to others. Sizes and styles of print can vary in acceptability under specific conditions. Magnification and projection devices are useful with some types of material or in some situations but not in others.

The attitude, personality, mental capacity, physical stamina, and motivation of individuals are suspected to have a close relationship to visual performance. Seldom identifiable as specific variables, their impact on behavior is difficult if not impossible to measure; furthermore, their behavioral effect is likely to fluctuate within one person according to family and teacher attitudes. A child who has been told he is "blind," even though he has some visual capacity, is likely to think of himself as unable to see at all and will demonstrate little motivation to use his limited vision. Teachers and parents find it necessary to arouse the child's latent curiosity. The availability of enticing pictures, puzzles, and games coupled with encouragement (rather than pressure) offers a challenge which most children will accept. Experiencing success and deriving satisfaction on his own enables the child to accept the stimulating guidance necessary for actual visual learning and perceptual organization. Once he has developed some degree of visual efficiency, he is able usually to maintain his visual abilities on his own as long as he has the opportunity to "look." Groups of low-vision children who have participated in experimental visual stimulation programs have been reevaluated after periods of 6 months and 1 year. No significant loss in visual abilities was noted; in fact, some children had actually increased in visual performance (Ashcroft et al., 1965; Barraga, 1964).

Illumination

Visually handicapped children are able to function more comfortably and effectively under optimal conditions of lighting, both natural and artificial. The quality of light is not necessarily related to the quantity, since many impairments are such that strong light interferes with maximum functioning. In such conditions as cataracts and macular degeneration, receptor cells in the peripheral retina are more responsive to less intense illumination; therefore, the light source and quantity should be controlled for effective functioning. Lacking skin pigmentation and the ability to filter light rays through pupillary actions, the child whose problem is albinism may actually be "blinded" by bright light. On the other hand, some refractive errors and defects in the central retina need greater quantities of light to stimulate the foveal cells which provide the highest quality of sharpness and clarity; otherwise their visual performance is reduced critically. An overall diffusion of light from all angles minimizes the effects of glare and shadows which interfere with efficiency and may provoke physical fatigue. Lighting conditions in the classroom should be controlled through multiple switches, indirect light sources, and nonglare glass in windows, as well as adjustable desk lights, in order to provide for the individual needs of all visually handicapped children.

Contrast Factors

Although studies in the past have suggested that black figures or symbols on white background provide the most desirable contrast for visibility, little attention has been given to the use of selective color combinations and their perceivability by visually handicapped children. Observation and empirical evidence indicate that discrimination of objects and symbols may be enhanced by the use of color. Form and contour appear to acquire dimensional and spatial qualities not discernible in black and white materials. The importance of the total perspective in pictures may be paramount, and when this (rather than distinct features) is the desired information to be conveyed, the use of color might be very helpful. Although experimental evidence has not yet been reported, several color combinations appear to provide contrasts equal to or better than black on white from the point of view of discrimination and recognition. Some of the combinations suggested are yellow on black; yellow on blue; yellow on purple; blue on yellow; green on yellow; and purple on yellow. Colors easily distinguished on white backgrounds seem to be green, blue, and purple. Perhaps the degree of contrast is the crucial factor rather than the colors themselves. Consideration may need to be given to the use of colored materials with visually handicapped children, especially after visual perceptual development has been well established.

Variations in Printed Materials

Inconclusive evidence exists in regard to the size of type most easily read by persons with limited visual functioning (Eakin, Pratt, & McFarland, 1961; Nolan, 1959). Less attention has been given to the style of print, the density of discrete elements, and the interletter–interline spatial relationship; however, these are important factors in the legibility of symbols. No relationship has been found to exist between reading speed and comprehension and type size or measured visual acuity of children (Birch, Tisdall, Peabody, & Sterrett, 1966). In an evaluation of large type, Fonda (1965) suggested that many children were forced to read large-type books when they could have more easily read material in regular print size. Perhaps a logical procedure would be to use a wide variety of type and style combinations in printed materials (once the visual perceptual abilities have been developed) and assess their usefulness on the basis of the information which is processed and interpreted by each child.

Magnification and Projection Devices

Recent research and development of optical devices is enabling increasing numbers of visually handicapped persons to function with higher degrees of efficiency and more satisfying experience than was ever thought possible. Optical aids and projective devices are many; some are more suitable than others for specific purposes; different individuals find discrepancies in the effectiveness of similar types of magnification. The estimation that three out of four persons who have visual acuity of 1% or greater can have their visual abilities improved through devices poses a challenge to educators and optical specialists alike. Both telescopic lenses (for distance viewing) and microscopic lenses (for close vision) can be designed to be worn on the face as glasses, although two separate pairs of spectacles are often necessary. Lenses can be clipped on glasses for use in specific situations, or contact lenses may be helpful to some people. Single, doublet, and triplet magnifiers may be held by hand over the material to be observed, permitting the individual to adjust the distance to the focal length of the device. Still others are made on stands with the distance fixed in keeping with the focal length of the magnifier. Some magnifiers are mounted on stands which can fit beside desks or tables, in which case both the device and the material may be adjusted for individual use (Sloan, 1966). For more detailed information regarding aids and devices, the reader should consult such agencies as the National Society for the Prevention of Blindness, the American Foundation for the Blind, or the American Optometric Association.

Perhaps more critical than the variety of aids themselves are the personal, perceptual, and psychological variables influencing their use by low-vision persons, especially children. Studies have show that several personal characteristics, such as age, nature of visual impairment, and general health, influence the effective and efficient prescription and use of optical aids. How important these factors are with young children is yet to be determined, but observation suggests that they may be of less consequence than perceptual and psychological variables, which are the major considerations.

The ability to use whatever degree of vision one has grows through a series of learned skills, the purpose of which is to feed greater quantities of usable information to the brain. The development of the visual perceptual process (the ability to interpret what is seen) may require considerable time, since coding and associating the information acquired through the other sense channels with the limited or distorted visual patterns can consume a great deal of time. Until older children (elementary and high school) have achieved some degree of visual perceptual development through a planned and orderly period of training, the attempted use of strong magnification may be less than a satisfying experience; in fact, attempts to fit visual aids without the child's being aware of how objects or symbols look may be detrimental to the development of increased efficiency. Perhaps the perceptual development has to have reached a point of stability and constancy in visual activities in order for the child to be qualified to assist the specialist in deciding whether or not magnifying lenses may be helpful to him.

A possible alternative to head-fitted or hand-held aids is the utilization of various projection devices to enlarge images, provide greater contrast, or permit the child to hold or turn his head at any angle and still be able to have the material close but without casting shadows. Rear-view projection screens, televiewer projectors, and the IBM microfiche viewer, all of which have possibilities for decreasing the need for enlarged-type books, are available for use.

The overhead projector with commercially available or specially made transparencies is often overlooked as a means of visual learning for low-vision children. Those who may be unable to derive meaning from the projected material may be able to see quite well by looking directly into the projector to gain a clear, sharp contrast of forms, objects, and/or symbols. Teachers may find it helpful to experiment with many of these devices in order to find the most effective means of contributing to the visual perceptual development of visually handicapped children who may have visual potentials previously undetermined.

The range of individual psychological factors influencing visual development and the use of magnification and optical aids in school-age children with low vision is extensive. If a child has been taught that he is "blind" (by parents and others) and has accepted this as a fact, he may be unwilling to try "to look with his eyes"; never having gained satisfaction through "seeing," he has no way of knowing what he may experience; another may be fearful that he will fail in his efforts; still another may assume the attitude that seeing could mean that he would have to work harder, and he really is not that interested in learning. The curiosity, motivation, and drive of the child (and the teacher) to know and experience appear to be influential determinants of the predictive capacity for visual development when impairments of the eye limit visual acuity to a marked degree.

Ideally, every child with a severe visual impairment who so much as responds to light should be carefully examined, and attempts should be made to fit him with appropriate lenses to enable him to experience his world visually from the earliest stages of perceptual development. The postulation that 80% of babies suspected of being blind at birth eventually develop some useful vision (Law, 1960) was based on a longitudinal study of babies who would ordinarily have been classified as "blind" by ophthalmologists. Evidence such as this is sufficient cause to reject the legal-medical definitions as relevant indicators of potential visual perceptual development.

Unfortunately, far too many eye specialists fail to discuss the possibilities of visual development with parents; accepting the diagnosis of medical authorities, parents are unaware of the importance of visual stimulation or of the advantages of strong magnifying lenses for future visual abilities in their children. More recently, Dr. Faye (1970) has stressed that "some children have to be encouraged to use their vision because they are used to their visual limitation and adults assume that there is no point in visual stimulation" (p. 142). Much research is needed to clarify the present knowledge regarding sensory defects in young children. Even more critical is the need for dissemination of present knowledge to all medical persons and to parents regarding children with visual impairments which will limit or interfere with optimal visual efficiency.

Summary

This section has focused upon an understanding of "vision" as encompassing far more than a single organ; it is rather a process which enables human beings to refine their impressions of the environment; code the discriminations into interpretable images as a means of associating them with other sensory data; and foster the articulation of the environment with the individual. "Learning to see," especially in visually handicapped children, is closely related to opportunity for visual stimulation; transmission of information to the brain, even when data are limited in quantity or distorted in quality; greater attention to clarification of information by verbal cues and practice in trying to gain meaning visually; freedom and encouragement to search for visual knowledge; guidance in associating, processing, and responding to a variety of visual activities. The determination of how much vision is sufficient for visual functioning and what degree of efficiency individuals with impairments may achieve is not clearly specified. In the meantime, educators must accept the challenge to provide constant visual stimulation, sequentially planned programs in visual perceptual development, and encouragement in visual learning for all visually handicapped children who are not totally blind.

TACTUAL–KINESTHETIC, AUDITORY, AND OTHER SENSORY SYSTEMS

When the visual sense is functioning with a high degree of efficiency, the intake of information through vision is such that sight is used as the fundamental sense for understanding and expanding one's environment. Sensory data from other channels provide supplementary knowledge. Children who are visually handicapped find the world inaccessible or less accessible to them through the visual sense and may need to rely primarily on other senses while developing the visual sense as supplementary to the others (see Chapters 2 and 3).

Children who are totally blind need to involve their whole bodies in searching for and receiving information about themselves and the objects available to them in their environment. By exploration with hands, feet, and the entire body, infants and young children can be actively engaged in bringing knowledge of the world to themselves instead of having their senses "acted upon" (Fraiberg, 1968).

The interrelationship between the tactual and kinesthetic senses in seeking and conveying information to the brain for coding, association, and interpretation is such that these two systems will be discussed simultaneously. "For successively progressing impressions and their connections, movement is indispensible" (Révész, 1950, p. 97) suggests that clear impressions can be gained tactually only when touching involves movement.

The following section will focus specifically on development of tact-ual–kinesthetic perceptual abilities and their effectiveness in supplying information. The critical factors involved in the refinement of "listening perceptual" abilities will be discussed briefly, since a more thorough coverage of this topic can be found in Chapter 7. Finally, attention will be directed to the major functions of the other sensory systems in the total learning process.

The Tactual–Kinesthetic Senses and Physiological Development

During the early weeks of life there are two main sources of stimulation for the "skin senses" of the baby: the reflexive movements of his own body, and the touch and tender handling of those who care for him. The nurturance and cuddling offered through contact with firm and stable hands and bodies bind him to the world beyond himself. Fraiberg (1971, p. 115) found that "the most reliable stimulus for evoking a smile in blind infants was gross kinesthetic stimulation," suggesting the possibility of establishing an early relationship between tactual–kinesthetic awareness within the child and external influences on his development. Movement of the arms, legs, head and neck, and trunk (even passively by an adult) may be considered a counterpart to illumination for visual development in stimulation of the tactual–kinesthetic system. In the blind infant, manipulation of the limbs provides information from the kines-thetic receptors about body space and awareness of the possibilities of move-ment within that space (Cratty, 1971). Even though such manipulation may be passively received at the unconscious perceptual level, storage of motor patterns may contribute to later cognitive development.

Gradually, the muscular system is strengthened to the point where exercise of some voluntary control over movements is possible. Lacking the sense of vision to guide his movements and to coordinate the use of his hands to explore and seek out information, development of the blind child is dependent on planned stimulation to enable him to progress in the handling of his body, and to begin to note the differences among the things he touches and that touch him. Prior to using his hands to explore, the infant gains a wider variety of information through the mouth and the blind child needs many opportunities to suck and mouth foods of different consistencies and any objects he finds pleasing and which are safe for him.

A variety of textures which are soft and warm to the touch are excellent for initial stimulation of the hands. Until the baby has developed voluntary grasp-ing functions and has begun to explore with purpose, the primary concern should be to provide encounters with soft stuffed objects with little variation in contour—the emphasis being only on texture. Careful observation will indicate the textures which have the greatest appeal to the sense of touch.

"Chance encounters" with one or two new textures at a time may arouse the desire for expansion of the touch sense. Contacts with the environment begin to provide more than pleasant sensations; they begin to feed the brain with knowledge and initiate the perceptual development.

Tactual–Kinesthetic Perceptual Development

Although little evidence is available upon which to define clearly the progressive sequence (if such occurs) of tactual–kinesthetic perceptions in visually handicapped children, some basic principles have emerged from comparative studies with sighted children. The inability to differentiate the effects of vision in supplementing tactual–kinesthetic reception necessitates many assumptions for which no verification can be offered.

The speculation that stimulus thresholds of the skin are lower in blind children than in sighted children has not been clearly substantiated (Axelrod, 1959); however, if, and in instances when, such a difference is found, several possibilities deserve consideration.

1. Practice results in reduced threshold values for skin receptors.
2. Practice affects only the receptors for a certain sense modality.
3. Different sensory impressions are based upon different combinations of the functions of the cutaneous sense modalities, ·and the recognition of and memory for these combinations improves with accumulating experience.
4. An unusual motivation (such as is present, say, in cloth assorters) or an imperative need may bring into consciousness sensations that are of no use under ordinary conditions and are, in that sense, subliminal (Juurmaa, 1967, p. 11).

Cutaneous receptor sensitivity, according to Juurmaa (1967, p. 12), involves at least five distinguishable activities:

1. A receptor is moved along various surfaces (differentiation is most often in the rough–smooth dimension);
2. Estimation of the distance between two receptors located opposite to each other, with an object in between (estimation of the thickness of an object);
3. Estimation of the distance between two points on the skin (two-point discrimination);
4. Observation of differences in degree of static pressure;
5. Observation of differences in movable weights.

The differences or analogies between visual perception and tactual perception have not been clearly distinguished, but several logical hypotheses have been suggested. Révész (1950) distinguishes between visual form recognition and tactual structure recognition; form is primary in visual perception as an immediate impression, whereas structure predominates in tactual perception and is an analysis of the relationship of parts. Juurmaa (1967) considers the difference a quantitative rather than a qualitative one.

Distinction in tactual–perceptual performances is that of simultaneous general impressions (stationery hand) for global perspective and successive tactile perceptions (moving or grasping hand) for detailed analytic information (Fieandt, 1966). Principles to be followed in the development of tactual–kinesthetic perceptual abilities are suggested by Fieandt (1966, p. 252).

1. Stereoplastic principle—the grasping of an object for textural discrimination and simultaneous assessment of its dimensional qualities (shape perception);
2. Successive perception—construction of analytic information into recognizable qualities;
3. Constructive synthesis—discrete perceptions of details gradually added to total form (accommodation and assimilation).

In order for the visually handicapped child to feed information to his brain (through his tactual–kinesthetic channels), the range and variety of tactual experiences should be structured and controlled to facilitate a sequential progression of perceptions and to minimize confusion. Relationships were found to exist between tactual ability, mental age, and measured intelligence; but chronological age was unrelated to tactual ability, suggesting that the ability to discriminate tactually is developmental in nature and a learned skill (Hammill & Crandell, 1968). Many sizes and various textured objects of the same class or category must be manipulated and handled to facilitate discrimination and in order to provide knowledge about changes in spatial position. Hands which grab and cup around objects, feet which encounter many surfaces, legs which walk up and down steps supply many variable impressions regarding the differences to be interpreted and adjusted in accordance with the tactual perceptions received.

By manipulation of easily handled objects (both large and small) the child learns that he is able to make them behave in specific ways and can exercise control over them at will. Tactual discriminative and kinesthetic manipulative skills develop more rapidly with the use of language (word names and action verbs); words give meaning to objects and activities of the blind child in the same way that meaning is furnished to the sighted child through vision. Explaining, and at the same time guiding, tactual exploration and manipulation of objects gives the child knowledge of the way he can use things to foster the organizing of information in order to clarify and strengthen the growth of a pattern of "tactual strategies."

Manipulation of objects enables the blind child to gain skills in manual inspection which are imperative for concept development. Seven general qualities of the object world have been identified as closely related to tactual–perceptual understanding: rigidity, unity, stability, weight, shape, thickness, and texture. Objects need to be pressed between the hands and fingers to find how far in they can be moved. Holding an object simultaneously in both hands allows it to be felt by all fingers in rapidly changing combinations and gives a concept of perceived unity. The sameness or stability of the object may be interpreted even when the hands move over it. Perhaps this is analogous to the visual experiences of viewing an object from many angles and at variable distances, yet understanding the stable nature of its size and shape. The constancy of object weight can be perceived by lifting, moving, and balancing the object within the hands. Fingers and hands also provide the most accurate perceptual information available to the blind child for discrimination and recognition of shape, thickness, and texture. (Cratty, 1971).

Teaching aids have been designed which introduce appropriate activities in a programmatic fashion (Dorward & Barraga, 1968). The materials present exploratory and discriminatory puzzles, followed by spatial orientation boards. Symbol recognition and association can be developed by manipulation of more complicated puzzles.

The toddler and preschool child who is blind uses his body to understand spatiality, a perceptual ability more easily acquired through vision. As he is taught to reach up to find objects, he has a reason to raise his head and to organize the space world in relation to his own body. In reaching out with his hands and in moving forward with his feet, he is receiving information to help him form body concepts. Bending down, crawling under, and climbing over increases understanding of body space in relation to the large space world. If he never crawls into a box or under a table, how can he relate his body size to that of larger objects? Lack of body concept is a deterrent to spatial orientation and freedom of movement.

Children perceive their bodies as vehicles for movement, and the visually handicapped child is no different in this respect. Because of the limitation in visual ability, meaningful body movement is difficult to learn. Objects can be moved in relation to body planes more easily than the body can move in relation to objects; similarly, movement of the total body is learned prior to accurate movement of individual limbs. Cratty and Sams (1968) suggest that children be taught manipulation of their own bodies, then manipulation of dolls, manual examination and manipulation of sighted persons, and last the simulation of body positions through clay modeling. The verbal discussion of each movement is necessary for understanding what the body is doing. The visually handicapped child must learn to think about *what* he is doing, and *why* he is doing it.

A sequence of training in body image and kinesthetic perceptions is suggested, with activities for progressive levels of mental development:

1. Body planes, parts, and movements—mental ages 2 to 5.
2. Left–right discrimination, which actually involves movement of the body in response to verbal directions followed by object-to-body movements,

such as "lift the ball with the left arm stretched from the shoulder and to the front of the body"—mental ages 5 to 7.
3. Complex judgements of body and body–object relationships, such as "touch left ear with right hand" or "touch your left foot to my left foot as I face you"—mental ages 6 to 8.
4. Another person's reference system, which requires that the child be able to identify left and right body parts of someone when face to face with the person—mental age 8 or 9 (Cratty & Sams, 1968).

The gradual coordination of body movement with tactual experiences provides stronger perceptions so vital to mobility training in later years. Additional activities should include mat rolling, wall sliding, body stroking with the child's own body; then inspection and manipulation of other human bodies upon verbal cue ("roll him over"); manual activities which involve body and object ("hold this block and find its twin in this box"); obstacle courses and mazes; trampoline games; rhythmic games and singing games which give direction for body activities and movements.

The overlap of tactual–kinesthetic movement activities from birth to independent travel at adulthood is portrayed in the following diagram (Cratty & Sams, 1968, p. 41).

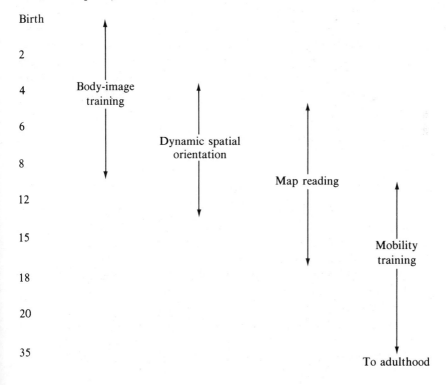

With the acquisition of facility in tactual–kinesthetic activities and knowledge of the qualities of his object world, the visually handicapped child should be ready to organize information for himself and to find satisfaction in directing his own search for new ways to expand his perceptions. More complex activities can be introduced, such as fitting household objects into each other (lids on pans, keys in locks, screwdrivers into heads of screws); putting shoes and socks in pairs according to shape and texture; sorting and matching objects (blocks, beads, silverware, buttons, etc.) according to size, length, or other differences or similarities (Kurzhals, 1966). As the child engages in more and more energizing functions with his hands and fingertips, his ability to make tactual recognitions increases rapidly. The finer the discriminations he can make, the more ready he will be to transfer these abilities to symbolic materials when he prepares for academic learning. Discussing perceptual factors in braille word recognition, Nolan and Kederis (1969) stressed the need for great emphasis on tactual perceptual development. "Introduction of finer discriminations can be parallel with experiences calling for orderly categorization of materials according to their variety of attributes" (p. 50). A high level of tactual perceptual development is essential for the derivation of meaning from braille symbology; the association of words and language (vocabulary) permit him to relate his dynamic real-life experiences to the stories he reads. (A discussion of tactual reading will be found in Chapter 7.)

The development of tactual–kinesthetic perceptions is never complete; unfortunately, there is a tendency to reduce the emphasis on tactual learning as the child progresses in schoolwork and to replace it with verbal skills "about" the world. The need for continuing practice in coding, organizing, and responding to tactually perceived information is evident. Maps for environmental orientation prior to mobility training (Groves & Wiedel, 1968) and charts and diagrams for representation of ideas not easily described in words will challenge the tactual perceptual abilities of the blind person throughout his life.

Raised Line Drawings and Embossed Pictures

The more complex perception becomes, the greater is the need for means to present tactually the component elements for analysis into sequential increments for processing and interpretation. Raised illustrations are valuable in that they bring together a large body of information in a form that can be interpreted easily, and they can communicate observed structures of objects or sets of objects for comparison (Vermeij, 1969).

Nevertheless, the construction of effective tactile (embossed) materials entails the problem of discovering at which point enough, but not too much, information appears in display. Too little information creates a void in the processing attempt and too much results in "tactile noise" or confusion. Schiff and Isikow (1966) found that the mode of presentation of histograms (to blind students) which included the greater stimulus redundancy resulted in fewer errors, suggesting the possibility that a certain degree of difficulty is required to lead the tactual perceiver to utilize more potential information; if the task is too easy, there is a tendency to use the first information available and ignore some other which could facilitate rapid and accurate interpretation; when the tactual task is moderately difficult, the perceiver seeks and acquires more information (Schiff & Isikow, 1966).

The efficacy of the systematic teaching of perspective and principles of graphic representation was established in a study by Merry and Merry (1933). Geometric figures were most easily recognized (as suggested on visual perception), but two-dimensional figures were more difficult. When the blind children were given a cue (perceptual or psychological set), the recognition of the signs increased. Following a period of instruction in how to recognize embossed pictures, younger and older children showed significant improvement in recognition, which is a finding similar to that obtained in the experiments in training visual perceptual abilities previously mentioned. No relationship between chronological age and performance has been found in any of the studies in visual or tactual perception (Merry & Merry, 1933; Morris & Nolan, 1961), but some indication of a correlation between general intellectual functioning and recognition of symbolic material was suggested. Patterns embossed in small scales seemed to be recognized even in very small sizes, whereas large-scale patterns required a much larger symbol for recognition (Morris & Nolan, 1963).

Greater attention should be given to organized teaching of tactually involved symbols (other than words) by exposing the blind child to raised line drawings early in his educational program. Providing the opportunity for him to make his own tactual drawings could enhance the understanding of orientation and directionality (Vermeij, 1969). Certainly, research studies designed to increase tactual perceptual efficiency in blind children through a planned sequence of activities would supply knowledge which could be of great value in the education of all visually handicapped children.

Auditory Perceptual Development

The sense of audition is considered next in importance to vision because of its relationship to language and communication. Maintenance of human and environmental contact is more easily maintained and may provide more satisfying interaction in early and later life through this sense.

Infants may begin to assume a listening attitude to the sounds of voices (to which they are most susceptible) within a few weeks. Low-frequency sounds evoke greater responses at first, but sensitivity to a wide range of and much higher-frequency sounds emerges rapidly. Babies between 6 and 12 months appear to be able to localize sound sources and move directly toward them. Hearing is a distance sense through which human beings project themselves into space. The first functional level of sound is that of primitive environmental noises; the signal and warning level follows, after which the symbolic level for reception of speech sounds becomes functional (Frisina, 1967).

Stimulation of the auditory sense is important for a blind child even before he is able to make use of his tactual–kinesthetic senses. The soothing sound of voices and contact through cuddling are his first means of establishing and maintaining contact with his environment. Consequently, the auditory sense is of prime importance to him in his early development. Since he lacks the visual sense to stimulate him to reach out to the world, the sooner he is taught to reach on sound cues, the more rapidly he will begin to develop ear–hand coordination to stimulate and guide his body movements (Fraiberg, 1968).

Paramount in the development of auditory discrimination skills (as with other sensory skills) is the factor of attention; the child seeks and attends to sound stimulation as it is useful to him or contains information he needs or wants. If the auditory stimulation does not provide information beyond the level of pleasant sensation, the child may, of necessity, remain at a mechanical level of sound reception; no useful or meaningful information reaches the brain to be coded, processed, and responded to through action and no contribution is made to perceptual development. For example, too often the blind child is left alone to "be stimulated" by "auditory noise" (meaningless sounds from radio or television); he receives sound sensations and responds by repetition of rote-learned words, phrases, and jingles (Elonen & Zwarensteyn, 1964). True, the development of auditory acuity is possible without auditory perception, but it is only one facet of discrimination; probably it bears no greater relation to information useful to the brain than does visual acuity to visual perception.

In order for auditory discrimination skills to contribute to knowledge about himself and the world, the child who is visually handicapped needs more frequent vocal stimulation and interaction, first with adults, and then with other children, so that he can associate names with objects and learn useful words relating to the manipulation of his own body and his actions on the things he encounters. A tactual–auditory dialogue interaction forms the basis for his "learning to know" and helps him establish a perceptual frame of reference. Clarification of auditory perceptions comes through others listening to his responses and answering his questions about himself and the environment. Permitting the child to engage in meaningless auditory self-stimulation or nonsense vocalization without the interjection of thought-provoking conversation makes no contribution to his perceptual development.

Toys and activities which combine texture or shape with sound enable associations to be made between things, so that eventually recognition of specific sounds is indicative of identifiable objects or actions within the environment. When meaning is derived from sound, the child is guided in his exploration, can develop purposeful freedom of movement in satisfying his curiosities, and can contribute to his store of auditory knowledge which is so necessary if he is to travel with confidence independently in his world.

Indication that auditory discriminative ability developmentally increases to age 7 or 8 (Hammill & Crandell, 1969) is particularly germane to the acquisition of sophisticated listening skills for learning of academic material. Studies indicate (Nolan & Kederis, 1969) that growth in both auditory and tactual discrimination may still be underway in the upper elementary grades. Suggestions that listening skills can and should be taught to blind children (Foulke, 1968) in order to increase their intake of information that is either unavailable in braille or too slowly read tactually necessitate consideration of the perceptual factors related to aural reading. Reading aurally is a very different perceptual task from reading visually. The acoustical display to be coded and processed is controlled by the rate of input of the reading medium and not by the reader himself (Foulke, 1969). The only information available to the aural reader, in one time dimension, is the singular word presented in sequence; once the sound has passed, it cannot be recalled for consideration. Unless the words are remembered, processed and coded as heard, the resultant perception may be inaccurate, distorted, or totally without meaning. Although aural reading offers many advantages for the blind student, far more attention should be given to the maximizing of listening ability for the most efficient organization of word sequences into chunks of information to be associated with previous and subsequent learning (Miller, 1967). (Additional discussion of auditory learning will be found in Chapter 7.)

Perceptual Development of Other Senses

Although extensive use of the senses of smell and taste becomes socially unacceptable as human beings increase in age, the utilization of them has great significance to the person who is visually handicapped. Because of their close physiological proximity, these two sense organs work in unison with each other. As a person tastes, he also smells the object or food; indeed the smell often determines or influences the taste. This phenomenon provides a measure of guidance and safety to the growing infant. Some things with pleasant odors are not equally appealing to the taste, nor is an unpleasant smell always indicative of displeasing taste or of something to be avoided. Nevertheless, the opportunity to explore the environment through the use of these senses provides valuable information to be processed and utilized with other sensory data in perceptual development. Pleasant odors are a means of leading the child to move toward objects or events to which he cannot be drawn by vision. As he grows older, the perception of certain odors are a source of spatial orientation to indicate his position is relation to objects or as cues in independent travel. For these reasons, attention should be given to assisting the child in his use of the sense of smell, explaining to him and directing his movements so that olfactory cues serve as a means of supplementing his knowledge of the environment. The association of perceptions through the various senses enhances the development of "processing strategies" so valuable in the utilization of one's capacities.

Summary

Although definitive evidence is not yet available to permit conclusive generalizations regarding the independence or corporate development of perceptual processes, it is reasonable to assume that some relationship exists between the sensory information processed by the brain. At the same time, the type and nature of sensory stimulation may contribute to the coding of specific data by several senses simultaneously. Some evidence indicates the possibility of interrelationships of various senses with regard to discrimination sensitivity and eventual perceptual ability. The emergence of sensitivity discrimination variables in mental arithmetic, memory functions, and word groups (presented aurally) suggests a common variance due to immediate memory connected with audition (Juurmaa, 1967). The associative perception of qualities which are tactually–kinesthetically perceived appears to contribute less to visual imagery than visually perceived qualities furnishing information regarding the tactual world (Hulin & Katz, 1934; Juurmaa, 1967).

Mills and Adamshick (1969) found that a period of training in discrimination and interpretation of all sensory stimuli had a noticeable effect on subsequent progress in orientation and mobility training and enabled students so trained to perform with facility and accuracy far exceeding that of students who had not had structured sensory training. The implication that practical attention can enable persons "to orient more exactly, listen more carefully, touch more acutely, smell and taste more precisely, and look more perceptively" (Gibson, 1966, p. 51) challenges us to discover and refine the regularities and lawful connections governing the central coding and experiencing of sensory messages (Fieandt, 1966).

In suggesting guidelines for research, Nolan (1969) designated perceptual development as an area of high priority. Delineation of the effects of visual handicaps on the perceptual development of the child, and the detailed analysis and description of his characteristic modes of perceptual behavior, are data sorely needed to guide educational planning for visually handicapped children.

CONCEPT DEVELOPMENT AND COGNITIVE ORGANIZATION

Concept Formation

Prior to the discussion of the processes involved in learning to think about things and to formulate ideas for oneself, some understanding of the various words used to describe thought patterns may be helpful. Bruner, Goodnow, and Austin (1956) suggested a working definition of a concept (thought):

> A concept is a network of significant inferences by which one goes beyond a set of observed criterial properties exhibited by an object or event to the class identity of the object or event in question, and thence to additional inferences about other unobserved properties . . . the network of inferences that are or may be set into place by an act of categorization [p. 244].

Piaget (1966, p. 53) says that "perception is the knowledge one has of objects or of their movements by direct and immediate contact" and in one way or another consists of a structuring of the relations between the environment and the organism. Conceptual thought (concepts) emerges as perceptions are related to each other through "assimilation" of the whole of reality to an "accommodation" or modification of the knowledge into action.

In making a differentiation between perceptions and concepts, Mussen (1963) says that "perceptions are organizations of simple sense impressions; concepts are derived from discovering and defining critical features common to a group of objects or events. [p. 36]."

Following a series of studies, Bruner, Olver, and Greenfield (1966) suggested that "cognitive growth is a series of psychological events [p. 2]." The young child's perceptions are organized around a minimal number of cues, usually the ones which he can acquire most readily. To actually *know* something (be able to think about it) the child must have done it (kinesthetically), formed a mental picture or image of it (visually or tactually), or have understood it through some symbolic means such as language. Arnheim (1969) says it quite clearly: "Unless the stuff of the senses remains present the mind has nothing to think with since nothing is in the intellect which was not previously in the senses [p. 1]."

Other definitions could be cited, but the general feeling expressed is that concepts are achieved through a process of associating numerous perceptions developed from all sensory data, and from the processed information, formulating ideas about the world; the nature of the concepts may range from functional to abstract, depending on the quantity and quality of information upon which the ideas are based. Concepts serve human beings in adapting to the environment and are never static, unchanging units, but are formed, reformed and interrelated continually.

Cognitive Organization

Often referred to as "cognitive patterning" or "cognitive styles," the manner in which the brain groups or codes and relates incoming data to previously received information may be considered a constructive process resulting in the formation of individualized "cognitive structures" in the higher brain centers. Regardless of the inadequacy of knowledge about actual brain functioning, theorists have considered conceptual development and cognitive organization to be the basic functions of the higher brain (which most probably determines the capacity for intellectual development—Bruner, 1957).

Numerous speculations have been offered relative to the possible effect of visual impairments on cognitive functioning and whether or not conceptual development is in fact different in totally blind persons. In Chapter 2 Lowenfeld has identified the factors which may influence cognitive development. Corso (1967) found that sensory deprivation did not, in general, affect cognitive functioning. Blindness itself is not seen to be a "factor hindering differentiation" of mental ability, and if the information processor (brain) and output systems (expressive abilities) are intact and normally operative, cognitive function should not be affected (Bateman, 1967; Juurmaa, 1967). Ability to conceptualize appears to be dependent on all of the concomitantly developing skills and experiences of each child through all his senses (Elonen & Zwarensteyn, 1964).

Some studies have attempted to identify differences among blind children and between blind and sighted children in areas of cognitive functioning. Nolan and Kederis (1969) reported that blind children with lower intellectual measurements were less able to utilize the characteristics of language, context, or peripheral cues in braille word recognition than were those whose measured intelligence was normal or higher. They suggested a slower central processing of information as an explanation.

As a part of a well-designed and controlled study on cognitive patterning in congenitally totally blind children, Witkin and his associates (1968) offered many suggestions regarding cognitive functioning. To form impressions of objects as discrete and of field as structured through senses other than vision may be possible but much more difficult. He stressed the dependence on others for exposure to and interpretation of activities through language. On a series of tasks involving analytic abilities in perception and problem solving, body concepts, and verbal performance on Wechsler scales, Witkin found a consistency among individual blind children in tactile performance and body concepts; marked individual differences were evident in the extent to which cognitive functioning was articulated (analytic and structured) or relatively global. As a group, blind children had less developed articulation than did a matched group of sighted children, but the difference was not as great as might be expected. Some blind children showed highly developed abilities to analyze and structure their thinking. In discussion, the explanation offered was that blindness may serve as an "impetus to the development of differentiation. . . . The idea of individual cognitive styles of the same basic kind unrelated to sensory or intellectual factors, acquires greater generality" (Witkin et al., 1968, p. 780).

A more recent study (Witkin, Oltman, Chase, & Friedman, 1971) postulated that the lack of vision slows the pace in the usual progression in cognitive development from global to articulated. However, the slower development was not as great as expected. The conclusion was that if there are negative influences of blindness, there may also be positive ones which exceed the negative ones. An unexpected finding was that there was much less correlation between sighted and blind children on an auditory embedded-figures task which seemed to measure different kinds of ability in the two groups. In sighted children it appeared to assess the ability to overcome an embedding context, but in blind children, it was mainly a test of the capacity for sustained attention in the auditory realm. Congenitally totally blind children were equivalent to sighted children in verbal comprehension ability but were superior in tasks requiring prolonged auditory attention.

To gather information about the development of scientific thinking in blind children and adolescents, Boldt (1969) presented some interesting views in regard to the way blind pupils develop abstract thought patterns. Ten different modes of concept formation were identified and explained: (1) sensory associative, (2) magical, (3) anthropomorphic, (4) proposive (these modes were identified as Level I, signifying a naive subjective relation to the phenomena, which are understood from the meaning received from experiences important to the child); (5) substantive, (6) dynamic, (7) uncritical functional (these modes were indicative of Level II thinking, which showed a certain change of objectivity of the phenomena, but the kind of explanation was still bound to the actual experience, the children were still uncritical in attributing their causation and were satisfied with evidence from singular problems); (8) analogical, (9) critical functional, (10) causal (these modes constituted Level III, real abstract thinking, or conceptualizing).

At 10 years of age blind children were 2 years behind sighted children in concept development, but had progressed to a level comparable to sighted children by 15 years of age. Suggestions for interpretation of the findings were presented. The development of concepts in blind children can be understood as a process of progressive disassociation of subject and object, and only toward the end of this disassociation is real conceptualization attained. The focus in elementary school should be on the *what* and *how* of environmental experiences and not on the *why*. The junior high level prepares the way for "scientific thinking" by observation and classification of the environment; the primary goal should be to discover the principles of quantification and causality. No doubt the level of concept development and the capacity for cognitive functioning in blind children is more related to learning opportunities, range in variety of life experiences, and attention given to explanation and clarification of the environment than to the fact that information is unattainable through the visual sense. In a big group, however, blind children seem to find it more difficult to determine when they have sufficient knowledge for perceptual closure and for the formation of complete concepts. The relationship between general intellectual capacity and the inability to "know what is possible" has not been substantiated.

The performance of blind children on the verbal section of the Wechsler Intelligence Scale for Children (WISC) shows considerable differences between the various subtests—more than the differences observed for sighted children with the same overall intelligence quotient (Tillman, 1967). Groups of blind and sighted children do not have the same WISC profiles; blind children tend to score higher on Digit Span at all age levels and lower on Similarities at all age levels and frequently on Comprehension. The specific differences between blind and sighted children are found in conceptual development and in short-term memory (Tillman & Osborne, 1969). If definitive information about cognitive behavior of blind children is to be acquired, the manipulation of task variables under different conditions, varieties of materials, and a wide sampling of children must be studied.

Deficits in vocabulary development have been reported by numerous investigators (Barraga, 1964; Nolan & Kederis, 1969). The consensus seems to establish a need for stress on vocabulary (with careful attention to full interpretation of meaning) and development of complete concepts very early in the child's life in both verbal and written contexts. Tisdall (1968) has hypothesized that "certain cognitive skills can be trained and can enhance the overall learning style and capacity by purposeful intervention into the child's limited range of background experiences" (p. 129).

Summary

The process through which concepts are formed and cognitive styles (thought patterns) are developed by children with severe visual impairments is still a matter of speculation. That differences between blind and sighted children may exist in the early years is suggested, and is reflected primarily in the time required for processing and coding of information. Perceptual closure and stability in the formation of abstract concepts seem to require more time for those without vision. However, no evidence is available to indicate that the nature and quality of cognitive organization, once achieved, is noticeably different than in sighted children.

Providing a range and variety of concrete experiences and materials in early life and in all academic learning during the elementary years is of primary importance. Also essential are marked attention to meaningful vocabulary development and opportunities for daily conversational interactions about ideas encountered. These factors can markedly enhance the organization of thinking patterns of visually handicapped children.

REFERENCES

Allport, F. *Theories of perception and the concept of structure.* New York: Wiley, 1955.

Arnheim, R. *Visual thinking.* London: Faber & Faber, 1969.

Ashcroft, S. C., Halliday, C., & Barraga, N. *Study II: Effects of experimental teaching on the visual behavior of children educated as though they had no vision.* Nashville: George Peabody College, Grant No. 32–52,0120–1034, 1965.

Axelrod, S. *Effects of early blindness—Performance of blind and sighted children on tactile and auditory tasks.* New York: American Foundation for the Blind, 1959.

Barraga, N. *Increased visual behavior in low-vision children.* New York: American Foundation for the Blind, 1964.

Barraga, N. C. (Ed.). *Teacher's guide for development of visual learning abilities and utilization of low vision.* Louisville: American Printing House for the Blind, 1970.

Bartley, S. H. A glance at vision. *Journal of the American Optometric Association,* 1971, **42,** 665–671.

Bateman, B. D. Visually handicapped children. In N. G. Haring & R. L. Schiefelbusch (Eds.), *Methods in special education.* New York: McGraw-Hill, 1967. Pp. 257–301.

Bier, N. *Correction of subnormal vision.* London: Butterworth, 1960.

Birch, J. W., Tisdall, W., Peabody, R., & Sterrett, R. *School achievement and effect of type size on reading in visually handicapped children.* Cooperative Research Project No. 1766, Office of Education. Washington, D.C.: U. S. Department of Health, Education, & Welfare, 1966.

Boldt, W. The development of scientific thinking in blind children and adolescents. *Education of the Visually Handicapped,* 1969, **1,** 5–11.

Bruner, J. S. On perceptual readiness. *Psychological Review,* 1957, **64,** 123–152.

Bruner, J. S., Goodnow, J. J., & Austin, G. A. *A study of thinking.* New York: Wiley, 1956.

Bruner, J. S., Olver, R. R., & Greenfield, P. M. *Studies in cognitive growth.* New York: Wiley, 1966.

Buddenbrock, W. Van. *The senses.* Ann Arbor: University of Michigan Press, 1953.

Buktenica, N. A. *Visual learning.* San Rafael, Calif.: Dimensions Publishing Co., 1968.

Corso, J. F. *The experimental psychology of sensory behavior.* New York: Holt, 1967.

Cratty, B. J. *Movement and spatial awareness in blind children and youth.* Springfield, Ill.: Charles C Thomas, 1971.

Cratty, B. J., & Sams, T. A. *The body-image of blind children.* New York: American Foundation for the Blind, 1968.

Day, R. H. The physiological basis of form perception in the peripheral retina. *Psychological Review,* 1957, **64,** 38–48.

Dorward, B., & Barraga, N. *Teaching aids for blind and visually limited children.* New York: American Foundation for the Blind, 1968.

Douglas, A. G. A tachistoscopic study of the order of emergence in the process of perception. *Psychological Monographs,* 1947, 61.

152

Drury, M. B. Progressive changes in non-foveal perception of line patterns. *American Journal of Psychology,* 1933, **45,** 628–646.

Eakin, W. M., Pratt, R. J., & McFarland, T. L. *Type size research for the partially seeing child.* Pittsburgh: Stanwix House, 1961.

Elonen, A. S., & Zwarensteyn, S. D. Appraisal of developmental lag in certain blind children. *Medical Progress,* 1964, **65,** 591–610.

Faye, E. E. *The low-vision patient.* New York: Grune & Stratton, 1970.

Fieandt, K. *The world of perception.* Homewood, Ill.: Dorsey Press, 1966.

Fonda, G. *Management of the patient with subnormal vision.* St. Louis: C. V. Mosby, 1965.

Foulke, E. Non-visual communication. *International Journal for the Education of the Blind,* 1968, **18,** 77–78.

Foulke, E. Reading by listening. *Education of the Visually Handicapped,* 1969, **1,** 79–81.

Fraiberg, S. Parallel and divergent patterns in blind and sighted infants. *Psychoanalytic Study of the Child,* 1968, **23,** 264–300.

Fraiberg, S. Smiling and stranger reaction in blind infants. In J. Hellmuth (Ed.), *Exceptional infant—Studies in abnormalities.* New York: Brunner/Mazel, 1971. Pp. 110–127.

Frisina, D. R. Hearing disorders. In N. G. Haring & R. L. Schiefelbusch (Eds.), *Methods in special education.* New York: McGraw-Hill, 1967. Pp. 302–350.

Gesell, A., Ilg, F., & Bullis, G. *Vision—Its development in infant and child.* New York: Harper, 1950.

Gibson, J. J. *The senses considered as perceptual systems.* Boston: Houghton Mifflin, 1966.

Gibson, J. J., & Gibson, E. J. Perceptual learning: Differentiation or enrichment? *Psychological Review,* 1955, **62,** 32–40.

Groves, P. A., & Wiedel, J. W. Tactual mapping: Problems of design and interpretation. *International Journal for the Education of the Blind,* 1968, **18,** 10–16.

Gurwitsch, A. The phenomenology of perception: Perceptual implications. In P. Tibbets (Ed.), *Perception.* Chicago: Quandrangle Books, 1969. Pp. 248–260.

Hammill, D., & Crandell, J. Implications of tactile-kinesthetic ability in visually handicapped children. *Education of the Visually Handicapped,* 1968, **1,** 65–69.

Hulin, W. S., & Katz, D. Transfer of training in reading braille. *American Journal of Psychology,* 1934, **46,** 627–631.

Juurmaa, J. *Ability structure and loss of vision.* New York: American Foundation for the Blind, 1967.

Kurzhals, I. W. Reading made meaningful through a readiness for learning program. *International Journal for the Education of the Blind,* 1966, **15,** 107–111.

Lancaster, J. E. The learning process in orthoptics. *American Journal of Ophthalmology,* 1949, **32,** 1577–1585.

Law, F. The problem of the visually defective infant. *Transactions of the Ophthalmological Society of the United Kingdom,* 1960, **80,** 3.

Margach, C. B. Spatial perceptions in low-visioned persons. *The Optometric Weekly,* 1969, **60,** 21–24.

Merleau-Ponty, M. The sensation as a unit of experience. In P. Tibbets (Ed.), *Perception*. Chicago: Quandrangle Books, 1969. Pp. 234–247.

Merry, R. V., & Merry, F. K. The tactual recognition of embossed pictures by blind children. *Journal of Applied Psychology*, 1933, **17**, 148–163.

Miller, G. A. The magical number seven, plus or minus two: Some limits on our capacity for processing information. In N. J. Slamecka (Ed.), *Human learning and memory*. New York: Oxford University Press, 1967. Pp. 219–234.

Mills, R. J., & Adamshick, D. R. The effectiveness of structured sensory training experiences prior to formal orientation and mobility instruction. *Education of the Visually Handicapped*, 1969, **1**, 14–21.

Morris, J. E., & Nolan, C. Y. Discriminability of tactual patterns. *International Journal for the Education of the Blind*, 1961, **11**, 50–54.

Morris, J. E., & Nolan, C. Y. Minimum sizes for areal type tactual symbols. *International Journal for the Education of the Blind*, 1963, **13**, 48–51.

Mussen, T. H. *The psychological development of the child*. Englewood Cliffs, N. J.: Prentice-Hall, 1963.

Myklebust, H. *The psychology of deafness*. New York: Grune & Stratton, 1960.

Nolan, C. Y. Readability of large types: A study of type size and type styles. *International Journal for the Education of the Blind*, 1959, **9**, 41–44.

Nolan, C. Y. Research in education of the blind. In M. H. Goldberg & J. R. Swinton (Eds), *Blindness research: The expanding frontiers*. University Park, Pa.: Pennsylvania State University Press, 1969. Pp. 240–249.

Nolan, C. Y., & Kederis, C. J. *Perceptual factors in braille word recognition*. New York: American Foundation for the Blind, 1969.

Piaget, J. *Psychology of intelligence*. Totowa, N. J.: Littlefield, Adams, 1966.

Renshaw, S. The visual perception and reproduction of forms by tachistoscopic methods. *Journal of Psychology*, 1945, **20**, 217–232.

Révész, G. *Psychology and art of the blind*. New York: Longmans, Green, 1950.

Schiff, W., & Isikow, H. Stimulus redundancy in the tactile perception of histograms. *International Journal for the Education of the Blind*, 1966, **16**, 1–11.

Sloan, L. L. *Aids for the partially sighted*. New York: National Society for the Prevention of Blindness, 1966.

Tillman, M. H. The performance of blind and sighted children on the Wechsler Intelligence Scale for Children: Study 1. *International Journal for the Education of the Blind*, 1967, **16**, 65–74.

Tillman, M. H., & Osborne, R. T. The performance of blind and sighted children on the Wechsler Intelligence Scale for Children: Interaction effects. *Education of the Visually Handicapped*, 1969, **1**, 1–4.

Tisdall, W. J. The visually impaired child. In G. O. Johnson & H. Blank (Eds.), *Exceptional children research review*. Washington, D.C.: Council for Exceptional Children, 1968. Pp. 110–134.

U.S. Department of Health, Education, & Welfare. *Vision and its disorders*. Bethesda, MD.: National Institute of Neurological Diseases and Blindness, Monograph No. 4, 1967.

Valvo, A. *Sight restoration after long-term blindness: The problems and behavior patterns of visual rehabilitation*. New York: American Foundation for the Blind, 1971.

Vermeij, G. J. Observations on raised-line drawings. *Education of the Visually Handicapped,* 1969, **1,** 47–52.

Vernon, M. D. *A further study of visual perception.* London and New York: Cambridge University Press, 1954.

Wilman, C. W. *Seeing and perceiving.* New York: Pergamon Press, 1966.

Witkin, H. A., Birnbaum, J., Lomonaco, S., Lehr, S., & Herman, J. L. Cognitive patterning in congenitally totally blind children. *Child Development,* 1968, **39,** 767–786.

Witkin, H. A., Oltman, P. K., Chase, J. B., & Friedman, F. Cognitive patterning in the blind. In J. Hellmuth (Ed.), *Cognitive studies—Deficits in cognition.* New York: Brunner–Mazel, 1971. Pp. 16–46.

CHAPTER 6

Educational Programs

Josephine L. Taylor

Bureau of Education for the Handicapped
U. S. Office of Education, Washington, D.C.

INTRODUCTION

The historical development of educational programs for visually handicapped children has been presented in Chapter 1. Therefore, this chapter will be limited to a consideration of present educational services as based on recent literature and observations by the author.

The variety of programs and the diversity of services developed may be interpreted as an indication of the desires and efforts of educators, parents, and others to (1) provide all visually handicapped children with an education appropriate to their individual capabilities; and (2) be aware of interests and needs, and consider feasible goals compatible with the life patterns, of the child, his parents, and the community of which he is an integral part. The variety, scope, and quality of services available to a visually handicapped child differ according to the community in which he lives and the services it provides for all children. If psychiatric services are not available to any children in an area, it is highly improbable that they can be developed for visually handicapped children. Likewise, some organizational patterns that may be quite efficient in the more densely populated parts of the country might be quite impractical in sparsely settled locations.

Since there appears to be confusion in the literature relative to different interpretations of terminology, the definition of some terms may help to clarify understanding.

In this chapter the term visually handicapped is used to describe those children who, after correction by all possible means, have such severe limitations in vision and their use of it that they are handicapped in their school programs. Visually handicapped children who use sight as their chief avenue of learning are referred to as "partially seeing" when it is necessary to differentiate between them and those who rely chiefly upon touch and hearing, the "educationally blind." The term multihandicapped indicates a child who, in addition to a visual impairment, has at least one other disability; it is applied without regard to the extent of either disability, when the combination of handicaps causes such severe educational problems that the child can receive adquate services neither in programs for visually handicapped children nor in those established for other handicapped children. Special programs for multihandicapped children may be developed in facilities for handicapped children as well as elsewhere. "Multihandicapped" is used only when the discussion requires a distinction between these and other visually handicapped children.

Visual acuity readings, IQ levels, decibel loss figures, or other common determinants formerly used to place children in special education categories are not part of the foregoing definitions. This should not be interpreted as a denial of the importance of knowledge of these as well as of other medical factors (cause of visual deficit, age of onset, prognosis, etc.) nor of the value of a full psychological evaluation, but rather as a recognition of the need to combine these with an understanding of the visually handicapped child's family and community situation and a competent educational diagnosis. Since any or all of these factors may change, flexibility in planning educational services, including choice of school placement, is necessary throughout the child's education.

Some children with relatively high visual acuity and others who are able to function visually efficiently despite very limited sight may not need special educational services at the beginning of their school life. Careful observation and educational diagnosis may be used to ascertain when or if special services are needed. Placement in a program for the visually handicapped on the basis of low visual acuity readings alone may handicap a child who is able to function adequately in a regular classroom without special services or materials by causing him or his parents and the teachers to overemphasize the visual impairment. In addition, continuous educational evaluation may indicate that the child's learning problems are not related to his visual impairment but to another disability for which other special educational services might be more beneficial. The continuing study of the child may also indicate a time when transfer to another program for the visually handicapped may be in his best interest.

Flexibility in school placement ideally begins during the preschool years and extends throughout the child's school life. It takes into consideration several principles brought out by Taylor (1947) as essential to an individualized program:

1. Constant consideration should be given to the life pattern of the child and his family. This involves seeing the immediate problem in its relationship to the total situation and the whole life pattern.
2. The recognition that the child is an integral part of the family and also of the community. Selection of facilities according to individual needs should, therefore, consider the needs, resources, and the life pattern of the family and the community from which the child is inseparable. Correlated with this is the advisability of sustaining and, if necessary, stimulating the parents' and the community's interest and activity on the child's behalf.
3. The need for flexibility in selecting facilities. That facility should be selected which fulfills a particular need, at the time of the need, and for only as long as—in the light of the total situation—it is fulfilling this need [pp. 119–120].

NURSERY–KINDERGARTEN EXPERIENCES

For children living in more densely populated areas, where preschool counseling and diagnostic services are usually available, the first school placement may be in a nursery school. This experience is especially advantageous for those with very little or no vision and for those who are multihandicapped. Due to the greater dependency on the mother and the other developmental problems (Imamura, 1965), it may be advisable to begin with small groups of two or three children, with the mother gradually withdrawing from the situation as the child becomes more comfortable with the others.

Children with very little or no vision, particularly those with additional handicaps, may not be ready for nursery school experiences until they are 4 or 5 years of age, or older. The child's interaction with the children in the small neighborhood play group may give some indication of his readiness for nursery school. Even when he may not appear to be ready for group interaction, a carefully selected nursery school with a well-trained, warm teacher often provides a therapeutic environment in which the handicapped child is given the opportunity, encouragement, and guidance to develop his physical, emotional, and social skills.

The most common, and for most children probably the most beneficial, placement is in a nursery school with normal children. For some of the multihandicapped a special nursery school may provide a richer learning situation and may be less stressful. If a residential program seems indicated, the advantages need to be weighed against the possible emotional trauma of separation from the mother at such an early age.

Some parents may need to be encouraged to assume a major role in choosing a school for their child. One of the services they may expect from their preschool counselor is guidance regarding the child's readiness and recommendations of appropriate schools to consider. A helpful procedure is for the preschool counselor to make the original investigation, as she is usually able to be more objective in discussing the child and can assure the school personnel of the assistance she can provide to them and to the child during this period. In rare instances the nursery school may not prove to be a healthy climate for a specific child. Such circumstances indicate the need for a reevaluation of the child's readiness and of the suitability of the school for him.

After a successful experience in the older nursery school group, acceptance in and adjustment to the kindergarten the child would have attended if he had normal vision is usually not too difficult. The placement will probably be more effective if the classes are not overcrowded and the kindergarten teacher has had an opportunity to observe him in nursery school. For totally blind children or those with very little useful vision who are attending local kindergartens, provision should be made for appropriate materials, individual instruction when indicated, and suggestions to the teacher from an educator of visually handicapped children. During this period even greater emphasis should be given to helping the child attain maximum utilization of his tactual, auditory, and visual senses, and to orientation, mobility, and daily living skills.

The neighborhood kindergarten is probably the first school experience for the large majority of visually handicapped children. Some of those with less severe handicaps may not be identified until they begin to experience difficulty in school. Others may live in communities where programs for the visually handicapped do not begin until after the kindergarten year. In the 1962–1963 school year, only 43% of the local school programs and 70% of the residential school programs included the kindergarten level (Jones & Collins, 1966).

Educational services on the kindergarten level were reported in only 23% of the local school programs serving partially seeing children only, and in 39% of those serving both blind and partially seeing in combination.

Another national study (Peabody & Birch, 1967) involving 1,084 partially seeing fifth and sixth grade children found that

> the academic level of the subjects was two and one-half years behind that which would normally be expected, . . . placement in special education programs took place, on the average, when pupils were between seven and seven and one-half years of age. . . . the disability occurred prior to the subject's second birthday for more than 70 percent of the subjects, and that nearly four out of five disabilities were diagnosed before the fourth birthday. thus, *this investigation's results*

and conclusions imply strongly the need for increased emphasis on two educational procedures. First is preschool identification and planning for partially seeing children. The most important parts of the preschool assessment should be a full delineation of the nature, extent and prognosis of the vision disability and a thorough analysis of the educational needs and potentialities of the child. Put together, these should point the way to a second procedure, a special education plan to be initiated when the child begins school. This should be a considered decision, with progress being observed and aided as necessary through special education, rather than just a placement "to see how he gets along," with special education to be called to the rescue after failure behavior becomes apparent* [p. 94].

The need for early intervention through planned educational programming for those with some residual vision who behave as though blind is obvious from studies by Barraga (1964) and Ashcroft, Halliday, and Barraga (1965), as described in Chapter 5.

For children with very low vision and for those who are totally blind, the kindergarten experience may offer the opportunity to grow in an understanding of everyday activities and objects in the environment that others learn through observation; to become a participating member of a peer group; to further develop language and listening skills; and to develop concepts and behavior patterns essential to a successful more formalized school program. Detailed discussions of school readiness may be found in several recent publications (Lowenfeld, Abel, & Hatlen, 1969; Kurzhals, 1966).

In a study on braille reading (Lowenfeld et al., 1969) a finding especially important in planning first school placements for educationally blind children was discussed:

The replies show that the majority of local and residential schools began braille reading instruction in the first semester of the first grade. However, almost one-third of the residential school questionnaires indicate that braille reading instruction was already begun in the kindergarten. In local schools only one-sixth followed this practice. . . . Most of the comments stressed the importance of readiness for the beginning of reading instruction and reported that such readiness programs are carried on at the kindergarten level [pp. 44, 45].

In local school programs where the visually handicapped child becomes a member of the regular first grade, beginning reading activities may make a difference in his acceptance as a group member by the other children, the teacher, and the child himself. Beginning reading for blind children, and for some partially seeing children, is a much slower process. If the blind child cannot share in this most exciting part of the first-grade program, he may

*Reprinted from *The Sight-Saving Review,* Volume 37, No. 2, Summer 1967, by permission of the National Society for the Prevention of Blindness, Inc.

develop feelings of not belonging or inadequacies which may affect his entire school and social development. To overcome this problem, several variations in beginning school programs have emerged. One mentioned earlier, in which a child attends an older nursery school group at age 5, entering kindergarten at age 6, with beginning reading instruction provided during the latter part of that year, gives him the head start that may permit him to actually participate as a member of the group. This plan has the advantage of permitting the child to continue relationships established in the smaller nursery school into the larger kindergarten class with a slight age advantage to compensate for the additional requirements the handicap imposes. Another pattern uses 2 years of kindergarten with greater concentration on beginning reading during the second year. Still another pattern places a special year, a combination kinder-garten and first grade (sometimes referred to as preprimary), after the regular term. In all of these arrangements the child receives the head start that may enable him to participate well with a group in the regular first grade. In the latter two arrangements, however, the child is required to establish a relation-ship with two separate groups of children, which may prove to be a difficult task for many blind children.

In addition to helping the child develop the skills and concepts noted earlier in this chapter, the teacher of visually handicapped children plays an impor-tant role in helping him, his parents, his schoolmates, and other teachers to acquire and retain wholesome attitudes toward the handicap. Full acceptance of the realities of the limitations imposed by the handicap and viewing these limitations as they apply to the immediate problem, the whole life pattern, and present total situation, may forestall incidents that cause the child and others to experience feelings of failure. Parents, teachers, and others whose relation-ship with the child is based on a need to extend their own success feelings through his accomplishments rather than on a desire to nurture his growth as a unique personality may not be able to fully accept the handicap without extensive help, if at all.

ADMINISTRATIVE PLANS

No census has been taken of the number of visually handicapped children in the United States. Although several "studies" have provided ratios which cover a broad range, this author believes that the findings of Jones and Collins (1966) are probably the most accurate in attempting to determine those chil-dren who require special educational services: "Visually handicapped children in these school systems therefore were found at the rate of about 1 for every 1,000 of the school-age population [p. 23]."

Using this ratio it can be assumed that there are between 50,000 and 55,000 visually handicapped children who require special educational services. Although no count has been made of the number of children receiving such services, it is known that there are at least 493, and probably over 500, different administrative units maintaining programs for such children (OE/BEH, 1968). Since the attendants of such programs vary in numbers, from only a few in smaller districts to almost 2,000 in the largest cities, the actual number of children served is unknown. The most accurate count, probably low, is that which includes the school children registered with the American Printing House for the Blind as "legally blind." As of January 3, 1972, their number was 20,048. Of this number 7,701 (35%) were registered by residential schools for the blind and 14,347 (65%) by local schools (American Printing House for the Blind, 1972).

Educational Evaluation

Decisions regarding the original school placement and later transfers from one school program to another are made through the assistance of evaluation and placement teams, on either the local, county, state, or regional level. The team makes its recommendations to the school administrators based upon up-to-date evaluations of the child's educational requirements, physical abilities and disabilities, personality, intelligence, and social competence, with such data having been derived from testing, interviews, and observations. Basic to the consideration are the availability of facilities and the wishes of the parents. Although the final decision must be made by the school administrators, educational advisors have a professional responsibility to give the parents a complete understanding of the choice of facilities and the reasons for the team's recommendations. Professional counseling must be based on a full understanding and consideration of the thinking and desires of the parents and the child.

Membership on the team varies widely but usually includes the child's regular classroom teacher or preschool counselor, psychologist, social worker or parent counselor, the local director of special education, and representatives of those programs for the education of the visually handicapped who may be or may become concerned, including the special teacher. Others may be added when indicated, such as the school nurse, ophthalmologist, school principal, guidance counselor, or vocational rehabilitation representative. The findings and recommendations of the team are not only useful to the administrators involved in the decision making but will also provide assistance to the teacher of the visually handicapped child in planning for his special needs.

A recent expansion of the evaluation-team concept has evolved through the establishment of county child-study teams and resource centers serving specific geographic areas. Among these are the Regional Resource Centers sponsored

by the Bureau of Education for the Handicapped of the United States Office
of Education, which are described as follows.

> A regional resource would provide a bank of advice and technical services upon
> which educators in the region could draw in order to improve the education of
> handicapped children. The primary task of the center would be to focus on the
> special educational evaluation of the child, and in light of this evaluation would
> develop a program of education to meet the child's particular requirements.
> Working closely with the handicapped child's parents and teachers, the center
> would then assist the school (or other appropriate agency) in providing this
> program, periodically reexamining and reevaluating the program, and making
> any adjustments which are necessary to keep the program responsive to the
> educational needs of the handicapped child [Senate Report No. 726, 90th Con-
> gress, First Session, p. 87]

The need to develop individually prescribed educational programs for visually handicapped children has been emphasized. Abel (1959a) noted that the
resource teacher "often has to act almost as a clinician [p. 55]," and that

> the goal of the resource type of program is to find for each child the adequate
> educational service which he needs, and for the resource teacher to help the
> school administration to pool all efforts in behalf of the child [p. 56].

Karnes and Wollersheim (1963) suggest:

> One of the implications of this study is that some partially seeing children need
> a clinical type of teaching utilizing special methods and techniques to facilitate
> achievement commensurate with their ability [p. 25].

Peabody and Birch (1967) emphasize the role of remedial and corrective
teaching and the need to develop new knowledge and procedures.

Regarding the application of these principles to the functions of the evaluation and placement team, Taylor (1960) notes:

> If children who happen to have a visual handicap are to be given an opportunity
> to develop to their fullest capabilities, there must be flexibility in the selection
> of educational facilities according to the individaul needs. Provision must also
> be made for a change from one facility to another when the first has solved the
> problem for which it was selected or is no longer the most suitable as an out-
> growth of new developments or because new facilities have been developed. This
> continuing evaluation of the child is one of the major functions of the Educa-
> tional Services. . . . It involves the drawing together of the team to pool knowl-
> edge, skills, imagination and creativity in order that a program may be selected
> or established through which each child may have the chance to develop his own
> particular gifts as fully as possible [p. 68].

Organizational Patterns

With the continuing increase in the number of visually handicapped children receiving educational services, new programs are being established and others are being modified, sometimes drastically, to offer more appropriate services to a changing school population and to individualize their services to meet the needs of all of their pupils.

Types of Programs

Before discussing these trends and changes, some additional definitions are given to avoid confusions in terminology:

The *residential school* is an organizational pattern whereby a boarding facility is provided for some or all of the visually handicapped children who either may attend a segregated school on the campus or may receive some of their educational services through a cooperative arrangement with the public or private schools of the community in which the residential school is located. Usually most of the students live at the school at least 5 days a week and attend classes on the campus. Some pupils may live in the community and be enrolled as day students at the residential school.

A description of *local school programs* is given by Jones and Collins (1966):

Five basic types of organizational pattern have evolved since the inception of special local school programs for visually handicapped children. Two or more patterns are often used in the same school program. These programs were defined for purposes of this study as follows:

Full-time special class—A specially staffed and equipped room in which blind and/or partially seeing children receive three-fourths or more of their formal instruction.

Cooperative special class—A specially staffed and equipped room in which blind and/or partially seeing children are enrolled or registered with the special teacher, but receive less than three-fourths of their formal instruction there. The remainder of their school day is spent in regular classrooms.

Resource room—A specially staffed and equipped room to which blind and/or partially seeing children who are enrolled or registered in regular classrooms come at scheduled intervals or as the need arises.

Itinerant teacher—An organizational pattern whereby blind and/or partially seeing children spend most of their school day in regular classrooms but receive special instruction individually or in small groups from itinerant teachers who travel among two or more schools devoting more than half their time to the instruction of such children.

Teacher-consultant—An organizational pattern whereby special teachers serve as itinerant teachers part of the time but spend 50 per cent or more

of their time in more general duties, such as consulting with regular school
personnel and distributing aids [p. 6–7].

In recent years there have been many changes in the services offered through
these administrative program patterns and in the ways in which they are
coordinated for the education of all visually handicappped children. Although
for many past years there persisted a dichotomy between programs for the
blind and those for the partially seeing (usually separated on the basis of
visually acuity measurements), according to the *Directory of School Programs
for Visually Handicapped Children—Fall 1968,* 89% of the programs served
both blind and partially seeing children. However, in many programs there is
a separation of units for the partially seeing and those for the educationally
blind. This is particularly evident in the larger city systems where there are
large numbers of partially seeing pupils and where there may still be some
teachers who were trained during the "dichotomy days" when teacher preparation programs also were separated by the Snellen chart divider. An opthal-
mogist's statement regarding a child's visual acuity, and whether or not he falls
within the legal definition of blindness, is still a common eligibility denomina-
tor for admission to most residential schools, thus limiting the number of
partially seeing children in attendance. If at all feasible in many places most
partially seeing children are retained in their local schools, partly also due to
the greater tendency toward use of braille in teaching children with useful
vision in the residential schools (Jones, 1961; Nolan, 1965, 1967; Nolan & Bott,
1971). Although some residential schools may have been remiss in that they
have not provided a program for visual stimulation or encouraged print reading, a case-by-case analysis of the subjects involved in the surveys just listed
might indicate that more children with special visual efficiency problems are
referred to residential schools.
    Since acuity reading rather than the child's ability to function visually is still
used in determining placement in some local school programs, which usually
accept children with higher degrees of visual acuity than do most residential
schools, it is quite probable that a substantial number of children enrolled in
such programs might be better served in regular classrooms. The ongoing
reevaluation of the child should be useful not only in planning for changes in
special education placement, but also in preparing for a child's return or
admission to a regular education program.
    After a long arduous period of program prejudice, which included not only
the controversy over residential versus local school programs, but also attacks
on and defenses of the various patterns of local school programs, present
practices show a definite trend toward recognition that each may be beneficial
to some children at some periods of their school careers. At the time of the
Jones and Collins study (1966), 16 residential schools reported that they
regularly send some of their pupils to some classes in the neighboring local

schools. This was usually arranged for all or some on the high school level, though two schools indicated that they send selected children from Grades 1 through 12. Lowenfeld (1965) makes these observations:

> It is most important that pupils of the residential schools are transferred to the local public schools whenever they are ready for it or when a public school facility for blind children becomes available in their home community. High school students should attend the public high school of the community in which the residential school is located, although they may reside at the latter which should provide reader service, guidance, tutoring in subjects which the blind student might find difficult to master without help, and mobility training. In short, it should function as a resource facility and boarding place for these public high school students. . . . Under this program the blind student has an opportunity to become a fully participating member of a high school community of seeing students while he can still be assisted and guided by a residential school staff which is familiar with the problems of blindness. . . .Besides its social values, it offers blind students a variety of high school courses which schools for the blind —small as they are in comparison with most public high schools—cannot possibly offer [p. 119].

Since there appears to be a relatively small number of normal severely visually handicapped children at the preschool and lower school levels at the present time, it is possible that this policy may become more widely accepted for those children who need a residential facility, whether because of unusual home conditions, the impracticality of providing a special program in some sparsely populated areas, or other reasons. Two recent developments would seem to be pointing in this direction. The first of these is an attempt by the California School for the Blind to extend the program described by Lowenfeld into the lower grades. If at all feasible, normal visually handicapped children would be returned to programs in their home communities, with arrangements made for the few who are unable to do so to commute to the program for visually handicapped children in the Berkeley public schools. The residential school would serve those on the elementary grade level in the same capacity as it has for many years its high school students. This transition must be expected to take some time, but it could prove to be a solution to the problem of providing sufficient motivation and competition to normal and bright visually handicapped children in a school that at present is largely serving multihandicapped children.

Another recent development pertains to the Nebraska School for the Visually Handicapped and the expansion of its role through an act by the State Legislature (Nebraska Legislative Bill 242, 1969) which includes the following.

> The Nebraska School for the Visually Handicapped, upon approval of the Commissioner of Education, may contract with a local school district, educational

service unit, or public institution of city, county or state government for educational services which cannot be provided more effectively by the school [p. 20].

Legislatively Bill 241 (1969) further delineates the new role of the school:

> The purpose of the Nebraska School for the Visually Handicapped shall be to provide general and special education for persons not to exceed twenty-one years of age for whose benefit such school was created until completion of a general or special program. The school shall be the state resource center for all educational programs for visually handicapped children in Nebraska and shall provide services such as in-service training of teachers, itinerant teaching, counseling services, the loan of equipment, books and learning media to local school districts and educational service untis [p. 20].

The latter provision is noteworthy since, with the exception of full-time special classes which are in this respect similar to residential schools, local school programs have a common frustration: the difficulty of providing their pupils with appropriate and sufficient educational materials and textbooks. The deficiency is most noticeable where programs are small and scattered. Several other residential schools in sparsely settled states have assumed similar responsibility in an informal way. In the more densely populated areas the problem may be more difficult to solve since it involves more individual children. Recognizing the greater efficiency in services to children and in monetary outlay obtained through statewide instructional materials and textbook centers, as exemplified by those maintained by the New Jersey Commission for the Blind, the Industrial Home for the Blind in New York, and the Hamm Foundation in Minnesota, three Ohio state agencies concerned with visually handicapped children and youth joined together to establish a Central Registry of Educational Materials for the Visually Handicapped.

> The Registry was established through the cooperative efforts of the State Department, the Ohio State School for the Blind, and the Services for the Blind, Ohio Department of Welfare. The Registry is located at the Ohio State School for the Blind [Grover, 1965, p. 5],

The main purposes of the Registry were defined as follows.

1. To establish a state unit for the registration and distribution of educational materials used in the education of blind and partially seeing children.
2. To prevent waste and duplication and to minimize the time required in matching available materials to the needs of the children.
3. To co-ordinate all available resources within the state and provide loan and information service to schools enrolling blind and/or partially seeing children [Overbeay & Eisnaugle, 1965, p. 51].

The Ohio Registry exemplifies the cooperation that can exist between residential and local school programs. However, so universal is the problem of providing adequate textbooks and other materials to children attending local schools that several other facilities have been developed to alleviate this situation. In some instances, as in the center maintained by the California State Department of Education, a combination clearinghouse and repository has been found expedient. There, as in many others, an additional function includes the coordination of recording and transcription of textbooks.

The inability of local school programs to provide visually handicapped pupils with essential equipment, identical texts, and other books in usable media, and with other instructional materials, has evoked criticisms that are too frequently justifiable. Although the adverse effect on scholarship and self-esteem resulting from this predicament is obvious, the situation remains acute in many parts of the country. Great impact has been made by local and national organizations of volunteer transcribers and recorders. Of inestimable assistance has been the provision of a reference catalog service for volunteer-produced textbooks in all media through the Instructional Materials Center of the American Printing House for the Blind. The further expansion and coordination of the network of the Instructional Materials Centers initiated by the Bureau of Education for the Handicapped, and the increasing number of centers funded by state and local districts offers hope for improving this service to visually handicapped children. The American Printing House for the Blind, quite apart from its participation in the Instructional Materials Center network, has experienced constant growth and adaptation in its efforts to meet the diversified needs of an ever-increasing number of children in the whole range of educational programs.

Through conferences for educators and volunteers sponsored by the American Printing House for the Blind, and especially through its annual meetings when representatives of both residential and local school programs serving children along the whole continuum of visual handicaps have opportunities to exchange views, much has been accomplished in bringing about greater unity in this relatively small area of special education.

Additional New Trends

Further Coordination

Concern for the welfare of all visually handicapped children in the state has been evidenced by summer programs at some residential schools that include children who attend local school programs during the regular school year. Use of the residential schools for periods during the summer months has become more common since Federal funding to expand and improve educational services for the visually handicapped has become available. The program described in the following extract has been selected as an example of close cooperation between the state education agency that provided funding (through a Title VI-A ESEA State Project) and shared in the administration with the state residential school. It also included participation by the rehabilitation services of the state Commission for the Blind.

"Vocational Evaluation and Development of Skills in Mobility, Efficient Living, Social Adjustment, and Recreation Through Summer Instruction for Blind Students Who Attend Public and Private Junior and Senior High Schools." This project brought together 50 blind pupils enrolled in both public and private schools in Texas for 10 weeks of intensive training which they would not have received in their present educational setting. Several aspects of the program were especially successful. These are: (1) pupils gained new insights about themselves and their relationships to others; (2) the development of independence not previously achieved; (3) the production of a film concerning the program that will be shown to the participants, parents, and teachers, to other parent groups, to educators in teacher training programs, to legislators and to the public; (4) the development of an awareness among educators that training of this type is needed in the regular programs for the blind in our schools; and (5) fifty blind students were given help to develop needed skills that they would not have otherwise have received [Bureau of Education for the Handicapped, 1969].

Despite the many benefits that accrue to most visually handicapped children and youth who attend local schools, the problems mentioned above are quite common among those who attend smaller programs, especially if they are educationally blind or have very low vision. Some residential schools have added intensive tutoring in academic areas to their summer programs, somewhat similar to the Oregon Plan (Jones, 1953).

Residential Schools

In addition to the utilization of local schools for some of the children living in residential schools and the extension of residential school services to those attending their local schools, the trend toward accepting day pupils has increased to a point where in some urban areas arrangements have been made for school bus or station wagon service from the child's home to the residential school. This adaptation may be especially practical for some children for whom the highly specialized segregated school program seems wise, but who still need or would enjoy the advantages of family life.

One of the most striking differences between the residential school of today and that of a decade or more ago is the closer relationship it maintains with the child's home and community. Possibly, this rapport was initiated even before the child entered school. Through counseling and active participation in parent discussion groups and cooperative nursery schools, families of visually handicapped children may have gained greater insights into their responsibilities in fulfilling the children's needs and a deep concern about the social, emotional, physical, and educational welfare of all handicapped children. These parents have brought force into the development of active parent–teacher organizations where schools have fostered such a partnership. Some schools have employed home counselors whose main function is to continue this bond. Some schools have initiated institutes or workshops for parents of school-age children as well as for those of the preschool group. Parents are encouraged to visit the schools, participate in planning the child's school program, and discuss his progress and problems with teachers and other personnel. Weekends at home are encouraged to the extent that some schools have arranged for bus transportation from the campus to convenient centers throughout the area every weekend, and have scheduled "long weekends" periodically for the sake of those pupils who live too far away for weekly trips home.

Another sharp contrast between the residential schools of some years ago and those of today, illustrative of a current trend in all special education, is the schools' concern for and development of specialized programs for multi-handicapped children. Increased services for visually handicapped children with additional disabilities are found in all of the administrative patterns. Itinerant and resource teachers, and even more frequently teacher-consultants, are working with children enrolled in programs for other handicaps. In local school districts throughout the country special classes have been established or converted to serve this group. Programs for the visually handicapped may be found in institutions for the retarded and in day and residential programs for other handicaps. However, the residential schools for the blind have led the way in the development of special programs and in the numbers of children enrolled (Jones & Collins, 1966). There are some who believe that service to this group of children may be the major role of these schools in the future (Wolf, 1967; Lowenfeld, 1969).

Although this change in programs of many schools may be considered an outgrowth of (1) the apparent decrease in the number of young visually handi-capped children without additional handicaps, (2) the expansion of local school programs, or (3) pressures from preschool counselors and parents, a review of the various projects for the visually handicapped established or improved through funds from the United States Office of Education since 1965 suggests that additional money and the availability of more trained teachers have provided a strong impetus (OE/BEH, 1966, 1967, 1968).

Concomitant with new or expanded programs for the multihandicapped was the initiation or furthering of other services to all children in the school and, in some instances, to other visually handicapped children in the state or region. Among these have been evaluation, diagnostic, and treatment services. Per-haps because of their concern regarding the unusual behavior of some of the multihandicapped children, some schools have added such staff as consulting psychiatrists, full-time psychologists, speech therapists, school social workers, and other professional personnel. Some schools have developed a closer working relationship with similar community services available to all children. The use of teacher aides, teaching assistants, recreation aides, and houseparent aides in some schools has extended beyond the multihandicapped to other groups, so that teachers and others may use their special skills more fully (OE/BEH, 1966, 1967, 1968).

A recent movement involving utilization of the residential school on an 11- or 12-month basis has enabled schools to undertake a wide variety of services and projects which limitations of time and space make difficult or prohibit during the academic year. In addition to some of the already noted institutes and workshops, these projects include intensive diagnostic and therapy programs for multihandicapped children not attending any school; extensive uninterrupted time for teachers to work together on curriculum planning; remedial and tutorial services to enable selected children to experience success in areas which have been stumbling blocks; intensive training in mobility, daily living skills, academic preparation, and study skills for college-bound youth; a special workshop for blind homemakers; school camping; and many others.

With the changes in the school population, the expanded school year, and the availability of more specially trained personnel have come other pertinent innovations. In recognizing the need to consider individual differences, the ungraded lower school is now a well-established program at the Maryland School for the Blind. Curriculum changes which facilitate transfer to local schools, as well as provide the "plus factors" described by Abel (1959b), are making possible more relevant training for the multihandicapped. Work–study programs previously enjoyed chiefly by those attending local high schools are being tried by residential schools. Many new building programs have brought changes from poorly lighted institutional-type facilities to modern, cheerful, utilitarian schools with special consideration for today's students through ramps, lighting, expanded library and instructional materials centers, etc. The Michigan School for the Blind may be leading toward a new trend through its large-type printery.

Other trends in curriculum advances and service changes will be noted later in this chapter and in other chapters.

Local School Programs

With the development of newer patterns of local school programs, such as resource rooms, itinerant services, and teacher-consultants, new apprehensions troubled the partisans of local school education of the visually handicapped. Chief among these were concerns that the pupils enrolled in these programs would not receive adequate special services and that they would not become full members of the group. In some of the sparsely settled areas and smaller communities, these fears have proved to be well justified. The inability to make certain that students have the necessary textbooks and other materials, discussed earlier, remains a problem in many communities. Some local programs, especially those in California, have made progress in solving this problem through employment of paid volunteers. In some places, chiefly in New Jersey, supplemental instruction is supplied through employment of part-time teachers, certified for the grade level or subject but not as teachers of the visually handicapped, who give individual instruction and other services under the joint supervision of the teacher of the visually handicapped and the regular classroom teacher. Use of paid transcribers, supplemental instructors, and teacher aides relieves the special teacher of activities that do not require the skills and knowledge acquired through special training as a teacher of the visually handicapped. Provision of paid readers also enables the special teacher to devote more time to tasks directly involving instruction and guidance of pupils.

The problem of providing services appropriate to individual needs is being dealt with in those programs that have found it possible to utilize more than one pattern. In smaller communities one teacher may serve as a resource teacher for a part of the day and as an itinerant teacher or teacher-consultant for the other. In larger cities, or in county, regional, or statewide programs in densely populated areas, several patterns may be used effectively. Self-contained classes may be available for those children who, because of special problems such as emotional disturbance or learning disabilities, are currently unable to participate in regular classrooms. Resource and itinerant programs may be provided for others, including those enrolled in classes for other handicapping conditions as well as those in regular classrooms, with the possibility of transferring from one to the other according to the needs of the child and the facilities of the neighborhood school. In larger programs the teacher-consultant may play an important role in serving those children who do not require regularly scheduled special instruction.

Another variation in local school programs is the multiclass public school for the visually handicapped. This is an outgrowth of the earlier segregated special class programs in the larger cities which were initiated in an effort to ensure greater service to pupils as well as for the purpose of administrative expediency. This pattern, in which most or all pupils are placed in one building, has been replaced in a number of cities by other types of patterns.

A serious problem of the itinerant teaching pattern is the amount of time the special teacher spends traveling between schools. The time spent driving from one community to the next may be poor use of skilled professional personnel, from the points of view of both administrators and the teachers themselves. This pattern has been adopted effectively in smaller cities and suburban areas. Paradoxically, the larger, most densely populated cities have been slow to inaugurate itinerant teaching services. The observations of Stephens and Birch (1969) may provide an explanation:

> Educators have devised many procedures, through the years, to provide for intellectual, academic, and physical differences of students. While present innovations in organizational modifications for instruction are made primarily to facilitate learning, Goodland (1960) has noted that other purposes are also served. These include financial considerations, administrative ease, and teacher satisfaction. The present authors would add the influence of individuals who have strong views and who are in leadership positions as another factor to consider when attempting to account for the organizational patterns which have developed in the education of partially seeing children and youth [p. 482].

There also seem to be geographic and parental influences. It is not surprising that parents who have moved to suburban communities for the sake of their children do not wish to have the one who happens to have a visual handicap transported back into the city to attend school.

Jones and Collins (1966) found the following concerning geographic differences.

> Some distinct regional differences appeared when estimates of pupils served in each were compared. Nearly 75 percent of the pupils in the North Atlantic Region of the United States were enrolled in school systems served by special teachers of visually handicapped children while less than 25 percent of those enrolled in the Southeastern Region had such services available at the local level. Such teachers were readily available in the home communities of about half the pupils in the West and Southwestern Region and to more than one-third of those in the Great Lakes and Plains Region [p. 25].

In the same report it is observed that efforts to serve visually handicapped children in local schools in small communities also vary according to where in the nation they happen to live. Regional programs, including those administered by counties, were found quite commonly in New York, California, Pennsylvania, Maryland, and Florida. Statewide programs also differ considerably. In the small densely populated state of New Jersey, the Commission for the Blind provides a continuum of services to all visually handicapped infants, children, and youth, through which about 85% of the children are served by itinerant teachers or teacher-consultants. The remainder attend selected residential facilities in neighboring states or special classes in the larger cities. The agency also provides psychological and other evaluations and treatments, mobility instruction, a variety of summer programs, and an instructional materials and textbook center. This program and a somewhat similar one in Connecticut are unique in states of such small size and dense population. Moreover, the program in New Jersey, because it is in an agency for the blind rather than a state education agency, suffered certain disadvantages to children and to professional personnel. Several programs maintained by local districts were discontinued. Only one new program, a partial county effort, was established under local auspices. Efforts to have the state education agency assume some responsibility for the total program or any parts of it failed. It would appear that although the education of visually handicapped children is believed to be a basic responsibility of local districts and state education agencies, it is very difficult to transfer the role once another arm of state government has assumed this function.

In other states, such as California, Oregon, Rhode Island, and Wyoming, state education agency consultants for the visually handicapped have assumed some direct services.

One of the numerous advances in education of visually handicapped children that has come about with the availability of additional finances through Federal funding programs is the addition of state consultants for the visually handicapped to coordinate and assist in the improvement and expansion of local and residential services. Jones and Collins (1966) made the following evaluation of this arrangement.

> The most comprehensive programs for visually handicapped children and youth often are found in States which employ specialists in the education of these children at the State level either in education agencies or in commissions or boards of education of the visually handicapped [p. 30].

Although the literature is replete with opinions of the advantages of one administrative pattern over the others, usually by persons with limited experience in the others, there has been little substantiation of these assertions in the research findings. The practical approach, therefore, suggests a continuing study of the child and his total situation together with a careful evaluation of the facilities available to him.

Assessment of Program Effectiveness

Elementary Pupils

Recent research pertaining to children on the elementary school level, if read without consideration of the limitations of the studies, might point to advantages of one program over another.

Lowenfeld et al. (1969), in a study of braille reading, determined that

> On the fourth grade level, blind children in local and in residential schools were equal in braille reading efficiency, since neither in reading comprehension nor in reading rate significant differences were demonstrated.
> On the eighth grade level, no significant difference in reading comprehension

was shown between local and residential schools, but the significant difference in reading rate indicates that eighth grade students in local schools were more efficient readers than their peers in residential schools* [pp. 112–113].

So far as chronological age is concerned, the study indicated that "On the eighth grade level, students in residential schools were 5.1 months older than those in local schools" (p. 81). Differences in IQ showed for eighth graders that "the difference, though only 3.4 IQ points and therefore not very meaningful, was in favor of students attending local schools" (p. 84). The study also found that the percentage of students in the upper IQ range (110 and above) in both fourth and eighth grades was greater in local schools than in residential schools. Regarding this phenomenon the authors (Lowenfeld et al., 1969) comment

> . . . it could be assumed that the more capable blind students tend to be referred to local schools, while the less capable ones are more often placed in residential schools. The latter may perhaps be done in the hope that less capable students will develop better in an environment which is completely geared to the needs of blind children, and in competition with blind children rather than with those who can see. The data of the study as such, however, give only the facts but no explanation for them* [p. 66].

There is no surprise in the findings that the eighth-grade students attending local schools were faster readers, since it would have been advantageous for them to develop reading speed in order to keep up with their faster-reading classmates and to cover the possible additional amounts of required reading. It is also worthy of note that the seventh and eighth grades are common periods for transfer from one pattern of education to another. Therefore, it is quite possible that the more academically able students may have at this time been placed in local schools, whereas others, needing more adapted programs, may have remained in or been transferred into residential programs.

In a study of 97 totally blind fourth-, fifth-, and sixth- grade pupils, McGuiness (1970) found that children in integrated and special school settings did not differ in their braille reading skills. However, in a summary of the conclusions from the study it is stated that

> The more highly integrated itinerant teacher setting surpasses the resource room setting in fostering friendships and participation in activities with sighted children. This is true also in active types of activities which might be, at first glance, seemingly too difficult for blind children.

*From Lowenfeld, B. et al. *Blind Children Learn to Read,* 1969. Courtesy of Charles C Thomas, Publisher, Springfield, Illinois.

The resource room setting, while not differing from the itinerant teacher setting in the fostering of independence and social maturity, is less effective than the itinerant teaching setting in fostering friendships with sighted children. While surpassing the special school setting in these respects, the resource room setting does not differ from the special school setting in the degree to which it fosters participation in activities, especially in active activities with sighted children.

While not differing from the other settings in the ability to communicate braille skills, the special school setting would seem to promote friendships with other blind children and participation in activities with blind children more than do the other settings [p. 45].

The McGuinness study does not indicate the extent of acceptance of the blind children in the integrated programs. In a study involving 63 visually handicapped children in resource or itinerant programs, Havill (1970) found, as have other studies, that the visually handicapped were less well accepted than their normally seeing classmates, but that those in itinerant programs had a higher sociometric status than those in resource room programs. This study also showed those who were blind to have a higher degree of acceptance than the partially seeing, and that there was low status for those at the junior high school level and for average achievers.

The Peabody and Birch report (1967), in which most of the pupils were attending self-contained classes for the partially seeing in the elementary grades, makes the following statements regarding academic achievement.

Educationally, the most important feature of the portrait of the typical partially seeing sixth grader is his underachievement. Since his intelligence is probably average, his grade expectancy can be determined by reference to the grade in which he would be for his age. That, for a child of 12 years and nine months age, should be the end of seventh grade or the beginning of eighth grade, depending upon the minor differences in admission age from state to state. Considering that his actual measured achievement of grade 5.4 was made at midterm it becomes clear that the youngster is approximately two and one-half years retarded academically, as based on age and mental ability* [p. 93].

Two other recent studies, both utilizing children enrolled in resource or special classes for the partially seeing in Illinois (Bateman, 1963; Karnes & Wollersheim, 1963) include among the findings statements which indicate that children who had milder visual defects, in the nature of refractive or fusion disorders, were "markedly underachieving" and were poorer readers for their grade placements than those with more severe anomalies or lower acuities. The question again arises whether these children found their way into a program

*Reprinted from *The Sight-Saving Review,* Volume 37, No, 2, Summer 1967, by permission of the National Society for the Prevention of Blindness, Inc.

for partially seeing children because of their visual problem or because of their educational problems, which may involve learning or other disabilities not associated with visual defects. Since children with mild or moderate refractive and fusion errors are less easily identified in early childhood, there is also the strong possibility that they did not receive correction for the refractive errors or orthoptic training until after beginning instruction in reading. There may be some doubt about the suitability of their placement in a program for visually handicapped children, but there would seem to be no question about their need for a thorough educational evaluation and intensive individual instruction.

Stephens and Birch (1969), reporting on a survey of opinions and research regarding the merits of the special class, resource, and itinerant plans for teaching partially seeing children, were able to cite much opinion but gave only one research finding that might show an advantage of one over the others.

> found a significant difference when mean scores on the Metropolitan Achieve-
> ment Test were compared among the three organizational plans, with subjects
> in itinerant plans having a higher mean score than the children in the other two
> plans [p. 484].

In the same survey it is noted that there was a "significant difference in mean IQ scores ($p < .01$) in favor of the itinerant group" (pp. 483–484). This suggests that the child's ability to achieve at the expected level may have been taken into consideration in the choice of an educational plan for him. The higher scores could also be due to the greater demands of competition in a regular classroom. It is also possible that itinerant teachers, who usually work with one child at a time, give more attention to educational diagnosis and a clinical type of teaching.

Secondary School Pupils

Since it was suggested early in this chapter that formal school placement might be later than normal as an advantage to some visually handicapped children, underachievement if measured solely by age in grade may not be reason for much concern. When considering the extra demands imposed by the handicap in such areas as social and emotional adjustment, mobility, acquisition of information, and career decisions, it is probably to the visually handicapped secondary student's advantage to be somewhat older than others at the grade level. However, these problems, coupled with the probabilities that many may be reading at a slower rate and with below-grade comprehension, many may test below grade level in arithmetic, and many may show poor writing communication skills, suggest that the selection of the secondary school placement requires most careful consideration.

According to Dauwalder (1964, p. 19), "Nearly one-third of the visually handicapped graduates of residential and day high schools throughout the United States attend some college or university." Due to problems caused by the small enrollment in high school departments of residential schools for the blind, local high school placement is often recommended for those who are college bound. However, such placement should be made on an individualized basis, making sure that each student is academically and socially prepared and has at least:

1. A high school that has a strong, broad college preparatory course of study.
2. A home free of such serious problems that he will not be able to progress satisfactorily in his academic and personal growth.
3. Basic textbooks for each subject available to him in a reading medium he can handle efficiently at the time that he needs them.
4. All equipment and special materials that he needs for the study of his various subjects at home, with duplicates of heavy or bulky articles to keep at school.
5. Adequate reader service (preferably paid readers, so that he will not need to feel in debt for the privilege of having at his command the same information others are able to obtain).
6. A teacher-consultant who will arrange for the three preceding requirements, and who will be able to advise the student, his parents, and school personnel, as well as to arrange for additional services, such as tutoring, mobility instruction, or vocational counseling, at the time the need occurs.
7. Opportunity for and encouragement to participate in extracurricular activities that may enhance his social, emotional, and physical development.

For those college-bound students who do not have the first two necessities listed, a more suitable placement should be sought. With the exception of the teacher-consultant for some children living in remote areas, the other items on the list can usually be obtained. If they are not provided, there should be some serious questions about the suitability of the selection of local high school placement for a college-bound student.

For the remaining largest percentage of visually handicapped students, the needs are much the same as those listed above except that the school should have a curriculum which will accommodate to the student's interests and abilities. If the student's home is in a community that has a large comprehensive high school program, it is quite possible for him to have a stimulating and satisfying experience. In a local high school with limited curriculum choices and major emphasis on college preparation, the student may be given a "modified academic" program which eliminates the more difficult courses, substituting "minor" courses when feasible, or even reducing the amount of work required of the student. For many this may provide a good learning experience as well as an opportunity for social and emotional maturation. For

some, when the school is not able to modify the program adequately, the
competition may be too great, so that a breakdown in morale and self-esteem
may ensue. For others a modified academic plan is not relevant, whereas a
technical, vocational, business, or other curriculum might be very challenging.
The foregoing comments regarding secondary school programs pertain equally
to local and residential school programs, and for the students' sake should be
considered objectively in planning with him and his parents regarding any
possibility of changing or continuing in a particular program. Too often a
student is moved from one program to another with the faint hope that he may
do better or be happier elsewhere.

Since the selection of the school is so crucial at this particular age, it seems
appropriate to cite the following quotation from Conant (1959).

> The enrollment of many American public schools is too small to allow a
> diversified curriculum except at exorbitant expense. The prevalence of less
> than one hundred students—constitutes one of the serious obstacles to good
> secondary education throughout most of the United States. I believe such
> schools are not in a position to provide a satisfactory education for any
> group of their students—the academically talented, the vocationally oriented,
> or the slow reader. The instructional program is neither sufficiently broad
> nor sufficiently challenging. A small high school cannot by its very nature
> offer a comprehensive curriculum [p. 77].

Fortunately, for most visually handicapped secondary school students the
possibility of attending an appropriate high school is or could be greater than
for many normally seeing students. According to Jones and Collins (1966):
"Approximately 80 percent of the 143 local school systems which enrolled
25,000 or more pupils [the 1962–1963 school year] were served by full-time
special teachers of visually handicapped children" (p. 24). At least half of the
residential schools are in or near large cities or regional high schools providing
comprehensive programs. Some small revisions, or merely updated interpretations, of present school laws or regulations could enable visually handicapped
students to attend high schools that would provide a relevant curriculum for
those for whom such is not available in their local home community high
schools or state residential schools. The policy of payment of tuition and
transportation costs for handicapped students to attend a facility in another
community is long established. Where the distance would be impractical for
daily commuting, the residential school might be used as a boarding facility,
or another may be found. The possibility of regional planning might also be
considered with those schools able to provide the service of accepting boarding
pupils from other states and serving them in much the way described earlier
in this chapter.

The suggestion for regional services is not new to educators of the visually handicapped, but is probably nearer to realization today than previously thought possible. The expanded use of helicopter service to bring special education to children in remote areas, which is predicted for the immediate future, could easily be reversed to bring students to needed services or to provide weekends at home. As indicated earlier, there has been an increasing cooperation between residential and local school programs in many places. Steps toward interstate planning have already been taken through the establishment of centers to coordinate regional services for deaf–blind children, Regional Instructional Materials Centers and Regional Resource Centers. Considerable attention is given to the need for regional planning in a report of the National Research Conference on Special Education Services in Sparsely Populated Areas (Jordan, 1966).

Moreover, the principle of regional planning might well extend below the high school level, particularly if consideration is given to the size and locale of some local and residential programs. A map plotting of the locations of residential schools and those cities large enough to employ several teachers and auxiliary personnel shows that in many parts of the country children are traveling great distances due to state boundary restrictions. Even more serious is the problem of very small schools or local programs. How can a school with 20 to 50 pupils give a full curriculum to pupils ranging from kindergarten to Grade 12? What happens to the child in a local program that employs only 1 teacher, who happens to be inadequate?

Broadened Curriculum

During the past two decades, while educators of the visually handicapped were coping with the problems attendant on a rapid increase in the number of children requiring highly specialized services, other developments were taking place. Greater emphasis was given to orientation and mobility skills through the emergence of college-trained specialists who were employed by agencies serving the adult blind, residential schools, and day schools, often by a shared arrangement. Teachers, through new emphasis in their training and through cooperation of the specialists, gave more intelligent assistance to younger children in the basic elements of physical, emotional, and social development. Efficient mobility students were able to participate in more community activities, thus extending their learning environment beyond the campus. Greater independence was fostered among children when daily living skills became part of the recognized curriculum for all ages, rather than something taught only informally and casually, if at all. New emphasis was placed on more efficient utilization of residual vision through low-vision clinics and private practitioners specializing in better refraction. The use of optical aids and changing attitudes toward use of them enabled many students who had previously read only braille to read print, understand diagrams and pictures, or use their improved vision as an aid in mobility. Some teachers began to train children with extremely low vision through a planned sequential program. In some schools, guidance and counseling services were extended down to younger children, and other pupil personnel services were expanded as additional funds became available through Federal programs.

The broadening aspects listed above were greatly influenced by developments in services to handicapped adults. A current trend that invites emulation centers on developing a curriculum that is more relevant for noncollege-bound pupils. Work–study programs are appearing in several forms, according to needs and resources. Some are part of an established program available to the nonhandicapped students in local schools; others have been organized especially for visually handicapped students and may include both college-bound and other students. Whether originated by the local schools, as in Portland, Oregon (McGee & Edwards, 1969), by a private agency for the blind, as in the Industrial Home for the Blind (Maloney, 1965; Richterman, 1963), or by residential schools, as in Maryland (Spurrier, 1968), the program usually evolves into a cooperative venture cosponsored by the school, the rehabilitation agency and, in some instances, the state education agency vocational education department. By considering the needs of the students emphasized in these programs and the inadequacies found in special programs for college-bound students (Kumpe, 1968; Paul & Goione, 1968; Pumo, 1970), it becomes apparent that the curriculum of many residential and day school programs needs to be broadened to include more of the following.

1. Social competency and personal adjustment. This encompasses a wide range of skills, the development of which begins in the preschool years and continues as part of the required school subjects until graduation. These skills are discussed in Chapters 8 and 9. They can be summarized under the following headings: skills of personal care, household skills and tool use, recreational skills, orientation and mobility skills. To these must be added mental health and emotional adjustment.
2. Communication skills. The need for increased reading speed and comprehension is discussed in Chapter 7. Reports of summer programs specifically arranged for college-bound high school graduates emphasize the need for more effective typing instruction, even though many of the students had had such instruction beginning as early as the third grade, and presumably had been typing many of their school assignments. Likewise, many of the blind students had not been taught handwriting, even to the extent of signing their names. Many partially seeing students had barely legible handwriting.

    It was also found necessary to provide these students with instruction in spelling and in the writing of themes and of term and research papers, as well as in the proper format for typing these assignments. All students needed further instruction in writing business letters; use of banking facilities, including checkbooks; and keeping accounts of personal expenditures. It was necessary to train the students in note taking, especially as used with tape recorders. Many of the students had had no experience in dictating notes, nor in the use of tape recorders in the preparation of term papers, etc. Some had not had experience in learning through listening to recorded textbooks, although this is the chief source of college textbooks. Little had been done to assist these students in the time-saving use of compressed speech. Many needed basic library information for use with college libraries as well as with those facilities for obtaining materials for the visually handicapped.

3. Prevocational and vocational guidance and experience. The development of good work habits, of attitudes toward work, of a self-concept that includes himself as a participating member in the everyday world, and of occupational goals that are realistic, begins in early childhood. Therefore, guidance in this area should be an intrinsic part of the school curriculum at all levels. Role playing, spontaneous among young children, provides opportunity for guidance and later may be stimulated even to the point of preparation for the first job interview.

The Dauwalder (1964) survey, after enumerating many shortcomings in guidance services, prevocational and vocational training, concludes

> It may not be practical for every school, residential and/or day, to offer all of the industrial arts experiences and levels of work which should be made available in training visually handicapped students. In the event that a school is not able to provide a complete program, ways must be found to make this service available through a large residential school or a large special education day facility to such students after regular school hours, on weekends, or during vacation periods [p. 55].

This author would disagree with the suggestion that additional hours be added to the school day, especially for those attending local schools. For them so much time is already involved in commuting, and visually handicapped children as well as others need to have time to pursue their own interests, even though these may be merely enjoying quiet idleness, or listening to a favorite radio program.

Extension of the school program might well be made through summer programs or through scheduled additional years to allow for a spreading out of academic subjects, thus giving time for more guidance and attention to social competency and personal adjustment, as well as to prevocational training, throughout the school program.

The Dauwalder (1964) survey is filled with data indicating severe inadequacies in the vocational counseling and training provided in both local and residential schools. With the passage of the 1963 Vocational Education Act and the 1968 Amendments to the Act, which earmark 10% of the basic allotment to each state for vocational education of handicapped persons, some improvement has been noted. However, there is need for greater effort and cooperation among all schools and rehabilitation agencies to further the development of innovative, quality programs adapted to the employment needs of today and tomorrow and to the abilities and interests of the students.

SUMMARY

In communities where a selection of educational facilities is possible, the decision regarding placement should be based upon a careful evaluation of the child and of the schools to determine which has a program and the emotional and social "climate" most suitable for him. An ongoing reevaluation from nursery school through high school and flexibility in changes from one facility to a more suitable one are recommended. The use of an evaluation team has been found to be advantageous.

More appropriate curriculum offerings, including those for multihandicapped children, might be feasible if statewide or regional planning and programming were established.

Various studies indicate that many blind and partially seeing children require more intensive and extensive special educational services than they are now receiving. Extension of the program through a longer school year, additional school years, or both, seems indicated. Many residential and local schools have begun to adopt this policy.

Greater cooperation among the schools, state vocational education services, and rehabilitation agencies is apparent but still inadequate in some areas.

REFERENCES

Abel, G. L. Growth of the resource room. In G. L. Abel (Ed.), *Concerning the education of blind children.* New York: American Foundation for the Blind, 1959. Pp. 49–58. (a)

Abel, G. L. Problems and trends in the education of blind children and youth. In G. L. Abel (Ed.), *Concerning the education of blind children.* New York: American Foundation for the Blind, 1959. Pp. 79–101. (b)

American Printing House for the Blind. Distribution of January 3, 1972 APH quota registrations by school grades, and braille and large type reading. Mimeographed report.

Ashcroft, S. C., Halliday, C., & Barraga, N. Study 11: *Effects of experimental teaching on the visual behavior of children educated as though they had no vision.* Nashville, Tenn.: George Peabody College, Grant No. 32–52, 0120–1034, 1965.

Barraga, N. *Increased visual behavior in low-vision children.* New York: American Foundation for the Blind, 1964.

Bateman, B. D. Reading and psycholinguistic processes of partially seeing children. *CEC Research Monograph,* Series A, No. 5, 1963.

Bureau of Education for the Handicapped. *Selected projects for handicapped children.* Austin, Texas: Texas Education Agency, VI-A State Project, 1969.

Conant, J. B. *The American high school today.* New York: McGraw-Hill, 1959.

Cowen, E. L., Underberg, R. P., Verillo, R. T., & Benham, F. G. *Adjustment to visual disability in adolescence.* New York: American Foundation for the Blind, 1961.

Dauwalder, D. D. *Education, training, and employment of the blind.* Pittsburgh: Western Pennsylvania School for Blind Children, 1964.

Directory of school programs for the visually handicapped—Fall 1968. Washington, D.C.: Bureau of Education for the Handicapped, U.S. Office of Education, 1968.

Grover, E.C. *Ohio programs for visually handicapped children.* Columbus: Ohio Department of Education, 1965.

Havill, S. J. The sociometric status of visually handicapped students in public school classes. *Research Bulletin No. 20.* New York: American Foundation for the Blind, 1970. Pp. 57–81.

Imamura, S. *Mother and blind child.* New York: American Foundation for the Blind, 1965.

Jones, J. W. Developments in Oregon's program for educating blind children. *Exceptional Children,* 1953, **19,** 131–134, 142.

Jones, J. W. *Blind children: Degree of vision, mode of reading.* Washington, D.C.: U. S. Government Printing Office, 1961.

Jones, J., & Collins, A. *Educational programs for visually handicapped children.* Washington, D.C.: U. S. Government Printing Office, 1966.

Jordan, J. B. (Ed.), *Special education services in sparsely populated areas: Guidelines for research.* Boulder, Colo.: Western Interstate Commission for Higher Education, 1966.

Karnes, M. B., & Wollersheim, J. P. An intensive differential diagnosis of partially seeing children to determine the implications of education. *Exceptional Children,* 1963, **30,** 17–25.

Kumpe, R. College preparation of blind prospective college students. *New Outlook for the Blind,* 1968, **62,** 319–320.

Kurzhals, I. W. Reading made meaningful through a readiness for learning program. *International Journal for the Education of the Blind,* 1966, **15,** 107–111.

Lowenfeld, B. The blind child as an integral part of the family and community. *New Outlook for the Blind,* 1965, **59,** 117–121.

Lowenfeld, B. Multihandicapped blind and deaf-blind children in California. *Research Bulletin No. 19.* New York: American Foundation for the Blind, 1969. Pp. 1–72.

Lowenfeld, B., Abel, G.L., & Hatlen, P.H. *Blind children learn to read.* Springfield, Ill.: Charles C Thomas, 1969.

Maloney, E. Examining the adequacy of programming for blind children. *New Outlook for the Blind,* 1965, **59,** 54–57.

McGee, J., & Edwards, J.P. Work experience for the visually impaired. *CEC Selected Convention Papers.* Washington, D.C.: Council for Exceptional Children, 1969. Pp. 302–307.

McGuinness, R.M. A descriptive study of blind children educated in the itinerant teacher, resource room, and special school settings. *Research Bulletin No. 20.* New York: American Foundation for the Blind, 1970. Pp. 1–56.

Nebraska Legislative Bills 241 and 242. *DVH Newsletter,* 1969, **16,** 20.

Nolan, C.Y. Blind children: Degree of vision, mode of reading, a 1963 replication. *New Outlook for the Blind,* 1965, **59,** 233–238.

Nolan, C.Y. A 1966 reappraisal of the relationship between visual acuity and mode of reading for blind children. *New Outlook for the Blind,* 1967, **61,** 255–261.

Nolan, C.Y., & Bott, J.E. Relationship between visual acuity and reading medium for blind children—1969. *New Outlook for the Blind,* 1971, **65,** 90–96.

OE/BEH. *Resumés of projects for handicapped children.* Washington, D.C.: Bureau of Education for the Handicapped, U.S. Office of Education, 1968.

Overbeay, D.W., & Eisnaugle, E.E. The central registry: Ohio's plan for service to visually handicapped children. *International Journal for the Education of the Blind,* 1965, **15,** 50–51.

Paul, R., & Goione, P.W. Composition through typing: Instruction in communication for the blind. *Exceptional Children,* 1968, **35,** 154–158.

Peabody, R.L., & Birch, J.W. Educational implications of partial vision. *Sight-Saving Review,* 1967, **37,** 2, 92–96.

Pumo, B.J. Prevention of vocational disabilities through comprehensive planning. *New Outlook for the Blind,* 1970, **64,** 53–59.

Richterman, H. A personal adjustment and orientation program for children. *New Outlook for the Blind,* 1963, **57,** 389–392.

Spurrier, E. A work-study program for students in a residential school for the blind. *New Outlook for the Blind,* 1968, **62,** 319–320.

Stephens, T.M., & Birch, J.W. Merits of special class, resource and itinerant plans for teaching partially seeing chldren. *Exceptional Children,* 1969, **35,** 481–484.

Taylor, J.L. Selecting facilities to meet educational needs. In B. Lowenfeld (Ed.), *The blind preschool child.* New York: American Foundation for the Blind, 1947. Pp. 117–120.

Taylor, J.L. Educational services. *The Welfare Reporter,* 1960, **40,** 64–75.

Wolf, J.M. *The blind child with concomitant disabilities.* New York: American Foundation for the Blind, 1967.

CHAPTER 7

Communication Skills

Freda Henderson

Tennessee School for the Blind and
George Peabody College for Teachers
Nashville, Tennessee

INTRODUCTION

For the visually handicapped child, as for every student, the school has no greater imperative than the development of the communicative skills. Effective communication is a tool as well as a goal of education. If the school is to fulfill its function as a learning laboratory, it must nurture a spiraling proficiency in the use of this tool. Effective communication skills are essential in order to give the student adequate foundation for his attainment of self-realization, economic sufficiency, positive human relationships, and worthy citizenship in society.

Language is vital to self-realization. It is uniquely human and is necessary for the normal growth and development of the individual as a member of the human race. The child's self-concept is largely a product of his interaction with others. As he expresses himself and receives the feedback from other individuals in his environment, there gradually emerges a self that will affect all his future accomplishments. The child who does not have a wealth of opportunities to discover the power of language as a tool for needed fulfillment may become psychologically dwarfed.

In order to discover, mature, and maintain the self, every individual must have opportunity to develop skills for interaction with his social group. The day on which Helen Keller first discovered the meaning of language marked the birthday of a personality. Language, although limited for her, nourished a world citizen.

Language can stimulate the individual to cultural awareness. It spans the barriers of time and space, enabling him to react to a wide variety of conditions and to participate vicariously in a broad scope of activities. Language stimulates his growth from egocentricity to social integration.

Communication controls the pulsebeat of economic activity. A strike halting newspaper production almost paralyzed the entire economy in one of our major cities. Hotel reservations decreased sharply; department store sales declined drastically; restaurants suffered financial loss; and taxicabs were idled. Stage plays that had once drawn capacity audiences played to empty houses or closed out entirely. Virtually every phase of life was affected by the break in this one line of communication.

On the average, every third person in the United States—man, woman, or child—subscribes to a daily or Sunday newspaper. A news commentator recently stated that during a 12-month period the people of our nation consumed over a quarter of a ton of paper per person. Advertising itself is big business. From magazines, newspapers, billboards, radio, and TV the public is constantly bombarded with assertions of the efficacies of every imaginable product. Unfortunately—or fortunately—the person with a serious visual limitation is protected from some of this deluge. However, to become an effective consumer as well as producer in our economy, he must appreciate the selling power of language. He must be able to extract from the deluge of words those claims which are valid and relevant.

Communication energizes the moral fiber of society. It is a cosmic thread running through all cultures, knitting mankind into one world community. Through symbols man transmits, interprets, and vitalizes his heritage of ideas and ideals. He discovers his place in the history of mankind—past, present, and future. Language puts man's mind into operation in the service of society. Discussion is basic to mutual understanding and social action. It is chiefly through effective communication at home and abroad that men will come to appreciate the inherent dignity of every human being and will learn to live together in peace and harmony.

Words are power. They soothe, anger, excite, tranquilize, stimulate, intimidate, energize, stultify, create, destroy, assassinate, or immortalize. Word power is the one measurable element that has been found to be present among men who have become leaders in any and all areas of endeavor.

The school should formulate its major goals so as to help every student realize his potential in word power. For the visually handicapped student, however, the pattern of behavior leading to those goals may have some unique aspects. This chapter will help to analyze the desired behavioral pattern, determine the essential skills, and formulate specific, measurable, behavioral objectives to ensure a sequential program. These objectives, formulated in terms of specific desired behavior, give direction in both planning and measuring the student's growth. The visually handicapped individual has both the right and the responsibility to achieve to the full his potentiality in the use of language power.

ESSENTIAL FACTORS IN COMMUNICATION

Speech is man's most distinctive behavior. What is speech? Why is language such a powerful tool?

The Core of Experience

Man's experience spawned his desire to communicate. There was a need that demanded gratification. Therefore, man created a tool—the sound symbol—whereby he could compress his experience, analyze it, dissect it, and share it, in part or in whole, with his neighbor. These sound symbols, or words, were manageable tools that man could store in his mind. They became keys that would unlock his memory and call forth segments of previous experiences to serve a new need. The symbols became links that would connect a man's experience with that of his neighbor so that they might interact and cooperate to satisfy their needs. Word symbols served as small shells, or capsules, with which man could manipulate his experiences and in which he could condense and store their ingredients for future use. Thus, experience was always the core of communication. It was the motivation, substance, and result of the communicative act.

Speech alone did not entirely satisfy man's need. It was limited to the immediate in space and time. In order to conquer distance and to leave his record for posterity, man had to create some tangible vehicle to convey his thoughts, actions, and feelings. To meet this need, he initiated the graphic representation of language—even in prehistoric days. Thus, experience gave birth to and nurtured communication.

In any form, communication is an interactive process involving both expression and reception. Since experience is the core of communication, there must exist between the communicators some commonality of experience. This core of experience must receive foremost consideration in any analysis of the communicative skills of a visually handicapped person.

Without question, the school in its program for the visually handicapped student must constantly be involved in the enrichment and expansion of experience—the core which gives birth to the desire and the skills for communication. The program should capitalize upon the strengths of tactual, kinesthetic, aural, and olfactory perception. It should maximize the use of even a relatively small degree of remaining vision. Whether the child is totally blind or has some degree of vision, it is essential that he learn to appreciate his preceptual strengths and to appraise his limitations realistically, so that he can and will develop his optimum functional efficiency.

Facets of Communication

For convenience the communicative complex may be segmented into a quadrangle—listening, speaking, reading, writing. Within this quadrangle, there is a constant two-way expressive receptive process. The receptive, or decoding, aspect of the process is always linked to the expressive, or encoding, aspect. Listening and reading function receptively; speaking and writing serve as expressive channels. Generally speaking, the elements of oral language precede those of written language, and the receptive skills precede the expressive skills. The child listens and patterns his speech after the sounds he hears. He observes the graphic forms of letters and begins to copy those patterns.

Although it is possible to identify the facets of communications as listening, speaking, reading, and writing, and to indicate that they develop in that order, such segmentation is a gross oversimplification of reality. These four facets intertwine and mold into the complex act of communication. In one sense, these four are peripheral. The focal act is cognitive; it is the action that takes place within the data network of the brain.

Listening and reading are channels of reception. They are decoding acts involving the extraction of ingredients that fill or alter the contents of the network capsules. Encoding is the formation of the new symbolic pattern emerging from the action within the capsules and the associated links. Speaking and writing are the channels for the expression of this mental action.

The language–thought process is uniquely human. It is a spiraling complex, inseparable from the total developmental pattern of the individual. It involves an intricate complexity of skills. For example, the reading process alone has been analyzed into as many as 83 component skills.

Perception, the first step of communicating, utilizes abilities which vary according to whether the sensory channel be aural, tactual, kinesthetic, visual, or olfactory. *Cognition,* the second step, takes place within the data network of the brain and includes all of the higher mental activities: observing, comparing, analyzing, synthesizing, evaluating, inferring. These mental activities are intact regardless of the individual's degree of vision. The thinking process is similar for individuals with or without vision. The difference lies in the kind and quantity of input. The third step in communicating is the act of *expression* resulting from the network activity. Although this output may take any of several forms, our primary concern is with words—spoken or written.

SYMBOLS OF COMMUNICATION

Experience is the heart of communication; the symbol is the tool. The brain carries on a continuous process of data transformation. It takes the impressions of gross experience and analyzes, abbreviates, and stores the ingredients in manageable units, or symbols. This symbol-making process, unique to man, is common to all human cultures. It is as much a part of man's development as are eating, sleeping, or moving about. A symbol is a sign that represents some element of experience—an object, an action, an idea, a thought, or a feeling. The symbol may be gestural, verbal, pictorial, rhythmic, tonal, or graphic.

Nonverbal Symbols

Although this chapter is concerened primarily with communication as it involves verbal and graphic symbology, some consideration of nonverbal communication (tone, posture, gesture) is pertinent.

In his receptive or encoding process of oral language, the individual with an extreme visual loss may become very sensitive to the tonal quality of the speaker's voice. He may detect weariness, slight irritation, or boredom, even though the speaker is confident that such feelings are well masked. He may be just as quick to catch the slightest note of excitement and enthusiasm. Thus, signals of a nonverbal nature may either enhance or deter the intent of the speaker.

The child who is blind lacks the advantage of the visual patterns that are subconsciously imitated by the sighted child in his habit formation. He may develop poor postural habits and an expressionless countenance that are in opposition to, or at least detract from, the desired verbal communication. Two guests, one of whom was totally blind, were visiting in a home. After they had departed, the little 3-year-old child questioned, "Why did that one man wear a mask?" Although this man was an accomplished, well-adjusted, pleasant person, his expressionless features had communicated adversely.

It is possible that the child or the parent may become overly anxious concerning some aspects of nonverbal communication that are associated with visual handicaps. The child with partial vision may be so concerned at having to hold his book very close to his eyes or to use a magnifying lens that he will attempt to avoid reading in the presence of sighted companions. A parent may discourage the child's efforts to investigate through close examination because she wishes him to "look normal." The person who is blind may try to avoid the use of the travel device or the slate and stylus because he feels that such aids draw attention to his blindness.

Individuals who are visually handicapped need the training necessary to handle their aids with ease. They need to be guided to discover and appreciate their strengths so that they can accept themselves. If they capitalize upon attractive strengths, these positive factors may dominate their nonverbal communication. Through helping the child to achieve a vital interaction with his environment; through discussion and the establishment of standards for his self-evaluation; and through direct demonstration, the teacher should encourage him to incorporate into his behavior acceptable, positive aspects of nonverbal communication.

Oral Symbols

The primary communicative tool is the verbal symbol—the word. The word is a time–space pattern of sound. It has no meaning within itself; it is a storage capsule, or shell, for some element of experience. As Smith (1950) says: "Symbols are but empty shells. It takes experience to fill them with the meat of meaning" (p. 99). The mind is involved in a continuous process of data transformation. It abbreviates and abstracts each gross experience, storing the ingredients in many capsules, or word symbols. As the elements are associated within the gross experience, the mind establishes connective links among these storage capsules. From each new experience additional capsules are stored; ingredients are added to or altered within the existing capsules; new links are formed which intensify the interaction and interdependence among the capsules. Thus the brain constructs an intricate data network.

The capsule, or word symbol, has no meaning of its own. The meaning lies within the experience of the individual. However, in order to have a basis for interpersonal communication, there must be some common agreement as to the element of experience symbolized by each word. These common agreements are recorded in a dictionary, which may be used by individuals to discover the "meaning" of a word. But there is no real meaning in the dictionary. There are merely more symbols, some of which are already stored as well-filled capsules in the reader's mind. His mind draws upon the ingredients of these capsules and establishes new links. Thus, the real meaning of the new symbol stems not from the dictionary but from the reader's past experience.

Common agreements concerning word meanings based on man's experiences do not remain constant. No symbol contains exactly the same ingredients for any two individuals. Even for the same individual a given symbol may not contain the same ingredients twice in succession, since each act or experience exerts a subtle influence on the ingredients stored within his data network. For

the individual and for society, language is an ever-evolving process, functioning with an ever-evolving set of tools.

Communication is a process of expression and reception. In order for this
process to function, there must exist between the communicators some commonality of experience. The cycle breaks if one of the communicators has
stored an insufficient number of symbolic capsules, or if he lacks an adequate
processing into the existing capsules. The core of communication is then
lacking.

A speaker or author draws from the symbols within his brain network
of processed data. Each capsule that he taps, in turn tugs upon the many
associating links within his own network. He rearranges the symbols to express his thoughts, and in so doing he may create new linkages and make
subtle alterations in his capsule ingredients. In turn, the listener or reader
receives the set of symbols, each of which triggers reaction within his
mind. Associated ingredients within his symbol-storage capsules are activated, strengthened, or altered. All connecting links within his network
feel the tug, and new links are formed. Any ingredient in the speaker's
symbols that does not attract some associated ingredient in the listener's
storehouse is lost in the act of communication.

Typographic Symbols

Man has developed an ingenious system for representing his communicative
symbols in written form. The first pictorial messages were gross expressions
of events and ideas. With the expansion of man's world and the extension and
refinement of oral language, the pictographic writing was inadequate. It was
necessary to create a graphic system that would provide for more accurate
reproduction and interpretation. Common agreement on these graphic symbols was essential to communication.

The history of the evolution of graphic symbols is common knowledge and
need not be detailed here. Various cultures progressed along devious lines from
ideographic to logographic to syllabic and finally to alphabetic representation.
In general, the development has moved toward a one-to-one relationship between graphic symbol and voiced sound. Such a basic set of graphics (alphabet)
can be rearranged to represent any number of sound patterns or words. It is
obvious that there is not a pure one-to-one sound–symbol relationship. Often
several graphic symbols compose a single voiced sound, and certain voiced
sounds may be represented by more than one graphic pattern.

The time pattern of oral language, involving both sequence and break, or
pause, became a space pattern in print. Symbols of punctuation were created
to assist in the graphic display of such voice elements as tone, inflection, and
timing.

With man's technological advance in the rapid and inexpensive reproduction and storage of typographic symbols, the ink-print code has become an effective tool for the colossal task of graphic communication. Through utilization of magnification and variations in type, the individual with partial vision and even the person with very low visual acuity can use print as a medium for communication.

Robert Irwin first provided large type, 36 point, for pupils in the Cleveland, Ohio, schools in 1914. This type proved to be too large and was soon abandoned for the more popular 24 point. Research sponsored by Irwin in 1919 indicated 24-point type to be the most readable of the sizes evaluated. Further research by others in 1952 and 1959 supported the efficacy of 18- or 24-point serif type. (Measure of type size is based on 72 points per inch.) Spacing, or leading, is also important; greater space between lines is needed with large type. Black type on white nonglare paper is used. The paper must be of sufficient weight to prevent shadowing from another page.

Punctographic Symbols

For the blind the graphic symbol must be tactually perceived. Braille, the graphic form of communication now in common use by the blind, derived its name from the originator, Louis Braille.

Irwin (1955) and Lowenfeld, Abel, and Hatlen (1969) have traced the fascinating history of developments leading to the adoption of a uniform braille code. There was a stormy interval which may be characterized as "the war of the dots." Another period, which Lowenfeld calls "the battle of the contractions," saw the transition from braille Grade 1 (in full spelling) to Grade 1½ (with some contractions), and finally to braille Grade 2, which is in common use today.

In 1932 a uniformly contracted code, Standard English Braille Grade 2, was officially adopted on both sides of the ocean. It was argued that conformity would open the door to the exchange of books and so increase the available supply of the very costly braille materials. Since that time, by agreement, the code has been international in nature—which proves to have both advantages and disadvantages. Some revisions were accepted in our country in 1959 and are included in our official code manual, *Standard English Braille, American Edition, 1959* (available from the American Printing House for the Blind).

Braille is embossed in standard spacing: .090 inch from center of dot to center of dot within the cell, and .160 inch between cells. The standard page is 11 by 11½ inches.

Braille is bulky. (The Bible requires approximately 5 feet of shelving space.) By incorporating contractions—symbols representing groups of letters—and short forms in which only a few significant letters represent a word, an appreciable amount of space is saved. The code using these space savers is designated as braille Grade 2. The shortcuts within the code facilitate the speed with which the fingers can traverse the word symbols and the speed with which braille can be written. They reduce the storage space needed. However, they have also created certain problems.

In braille Grade 2 such a burden is placed upon the 63 possible dot combinations that many of them have been assigned a multiplicity of meanings. As a consequence the reader must not only perceive the accurate configuration of a given character, but must also interpret its meaning in the light of its context and spatial relationship to surrounding characters. This interpretation often depends on the tactual discrimination of a distance of only .090 inch. For example, one character—two adjacent dots on a horizontal plane—has eight different meanings in literary context, all determined by spatial relationships (*c, can, con, com, cc,* hyphen, dash, colon). The problem is confounded by the fact that these same 63 symbols must also serve for mathematic, scientific, and music notation.

Although there are possible pitfalls inherent in the braille code that have implications for instructional techniques, braille is the most effective graphic tool in existence for communication by individuals who are blind.

LISTENING

Rankin (1930) showed that of the total time that all adults spend in communicating, 45% will be occupied with listening, 30% with speaking, 16% with reading, and 9% with writing. (These percentages are probably still typical.) More than one study has indicated that the sighted student spends approximately two-thirds of his school day in listening. For the person who is blind, listening is of paramount importance. It is his chief avenue of learning from his extended environment as well as from other people. The school should motivate and train the student to maximize his listening efficiency.

For the infant, the ear is the first receptive channel that is activated. For most individuals the ear and the eye function as major input channels. Usually the eye is dominant, but as vision decreases, more dependence must be placed on hearing. There is no compensatory increase in auditory acuity. However, as attention is focused upon auditory stimuli, the brain becomes more sensitive to ingredients fed through the aural channel. When a person has little or no sight, it is his auditory and olfactory senses that serve to extend his reach beyond arms's length.

The erroneous opinion is sometimes expressed that blind children naturally learn to listen more keenly than do sighted children. Hartlage (1963) found no significant difference in listening ability between the sighted and the blind subjects in his group.

Aspects of Listening

Listening is not a simple process. It involves auditory acuity, awareness, identification, selection, and interpretation.

Auditory acuity is the physiological basis for good listening. This physical readiness should be measured by means of audiometric screening and testing. Hearing losses that do not fall within the voice range, and therefore do not affect the audition of speech, may be significant for the blind individual, since they may seriously affect his ability to detect objects within the environment.

Normal auditory acuity per se does not ensure good listening. An individual may have the ability to hear, yet he may lack *awareness* of the sounds in his environment. Auditory awareness differs greatly among individuals. Recently a group of five young people were asked to listen for 1 minute and to report the sounds they heard. Their responses ranged from three to ten, and no one of them had been aware of all of the sounds. Awareness of sound is related to the meaningfulness of the sound. Sound has meaning only if it is associated with some object or activity or if it has some strong emotional connotation, such as the stimulation of fear or the anticipation of pleasure.

Unawareness may be a shield. In sheer defense the mind must mask out many of the sounds constantly bombarding our ears in this age of technology. Should our minds attend to all of the noises, many of us would become sonic wrecks. Children living in a noisy environment can become oblivious to sounds that have no meaning to them. Studies show that adults who grow up in noisy, culturally deprived surroundings tend to be unaware of environmental sounds even though their auditory acuity is normal.

Observation has indicated that a blind child may be extremely unaware of sounds. Early environmental conditions may have seriously affected his listening ability. The young blind child who has not established meaningful contact with his environment may habitually mask out most sound. When this child enters school he may sit in the classroom, oblivious to all the conversation going on around him as well as to the teacher's voice. He needs training in sound awareness.

Sometimes the individual with a low degree of vision focuses his attention so acutely on hazy visual stimuli that he becomes unaware of aural stimuli that would be more helpful. Such an individual needs to develop an awareness and effective utilization of all his sensory input.

Awareness of sound is not sufficient; there must be *identification*. Through the normal sense of hearing a person can perceive the presence of an object within a range of several feet and can gain some concept of the mass of that object. Through hearing he can also gain a concept of the direction and distance of the stimulus. None of these concepts necessarily identifies the object. When tactual contact with the stimulus is not practical, a parent, teacher, or sighted companion can make the identification meaningful through verbal description.

Inasmuch as the mind cannot tolerate attention to the daily deluge of sounds, it must exercise *selection*. Usually it selects those sounds that it can identify as having some meaning at that particular time. The child must not only become aware of and identify sound; he must also discern which of those sounds have meaning for him. He must learn to distinguish the figure—the important sound—from the subordinate background noise. The individual who has not developed this ability is usually very distractible and nervous. He cannot concentrate on the assigned task.

Selectivity is an important aspect in the use of listening as an educational channel. Before pupils are asked to engage in a listening activity, teachers should help them to clarify their purposes as guides to selectivity. Students should be encouraged to formulate their own purposes before approaching independent listening activities.

Finally, auding also involves *interpretation*. Interpretation gives direction to response. It assigns the meaning that words or sounds will have for the individual in terms of his immediate purpose; it directs his thought, words, or actions. Acute awareness, rapid identification, meaningful selection, and intelligent interpretation characterize the effective listener.

The young child or the newly blinded individual who is keenly aware of sound may be very frustrated and upset in any large crowd or noisy surroundings until he begins to identify, select, attend to, and interpret those sounds that have meaning for him.

Avenue of Learning

For the student with serious visual limitation, listening usually becomes the most significant avenue of learning. In addition to obtaining information through discussion and verbal description, he often substitutes listening for reading. Frequent use is made of live reader service. A fellow student, a volunteer, or a paid reader may serve in this capacity. Much excellent recorded material is available through regular commercial channels. In addition, many books and magazines are produced on tapes or disks for use by persons with a serious visual handicap. These materials are made available through loan from the Library of Congress and the network of regional libraries established for this purpose. The talking book machine for playing the disks is also available on loan to the visually handicapped. Through volunteer services an individual may have any textbook of his selection recorded on tape or disk.

Auding is a receptive process that involves all of the comprehension skills required for reading. Within recent years the art of listening has received added emphasis in the area of general education, and most texts dealing with reading instruction include a section concerning listening. Accurate auding is more difficult than accurate reading because listening is more transitory in nature. It is more passive in that it lacks the physical activity necessary in reading. Concomitant physical activity can sharpen the effectiveness of auding skills. Since movement enhances learning, the teacher should frequently plan for some activity to accompany the receptive act of listening.

Efficiency in listening is not learned incidentally; it must be taught. Since auding is of such paramount importance as a receptive process for the visually handicapped, it should receive a major emphasis in instruction.

Although the word is the basic symbol common to listening, speaking, reading, and writing, the set of symbols, or vocabulary, differs for each facet of communication. For an individual, the listening vocabulary is usually the largest. He hears and understands more words than he uses in speaking, reading, or writing. Usually, especially for the child, the spoken vocabulary ranks second in size. His speech is an outgrowth of the language he hears. Smith (1941) reported that the child in the first grade may possess a basic speaking vocabulary of 17,000 words, increasing to 32,000 in the sixth grade. Reading vocabulary, in general, grows out of the oral vocabulary. There is, however, an interaction; as the student progresses he meets unfamiliar words in reading which become a part of his oral language. The store of words that a child uses in his written expression is usually his smallest set of symbols.

During successive years at school the gap between the vocabularies narrows. For some individuals the reading vocabulary may exceed that used in speaking and in some instances even that used in listening. However, for the visually handicapped child the vocabulary associated with the graphic facets of language is likely to be delayed. Because of the limited quantity of graphic materials available and the time necessitated for reading, he comes in contact with a relatively limited number of symbols. Usually auding remains his most extensive avenue of learning.

READING

Reading, the process of receiving information through graphic stimuli, is closely related to listening. The cognitive process within the data network of the brain is quite similar. In fact, if beginning reading materials are wisely selected, the only new element will be the perception of the graphic symbols. The child will already have developed an oral vocabulary—a set of capsules

—filled with ingredients from an adequate experiential background. Associative links will exist within his data network. However, in the reading process the key that unlocks the capsules and stimulates brain activity is different. Instead of being made up of sound it is comprised of graphic symbols—raised dots or marks made with ink.

Educational Environment

Current trends in organization, methodology, and learning media may affect the language arts program for the visually handicapped. Although the organization of the program may vary with educational systems, it is probable that during the primary years the development of reading skills will receive the major emphasis in time and effort. As the student progresses, the time devoted primarily to the teaching of reading decreases, but the time spent in the utilization of reading as a learning tool increases. Although there is a trend toward the inclusion of reading instruction as a subject in high schools and even in colleges, it is often true that on the secondary level reading assumes its place as a functional tool only. Every teacher of every subject needs to accept the responsibility for leading each student to acquire the reading skills required in his area.

Currently there are many approaches to the teaching of reading which are successfully implemented in various school systems. There is the individualized approach exemplified by Sylvia Ashton-Warner's work in New Zealand with the Maori children. The basal reader approach is typified in the instructional series published by such companies as Ginn and Scott, Foresman. Bloomfield and Fries are strong proponents of the linguistic approach. McCracken and Walcutt, in their series of readers published by Lippincott, are among the leaders who structure the learning process around the phonic approach. The language-experience approach, of which Van Allen's work is illustrative, is somewhat similar to the individualized organization. There are leaders who place emphasis on an early letter approach, advocating early visual identification of letter symbols by name. Other approaches are made through color coding, use of rebus material, and modified alphabets such as the Initial Teaching Alphabet (ITA).

Research has not established the superiority of any one methodology. Each system has its strong points. The teacher should be cognizant of all. Any one of the systems may prove to be the solution for some child having a specific reading problem. Most methods become modified through adaptation and inculcation of strong features from other programs. Almost every method provides the opportunity for some degree of individualization, self-selection, and self-pacing.

As a result of the differentiation in methodology and the rapid technological advance, the producers of educational hardware and the producers of software, such as books and pamphlets, have joined forces to produce an upsurge of audiovisual aids, structured kits of multilevel self-pacing materials, and a great variety of instructional media. These should be studied for their adaptability to work with the visually handicapped.

Within any educational environment the creative teacher who keeps abreast of current trends can make adjustments and innovations to provide the best possible learning program for the student who needs to use braille or large type.

A minor ferment in the field of reading instruction for the blind reflects a much broader ferment in the general field of reading instruction. Chall (1967) analyzed existing research and challenged its support of the whole-word method of vocabulary development. The whole-word method, according to a recent nationwide questionnaire reported by Lowenfeld et al. (1969), is the most prevalent in programs for braille readers. It has been challenged by Nolan and Kederis (1969) in their analysis of research.

It is possible that there is confusion in terminology. This writer has questioned a number of professional people concerning their understanding of the whole-word method and has reached the conclusion that the term encompasses such a wide variety of interpretation that it has lost its distinctive communicative value because it no longer holds a common ingredient of meaning.

Nolan and Kederis (1969) concluded that the cell rather than the total word is the perceptual unit and that word recognition is a sequential, integrative process which involves the accumulation of information over a temporal interval. They observed that "the task of identifying a word takes from 50 to 150 percent more time than the identification of the characters included" (p. 84). The presence and position of contractions within a word shortened recognition time for familiar words and increased it for unfamiliar words.

Ashcroft (1961) found through his analysis of oral reading errors that braille readers made the greatest number of errors in the recongition of short-form words (represented by only a few significant letters) and in the dual-cell contractions. These findings would indicate the need for a language arts program adjusted to ensure adequate knowledge of the full spelling of braille contractions.

Educational programs may differ widely in organizational pattern and in their approach to instruction in reading. However, to stimulate optimum development of each student any program of reading instruction must have three essential features: It must be *diagnostic, sequential,* and *developmental.* There must be continuity not only within the total school program but also for each individual as he progresses through that program.

It is important to realize that the program designed to be diagnostic and to provide developmental continuity for the readers of print may not accomplish the same purposes for the reader of braille. In order to modify the instructional

materials to meet the needs of the braille reader, the teacher must have sufficient mastery of the dot code to think in terms of tactual perception of braille
forms.

Regardless of the organizational pattern of the learning environment and
regardless of the approach to the instruction of reading, the effective program
will include five basic objectives: adequate readiness, word recognition power,
comprehension skills, personality growth, and diagnosis and evaluation. The
first four objectives are at a developmental stage at every level of the academic
program—and, hopefully, throughout life. In order to plan effectively for
optimum individual growth, there must be diagnosis and evaluation at each
level. Every teacher in every area of learning at every level must assume
responsibility for these objectives as a part of the educational program. He
must understand the implications of visual limitation and provide the necessary modifications.

Adequate Readiness

Code breaking, or the recognition of the graphic symbol, may be isolated
as the only unique element in the reading process. However, the teacher in
planning the program must perceive reading in its role as a receptive channel,
contributing to, and developing as, a part of the total language–thought process. In turn, language growth must be perceived as one thread, inseparable
from the total growth and development of the individual.

In assessing and nurturing readiness for any stage of reading, the teacher
must give attention to the student's mental age, physical maturation, social-
emotional development, experiential background, oral language skills, sensory
acuity and efficiency, and motivation.

The visually handicapped child may need an extensive readiness period. He
must be able to interact successfully with his physical and social environment.
He must participate in the give and take of group activity. The student must
acquire an adequate number of words—capsules well filled from an experiential background. Associative links must be formed within the data network of
the brain.

The child must get ready to use a new key, the graphic symbol, to unlock
the capsules and set his brain network into action. The child with even a very
low measurable degree of vision may develop the ability to use print as his
graphic tool. He may need to develop adequate eye movements; he may have
to learn to focus. It may be necessary for him to discover the importance of
form constancy and direction and to learn to discriminate between significant
details. He must learn to see. Provided with a visually stimulating environment
and given adequate training, he can learn to make maximum use of his vision.
Barraga (1964) demonstrated the efficacy of a sequential program of training
for individuals with low visual acuity.

The child who needs to be tactually oriented to reading must learn to see with his fingers. Prior to his entrance into school, he may never have learned the joy of discovery with his hands. As a reinforcement to his own observation, the teacher may use the Roughness Discrimination Test developed by Nolan as an aid in making early assessment of the child's tactual acuity. (This test is available from the American Printing House for the Blind.)

The child who has never been encouraged to explore with his hands may need an extended readiness program. He may require gross physical activities to develop muscle strength and tone. His environment must be tactually stimulating. It must include many opportunities for finger manipulation in order for him to develop coordination and dexterity. There must be activities that call for discrimination of texture and shape. Fingers must learn to touch lightly, to slide smoothly from left to right, and to move with ease from one line to the next on the page. They must begin to discriminate fine differences in spatial relationships in dot configurations.

If the child is to move with pleasure and ease into the act of reading, he must meet his graphic symbols in many informal, meaningful situations. The child with sufficient vision has from infancy been bombarded with typographic symbols. Books were probably among his first prized possessions. Before he enters school he may have connected graphic symbols with some of his spoken words. The sighted child of 3 who could identify the song on any given page in his book was well acquainted with graphic symbols. His was merely a gross interpretation of the entire page, but he was reading.

It is unlikely that the child who is blind has had any preschool contact with his braille symbols. His readiness program must foster appreciation of, and friendship for, his graphic reading symbols. During this initial period the teacher must be alert to capitalize on every opportunity to display the appropriate graphic symbols—braille or type—paralleling the child's oral expression of meaningful situations. The teacher should be as enthusiastic over the child's recognition of his first spoken word. This positive reinforcement will serve as a strong motivation for the reading process.

For the older student who is losing or has recently lost his vision, social-emotional readiness is a very important factor. His new reading medium may be to him a tangible symbol of his deficiency, and he may consciously or subconsciously build up resistance to it if it is introduced before he has made an emotional adjustment to his visual condition.

Word Recognition Power

In reading, the graphic symbol is the key that unlocks the meaning-bearing capsule to set the brain network in action. Every school reading program should assist the student in developing five means of increasing his power in the use of these keys. He must build a basic vocabulary—a set of keys that he recognizes instantly by sight or by touch. He must learn to use phonics, structural elements, and context as clues to new symbols. He must gain skill in using special aids such as glossaries and dictionaries to discover symbols.

The major aim in beginning reading is to establish skill in using a basic set of keys—to build a basic sight vocabulary. Producers of print materials have discovered ingenious methods to help the young reader recognize his keys. Clues are supplied through color coding, page format, pictures, and even modified alphabets such as the ITA. Few of these clues can be paralleled in the transcription of materials for tactual reading. There has been some experimentation in the application of the principles of the ITA to braille. There is at present insufficient research to indicate whether or not such alterations in the punctographic word forms will, in the long range, facilitate or hinder efficiency in braille reading.

In standard reading series the preprimers are designed to build basic vocabulary. Attractive pictures facilitate symbol recognition by suggesting the meaning of a given word. In many instances, the child with some degree of vision may find the type size used in primary readers sufficient for his needs. When this is true, he will profit from the illustrations in the regular print books.

When these books are transcribed into braille, there is no means of reproducing the picture clues in a form that is tactually significant. The teacher or a classmate may describe the pictures for the braille reader. However, at this early stage necessary dependence on sighted persons to supply the meaning is not conducive to positive attitudes toward self or reading. The child must have sufficient opportunites to discover and interpret graphic materials for himself.

The language–experience approach is in several ways advantageous to the braille reader. Experiential and tactual clues stimulate symbol recognition. Personal involvement strengthens motivation. Symbol introduction can be controlled in terms of braille readability.

Readability formulas used by authors in the preparation of print materials cannot be assumed to have equal applicability when the material is reproduced in the braille code. As yet, no series of reading books has been designed for a sequential development of the complexities of the braille code. When basal readers prepared for sighted pupils are reproduced in braille, they do not provide for gradation in the difficulties inherent in the code.

Regardless of the instructional materials utilized, there are many factors affecting the sight vocabulary of visually handicapped children. The child who can bring only one or two letters into visual focus simultaneously may need numerous contacts with his word symbols before he recognizes them quickly. His process will be one of word synthesis rather than immediate recognition of total word form.

From her study of partially seeing children in Grades 1 through 4 in Illinois, Bateman (1963) concluded that there is no reason why partially seeing children should be retarded in reading if adequate materials and methods are used from the outset of their educational program. Her findings suggest that a minimum sensory input can stimulate a near-maximal central network activity. Bateman recommends that the program include increased emphasis on discrimination of vowel shapes, training in close attention to each symbol to discourage the tendency to omit letters or words, and efforts to overcome faulty eye movements likely to accompany certain visual deficiencies.

For the blind child the numerous short forms in the braille code place a great burden on memory and immediate recognition. For example, the braille configurations for *have, here, his, had* contain only one sound symbol, the letter *h*, which stands alone or is modified by position or by prefixes composed of certain dots having no meaning of their own. Each of these words must be recognized immediately by memory.

Some braille words are composed of only a few significant letters, such as *fr* for *friend* and *pd* for *paid*. These, too, must become part of a "sight vocabulary." Other words are represented by arbitrary symbols for the entire word, with no component letters. Words such as *to, was,* and *were* require 2 different graphic symbols for the braille reader because each appears either as a one-cell contracted form or in full spelling, according to its relationship to other symbols.

Context functions uniquely as a clue to word recognition for the braille reader. Not only does he depend on clues from associated meaning, but he must also interpret many clues from the braille environment. For example, the braille configuration for *f* when there is a space on each side of it represents *from*. If it is moved into the lower part of the cell (a distance of .090 inch), it becomes *to* when it is adjacent to the beginning of another word, *ff* when within a word, or an exclamation mark if adjacent to the end of a word. Only the relationship of this character to the surrounding braille environment identifies it for the reader. If the context were mathematics, the same symbol would be the numeral 6, and in music it would represent the note E.

The structure of the braille code modifies the manner in which phonics serves as a clue in word recognition. Some of the examples already cited illustrate that many of the contracted forms lack a sufficient number of phonic elements to aid in identification. Because of the multiplicity of meanings stored in one symbol there is no sound–symbol constancy. The configuration for *j* also represents *by, was,* and the closing quotation mark. There is no phonic constancy. In the braille code the symbol for *tion* is composed of the letter *n* prefixed by two dots. There are 14 such contractions in which the only component letter is the final one. This feature tends to confuse the reader who is attacking a word phonetically unless he has mastered the code to the extent that he immediately associates the full spelling with the contracted form.

In some ways structural analysis is aided by the code. Common prefixes and suffixes are represented by single braille signs. However, contracted forms and general rules of usage in the code often obscure such structural elements as length, root words, and syllabication.

Glossaries and dictionaries, although cumbersome to use, serve the visually handicapped reader. The braille reader may gain his skill in the use of these aids more slowly than does the sighted child. For him, there are not the readiness materials and many simplified dictionaries available to motivate an early start.

From their research Nolan and Kederis (1969) hypothesized that the braille reading process matures more slowly than the print reading process. In the upper elementary grades pupils are still refining skill in character recognition. One bit of supportive evidence is the fact that no significant correlation is found between intelligence and braille reading rate below the secondary school level. For sighted readers, a positive correlation between these two factors emerges during the upper elementary grades. If such delayed maturation is typical of braille reading, instruction throughout the elementary grades should include continuous emphasis on perceptual factors related to the code.

It is quite evident that at each level of the child's development, his teacher must possess an adequate knowledge of the braille code in order to understand the implications for helping the student achieve optimum skill in the recognition and use of his graphic symbols.

Comprehension Skills

As measured on reading tests, there is no significant difference between the comprehension skills of sighted and visually handicapped children. Comprehension is the cognitive process that takes place within the brain network. However, when interaction between rate and comprehension is the measurable factor, a very significant difference is evident.

All available research supports the fact that the greatest discrepancy between tactual and sight reading lies in the rate of input. It is much slower for braille reading than for print. The differentiation is not too marked in the initial stage, but the gap consistently widens throughout the school years. Foulke, Amster, Nolan, and Bixler (1962) reported that braille readers in Grades 6 through 8 read science material at 57 words per minute (wpm) and literary material at 70 wpm. Nolan (1966) reported that 208 braille readers in Grades 4 through 6 read literature, science, and social studies for their respective grade levels at mean rates of from 52 to 57 wpm. In Grades 9 through 12, 174 braille readers read appropriate materials in these categories at mean rates ranging from 66 to 74 wpm.

Lowenfeld et al. (1969) reported that 50 fourth-grade pupils from residential schools and 50 from day-school programs (all braille readers) read the initial portion of the Sequential Test of Educational Progress at mean rates of 72 and

84 wpm, respectively. Fifty pupils from the eighth grade in residential schools and 50 from day-school programs read at mean rates of 116 and 149 wpm, respectively.

The apparent discrepancy in reported reading rates may be due in part to the test conditions. The slower rates reported by Nolan and Foulke were obtained on textbook materials, which characteristically tend to rank almost one grade higher in difficulty than do most standardized reading tests. The subjects were instructed to read carefully because they would be tested on the material. They probably employed the rate usually appropriate for study materials. The greater speeds reported by Lowenfeld et al. were derived from the initial portion of a standardized power test in reading (Sequential Test in Educational Progress).

In assessing braille reading rates, the difficulty of the material is of utmost importance. In administering the Gilmore Oral Paragraphs in Grades 3 through 6, this writer noted a consistent sharp decrease in rate of reading as the difficulty of the material increased. Pupils who read from 100 to 120 wpm on their basal level dropped to from 40 to 60 wpm as they approached their ceiling.

Comparison of the highest means in reading rate reported for braille readers with those recently being reported for sighted readers reveals a significant difference. For example, Taylor (1957) reported rate–comprehension studies of 5,000 children whose rates ranged from 75 wpm in first grade to 180 wpm in fourth grade and 255 wpm in junior high school. Reading rates for the individual with a low degree of vision are more comparable to those for braille readers than to those for the sighted.

Optimum reading rates are fostered by means of a good reading environment, the use of good reading mechanics, adequate mastery of the symbols of the code, and a high level of motivation.

A *good reading environment* is one that stimulates purposeful reading. Such an environment should include a wholesome learning atmosphere; objects and activities that arouse curiosity and raise problems to be solved; a broad scope of materials on many reading levels; and adequate equipment for comfortable reading. For the student using braille, the reading surface should be flat, of sufficient size to support his book, and no higher than his elbow level when seated. For the reader of print the surface should be adjustable to obtain sufficient height and an adequate angle in order that he may maintain comfortable posture while securing the best distance and light for his work.

For the sighted reader *good mechanics* include effective eye movements, the use of a marker if necessary to assist in focusing, and the skillful use of any advantageous magnification. The braille reader should have fingers lightly curved to allow contact with the full depth of the braille line. His hands should move with a light touch in a fairly smooth left-to-right sweep, with few regressive and scrubbing motions. In general, an independent yet coordinated function of the hands is typical of the fastest braille readers. As the right hand completes a line, the left moves to the next line and begins reading while the right hand returns to meet it. At the end of a page the left hand completes the final line while the right hand reaches to turn the page. Reading is most frequently accomplished by the index fingers or the first two fingers on each hand. Other fingers usually rest on the line and serve to check and to help maintain position.

Certainly an adequate *knowledge of the reading code* is essential. Print readers must learn to discriminate between similar letters. Braille readers must develop skill in rapid recognition of the configurations and rapid association of full spelling with each contracted form.

Motivation is a prime factor. In some of the studies conducted by Nolan and Kederis (1969) motivation alone produced rate increases of as much as 33% without any significant loss in comprehension. Interest and purpose provide motivation. Records kept on the results of timed tests and exercises stimulate interest in self-growth.

Diagnosis and Evaluation

Constant diagnosis and evaluation are essential to any sequential developmental program. Through this approach continuity can be provided for each student. Needs are analyzed and individual adjustments made to meet those needs. Remediation becomes an integral part of the regular reading program.

For group use, the Stanford Achievement Tests, Diagnostic Reading Test, and Sequential Test of Educational Progress are available in both braille and large type. For individual diagnosis, Gray's Standardized Oral Reading Paragraphs are available in braille. Although not commercially available in type adequate for use with visually handicapped children, batteries such as the Spache Diagnostic Scales that include measures for vocabulary, listening comprehension, oral and silent reading, and phonic skills are quite useful. Many reading programs have internalized diagnostic measures that can be transcribed. The Colorado Braille Battery has been used as a group test to make some assessment of accuracy in braille character recognition.

The administration and scoring of a test is not sufficient for diagnostic purposes. The student's responses must be analyzed to determine areas of strength or weakness. Errors must be studied to ascertain the type and the cause. The student's program must be adjusted to care for his specific needs.

Classes for the visually handicapped are usually sufficiently small in number so that the teacher may administer individual diagnostic measures. Oral reading from the textbooks can be used for this purpose. As the student reads orally, the teacher may record every error by indicating the word as the child calls it and later analyze these to determine their type and cause. The student may be given a list of words to read orally, attempting to work out orally any words that are unfamiliar. Weak points in his character recognition and use of phonetics should be recorded and analyzed.

The teacher should take advantage of the interdisciplinary approach to the analysis and remediation of reading difficulties. He must rely upon the medical profession for diagnosis and prescription for eye conditions and general health status. The teacher may detect signs of asthenopia that may be symptomatic of such conditions as hyperopia, hyperopic astigmatism, muscular heterophoria, or aniseikonia. Frequently, following referral, such refractive and motility errors can be successfully eliminated as causes of reading disability.

Vail (1959) suggests that reading disability is often erroneously attributed to visual problems when some type of learning disorder is the true cause. Bateman (1963) found that children with mild refractive errors were among the lowest achievers in her study of the partially seeing, which suggests confirmation of Vail's claim. The teacher must plan a thorough diagnosis to discover and treat the true cause of the difficulty for these cases.

Dyslexia represents a word-recognition disability so extreme that it has been termed "word blindness." The behavior pattern includes the inability to make association between sound and the letter form, inadequate retention of detail in visual memory, and frequent letter reversals. Although the term "dyslexia" implies a neurological dysfunctioning, similar symptoms may have educational and emotional etiology. A multisensory, aural–visual–kinesthetic approach, emphasizing direction and detail through tracing and writing is often prescribed.

Smith (1969), in the conference report of the International Reading Association, pictures the teacher of the future as a skilled diagnostician acquainted with a wide variety of materials as well as with many sources of materials; adept at operating many types of technological learning media; utilizing the skill of all types of specialists; and able to direct the services of unskilled aides in order to secure the best individualized learning program for each child.

Determining the Medium

The school has the responsibility for helping each student to assess his various receptive channels, maximize his skill in the use of each channel, and exercise wise discrimination in selecting the media most efficient for his various purposes.

Braille or Print

For the child with a low degree of visual acuity the question arises whether he should use print or braille as his major graphic medium. Certainly, every child with any residual vision should not only be encouraged to use it, but should receive training in its most effective use. However, braille may be this child's most efficient reading tool. There is no demarcation point in visual acuity that determines the child's mode of reading. There are several factors that may affect the choice:

What is his near visual acuity? The child's record may state only his far vision acuity, which is no indication of his visual efficiency at reading distance. A report of measured near vision can be requested from the ophthalmologist or optometrist.

What does observation reveal about his visual efficiency? The best clue to the child's reading medium is derived from the teacher's observation of his daily functioning. During the readiness period many games and activities can be designed to help the teacher determine at what distance and with what clarity the child sees details of objects and pictures. If more than one teacher works with the child, a staff conference is advisable in making the decision, in order to ensure consistency and continuity in the child's program. The same is true if there should arise any question concerning a possible change in medium during his years in school.

How does he rank in general ability? Some students who are above average in ability may find both braille and ink print useful media. Although a person may be able to accomplish his personal reading by holding his book very close to his eyes, he may find that he can take notes more rapidly and write more extensively by using braille. When he wishes to read or speak from notes in public, he can maintain better posture and a more pleasing appearance if he is using braille efficiently. On the other hand, the child who ranks toward the lower level of the scale in general ability will probably have very little life need for braille. In most cases this child should concentrate on optimum use of print, even if he has only a small degree of vision.

What will be the psychological effect if the student must later change his medium? If, after all other factors are weighed, there is still doubt concerning the child's best medium, consideration may be given to the effect of a possible shift in mode of reading at a later period. The child who finds it necessary to change from print to braille often loses a year in his academic progress. The child who changes from braille to print can usually make the transfer with greater facility and without interruption to his program. Psychologically, the change from braille to print is a success experience for the child, whereas the necessary shift from print to braille is often regarded as a failure experience.

Auding or Reading

As the visually handicapped student progresses, he is faced with the need to make wise selections between aural and graphic channels. During the elementary years the emphasis is placed upon the development of optimum reading skills. The use of supplementary recorded materials is guided by the teacher. By the time the student is in secondary school he must be led to establish standards for his own selectivity in the use of aural and graphic channels. In high school, in college, and as an adult the person who is blind or who has very low visual acuity may find it effective to depend extensively on recorded materials and live reader service. However, he should not neglect his reading skills.

Nolan (1966) found that intake through listening required only about one-third of the time necessary for tactual reading and that comprehension remained stable. Some studies have been conducted to determine the role of compressed speech in improving listening efficiency. Foulke et al. (1962) and Orr, Friedman, and Williams (1965) found that students could comprehend speech at rates of 275 wpm and in some instances at even higher speeds. This area of rapid speech needs further research. It has not yet been extensively applied to educational programs, but it seems to hold promise.

SPEAKING

Spoken language is an essential constituent of human growth and development. Speech is vital to the child's development of a sense of identity. Language may be thought of in terms of a sequence in which the first stage is direct sensory experience—hearing, seeing, tasting, smelling, feeling. This is followed by a stage in which there is comprehension. A child understands and follows the simple speech of others. Later the child differentiates his own speech sounds and so becomes able to talk with others. By the time he enters school he has a fairly good command of speech.

Speaking is the manipulation of sound symbols. These sound patterns are learned through imitation. Accurate articulation depends on the physical development of the mouth, tongue, teeth, lips, and vocal cords. Since there is a general articulatory developmental sequence, the child may not form all sounds correctly until he is 7 or 8 years old. In general, children express ideas in one- or two-word sentences by the age of 18 months and use sentences of about five words by the time they are of kindergarten age. As is true in any developmental pattern, the timing varies with the individual.

Speech Defects

Speech deviations may be somewhat more frequent among children who are blind than among those who are sighted, although research is not in full agreement on this point. Stinchfield in 1928 reported that 49% of students at Perkins and Overbrook residential schools for the blind evidenced speech problems. In 1958 Rowe surveyed visually handicapped children in northern

California and found that 6.7% would benefit from speech therapy. Miner (1963) surveyed 293 pupils classified as blind from the Michigan and Iowa residential schools and found 33.8% with some speech deviation. About 74% of these problems were articulatory. There was no significant difference in the magnitude of the problem between the totally blind and those children who had some remaining vision.

The child without sufficient vision to observe lip movement and facial expression has only the auditory pattern as a basis for his imitation. This limitation may result in faulty reproduction. It may be necessary for the child at some time to examine tactually and seek to imitate the lip formation, sound placement, and facial expression of one who is speaking to him.

The help of the speech therapist should be enlisted in the diagnosis and remediation of speech difficulties. The school staff must cooperate to correct faulty pronunciation and enunciation, as well as to stimulate creative thinking and vivid expression. It is important that the student learn to face the person to whom he is speaking and to maintain a relaxed but alert posture and expressive features. He must exercise control over voice volume, tone, and quality. He must observe socially acceptable patterns of speech. His ability in language will undergird his entire academic program. A courteous manner and pleasing, well-modulated, accurate speech will prove to be powerful assets to the visually handicapped person.

Motivation

The motivation for communication comes from within. It probably arises with the first vague awareness of some need. Need satisfaction is a constant stimulating factor. If the overconcerned parent anticipates and supplies every need, the child's language development may be delayed.

The child's growth in oral language is enhanced by the feedback that he receives. The adult enthusiasm over first attempts to talk is a strong motivation factor. However, if tension over the presence of the handicapping condition makes it impossible for the parent to enjoy his child and react normally to him, the child may not receive the feedback conducive to language growth.

The production of speech sounds is simply a physiological process. Words are mere sound patterns. If language is to have meaning, words must be filled with the ingredients of concepts, thoughts, ideas, emotions. Thought emerges from experience. Rich experiences and rich language growth go hand in hand. If the child's visual horizon is severely restricted, a number of experiences must be brought within the area of his sensory perception. Motivation must be provided to stimulate initiative and to develop the ability to move about and seek out new experiences. It must be remembered that it is difficult to discern how much the partially sighted child sees. He may miss out on many actions that are ordinarily observed from a distance.

Verbalism

Some authorities have identified verbalism as a trait common among people who are blind. Verbalism is merely the manipulation of empty words or those with very meager ingredients and few if any associative links. Everyone engages in verbalism to some degree. For example, every sighted person who employs the symbol "blind" is engaging in some verbalism, since no sighted individual can realize all of the experiential ingredients of total congenital blindness. Perhaps this degree of verbalism explains some of the faulty generalizations assigned to "the blind."

The handicapped child who has been sheltered from experience will have a meager supply of data processed within his brain. There will be relatively few capsules, a number of which will be inadequately filled and have few connecting links. The absence of capsules results in general retardation; inadequately filled capsules result in verbalism. Unless the child is provided with a rich environment and is guided in developing an adequate data network, verbalism may become a serious problem for him.

Cutsforth (1951) attributes much of the verbalism among the blind to educational programs which stress the visual qualities of experiences. For example, the child has had several objects described to him as *red*. He learns to manipulate this symbol linked to the symbols for the various objects. For him, there is no ingredient in this capsule *red* related to the visual quality.

However, *red* may not be an entirely empty shell. A little girl may have a favorite doll which has been frequently referred to as the doll with the red dress. For her, although the symbol *red* contains no visual ingredient, it does connote a feeling of pleasure derived from its linkage with the favorite doll. When this child uses *red* she is not engaging in pure verbalism. There is some element of experience within the symbol. However, the symbol is for her a faulty tool for communication because the elements stored by her brain digress too far from the ingredients stored by the brain that has been stimulated by sight. If this same child is given some red cinnamon candy that she finds disagreeable because it burns her mouth, her previous ingredient for *red* has been contradicted; the shell is emptied, or there is confusion.

If the child without vision continuously hears objects described in terms of color, his brain processes these associations as important linkages, even though for him one shell is empty. He may even begin to ask the color of objects. Such inquiry may erroneously be interpreted as genuine interest in color, whereas his real interest is in conformity. He has discovered that there is a very important set of symbols all linked to another symbol, *color*. Although these symbols represent elements that he cannot discern for himself, he can ask about them and pattern his symbology after that of his associates.

Harley (1963) found verbalism more often a product of paucity of firsthand experience than of imposed visual terminology. However, Dokecki (1966) points out that an educational program entirely dependent on firsthand experiences would indeed be impoverished. He suggests that there has been too much concern over verbalism.

Most individuals adopt symbolic patterns that contain some shells that are almost empty. Fairly good examples of this procedure can be found in some doctoral theses. A certain degree of verbalism is not harmful for the child who is blind. In fact, some of it does serve a useful purpose as he communicates in a sighted world. As long as the child's data network has many well-filled capsules with many meaningful linkages, he can incorporate a number of very shallow or empty capsules without damage. Danger exists when the network contains too large a proportion of shallow or empty shells. The child then loses the concept that language is a symbolic representation of reality. The speech pattern becomes verbalism. The child may have the ability to manipulate symbols well in a very acceptable oral pattern. He may read symbols with fluency, but there is no meaning; he is merely juggling empty shells. When language becomes meaningless, the child's self-concept fails to develop adequately and he may become emotionally ill.

The school must assist the student in developing a rich and meaningful vocabulary from a variety of stimulating experiences. Education should result in the addition of a maximum number of well-filled capsules within the data network of the brain. An intricate meshing of associated links should be established.

The spoken word, as never before, wields nationwide and even worldwide power. Words that a few years ago would have influenced an audience of several hundred people may now reach hundreds of thousands. McClellan (1969) states that in 1970 it is theoretically possible with all of the communication satellites for one man to speak to, and be seen by, six billion people. Theoretically, a laser beam the size of a pencil can transmit a million TV conversations at one time.

Society today challenges the schools to produce citizens possessing a vast storehouse of words, with the ability to select them wisely and speak them effectively and with the motivation to use them to strengthen mankind socially, economically, and spiritually.

WRITING

Written expression is a natural outgrowth from oral expression. Through his initial reading experiences the child learns that reading is "talk" written down. The next step is the natural desire to write his own thoughts. He must learn the operation of his writing tools, the formation of the graphic symbols for sounds, and the use of spacing and punctuation to represent the timing, pause, and inflection of oral speech.

Mechanics

For the child with partial vision, pencils that make a heavy black stroke are provided. Widely lined paper with a dull finish is used. Many children need extensive practice in correct letter formation, especially in relation to the position above or below the line of writing. Manuscript writing is usually easier than cursive. Even after cursive writing has been learned, many partially sighted people prefer manuscript for their personal use.

The child who ordinarily uses braille will, at some time during his school program, want to gain sufficient skill in handwriting to sign his own name and make brief notations. Letters can be formed in some manner that can be perceived tactually—such as with string, wire, or modeling clay. Engraved cards or boards may be used. The child can trace the grooves to get the kinesthetic pattern of the letter formation. Cursive writing will probably be easier for this child. The kinesthetic fluency of the uninterrupted pattern seems easier to learn than the isolated manuscript form.

For the student who uses braille, the mechanical braillewriter is his first tool, because this machine requires less muscular coordination than does the hand slate and stylus. The machine has seven keys along a horizontal plane. The large central key, operated by either thumb, is used to space between words. The three keys to the left, beginning with the one next to the central key, form dots one, two, and three, and are operated by the left index finger, middle finger, and third finger, respectively. The three keys to the right beginning next to the central key form dots four, five, and six, and are operated by the index, middle, and third finger of the right hand, respectively. On the Perkins Brailler, which is the one most commonly used, a round key to the right performs the function of back spacing, and a round key to the left positions the paper on a new writing line. All of the keys needed to form the desired braille symbol must be depressed simultaneously. The machine embosses the symbol in the correct reading position, where it can be checked immediately.

The standard Perkins Brailler is available with an adapter so that it may be operated by a person who has the use of only one hand. A Perkins Brailler may also be adapted for the reader who wishes to take notes. Extension keys may be attached to make it possible to span the keyboard with one hand while the other hand is used for reading.

For speed and accuracy in writing with a brailler, correct fingering is essential and should be encouraged throughout the school program. With the mechanical writer a braillist can produce about 15 pages an hour.

The most portable and least expensive braille writing tool is the hand slate and stylus. This equipment consists of a hinged metal or plastic frame into which the paper is clamped. The back section of the frame contains a series of braille cells, in each of which there are six depressions positioned to correspond to the dots in the cell. The front section contains a series of windows. Around the edge of each window are demarcations indicating the correct position for each of the dots. The person, using an awl-like stylus, presses the dots through from the back to the front of the paper. Writing begins at the right and proceeds to the left.

In the initial presentation of the braille characters, the teacher should be sure that one form is well established prior to the introduction of its mirror image. Thus, interference to learning is reduced.

This writer has found very effective results if the child, during the initial stages of symbol formation on the braillewriter, is taught to verbalize the dot numbers as he depresses the keys. Through this process his learning is reinforced by the simultaneous verbal and kinesthetic impressions, followed immediately by the tactual stimulus as he checks his work. If the child establishes this automatic association of dot numbers with braille configurations, he has little difficulty when he later learns to use the slate and stylus. He is told that, as he approaches the cell, the first dots are one, two, and three and that on the second side of the cell the dots are four, five, and six. Concentration on dot numbers as his guide establishes his new direction without any thought of reversed patterns.

Lowenfeld et al. (1969) suggest that the new direction can be established through practice in the formation of dot configurations not associated with letter names. Bourgeault (1969) feels that the kinesthetic image is sufficient, and that the learning of dot numbers is wasteful. There is no available research to support any one of these proposals.

Creative Writing

The mechanics of writing have been discussed extensively. However, the teacher must not lose sight of the fact that expression is the primary purpose for writing. Correct form and correct use of contractions are important, but they should never be stressed to the extent that they restrict or stultify creative thinking. Before the child has developed skill in writing, he may dictate his story to a scribe or record it on tape for someone else to copy. At all levels throughout the school program there should be periods when the only aim of writing is the expression of thoughts and feelings about some experience or topic of intense interest. Expression flows creatively. No criticism is made of form. There will be periods at other times for developing the mechanical skills, and emphasis will then be placed upon correct form.

If the child without vision is encouraged to process into his data network symbols filled with the rich ingredients of tactual, aural, kinesthetic, and olfactory perception, he may some day engage in creative writing that will add to our heritage of beautiful prose and poetry.

SPELLING

Braille readers, in general, are not very proficient in spelling. Whether or not they are less proficient than sighted people is a debatable question. The braille reader has fewer contacts with the graphic forms of words than does the sighted reader. His everyday world is not saturated with graphic symbols. He reads less extensively because he reads more slowly and because, even in his school program, far less material is available to him. Therefore, he may not have the mental image of the graphic form to aid him in his spelling.

There are certain teaching procedures that will help to ensure more skill in spelling. Teachers may increase the student's contact with words by providing vocabulary lists to accompany class discussions, recorded materials, and items in current news. They should encourage curiosity about the spelling of words so that the student assumes the responsibility for asking about new words.

Accurate articulation contributes to accurate spelling. Inasmuch as the child with low vision depends on the aural pattern, training in auditory discrimination is important. Speech patterns are learned through imitation. The teacher's speech must be exemplary. Oral spelling should be stressed in the primary grades. The contracted form of the braille code need not prove a stumbling block in spelling. If the language arts program includes a sequential plan for developing a knowledge of, and insight into, the structure of the code, good spelling habits can be developed.

Teachers must be sufficiently adept in their own use of braille to promote high standards of accuracy. They should provide the student with flawless copy. Through insightful instruction they should help the child to become proficient in the use of the braille code. Through careful checking of daily work, they should give the student constant reinforcement in strengthening habits of accuracy.

Early introduction of typing strengthens skill in spelling because it requires the full spelling of words. The typewriter provides the one means by which the braille reader communicates freely with sighted people. Typing is an essential skill for the visually handicapped person. The student should become so proficient in the operation of the typewriter and so familiar with acceptable forms that the mechanics do not inhibit his free expression of thought.

Authorities are not in full agreement concerning the grade level at which typing should be introduced. Mental development, muscle control, and coordination are important readiness factors. Cohoe (1960) reports:

Detroit's special teachers have found that the great majority of pupils are ready to learn typing when they reach the fourth grade. Some children in the third grade are ready and a few cannot type successfully before entering the fifth [p. 1].

Cohoe's program with its recorded lessons is designed for this early introduction of the skill.

SOURCES OF MATERIAL

The production of materials in braille and in large type is a costly and time-consuming process. Therefore, in comparison to the resources in regular print available to the sighted child, there is a dearth in these materials. The Federal government alleviates some of the expense on the local level through Aid to Blind School Children. Each local school system annually registers with the American Printing House for the Blind in Louisville, Kentucky, every pupil who falls within the legal definition of blindness. Annually Congress votes an appropriation to the American Printing House. The local school system may then order supplies on its quota account, which is determined on the basis of the number of blind children registered.

Some private agencies may subsidize a portion of the production cost of certain materials. However, when one copy of a reading book with its accompanying workbook costs over $30 in braille and $28 in large type, a single copy of an arithmetic text in braille costs about $40, a single copy of a science text with its accompanying student guide costs $135, and each braillewriter costs $100, it is easy to understand that schools have difficulty supplying a great variety of materials.

Neither the quantity nor the variety of materials in braille and large type is comparable to print supplies. Fewer than 700 titles were reported produced in braille during a recent year when, according to the *World Almanac,* there were 28,500 new titles in print.

Braille pages are embossed on zinc plates. A braillist can produce about 50 correct plates per day. The average book requires at least 100 hours of brailling time. Not only is the actual production of braille comparatively slow but, inasmuch as most braille publications parallel the ink-print copy, the print book is often on the market before the brailling begins.

Since the American Printing House for the Blind has computerized a portion of its production process, the time gap is not quite so great. Some publishers agree to let the Printing House have their compositor tapes, thus permitting braille production to begin before the original print copy is available in book form.

The American Printing House produces approximately 75% of the press braille in the United States. The Braille Institute of America in Los Angeles, California, Clovernook Printing House in Cincinnati, Ohio, and Howe Memorial Press in Watertown, Massachusetts also print braille books. There are about 20 agencies that supply braille material of some nature.

Stanwix House in Pennsylvania and the American Printing House for the Blind in Kentucky are the leading producers of material in large type. However, other publishers are beginning to enter the field of large type production.

In order to increase the supply of current educational materials, teachers must produce many of their own resources or depend on trained volunteer transcribers. As more visually handicapped students enroll in day-school programs and need single copies of texts paralleling those used by their sighted classmates, there is a growing demand for volunteers to produce both braille and large type. The National Braille Association, a group of volunteer transcribers and others interested in the production of braille, now numbers well over 2,500 in membership. Teachers from a school system or other qualified instructors may train these transcribers. The Library of Congress offers free correspondence courses for those desiring to become braille transcribers.

From an original clear braille copy, duplicates can be reproduced on a special kind of plastic sheet by means of a vacuum process on a machine known as a Thermoform. The National Braille Assocation maintains a book bank which is a storage center for college and technical materials. It also cooperates in the maintenance of a Central Catalog, housed at the American Printing House for the Blind, which contains a record of all texts that have been or are being hand transcribed. The Library of Congress keeps a corresponding record of all literary materials. Thus, an individual may discover the sources of original copies that may be reproduced in Thermoform or otherwise used.

Some materials are available on library loan. The Library of Congress, through its Division for the Blind and Physically Handicapped and through the network of regional libraries, offers services to the visually handicapped. Not only books and periodicals, but also tapes and talking book disks may be borrowed by mail, postage free. The disks may be played on a regular record player, or a talking book machine may be borrowed through a local rehabilitation center.

Some organizations offer individualized services. Recordings for the Blind in New York offers volunteer service for recording designated texts on disks. The National Braille Press in Boston offers volunteer service to record needed college textbooks on tapes for individuals. There are many excellent recorded resources now available to anyone through regular commercial channels.

One of the latest innovations in the provision of materials is the national network of Instructional Materials Centers. Three of these—located at the American Printing House, the University of Illinois, and Michigan State University—serve the visually handicapped. These centers are established for the purposes of experimentation, evaluation of materials, production of new instructional aids, and dissemination of information.

There is currently on the market an electric braile typewriter manufactured by IBM. It is hoped that this machine is indicative of more experimentation related to new writing equipment. The standard typewriter keyboard is employed, with the shift positions being utilized for the various braille contractions. No shift is necessary for the purpose of capitalization in the braille code. Inasmuch as all of the letters and punctuation symbols are in the standard position, a typist with no knowledge of the braille code can produce accurate braille in full spelling. Knowledge of the rules governing the use of braille contractions is necessary for full use of the machine. Perhaps the greatest disadvantage of the machine is that the keys strike the back of the paper, so that the embossing is produced on the underside and cannot be read until the line of writing emerges from behind the roller.

The American Foundation for the Blind makes available a series of leaflets, *Sources of Reading Materials for the Visually Handicapped,* prepared by its Publications Divison. This series includes lists of libraries and reference services; sources of various types of educational and recreational reading materials; names and addresses of publishers of books and periodicals in braille, large type, talking book, and tape; reference services; etc. It constitutes the most complete informational resource for teachers and users of such material.

SUMMARY

While considering the content of this chapter, the reader has no doubt frequently made the mental note that most of it is applicable to sighted children as well. Such comment emphasizes the fact that there are many more similarities than there are differences between the sighted and visually handicapped individual. Both have the same basic needs, rights, and responsibilities, as well as the basic potentiality for fulfillment. For both, the primary step in the communicative process, cognition, is similar. Deviations exist in the sensory input channels which necessitate adjustments in the communicative media.

Although in the communicative process for the sighted and the visually handicapped similarities far outweigh differences, there are four vital aspects that must be considered in planning the educational program for students with little or no sight. (1) The school must enrich the core of communication by stimulating incentive and initiative and by offering guidance in increasing the quantity and enhancing the quality of meaningful experiences. (2) The educational program must guide the student in a realistic appraisal of his communicative media—aural or graphic, visual or tactual—in order that he may appreciate his strenghts and select the most effective medium for his purpose. (3) Techniques of the teaching–learning process must be adjusted on the basis of the perceptual factors involved in symbol recognition during the receptive act and the mechanical skills involved in symbol production during the expressive act. Symbols are mere tools, but they may help or hinder the communicative process. Therefore, the school must meet the student's unique needs in achieving the skillful use of his symbols. (4) Above all else, the educational program must be one through which the individual develops a positive self-concept and self-motivation. It must open doorways and guide the visually handicapped student upon the threshold of a life in which he will be not only self-supporting but also self-contributing to a society demanding expanded knowledge, technical skill, moral values, and spiritual strength.

REFERENCES

Ashcroft, S. C. Errors of oral reading of braille at elementary grade levels. *Report of proceedings of conference on research needs in braille.* New York: American Foundation for the Blind, 1961. Pp. 16-31.

Barraga, N. *Increased visual behavior in low-vision children.* New York: American Foundation for the Blind, 1964.

Bateman, B. *Reading and psycholinguistic processes of partially seeing children.* Washington, D.C.: Council for Exceptional Children, Monograph Series A, No. 5, 1963.

Bourgeault, S. E. *The language arts.* American Foundation for Overseas Blind, Far East Regional Office, 193 Jalan Abdul Samad, Kuala, Malaysia, 1969.

Chall, J. S. *Learning to read: The great debate.* New York: McGraw-Hill, 1967.

Cohoe, E. (Ed.). *Typewriting for partially seeing and blind pupils.* Detroit: Public Schools Publication 5-344 TCH, 1960.

Cutsforth, T. D. *The blind in school and society.* New York: American Foundation for the Blind, 1951.

Dokecki, P. R. Verbalism and the blind, a critical view of the concepts and the literature. *Exceptional Children,* 1966, **32,** 525–530.

Foulke, E., Amster, C. H. , Nolan, C. Y., & Bixler, R. H. The comprehension of rapid speech by the blind. *Exceptional Children,* 1962, **29,** 134–141.

French, R. S. *From Homer to Helen Keller.* New York: American Foundation for the Blind, 1932.

Harley, R. K. *Verbalism among blind children.* New York: American Foundation for the Blind, 1963.

Hartlage, L. C. Differences in listening comprehension of the blind and the sighted. *International Journal of Education for the Blind,* 1963, **13,** 1–6.

Hayes, S. P. *Contributions to a psychology of blindness.* New York: American Foundation for the Blind, 1941.

Irwin, R. B. *As I saw it.* New York: American Foundation for the Blind, 1955.

Lowenfeld, B., Abel, G. L., & Hatlen, P. H. *Blind children learn to read.* Springfield, Ill.: Charles C Thomas, 1969.

McClellan, A. *The new times.* Nashville, Tenn.: Broadman Press, 1969.

Miner, L. E. A study of the incidence of speech deviation among visually handicapped children. *Outlook for the Blind,* 1963, **57,** 10–14.

Nolan, C. Y. *Reading and listening in learning by the blind: Progress report.* Louisville, Ky.: American Printing House for the Blind, 1966.

Nolan, C. Y., & Kederis, C. J. *Perceptual factors in braille word recognition.* New York: American Foundation for the Blind, 1969.

Orr, D., Friedman, H., & Williams, J. Trainability of listening comprehension of speeded discourse. *Journal of Educational Psychology,* 1965, **56,** 148–156.

Rankin, P. T. Listening ability: Its importance, measurement and development. *Chicago School Journal,* 1930, **12,** 117–179.

Rowe, E. D. *Speech problems of blind children: A Survey of the north California area.* New York: American Foundation for the Blind, 1958.

Smith, M. Measurement of the size of general English vocabulary through the elementary grades and high school. *Genetic Psychology Monograph,* 1941, **24,** 313–45.

Smith, N. B. Readiness for reading, II. *Elementary English,* 1950, **27,** 91–106.

Smith, N. B. (Ed.). *A forward look.* Newark, Del.: International Reading Association, 1969.

Stinchfield, S. M. *Speech pathology with methods in speech correction.* Boston, Mass.: Expression Company, Publishers, 1928.

Taylor, E. A. The spans: Perception, apprehension, and recognition. *American Journal of Ophthalmology,* 1957, **44,** 501–507.

Vail, D. *The truth about your eyes* (2nd ed.). New York: Farrar, Straus & Cudahy, 1959.

CHAPTER 8

Special Subject Adjustments and Skills

Grace D. Napier

The University of Northern Colorado
Greeley, Colorado

GENERAL ORIENTATION

This chapter deals with educational materials, curricula, course content, and methodology as they apply to special subject adjustments and acquisition of skills by students with visual handicaps. Special subject areas treated include mathematics, social science, science, music, foreign language, home economics, arts and crafts, physical education, and recreation. For a discussion of language arts, see Chapter 7.

Educational Materials

Educational materials employed with visually handicapped students fall into the following classifications.

1. Materials that are usable in the original form of the product (such as beads and blocks for stringing and counting).
2. Materials that require some modification or adaptation (such as braille wristwatch for touch reading).

3. Materials that have been designed and manufactured specifically for the visually handicapped (such as a variety of arithmetic slates, the Perkins Brailler, and enlarged print maps for the partially seeing).
4. Materials that provide substitute experiences for the visually handicapped (such as realia and models instead of pictures).

Models and Realia

Items classified as *realia* are to be preferred to *models*, when feasible. For example, a genuine screwdriver or ski (realia) is far more effective in teaching a concept than a toy screwdriver or ski. A *model*, on the other hand, is not the real thing itself but a three-demensional representation of it in modified size, texture, ability to operate, etc. Realistically, models of some objects are the only tangibles accessible to children who do not see. Models function to arouse awareness and to build comprehension of the physical environment. They must be accurate in detail and proportion in order to communicate correct information. They help to acquaint visually handicapped children with real things that are inaccessible because of inappropriate size, distance, or inherent danger (Lowenfeld, 1950).

Manipulative Devices

Sometimes manipulative devices might be things other than models and realia. For instance, in number work children gain a great deal in learning from handling objects for the purpose of simple enumeration grouping, outside the reading of textbooks or even before textbooks are introduced. Therefore, having various kinds of articles incorporated into the lesson facilitates cognitive processes. Such items might include common and inexpensive materials such as plastic spoons or large safety pins. Variety from day to day adds new interest for children though basic arithmetic facts are the same.

In the routine of classroom living, children can be afforded opportunities to use standard equipment such as staplers and paper cutters. Such experiences may result in two major benefits: (1) knowledge about and skill in using the device; (2) two-hand dexterity or coordination.

Curriculum

Curriculum "is the total experiences a learner has under the supervision of the school" (Smith, Krouse, & Atkinson, 1961, p. 969). Curriculum organization "is the method by which the best possible learning experiences and instruction are offered to a child throughout his school career" (Smith *et al.,* 1961, p. 385). When selecting a combination of knowledges and skills to be taught, educators must bear in mind needs common to all children and needs peculiar to children with visual disabilities.

Provision of information to familiarize students with their cultural heritage, to make products of schools employable, and to equip individuals to cope successfully with routine problems and responsibilities of living in human society are just a few of the basic justifications for educational programs and for requiring compulsory attendance by children. In type and quality, educational offerings should be commensurate with individual ability to learn and potential to apply what has been learned in meaningful, constructive, and contributory ways. Two American philosophies further supporting public school systems are

1. The state assumes responsibility for educating *all* the children of all the citizenry. This, then, includes visually handicapped children.
2. Education, though expensive, is less costly than total or even partial maintenance of the individual by the state for the remainder of his life. For reasons of human dignity, self-esteem, and mental health, supporting oneself is to be encouraged. Adequate and appropriate education constitutes preparation for and realization of that goal in adulthood.

Implicit in the latter philosophy is provision of educational programs to meet specific needs found in intellectually gifted or mentally slow youngsters, as well as those with physical or emotional differences. Visually handicapped children have the *same* needs as their seeing peers, though learning execution may differ. The major areas of need for both groups are academic competencies, self-care, and social skills (Shults, 1957), freedom of movement and independence, preparation for employment and placement on the job, recreation outlets, and family membership. Normally seeing and visually handicapped individuals execute some tasks in the same ways, while other tasks are done differently. For example, almost all children learn to write; both groups spell words in identical fashion, but seeing children use pencil or pen while visually handicapped children use braille writer, slate and stylus, or typewriter. Carefully organized curricula are sensitive both to restrictions or problems caused by visual handicaps and to realistic potentialities of the individual in spite of his visual loss (Olsen, 1963).

Content

Content deals with the *what* to teach at a given point in time according to the learner's level of readiness and maturity. The teaching–learning process begins with the child's sensorimotor–kinesthetic self and moves outward to encompass the abstract. The goal must be achievement of genuine comprehension, not merely rote memory of prescribed words devoid of meaning for the child. In keeping with reality, selection of specifics to be learned constitutes

wholesale adoption, adaptation, substitution, and deletion when the content
has first been geared for normally seeing learners. When these four processes
do not entirely meet the needs of visually handicapped children, additional
material may supplement the content.

Each child learns first from within himself or with himself and then moves
to the environment outside himself. However, normally seeing children have
one more aspect of the self—namely, vision—through which and with which
to learn. Visually handicapped children have little or no assistance in learning
from the visual self. Because vision is not a primary channel for these children,
the remaining senses and motor-kinesthetic avenues must be employed to
facilitate learning. Effective teachers involve as many aspects as possible of the
child's total self, so that learning will be comprehensive, enduring, and functional, and so that the child learns how to learn.

Meanings of words must evolve from experiences or lead to the introduction
of new experiences. Teachers cannot entirely control—and should not want to
—words to be learned or experiences to be lived. Words and experiences are
interrelated.

Parts of the traditional content for normally seeing children, usable with the
visually handicapped, are augmented by specially created bodies of knowledge
and skills. Degrees of success will vary from child to child in keeping with
individual differences other than visual limitations. Visual handicaps will
neither guarantee success nor predetermine failure.

Methodology

Too often even the otherwise sophisticated ascribe differences to the methodology in teaching visually handicapped children when, in fact, the difference
lies in the realm of materials. For instance, when a blind child solves a long
division problem on one of the arithmetic slates used for arithmetic, he sets
down the numerals in the same format as seeing children. Although he is using
braille and a slate with cubes or type instead of paper and pencil, his method
of solution is the same as for seeing peers.

Methodology, therefore, refers to *how* to teach. A competent teacher uses
a variety of approaches, sometimes merely for variety's sake and often because
certain subject matter or concepts are more communicable via one method
than others. Many of the same methods are practicable with both normally
seeing and visually handicapped children. Consequently, when working with
visually handicapped students, teachers must be selective in their procedures.
Visual approaches must be supplemented with other information or experiences. The type of educational program used will, in large measure, dictate the
choice of method. Methods used at residential schools for the blind concern
themselves exclusively with children having limited or no vision, whereas

visually handicapped children educated in day programs with normally seeing peers are exposed to methods that at times are inappropriate for the handicapped individual though suitable for the group.

Although this text is directed to prospective teachers of visually handicapped children (Carpenter, 1969) and not to regular classroom teachers (Napier & Weishahn, 1970), special education teachers cannot divorce themselves from methodology practiced by the general educators who are responsible for much of the handicapped children's education. Special education teachers are usually called upon to suggest how classroom teachers might modify their methods because of the handicapped child's presence in the group. The following are only a few ideas that may help the regular teacher to feel more comfortable and qualified to teach a child with a visual disability (Napier, 1966–1967).

1. Use the child's name when you speak to him in a group situation so that he will be sure that your words are directed at him and not someone else.
2. In giving directions for the location of something—furniture, door, personal property—be certain that "left" and "right" are in relation to his body, not yours.
3. When writing on the chalkboard, say what you are writing word by word so that he can follow you mentally.
4. Because the blind child works with an itinerant teacher or perhaps in a one-to-one relationship with the resource room teacher, he may not have need in such situations to raise his hand to gain the teacher's attention or permission to speak. Therefore, if seeing children raise hands, the blind child may need to be told this so that he will not call out and seem disrespectful or uncooperative.

If the child has residual vision, certain visual methods may be workable provided that the material is close enough, large enough, or distinct enough for visual inspection by him. Other methods appropriate with visually handicapped children are the following.

1. Carefully selected and planned field trips (Crockett, 1958) that involve a multisensory, and not solely visual, experience. Teachers should take the trip themselves before taking their group of children so that all details can be determined and explored. In this way, teachers can then prepare children for the combination of experiences.
2. Oral–aural presentations—panels, discussions, lectures, questions and answers, dramatizations, guests, etc. Visually handicapped children can participate in listening and speaking situations with as much ease as seeing members of the group.
3. Manipulation of materials—tactual examination for size, texture, opera-

tion, detail, etc. This necessitates the utilization of realia and models to supplement or replace pictures.

4. Audiovisual aids—films, slides, television (Dunkin, 1962), maps, pictures, etc. These necessitate supplying adequate narration in terms of explanations, factual information, descriptions, comparisons, and contrasts to known relationships, etc.

5. Exhibits—in school corridors, museums, public libraries, laboratories, etc. Displays that are other than pictorial and that can be handled can be meaningful to visually handicapped youngsters. Pictures may be described and captions read to the handicapped children to convey some of the meaning.

6. Active participation instead of passive listening only—visually handicapped children can make a contribution to classroom and school activities by reporting information, role playing, and participating in show and tell, holiday programs, etc.

7. Reading—braille, large print, sound recording, human reader. Handicapped children should be expected to use reading in the same way as other children—to gain understanding, to paraphrase, to answer questions, to compare sources, to define terms, etc. Reading for visually handicapped students entails preparation on the part of teachers to ensure that needed materials will be available at the right moment or that reader service is accessible when assignments call for materials not otherwise readable by students themselves.

8. Research—reading for information, asking the right people questions, telephoning for needed information, visiting librarians, writing letters, etc. Research methods can be introduced even in the primary grades as long as children use techniques suitable to their competencies and maturity.

9. Small group demonstrations—(a) conducted by a few students, each with his role or responsibility so that the total effort constitutes a completed task; (b) conducted by a teacher for a small number of students with ample time and space for individual attention. If children can work at the same table with the teacher, handle items, and are not rushed, visually handicapped children can participate with meaning and learning.

10. Team approach—in art, science, home economics, industrial arts, physical education, musical group performance, etc. In these situations the visually handicapped student has a seeing partner and the two share the task to be completed. In a science laboratory, the seeing student uses the microscope and shares his knowledge with his partner. In art the blind child might make the plaster of paris piece and the seeing student paint it. In home economics the two might clean vegetables, with the blind

child cutting or scraping, while the seeing child looks for spots that have been missed or inspects for foreign matter, such as sand or worms in the lettuce.

Perhaps the biggest problem in selecting appropriate methods is not knowing in advance where children have gaps in experience or vocabulary because of blindness and its imposed limitations or because of overprotection. For instance, a simple task might include use of scissors, although use of scissors is not being taught as part of that lesson. At this moment the teacher discovers that the visually handicapped child does not know how to use scissors. Although timing may be somewhat delayed, follow-up lessons or exposures to a specific aspect can be provided. In brief, if the visually handicapped child can hear it, handle it, pace it off with hands or feet, smell it, taste it when feasible, and generally involve his total being, he can learn from it. When a teacher deliberately tries to teach more meaningfully because of the visually handicapped child in her group, she is usually teaching more meaningfully for the seeing children as well.

MATHEMATICS

Mathematics, as treated in this chapter, encompasses the content of the subject as encountered in elementary and secondary schools. It includes arithmetic (traditional and "modern"), algebra, calculus, trigonometry, and geometry (plane and solid).

Arithmetic

Arithmetic involves mastery of basic number facts and processes, and then, the combination of both facts and processes for problem solving and computation. The step-by-step progression in content from grade to grade throughout elementary school is the same for both seeing and visually handicapped pupils, whereas materials and methods are likely to be different.

Reasoning and Problem Solving

When seeing children enter kindergarten or first grade, they bring certain learning with them based on prior number experiences. Although acquired incidentally, this learning is not unimportant or trivial; rather, it is essential as foundation for formal teaching. Lacking this background, children cannot begin at the usual level, that is, kindergarten or first grade. Children who are visually handicapped before entering school have not had enough of the same kinds of incidental experiences and concepts as their seeing classmates. Even worse, some types may be completely absent. Consequently, these children function at a lower level of readiness and may need to have built into the arithmetic program number experiences that seeing children usually have encountered during preschool years. Visually handicapped children may come to school teachable and ready for formal instruction, provided content is in keeping with their meager background relative to numberness. Just as other programs have been established to prepare some children for school, a special program for visually handicapped preschool-age children might be designed to include the following.

1. Stimulation at home by a teacher grounded in early childhood education.
2. Counseling parents so that they are better able to provide an enriched home environment.
3. Enrollment in a nursery school for either visually handicapped or normally seeing children.
4. Enrollment in such facilities as Head Start.

Teachers must use tactual, manipulative, and auditory materials. Vicarious experiences should be kept to a minimum. If three plastic spoons are mounted on a card, this is an example of tactual material. If a box contains a generous supply of spoons, these represent manipulative material. If the teacher deliberately drops spoons one by one on a table top for counting purposes, they constitute auditory material. Tactual and manipulative materials are, in general, more appropriate for partially seeing children if brightly colored or in sharp contrast to the background area. If the desk or table top does not lend enough contrast to items being handled and counted, a sheet of colored construction paper on the desk top will provide the contrast desired for improved visibility.

If materials are mounted on cards or pages, having enough loose or unattached items of the same kind is important for other number activities. Mounted and bound materials have limited usefulness. If materials are mounted, avoid presenting them to children in the same position. For instance, threeness should not always be presented in this arrangement: X X X but in a variety such as: X X X X X X etc. Cards or unbound pages have more flexibility for teaching, because the teacher can use the card or page in one of four positions by rotating it to show four different arrangements.

These same cards, once prepared, may also be used in reading readiness activities to show similarities and differences, etc. The following are some suggestions.

1. When mounting spoons, put two with bowls on top and one with handle on top, or use two big spoons and one little spoon. Concepts involved are top and bottom as well as big and little.
2. When mounting three combs on a card, place two with teeth pointing to the right and one with teeth to the left, or small comb pointing to the left and big and small combs pointing to the right. Concepts involved are big and little, left and right.
3. When mounting buttons on a card, use two large ones and one small button, and a buckle and comb. Concepts illustrated include big and little, similarity and difference in initial sound of the words, and classification of function. (For further treatment of reading readiness, see Chapter 7.)

Whether in arithmetic or reading readiness, when introducing a different item, always take care to vary its location so that the child does not relate to location (which is always a secondary consideration) rather than to the primary concept intended.

Use of a magnetic board has three advantages:

1. The teacher can make arrangements for the child to examine without disrupting patterns.
2. Children can do independent work for the teacher to inspect later.
3. The board can be used on desk, table, or lap.

A compartmentalized box or tray affords the child a definite place in which to put counted objects. For example, the teacher might assign the child to place four bottle caps in each section. Independent seat work encourages children to work alone and without constant supervision by the teacher.

Stringing beads has application for arithmetic when the student is required to count and follow a prescribed pattern, such as one big bead and three little beads or one round bead and three square beads. Color differences should be used if the child can use color.

Before any child begins computation in written form in the abstract, he must have much practice in handling and counting objects in order to solve problems in the concrete. Sufficient time must be allowed for manipulation of numbers before undertaking manipulation of numerals. Teachers should avoid mechanistic approaches in arithmetic and strive for mastery of comprehension.

An approach to the physical world through arithmetic includes such factors as size (big or little), dimension (two or three), weight (heavy or light), length (long or short), width (thick or thin), temperature (hot or cold), etc. In short, these characteristics can be estimated, measured, and compared with assistance from available adapted equipment, such as clocks, foot rule, yardstick, scales, and thermometers.

Computation

Computational processes (Nolan & Bruce, 1962) can be either written or mental. Numerals are used in both instances. Written computation is for one of two purposes:

1. To arrive at an answer when one cannot accomplish the same end via mental approaches.
2. To communicate or demonstrate to someone else. The teacher communicates on the chalkboard, while students demonstrate in homework or tests.

Partially seeing children (Auerbach, 1959) use chalkboard or heavy pencil and heavy-lined paper. If duplicated sheets are distributed, partially seeing students should be supplied with sharp, clear copies. If the teacher demonstrates work on the chalkboard, she might have identical work previously prepared on paper in large, dark numerals as a desk copy for partially seeing children to follow as she explains. These children should be encouraged to come close to the board if necessary when the teacher explains something and a desk copy is not available. If the teacher gives individual help to a child, her writing on his paper should be with the kind of pencil he uses in order that it be legible to him. Heavy-lined paper is available for purchase or teachers can make their own. Working on teacher-made work sheets rather than from the textbook eliminates the possibility of making errors in transferring material from book to paper.

Writing Devices

For primary grade blind children, the Perkins Brailler and two types of cube slate are used. The Perkins Brailler is more suitable than other braillewriters, because with it rolling the paper up and down does not crush dots or cause the paper to become misaligned. Both cube slates are basically alike—cubes with six facets and a board with depressions into which the cubes fit. The main difference is in the size of the cubes. The larger cube is easier for small hands to manipulate, read, and place in the board. Because the cubes can be turned or rotated, the six facets accommodate nine digits and zero.

The cube slate and Perkins Brailler have advantages and disadvantages. The cube slate is suitable when the child stays at a desk or table to work, but not when he must carry it from place to place with completed work on it, because cubes turn easily in their holes or may spill out altogether. If work is done on the brailler, paper can be removed and carried; however, cubes can be used indefinitely, whereas paper must be replenished. Both brailler and cubes use braille symbols. The brailler is considerably more expensive than slate and cubes.

In addition, some students, especially in upper grades, are exposed to the

Taylor Arithmetic Type Slate. Although this device does not use braille, many blind individuals have found it to be a satisfactory tool for computation. Conversely, many educators frown on its use, because it imposes another written code. Realistically, many blind students may not be able to purchase the Perkins Brailler for use at home, whereas one of the slates would be within their means. Someday educational programs will supply students with necessary equipment for use at home as well as in the classroom.

Blind students should not be required to do arithmetic with slate and stylus. Aligning columns correctly is extremely difficult and time consuming (Waterhouse, 1955).

A type slate using print numerals has extremely limited usefulness. A youngster who has recently lost his vision and already knows print numerals but does not yet know braille symbols might employ this device. However, the numerals are rather small for touch reading.

Occasionally a teacher who cannot read braille requires the child to submit his work in typewritten form. The child has to be proficient in typewriting in order to comply. This necessitates the child's having first to compute on brailler or slate and then to copy his work on the typewriter. Typewriting arithmetic involves obvious difficulties: counting spaces for proper alignment is not easy, even for the sighted; the visually handicapped child is unable to read his own work; some needed symbols are not included in the standard keyboard, hence, seeing help must be enlisted to insert these signs or symbols. If the child typewrites only his answers, the teacher cannot determine where or how errors occurred and cannot remediate the situation.

Work sheets and desk copies in braille require advance planning by classroom teachers and excellent communication between them and special education teachers. Allowing visually handicapped children to confer (in a whisper) with a seeing neighbor is another way for handicapped children to follow their teachers' work on the chalkboard.

The Adapted Abacus

Increasing numbers of teachers and visually handicapped children are using the adapted abacus. It is small and lightweight for easy carrying and is relatively inexpensive. Beads do not slide so easily on the adapted abacus, in order to permit children's fingers to touch and read the beads without distorting the work. Manuals (Gissoni, 1964; Davidow, 1966) and summer workshops are available to help familiarize teachers with the correct use of the abacus.

Showing Complete Work or Using Short Cuts

Using braille or slate consumes more time than working with pencil or chalk. One timesaving technique is assigning the child only selected examples or problems rather than the entire lesson. Another shortcut is to ask for only answers. Then, when a given answer is incorrect, the child can be asked to do that problem again, showing the complete work.

Mental Arithmetic

Wherever possible, teachers should include mental arithmetic (Hussey & Legge, 1956) for fast and accurate computation without the crutch of writing. This is especially helpful to blind persons, who have need to compute but cannot always carry writing equipment with them. Sometimes the format in mental arithmetic is different from that in written computation. The justification for this difference is the elimination of so many numerals to remember from step to step. Once a new numeral has been derived, all previous steps can be discarded. The child then has only one numeral to remember from step to step. Some children find it helpful to write down only certain numerals along the way. Another technique used in mental arithmetic is that of working with rounded numerals initially and then adjusting the answer in keeping with the original problem. For instance, 128×5 might better be considered $130 \times 5 - 10$. In mental arithmetic procedures, computation generally begins with operation of big numerals, progressing toward digits. Compare the two solutions in the accompanying illustration.

Mental Format	Written Format
123	123
$\times 456$	$\times 456$
$400 \times 100 = 40000$	738
$400 \times 20 = +8000$	615
48000	$+492$
$400 \times 3 = +1200$	56088
49200	
$50 \times 100 = +5000$	
54200	
$50 \times 20 = +1000$	
55200	
$50 \times 3 = + 150$	
55350	
$6 \times 100 = + 600$	
55950	
$6 \times 20 = + 120$	
56070	
$6 \times 3 = + 18$	
56088	

Speed versus Power

If a given lesson contains only one type of work, such as multiplying a whole number by a simple fraction, power is more important than speed. When speed means completing or not completing a whole assignment, the assignment might be abridged to include fewer problems if they are all of the same type, such as long division. One can assume that if the child does 10 problems correctly, he could probably do 15 correctly if given more time in which to work. In a mixed lesson, however, such as a review, the teacher cannot assume that if the child correctly works division by a fraction, he can also work correctly with percentages. The teacher might designate specific problems to do, so that the child's total lesson contains representative types. If the child is unable to do a certain type correctly, he can then have intensive help in that area.

Homework

In assigning homework, teachers need to consider several factors: Is it really necessary? How much homework should the child be asked to do? Should he show all the steps or only answers? What kind of computational equipment does the child have at home and at school?

Test Situations

The time for taking a test might be extended for visually handicapped students, or the number of test items might be reduced. The teacher must decide whether demonstration of speed or of power is the goal of a given test. The teacher should also consider whether the test is meant to prove what the handicapped child knows or does not know, or whether he is unfairly compared with seeing children by being asked to complete the same number of examples in the same amount of time.

Use of Graphs and Tables

Through use of the Sewell Raised Line Drawing Board, the American Thermoform Duplicator, embossed graph paper, graph board, Perkins Brailler, etc., charts and graphs can be represented tactually. Enlarged graph paper for partially seeing students permits them to read and make their own charts and graphs. Visually handicapped students need to learn how to use and interpret these illustrations.

Preparation of Textbooks

The following aspects of securing textbooks should be considered.

1. Can the book be purchased with quota or cash? If so, and if it is available in more than one mode, which is best for the student? Sometimes the book

may be only partially completed by the time the student requires it. Is this the section of the book that he will need first? The classroom teacher should be consulted for adequate planning of transcriptions.

2. Can a completed book be borrowed for a semester or a year? If not, can it be borrowed long enough to have it copied by the Thermoform Duplicator? What are the time deadlines? What expenses are entailed, if any?

3. Are volunteers available to transcribe the arithmetic textbook? Transcribing of mathematics is a specialized skill; many otherwise certified braillists may not be qualified to do arithmetic. Planning must begin well in advance of the student's requirements so that all ramifications of the problem can be explored.

4. In which subject areas—other than arithmetic—are books needed? Foreign language and music also demand special skills and only certain braillists are able to transcribe them. Textbooks, in general, are more difficult to transcribe than strictly literary material. Braille textbooks are less crucial in some course areas than others. Besides reading series, perhaps mathematics, foreign languages, and sciences that involve equations and formulas should be in braille rather than sound recording. A student can cope with other modes for other courses. That he is not altogether comfortable with sound recording and a human reader may indicate a student's need for help in learning how to use them better. As a blind reader, he will not have every book he wants to read available in his preferred mode.

If he is partially seeing, can a large-print edition be purchased or copied? Can the student read the regular edition with optical aids? Sound recording and human reader will be a partial solution. Is a human reader available on a scheduled basis or at least on call?

Special Braille Code

Both teacher and blind student must be familiar with the *Nemeth Code of Braille Mathematics and Scientific Notation,* revised in 1970, mandatory in mathematics textbooks. The manual is available in braille and print for reference purposes.

"New Math" versus Traditional

Whether in residential schools or day programs, teachers of visually handicapped children must be acquainted with "modern math" (Nolan & Bruce, 1962) and qualified to teach it. Uninitiated teachers owe it to themselves, their students, and their profession to learn new math through one or more of the following means.

1. Study new math textbooks for children along with their teacher's manuals (*Educational Research Council of Greater Cleveland,* 1962; *Minnesota*

ᵗgmentation

Mathematics and Science Teaching Project, 1968; Shuff, 1962).
2. Study professional books written for teachers (Larsen, 1958; Crescimbeni, 1965; Feldzamen, 1968).
3. Be taught in a formal way by enrolling in college courses.

In the new math, expressions that resemble algebra in format may often be seen in primary or middle grades. A typical grapheme might be

$$3 + (4 + 2) - (1 - 1) + 4^2 = 5^2$$

In preparing desk copies for partially seeing students, teachers might use paper with heavy and fine lines. The heavy line would serve as a base line, with the fine lines above and below it accommodating superscripts and subscripts, respectively. Initially, superscripts and subscripts might be written in red or green to contrast with writing on the base line. Contrast in color draws attention to the fact that such figures or letters are not on the base line and represent special functions.

Algebra, Calculus, and Trigonometry

These subjects may now first appear in junior high school, though a generation ago they were reserved for senior high school. Because expressions resembling algebra appear as early as in the primary grades, the format in algebra does not seem so strange when students encounter it later on.

Adapted Equipment

A variety of seamstress's tracing wheels and C.V.H. Relievo Paints can be used by illustrators for geometric figures and diagrams. Adapted protractor, draftsman's compass, foot rule, slide rule, etc., are available for use in mathematics. Current catalogs of specialized aids and appliances should be consulted.

Special Braille Code

Teachers of the visually handicapped should make available to students braille copies of the *Nemeth Code* manual for reference purposes when unfamiliar symbols appear in the text. Teachers should also acquaint students with how to read typical expressions, using correct terminology. Special education teachers will most likely not teach algebra, calculus, and trigonometry, but are responsible for teaching braille notation. The regular mathematics teacher might indicate to the special education teacher new work he plans to introduce, so that blind students might be exposed to the braille format in advance, thus enhancing the educational value of the classroom presentation. Realistically, on the secondary school level, a special education teacher may not be available for such assistance on a scheduled and frequent basis. In this case visually handicapped students and the regular mathematics teacher must find time to work together apart from the class for this kind of orientation.

Use of Typewriter

Whereas use of the typewriter for arithmetic is not recommended in elementary grades, typewriting algebra is feasible. Format in algebra is primarily linear, whereas that in arithmetic is columnar. For this reason, transposing algebra from computation in braille to typewritten form is less difficult. Work is expedited if the machine has the half-line spacer; this device allows blind students to show neatly superscripts and subscripts. Furthermore, the machine should contain the necessary symbols for algebra: $=$ and $+$ and others employed in notation. It may be necessary to use a combination of symbols to make the one desired, such as the hyphen and underscore to make the equals sign. If the machine does not have square brackets, the student may need to engage seeing help to insert brackets later, once the paper has been removed from the machine. Or he and the teacher might agree on another arrangement to represent square brackets, such as the double opening parentheses or double closing parentheses.

With regard to use of the typewriter in general, it should be noted that blind students run the risk that the typewriter ribbon may be worn or not working properly; consequently, their completed work may not be legible, causing frustration and extra work. However, if carbon paper is used between two sheets of paper, one copy will be legible as long as the carbon paper is changed frequently enough. Although this procedure consumes more paper, it is excellent insurance against that occasion when something goes wrong with the original copy without the student's knowledge until too late. Even if family members inspect papers before they are taken to school, the damage may already be done, requiring redoing and submitting assignments past the due date. In taking tests, the use of carbons is especially recommended.

Sources of Tutoring

If visually handicapped students do not understand the content in algebra, calculus, and trigonometry, they can best secure tutoring or remedial assistance just as their seeing peers do—by making appointments with classroom teachers for individual or small group help. This is preferable to expecting special education teachers to provide such instruction. First, special education teachers are not always available when help is needed on the secondary school level. Second, special education teachers may not be qualified or certified to teach mathematics. Special education teachers cannot teach every course taught in the modern high school.

Management in Classroom

Availability of desk copies of work to be shown on the chalkboard may be more likely for partially seeing students than for the blind, because the regular classroom teacher can make his own in print but not in braille. The special education teacher may not visit often enough to provide this service. Students should be expected to have their braille or large-print texts with them in class in order to benefit from references to specific pages or illustrations. Teachers and students might confer regularly to ascertain if material is being comprehended rather than waiting until much later to determine if need exists. If students demonstrate that they can cope successfully with the content to be learned, private meetings might be discontinued with the understanding that new appointments could be secured, should the need arise. Realistically, secondary school, besides providing academic training, also affords students opportunities to assume increasing responsibility for themselves; therefore, part of the responsibility of visually handicapped students is to know when they need help and how to secure it.

Since pagination in print and braille texts is the same, students should be able to locate the proper page when teachers announce specific numerals.

Access to Tables of Numbers

Basic to execution of mathematical procedures is access to tables of logarithms, square roots, etc. Because almost all mathematics textbooks in print include such tables, blind students should have these tables in braille for independent work. The American Printing House for the Blind and the Braille Book Bank of the National Braille Association have prepared quantities of these tables apart from a given textbook.

Geometry (Plane and Solid)

Plane geometry, as found in textbooks, is far easier for visually handicapped students to comprehend than solid geometry, because they are accustomed to examining one thing at a time rather than having a panoramic view. Also, tactual inspection of one article at a time restricts the area being experienced, whereas visual inspection encompasses large areas, with the accompanying perspective and angular relationships between the articles.

Meaningful Representations

Two-dimensional illustrations employed in textbooks can be meaningfully represented for braille readers when tactually different lines are used—smooth and dotted, finely dotted and coarsely dotted, etc. The American Thermoform Duplicator is an excellent aid for making functional illustrations, since a variety of materials—strings, wires, chains, tubings, etc.—can be utilized in the master copy from which Braillon pages are made. Parts of the diagram should be labeled with arrows or letters as in the print edition for communication purposes.

Partially seeing students will likely require enlarged copies and/or darkened drawings for ease in reading. Perhaps the teacher can draw over the lines in original illustrations to make enlargement unnecessary. Color might be added to an otherwise black and white diagram. For example, the illustration may have a solid line in black and also a dotted line in black. Adding red or green to the broken line might make the drawing more readable.

Meaningful illustrations for touch reading are all but impossible to produce for the three-dimensional or solid geometric figure. Instead, using solid representations is far more effective. The American Printing House for the Blind manufactures a set of geometric figures representing the plane, the outline, and the solid.

Homework

In the drawing of figures for homework assignments, visually handicapped students will encounter difficulty even with adapted tools such as compass and protractor. Besides, when figures are represented for touch reading (when made by the student), they will not be in ink or pencil for easy reading by the regular geometry teacher. If parts are labeled in braille, they will also have to be labeled in print for the teacher's convenience. The student may find it necessary to explain his work to the teacher in a one-to-one situation rather than merely to submit it as written work.

Test Situations

When time is a factor, students and teachers might arrange to meet at mutually convenient hours to provide opportunity for the former to explain those sections of the test that require drawings. The students may understand the theorems and principles involved and have a mental grasp of illustrations, but they nevertheless experience difficulty with the mechanics of making their own illustrations.

Source of Tutoring

The special education teacher has the responsibility of supplying the geometry teacher with specialized equipment, such as the American Printing House for the Blind set of geometric figures and the Sewell Raised Line Drawing Board. Having these at his disposal, the geometry teacher is prepared to offer remedial help should visually handicapped students need it.

Management in Classroom

In geometry, teachers frequently refer to illustrations in the textbook for discussion and elaboration. To facilitate following and comprehending such instruction, visually handicapped students have the responsibility of bringing their texts to class also.

SOCIAL SCIENCE

Many concepts are involved in the teaching of social science knowledge. Although seeing children may be able to use terms seemingly with comprehension, teachers discover to their chagrin that many of these terms have been incorrectly understood. The writing down of such commonplace Americana as the Pledge of Allegiance to the Flag or words to *America*—by children who supposedly know them—often reveals vast discrepancies between the actual and the children's meanings. This is true to a larger extent of visually handicapped children's concept formation in social science. Because of experiential deprivation, these children may use such words as wigwam, windmill, butter churn, canoe, or pump (Fulker & Fulker, 1968) without ever having examined real ones and sometimes having only the faintest notion what the thing is or does or how it might be classified. Not having pictures from which to learn, blind children especially need realia and models in the classroom in order to effect adequate communication between book and child or teacher and child. Because the word at best is only a phoneme without embodiment or concreteness, stress should be placed on actual experiences.

Orientation to Fixed Point in Space

Because of restricted movement, visually handicapped children have limited experience with space and distance. Just as there must be readiness activities to prepare for the teaching of reading, there must be readiness activities prior to the teaching of map reading. Before the most rudimentary map can be read, children must experience a given area with all its details and cues. Therefore, mastering a limited area, the classroom, is the logical place to begin. In this setting, children learn that coats are hung in the closet left of the main door, that the teacher's desk is straight ahead from the door, that the wastebasket is immediately inside the door on the right, etc.

As children move about in the room, they should be encouraged to touch things en route. For instance, as the child moves from his own desk to the teacher's, he may pass the piano. He should be directed to reach out a hand and touch the piano in order to reinforce the idea that this is a point in his route; it also serves as a landmark that he is on course and headed in the correct direction. Furthermore, later he will see "piano" on the map and should be completely aware of its existence and location. This technique conveys the truth that movement is not only two points—departure and destination—but many points along the way. In other words, it confirms the fact that a line is a series of points or segments. Later in his education the child needs to learn that a given point can usually be reached by a variety of routes; so he might experience numerous ways by which he might walk and eventually arrive at the piano. If a child cannot do this, he will inevitably encounter a barrier across his path and not know which other way to proceed. Only after children have lived this map by walking and talking it dare the teacher introduce a more advanced map.

Once spatial relations in familiar territory have been mastered through demonstrated ability, the same area can be represented by a map. The locale to be learned can expand from the classroom to a floor plan of the school, and later to the route between home and school. Similarly, the map will expand to encompass more area commensurate with experience. In this way, the map —an abstract representation—acquires functional meaning. Reading a map involves reading or interpreting symbols and points common to map making. Once the child can read a map of known territory, other maps can take on meaning even though the reader has not visited the places represented. First-hand, concrete experiences with space are imperative; otherwise map reading cannot succeed.

Estimation of Distance, Size, Time, and Weight

Although this topic relates to arithmetic, concepts of distance, size, time, and weight also apply to understanding of social science. Children might estimate measurement by walking distances, lifting objects, comparing sizes, and considering lengths of time, such as "How long does it take us to walk from the classroom to the cafeteria?" or "How long does it take for us to sing this song?" Only as children experience and comprehend the here and now can they begin to grasp terminology found in social science textbooks—300 miles, 50 years, 2 tons of wheat, mountain ranges, and relative sizes.

Map Study

Relief Maps of the Immediate Environment. A relief map is the most effective means to introduce map reading. A map of the classroom can be meaningful even though crude and simple. Such a map any teacher can make. It can consist of a rectangle to represent the floor with objects fastened on at appropriate points to represent main door, teacher's desk, coat closet, sink, storage cabinets, etc. Small blocks of wood, sponge, cork, etc., with braille labels affixed will convey the message. Compass points—north, south, east, west— can be labeled in appropriate margins. If specific areas are reserved for aisles, these can be shown with strips of sandpaper. A map of the school's general floor plan showing corridors with rooms, windows, and doors on either side can be similarly constructed. The description of these maps given here need not be followed precisely; rather, the intent is to emphasize the ease of their construction.

Somewhat different is the map showing the route between school and home. The bottom level signifies the street surface. On this level are fastened smaller squares representing city blocks; these might be made of sandpaper. On the city blocks are affixed specific structures representing post office, drugstore, gasoline station, etc. This kind of map shows visually handicapped children that the sidewalk is higher than the street and that buildings are set back from sidewalk and street. Street intersections are now obvious. One must be accurate, however, in showing correct angles of intersections. If a given intersection is not a right angle, the sandpaper must be shaped accordingly in order to communicate the true picture. Though constructed for blind children, these maps also provide partially seeing and normally seeing children with excellent teaching aids.

Reading Relief Maps. Relief maps should be placed and read on the horizontal, parallel to the floor, and not on the vertical or incline. Maps should also be oriented to compass points, with the northern end toward the northern end of the room.

Puzzle maps with pieces cut at random should not be used as teaching aids. However, if a puzzle map has been cut along state boundaries, children may be able to learn some of the distinctive shapes, such as Florida and Idaho. Many states and countries are roughly rectangular and, therefore, resemble other states and countries. Names, initials of names, or numerals (with a key) should be affixed for identification value. These maps are not strictly relief, since all pieces are level, but they are usable, nonetheless. The American Printing House for the Blind produces relief maps with states or countries as separate pieces that can be removed and examined more closely. The American Foundation for the Blind sells relief maps that are not separable into geographic areas.

Relief maps for touch reading necessitate exaggeration in order to convey the information intended. As represented on such maps, mountain peaks, for example, seem to the eye unduly pointed and higher in relation to surrounding territory than they are in real life. Without this exaggeration, however, the tactual sense may not recognize differences.

Reading Embossed Paper Maps. Embossed paper maps are less meaningful to blind students than relief maps. The latter are more abstract, requiring higher-level skills. Realistically, not every map can be in relief form. Books contain paper maps, which must be embossed. In contrast to maps intended for visual reading, embossed maps for tactual reading can present only a limited amount of meaningful information. Whereas one ink-print map contains many types of information, embossed maps can show only a few specifics. Visual representations utilize many types of symbology. On the other hand, embossed maps contain only a few different symbols, because too many of them would confuse the touch observer. Therefore, several embossed maps must be made to depict all the information attainable from one visual map.

Types of Embossed Maps. Students must learn to read a variety of embossed maps—outline maps with and without labels, and outline maps giving limited information, such as rivers or cities only. Another type shows topography without regard to state or national boundaries. Blind students must also learn to interpret scale. In assigning map study, teachers need to be aware that scale on a tactual map will differ from that on a visual map.

Map Making. Making an original map is all but impossible for blind students. Copying or tracing is not practicable. However, students can make floor plans or city streets maps on the Perkins Brailler. If supplied with outline maps, blind students can show certain information. Besides labeling, students might mount the map on cork, rubber, or soft wood and then, by using map pins and string, show the route of a river. If it is not accurate enough, the string can be adjusted. The student can use map pins and slips of paper to identify main industries or products, etc.

Access to Supplementary Reading

In social science, many books contribute to the students' knowledge—textbooks, biographies, fiction, exposition, etc. When practicable, visually handicapped students should be expected to read the same books assigned to their seeing classmates. When a title is not available except in regular print, two alternatives are to (1) provide a human reader, and (2) substitute another title.

To expedite matters, the special education teacher should supply catalogs from various sources to the social science teacher, so that he can early select and order appropriate titles. Usually titles for braille books, large-print books, and sound-recorded books are cataloged separately for convenience. Advance planning is imperative in order to maximize the students' success and development of desirable work habits. Visually handicapped students require more time to read a given passage; for this reason, teachers might arrange to give assignments to the visually handicapped students before giving them to the seeing students, thus allowing more time. This procedure is preferable to having visually handicapped students submit assignments late, which may foster an attitude of not taking assignments seriously or of being entitled to unreasonable allowances. If these conditions have been met, visually handicapped students should be expected to meet deadline dates for completion of work.

Preparation of Textbooks

Textbooks in the area of social science can be prepared in one of a variety of modes with satisfactory results. Sound recording is undoubtedly the fastest method of copying a book. If sound recording is chosen, special education teachers must alert recordists to the necessity for oral inclusion of pagination, spelling of difficult words, announcing new topic heads, indicating quoted material, footnotes, etc. If the social science teacher indicates before the book has been started that she will use the study materials in this text extensively —questions to answer, outlines, definitions, etc.—these particular sections might be brailled or typed in large print, so that students can have access to them in a form more easily usable than the sound recording itself. If a sighted reader is available on a fixed schedule, a regular edition, not otherwise transcribed, might be assigned to her with the understanding that she will not read books already brailled, typed, or recorded for the student.

How to Locate Books for Class Use

Well in advance of the beginning of a course (as early as January for the next September), teachers must determine which specific books will be used in each of the student's future courses, noting *complete* bibliographic information, including the number of the edition and whether it is a revision, for each. If the revised edition in ink-print form is not available in a special mode but an earlier edition is, comparison between the two should be made, because quite frequently revisions are so slight that the earlier edition will serve adequately. Current catalogs from several sources should be consulted:

1. American Printing House for the Blind (mass-produced titles).
2. Library of Congress, Division for the Blind and Physically Handicapped (mass-produced titles).
3. National Aid to Visually Handicapped.
4. Recording for the Blind, Inc.
5. Braille Book Bank of the National Braille Association.

Quite often a private agency or state library, though not having a published catalog, will nonetheless have the desired book and, therefore, should be contacted with a query. Other school systems in the state or the regional instructional materials center might possess the book and allow the student to borrow it.

If all the foregoing measures are unavailing three additional sources should be explored:

1. *Central Catalog of Volunteer Produced Textbooks* of the American Printing House for the Blind.

2. *Union Catalog of Volunteer Produced Books* of the Library of Congress, Division for the Blind and Physically Handicapped (nontextbook materials).
3. Director of Educational Services, Xavier Society for the Blind (Catholic school materials).

Those sources indicate if the book exists somewhere, even as a single copy, or if it is in the process of being copied. In either case, its location is supplied. The teacher can then contact that address to inquire if the book might be borrowed for a given period of time. If the book may not be borrowed for the specified period, it may be possible to borrow it long enough to make a copy from it. In the case of sound recording, it can be dubbed onto a blank tape or disk. If ink print, it can be photographed. If braille and on paper pages, it can be copied on the American Thermoform Duplicator. Unfortunately, if already on Braillon, it cannot be Thermoformed.

At this point, two alternatives remain if the book cannot be made available to the student:

1. Designate a reader to read it to the student while the course is in progress.
2. Locate a volunteer to copy and complete it before the student needs it.

To locate volunteers and those who offer special services, such as brailling foreign languages, Thermoforming, or typewriting, consult *Volunteers Who Produce Braille Books, Large-Type Books, Disc Recordings, Tape Recordings for Blind and Visually Impaired Individuals* compiled by the Library of Congress, Division for the Blind and Physically Handicapped.

Not to be overlooked in the searching are commercial publishers of large-print editions and commercial recording companies that produce spoken-word recordings. Although their titles are likely not to include textbooks, these companies may be sources of supplementary materials needed in the course.

Subscription to *Braille Book Review* and *Talking Book Topics* is imperative for teachers. These two publications, issued bimonthly by the Library of Congress, Division for the Blind and Physically Handicapped, announce recently circulated or acquired books and other pertinent information relating to books and library services.

A most valuable source of information is a series of leaflets, *Sources of Reading Materials for the Visually Handicapped,* made available by the American Foundation for the Blind (see Chapter 7).

Finally, regular classroom teachers should be informed by special education teachers that sometimes braille editions do not contain all the maps included in the print edition. Also, a sound-recorded text may not have maps accompanying the disks or tapes. A student using a reader will not have access to maps in the textbook except as the reader is capable of interpreting them for him.

Besides the sources for securing maps already mentioned, embossed maps may be secured from Howe Memorial Press, and these might supplement the sound-recorded editions.

Enrichment Activities

As a method of supplementing textbook materials, the following are suggested.

1. Arrange field trips rich in multisensory values (Crockett, 1958).
2. Invite staff members from a museum (Coon, 1953) to bring appropriate artifacts to the classroom and discuss them.
3. As some schools do, make an inventory of adults in the community to determine their hobbies and interests, what visual aids and artifacts they may have from previous tours relating to these hobbies, their line of employment, and their willingness to serve as guests in the classroom and share with the children their experiences and expertise.
4. Play REAL (Recorded Educational Aids to Learning) tapes from the American Printing House for the Blind. Most of these employ dramatizations and sound effects to depict historical episodes and other relevant material for a social science class. Commercial recording companies, on their spoken-word recordings, have reproduced famous speeches (some with original voices), appropriate poetry, etc. Free materials (Wittich, 1969) include radio transcriptions and other audio products, as well as scripts that might be the basis of dramatizations in the classroom.
5. Music typical of the period in history or the geographic area being studied can be played for the children to hear, and they can sing characteristic songs or play them in their band or orchestra.
6. Timely dance forms can be learned.
7. Relevant literature—biography, poetry, fiction, etc.—can be read. The teacher should not miss the rewarding opportunity of reading aloud to the class.
8. Children can bring articles to class for exhibits on a given topic. These would not be encased in glass but would be accessible for tactual examination. Cooperative relatives, neighbors, friends, and sometimes even merchants might be delighted to share their possessions for such displays (with cards identifying donors).
9. A variety of art activities will allow latitude for visually handicapped children to participate. For instance, if the American colonial period is being studied, handicrafts might include rug making, basketry, or pottery for visually handicapped children. Simultaneously, normally seeing peers can be engaged in other art experiences.
10. Debating teams can be assigned topics for research and oral presentation

of findings. Students may pretend to be political candidates and present original campaign speeches based on issues of the day being studied.

In short, teaching should be unit based, so that bodies of knowledge are demonstrated to children in their interrelatedness. Social science, especially, is an intermingling of all people and their total lives.

Available Periodicals

Periodicals in the realm of social science available for students' use include *Current Events, My Weekly Reader, National Geographic, Senior Weekly Reader, American Heritage, Changing Times, Holiday, Newsweek Talking Magazine,* and *Foreign Affairs.* Others may become available in the course of time.

SCIENCES

Science courses comprise more than definitions, formulas, and classifications. They should convey important scientific thinking and foster methodical, careful observation, and accurate recording of data to assist in formation of judgments and conclusions. Science must be demonstrably lived and learned in the real-life environment (laboratory) and not in the artificial realm of classroom or textbook alone. Visually handicapped scientists are living evidence that neither poor vision nor total blindness need be an insurmountable barrier to careers in science. Success for visually handicapped students rests on modification and enrichment of the science curriculum to include meaningful experiences and activities in keeping with total involvement.

Personal Hygiene

In personal hygiene, problems are the same for both visually handicapped and normally seeing students, namely, care of self to promote and maintain health and to impress favorably others one contacts in routine living as well as in unexpected or unusual associations. Although the problems are identical, handling and solving them are different for the visually handicapped because of reduced or absent visual feedback. Not having this feedback, visually handicapped persons must learn substitute techniques. The following are a few suggestions:

1. Adoption of the habit of routinely or mechanically taking care of certain tasks, such as care of nails, laundering of clothing, polishing of shoes, assuming automatically that they need attention rather than assuming that they are satisfactory or clean.

2. Assuming responsibility for washing hands more frequently and before beginning new activities, because visually handicapped individuals use their hands so much more than sighted people in many activities.
3. Frequent laundering of clothing increases the likelihood of socially acceptable standards. With present-day automatic laundry equipment and wash-and-wear fabrics, care of clothing is not the problem it once was. Dry-cleanable garments should have visual inspection to ascertain need of servicing before the next wearing.
4. Subscriptions to such periodicals as *Our Special, Seventeen,* or *Ladies Home Journal* serve as avenues for keeping informed about current fashions and personal care. (Consult *Sources of Reading Materials for the Visually Handicapped,* available from the American Foundation for the Blind.) Visually handicapped students need to know how their peers are dressing.
5. Constructive counseling by a seeing person (teacher) in whom the visually handicapped student has confidence regarding such problem areas as obesity, dandruff, dingy teeth, or poor posture might effect positive change without embarrassment or hostility.

Available Manuals

Fortunately, manuals are now available to guide teachers in techniques of personal hygiene applicable to their visually handicapped students. Sometimes they have been written for newly blinded adults, but even these (Bindt, 1952) have usefulness with school-age students. Eating correctly (Pittman, 1964) is a major problem without visual feedback. Having broad social experience (Barraga, 1958; Shults, 1957) yields at least two dividends in promoting motivation:

1. Students realize more vividly that classroom learning has valuable application outside the school setting.
2. Certain areas of need should be met to gain further acceptance in social situations as appropriate help is available at school.

Teachers might share manuals (Western Michigan University, 1966) with parents so that consistency between home and school management is achieved. Houseparents and teachers at a residential school must work cooperatively and communicate effectively with each other so that both groups instruct youngsters in a consistent manner. Observation of children at summer camp reveals areas of needed instruction:

1. Does the girl comb her own hair?
2. Can the youngster take his own bath or shower unassisted (commensurate with age)?

3. Can the child eat with a fork or only a spoon?
4. Can the child cut with a knife?
5. Can the child butter bread?
6. Can the child tie his own shoes?

Enrichment Activities

In order to implement learning beyond the verbal level, the following instructional procedures—among others—might be included.

1. Bring a variety of foods to the classroom for sensory experiences. They should be in various states: raw, peeled, sliced, cooked, etc. Food and nutrition activities might be conducted in the home economics room, where tools and equipment permit wider latitude for student involvement with washing, scraping, slicing, mashing, etc.
2. Arrange for exercises with spoon, fork, and knife used with *real* foods in the teaching of table etiquette. Ample time must be allotted for meals at school if children are to practice techniques taught. Children who are rushed through a meal may resort to outgrown and incorrect habits rather than forego the food. Eating correctly demands time and care.
3. Exhibit an assortment of packaging processes: plastic bag, box, can, bottle, carton, etc.
4. Discuss color of specific foods so that youngsters will be familiar with "yellow foods" and "green foods" and how color may change from the raw state to the cooked.
5. Set up a vanity table or a "bathroom corner" much like the "science corner" or "book corner" for toilet articles: brushes, razors, deodorants, mouthwash, etc., so that children become familiar with the containers, shapes, textures, scents, and utility of each.
6. Display a set of typical or basic face shapes so that children might examine faces other than their own. The art teacher may be of assistance in securing such a set.
7. Adapt sex education ('t 'Hooft & Heslinga, 1968) around frank and honest discussions, use of accurate models of the human body, examination of a pregnant cat or dog, and examination of such intimate articles as brassiere and sanitary pad (and dispenser machine).

Logically, activities should be selected for each grade level commensurate with the student's level of readiness and maturity.

Climate and Weather

Visually handicapped children are aware of weather conditions as they move about in the community. They also hear weather reports on radio and television. Instruments for measurement designed for touch reading are available in adapted form from the American Printing House for the Blind, the American Foundation for the Blind, etc. With specialized tools, blind students can determine readings on a thermometer, barometer, hydrometer, etc.

Clouds

Although totally blind students may acquire only vicarious information (except for some direct experience derived from walking through fog or being in a steamy bathroom or laundry), they can nonetheless learn factual information including technical names and characteristics of cloud formation. This is similarly true in astronomy.

Weather Map

If visually handicapped students can read other maps, they will have an understanding of weather maps. However, weather maps in braille are not likely to be available except as found in textbooks for illustrative purposes. Radio-presented weather reports are more easily comprehended by the blind than television reports, because the former is communication exclusively by audio means, whereas the latter is audiovisual.

Effects of Weather on Blind Persons

Whereas seeing persons are hampered by fog or darkness, blind individuals do not find these conditions limiting. By contrast, snow is "the blind man's fog." When snow is deep enough to obliterate familiar kinesthetic cues perceived through the soles of the feet or tip of the cane, blind persons become disoriented. They do not walk in straight lines automatically and tend to veer off course. Also, they cannot use cues to the side of the path, such as trees or telegraph poles or buildings, to keep in alignment. Since the dog guide operates as a seeing guide, it will usually stay on course, especially if it has traveled the path in question many times prior to the snowfall. Wind is a hindrance to the blind traveler, because the sound of it in trees and elsewhere generally masks auditory cues—sounds of vehicular traffic especially—employed in mobility. Wet pavements amplify sounds of tires on streets. Heavy rain, much like wind, masks helpful auditory cues. Snow on the ground deadens sounds so that a blind person is not aware of an approaching vehicle till it is quite close—unless the snow is hard-crusted or tire chains announce its approach. Icy pavements and piles of snow in the path are hazardous because blind people have no warning of their location until they step on ice or stumble on the pile. When using a cane or dog guide and carrying a parcel (or books), blind individuals cannot use umbrellas. Even in cold weather, blind persons do not like to cover their ears with a scarf or earmuffs because doing so would mask auditory information. After a severe storm—wind, snow, hurricane, tornado—when debris is strewn about, blind persons may and should be reluctant to venture out because of obstructions and dangers, such as fallen live electrical wires, whereas seeing persons can pick their way carefully to avoid dangers.

Weather Vane and Wind Chimes

The science class or the blind child's family might enjoy mounting a noisy weather vane or wind chimes near the building and low enough for children to reach them. Examination should reveal which way the weather vane is turned or the wind chimes are blowing. These sensory experiences increase interest in the study of weather. They also help clarify the names ascribed to winds—that the North Wind comes from the north, even though the wind chimes are blowing to the south.

Enrichment Activities

To make application of learned principles, children might be directed in the following representative activities.

1. Make bar graphs on Perkins Brailler, American Thermoform Duplicator, graph paper, and graph board, showing the percentage of rainy days in a given month.
2. Make pie graphs with pairs of paper plates of the same size: Cut out a section from one plate, and superimpose the cut plate on an intact one, sprinkle the portion of the bottom plate that is visible with glue and sand, so that the visually handicapped students can perceive it tactually. (Plates of different colors can accomplish the same ends.)
3. Construct make-believe thermometer similar to popular teaching aids that have an adjustable elastic loop, one segment red and one white, with red representing mercury. For blind children, use two textures of elastic, or make the red segment tactually different.
4. Hang wind chimes indoors over a radiator or ventilator, or near an electric fan, to demonstrate that wind is the factor and not the outdoors.
5. With a battery and mild electric shock and drums, demonstrate lightning and thunder—that lightning (shock) precedes thunder (roll of drums).

Astronomy

In the study of astronomy, visually handicapped students are held responsible for mastering the factual information of the content—names of planets; their relative sizes and relative distances from each other and earth; definitions of planet, comet, meteor, galaxy, etc. Carefully selected substitute activities will keep visually handicapped students profitably engaged while seeing peers are involved with map making, telescope viewing, etc. Substitute assignments might include the following.

1. Reporting on biographies of famous astronomers.
2. Reading science fiction and trying to separate reality from fiction.
3. Reporting on several astronomy textbooks, comparing their information, detail, dates, qualifications of authors, etc.
4. Visiting a weather station with a few classmates in order to bring back pertinent information to the class.
5. For a period of time, keeping track of predictions in the almanac as well as becoming familiar with the signs of the zodiac and astrology.
6. Reading Greek and Roman mythology, ascertaining the ascribed attributes of the gods whose names relate to astronomy.
7. Reporting on proverbs or adages relating to weather and astronomy.

Team Work

A partially seeing student and his seeing peer might use a telescope together, with the latter adjusting the lens for the other, and with the partially seeing child being responsible for basic information. Likewise, a seeing and blind student might constitute another team, with the latter supplying information and being held responsible for becoming familiar with the telescope and its parts.

Use of Heat

Some concepts can be conveyed with the use of a heat supply. Representing the sun, a lamp or heater remains fixed (on the table) while a student, acting as Earth, travels around the table to depict night and day or the complete year. Eclipses can be demonstrated equally well by imposing a barrier between heat source and child.

Laboratory Science (Chemistry, Physics, and Biology)

Chemistry, physics, and biology (botany and zoology) can most meaningfully be taught as laboratory courses. This, however, does not necessarily mean having a special room in the school to which classes go in order to have science classes. A laboratory course is more technique and procedure than place. Effective science teachers may be teaching laboratory courses in the same room where they teach spelling, history, or reading. Because many laboratory experiences tend to be visual, modification of approach and careful selection of activity are necessary if visually handicapped students are to derive maximal value from them. When teaching is thus adapted, it often becomes a richer experience for seeing children as well.

Employing Sensory Approaches

Many basic scientific constructs are taught in grades lower than senior high school, though not necessarily labeled "physics" or "biology," and by teachers who might consider themselves not highly trained in science. Some topics that lend themselves to successful presentation in these circumstances are simple machines, gravity, and fire and oxygen. Classroom teachers (especially in the elementary school), not highly skilled in science but vitally interested in succeeding in this area of the curriculum, can seek appropriate activities for their visually handicapped students through the following sources.

1. Examine a variety of textbooks for demonstrations and experiments that utilize more than the sense of vision. Access to even one copy of a textbook is sufficient; a copy for each child is not necessary. In fact, present-day teaching often employs several textbooks in the classroom in order to have a greater variety of material. Five or six copies of a given text may be sufficient if four or five other texts are similarly represented. Appropriate material can be drawn from several authors' expertise.

2. Confer with knowledgeable faculty members for suggestions regarding textbook material and laboratory manuals or kits, etc. Some kits are nothing more than a card file arranged by topic; yet the information on each card is valuable in guiding the teacher.

3. Having ideas is more important than having equipment. Even if the classroom is not supplied with much science equipment, effective teaching can result when the teacher has workable ideas; then he can make arrangements to borrow equipment from sources within and outside the school for a short period of time.

4. Science models designed for seeing students and obtained from usual supply houses are frequently appropriate aids for the visually handicapped, with little or no adaptation.

5. The Instructional Materials Reference Center affiliated with the American Printing House for the Blind has been developing prototype models demonstrating the operation of the screw, pulley, scales, etc. A similar facility at Michigan State University concentrates on collecting, adapting, and disseminating information about teaching aids.

6. Science for the Blind is another resource, through its magnetically taped material and its expertise in supplying helpful answers relative to science equipment and adaptations.

7. Fulker and Fulker (1968) provide many ideas accompanied by diagrams and pictures concerning inexpensive or homemade devices that convey concepts and principles, especially in the realm of physics. The authors capitalize on advertising models by requesting to have them when mer-

chants or salesmen have no further use for them, and then doing whatever adapting might be necessary, such as opening one side so that children can feel the inner mechanism.

8. *Report of Science Workshop* by the American Association of Instructors of the Blind (undated) concerns itself with materials of instruction. Regional meetings of the Science Workshop or the biennial conventions of the Association for Education of the Visually Handicapped deal with problems and solutions in teaching science to visually handicapped children.

9. *Experimental Science for the Blind* (Wexler, 1961) and "Secondary School Sciences for the Blind" (Bryan, 1956) come to the assistance of the earnest teacher.

Enrichment Activities.

To supplement textbook learning in either braille or recorded form (Borgersen, 1965; Helms, 1957, 1968; Recording for the Blind, Inc., undated), the following activities are suggested.

1. Employing nonvisual sensory approaches as ways of gathering data in science may help to awaken an awareness of detail.
2. Using the mechanical action of the human body through isometrics may convey the concept of opposing forces—actions and reactions.
3. Manipulating equipment brings meaning to textbook explanations and descriptions.
4. Substituting objects for diagrams helps demonstrate textbook theories and principles.
5. Subscribing to certain magazines for students (in a variety of reading modes) provides students with additional information that may apply to classroom activities. Some of these magazines are *Braille Science Journal, Braille Technical Press, Current Science, Popular Mechanics, Today's Health, Farm Journal, Natural History,* and *QST.*
6. Having plants and pets for which children assume responsibility can point up the importance of proper nutrition, ecology, and reproduction.
7. Conducting experiments by using sets of animals or sets of plants and giving different treatments for comparison purposes—potted plants kept in sunshine or shade, kept moist or dry, in rich loam or sand—to determine results may reinforce the scientific method (Boldt, 1969).
8. Studying electricity can be adapted by using heat or shock to demonstrate light.
9. Studying earth science involves noticing texture and odor of soil and weight and sound of rock when hammered.

MUSIC

In the area of music, visually handicapped children—contrary to lay belief —are not gifted merely as compensation for blindness. However, in residential schools especially, these children are exposed to music instruction and related experiences from kindergarten on (Thompson, 1957). Thus exposed, some children may reveal a genuine interest in and proclivity for music as an art form. If normally seeing youngsters were equally saturated with music, more seeing children might demonstrate musical ability, too. This is largely a matter of environmental stimulation.

Rhythm Band

Benefits derived from rhythm bands are the same for normally seeing as for visually handicapped youngsters. However, teachers must assume responsibility for acquainting children with every instrument—the sound of it, how it feels in the hand—because otherwise each student will acquire only a limited knowledge about the instruments played by other children.

If the teacher points or gestures to indicate when children should or should not play, blind children will not receive such signals; therefore, teachers must adopt audible cues.

Identification of Instruments

To facilitate recognition of tone quality, teachers play instruments or use recordings, thus familiarizing the children with identifiable and characteristic sounds. Awareness that a violin sounds like a violin and not like a tuba is the lesson objective. A second step is to allow visually handicapped children to handle and examine all the instruments. If the teacher plays a recording of a clarinet, children should have opportunity to examine a real clarinet in class.

Instruments in a given family—strings—should be compared for sound, size, number of strings, position held when played, etc. Since experimentation is a channel for learning, the child might hold a string while it is being bowed and note the difference when he removes his finger. Also, differences between heavy and thin strings should be explored. How does the performer achieve *legato* and *staccato* effects?

Combinations of instruments can be introduced once the children have become acquainted with individual instruments. If live performers can be utilized, they might place themselves in various parts of the room so that the individual sounds can be more easily distinguished. In this exploratory stage, the human voice—alone and in combinations—should also be included. Having felt vibrations in other instruments, the children might feel vibrations in their throat and diaphragm.

Music and Self-Expression

Self-expression to the accompaniment of music is desirable for all children. Blind children, however, may be limited in their experiences when required to depict certain behaviors, as when the teacher says: "Pretend you are a bear and walk like one," or "Make believe you are a daisy blowing in the breeze." Therefore, blind children must be shown how to perform the intended action. Instead, the teacher might try to draw out ideas rather than impose them. She might say: "Listen to the music, and then make your feet do what the music seems to say," or "What do you think your arms want to do with this kind of music?" Under these conditions, visually handicapped children experience no disadvantage.

Some blind children are reluctant to move out or do so only awkwardly or fearfully. Because of this, teachers might request such children to "act out the music" right where they are. If children learn enough freedom and confidence while staying in one place, they may learn, though belatedly, how to move in an enlarged area.

Music and Dance (Eurhythmics)

Eurhythmics involves following a prescribed pattern imposed by the teacher or choreographer. Children learn to coordinate bodily parts and work toward independence of separate members. Eurhythmics yields gains in muscular control and coordination, grace, poise, and self-confidence. However, more modern methods of rhythmical gymnastics give greater freedom of movement, encourage more self-expression through bodily movements.

Music Notation in Braille and Large Print

If normally seeing students are expected to read music notation on the staff at a given grade level, partially seeing students at that time should also have such competence in enlarged form. Teachers can use either specially prepared sheets with the enlarged staff, adding notation by hand, or can purchase ready-made enlarged sheet music if the desired title is available.

Music notation in braille is entirely different from the staff format. Regular classroom teachers who can use large-type music with little assistance from the special education teacher cannot use braille notation without help. Special education teachers are responsible for teaching braille notation even if they are not highly trained in music. Fortunately for such teachers, children learn only a limited amount of notations each year. Thus, instruction can keep abreast of children's needs. Occasionally a given community may have a seeing music teacher who knows braille music notation or a blind teacher of music with whom the child and his family might arrange private lessons for both notation and performance.

Careers in Music

Visually handicapped students, their parents, and their teachers must not jump to conclusions that careers in music are guaranteed and automatic. Frequently the presence of musical talent is overestimated. Interest and enjoyment are not enough to launch a career. Countless hours of arduous and lonely practice are imperative.

Visually handicapped students in music have one of three choices if contemplating a musical career:

1. Serious music based on use of notation and exactly prescribed performances.
2. Popular music, which calls for the development of a personal style distinctive from that of other performers. If the visually handicapped musician has a good ear for reproducing what he hears in live or recorded performances, he may have little or no need for notation itself.
3. Teaching music, which is similar to choice #1, though it does not demand performance in concerts.

The student using braille notation must memorize it before being able to play it. This consumes much time and restricts the performer's repertory. Unlike a seeing person, who can do a reasonably accurate job even on his first exposure to a musical composition, the braille reader cannot "sight read" music. Partially seeing students have similar difficulties. Because of their visual problem, they may not be able to read quickly enough to read and play simultaneously; so they may have to memorize also. Furthermore, the partially seeing may need to use a special music rack that brings the sheet close to the face so that it can be read.

It is hoped that the persistent will sell themselves on the quality of their musicianship and not on their blindness.

Attending Professional Concerts

Although attending live performances has the same values for both visually handicapped and normally seeing peers, one difference lies in the inability of the former to read program notes distributed to the audience. There may not be sufficient time before the performance to allow a seeing person to read in whispers. Without these notes, the listener misses vital information pertaining to historical setting or analysis of art form. To correct this problem, teachers might secure advance copies of the program—often advertised in newspapers —and then play the same compositions at school, discussing pertinent information. A culminating experience might involve listening again to the same compositions after the concert and sharing reactions to the live performance.

Group Participation (Chorus, Orchestra, and Band)

Visually handicapped students should be encouraged to assume active memberships in school organizations devoted to music. This type of integration with seeing peers may result in lasting friendships beyond the school years, in avocational channels (Bevans, 1965), and in keys that unlock social doors, making possible broader interpersonal relationships. Some modifications are necessary, as outlined in the following paragraphs.

Processions and recessions: Moving in straight lines equidistant from those in front and behind is important for aesthetic effects. If a blind student is paired with a seeing partner, they might link little fingers of adjoining hands in an inconspicuous way. An understanding teacher might have students process by twos instead of in single file when a blind student is a member of the group. When required to go in single file, a blind student might use a thin string held taut by the student preceding and following him with the string wrapped around his own finger halfway between the two. Being confronted with new territory poses the problem for blind students of not knowing distances or turns or the presence of steps, since rehearsals may be conducted in one place while the public performance is held elsewhere. If possible, arrangements should be made to take the blind student to the new site in order to orient him to it.

Marching band: Partially seeing students may succeed as participants in a marching band, whereas blind students might find it extremely difficult to keep in line while marching and playing. However, blind students should be permitted to try doing it in rehearsals. Perhaps blind students can orient to a particular sound preceding them, such as a drum or flute.

Pairing with partner: In chorus, band, or orchestra, visually handicapped students might be placed beside a capable musician singing or playing the same part. Such partners can serve as examples to emulate. In rehearsals, blind students can listen part of the time and later sing or play when the material has become familiar. The pair might work at times other than during rehearsals, with the seeing performer playing or singing the part for the other to listen to and learn. When several persons make up a given section (such as tenors), the blind student should be seated in the front of that group so that more of the sound of his part reaches him.

Use of recordings: If a student group is practicing a given composition already recorded by another group and with the same arrangement, visually handicapped students might be assigned to study by listening repeatedly to that recording. Furthermore, the Division for the Blind and Physically Handicapped, Library of Congress, is producing kits containing sound recordings with music in usual renditions, also at a slow rate for study purposes, with solos unaccompanied, and with notation in both braille and large type. These materials can be of utmost value if the teacher's selection and the titles thus made available coincide.

Signaling: Music teachers who are not accustomed to having a visually handicapped student in the group may need to modify their signaling procedures. A nod or hand gesture will not be noticed by him. Instead, a code of raps with the baton on the music stand might be devised.

Blind soloist and accompanist: Although use of the voice may be correct, blind soloists may need assistance with stance, facial expression, and gestures. If the soloist is blind, he can usually take his cue from the accompanist and the musical introduction, if there is one. If the accompanist is blind, he must be certain that the soloist is ready before beginning the introduction.

Available Periodicals

Periodicals in the field of music available for students' use include *Braille Musical Magazine, The Braille Musician, The Piano Technician, Keyboard Junior, Overtones, Young Keyboard Junior, Music Journal, High Fidelity, Music Quarterly.*

FOREIGN LANGUAGES

Speaking or comprehending spoken foreign language is no more difficult for visually handicapped students than for their normally seeing peers. Problems lie in such aspects as accessibility to written material that visually handicapped students can read and learning of correctness when having to write in a language other than English. Often, the grapheme does not seem to correlate with its phoneme (based on English pronunciation and spelling). For instance, the German word *vier* (four) sounds as if it might be spelled *fear.* Orientation to English sounds in another language is not especially helpful. A person is not considered truly educated in a given language unless and until he can, and with comprehension, speak, read, and write it correctly. If seeing peers are required to master these facets of language, the same level of expectation should prevail for the visually handicapped.

Braille Codes

Foreign language written in braille follows the *Code of Braille Textbook Formats and Techniques, 1965*. Although American readers of braille are familiar with contractions, these have different meanings or may not be used in languages other than English. Therefore, foreign-language books brailled in the United States do not utilize contractions. The only "signs" are those representing accented or modified letters, resulting in altered pronunciation. For instance, in the German word *Jahr* (year), only letters of the alphabet are shown. In the German word *Jäger* (hunter), the umlaut *ä* is shown by a special symbol, occupying only one cell. Whereas German has only few such symbols, French has many.

Another aspect of reading or writing in a foreign language is the basic alphabet characteristic for that language. Visually handicapped students must be provided with appropriate alphabets in braille or large print. Some languages, such as Swedish, have alphabets with more than 26 letters; others, such as Greek, have alphabets with fewer than 26.

Special education teachers, even if they do not teach foreign languages, have the responsibility to introduce such alphabets, accent marks, and related symbols, so that these students can profit from instruction with nonspecial education teachers.

Use of Labels

Some teachers of a foreign language employ pictures in the classroom or require students to keep scrapbooks of pictures or files on given topics, such as foods, furniture, or animals. Partially seeing students can see well enough to find suitable pictures, label them in the foreign language, and complete assignments in final form that strongly resemble those of their seeing peers.

Blind students, though, need to engage help from friends or relatives to collect pictures. In labeling them, blind students tell their scribes what to write in print. In addition, blind students add braille labels giving both English and foreign equivalents. Since they cannot see the pictures, the English word will help them to learn the foreign word.

Using braille labels in the classroom, such as on a door or wall, is cumbersome for blind students who would have to go to the item and touch it in order to read the label. If teachers use bulletin-board displays, they may rely on pictures; better, they may use real things, such as a spoon or napkin. Here braille labels would be valuable. Any print labels should be large enough for partially seeing students to read.

Preparation of Textbooks

For best results, foreign-language textbooks should be in braille or large-print editions rather than sound recordings. If the course is strictly for listening and speaking, as in primary grades, and not for reading and writing, assignments will involve listening to tape or disk recordings. If the recorded material has been prepared for seeing listeners, its labels will be in print; these must be transcribed into braille for easy location of specific sections to be studied. If the tape or disk album is accompanied by a print booklet, the text material in the booklet should be transcribed. Partially seeing students might be able to use the pictures that such booklets usually include.

If the usual print textbook is accompanied by a workbook, the latter should also be reproduced. Brailling such workbooks may be a problem if an abundance of pictures and a minimum of text constitute the content of the workbooks. Specially trained volunteer braillists and typists must be utilized for copies of foreign-language material.

A typewriter that writes both in large symbols and with the necessary foreign letters and accents is desirable for children who can read visually. Otherwise, typists must add special symbols by hand, a process which is time consuming, subject to error, and less attractive as a finished work.

Foreign-Language Audio Aids

Even when foreign-language recordings are not required, visually handicapped students may wish to use them. They help to accustom the ear to the pronunciation and rhythm of the language as well as to test the student's facility in comprehending oral expression in that language. Sources for such materials include the usual catalogs for the visually handicapped, local record shops, and catalogs from commercial recording companies, foreign-language teachers, local public libraries for the seeing, instructional materials centers, etc.

Radio and television broadcasts may include two kinds of foreign-language programs:

1. Those designed for adults proficient in the language.
2. Those designed for students learning the language.

A college town may offer foreign-language drama productions, useful to younger students for the auditory experience. Foreign movies often shown on college campuses may not be of much help to visually handicapped students, because most of the films are in the original language with sub-titles in English.

Some commercial companies (such as Bell and Howell, with its Language Master, and Electronic Futures, Inc., with its EFI Card Reader) have already prepared cards in some foreign languages. A single card is inserted into the machine, which then reads aloud a 30-second message, such as a word or phrase written in print on the card. Braille, large print, or pictures can be added to these cards. Blank cards are also available for purchase, enabling teachers to develop their own programs.

Foreign-Language Visual Aids

Access to visual aids—magazines, newspapers, menus, etc.—in foreign languages is less likely to materialize in braille or large print. Here the student can make valid use of a reader fluent in the relevant language. Though these items may be supplemental readings, they supply the flavor and color of a culture and are of utility to future tourists. These publications employ contemporary language and timely topics, in contrast to the classics being studied.

Typewriting Foreign Languages

Since writing a foreign language involves using letters and accents not common to English, typewriting poses a problem. Borrowing or renting appropriate typewriters may be a good solution. If this is not possible, students and teachers must improvise techniques to overcome such difficulties on an English-language typewriter. If students plan to do anything serious in their careers with their foreign-language skill, these improvisations will not be considered acceptable abroad. If students use foreign-language typewriters, special education teachers must teach them the new keyboard or deviations of it.

Foreign-language dictionaries and glossaries, consulted when writing, are available from the American Printing House for the Blind, separate from any given textbook. Some words used in the course may not be included in these elementary compilations, but they meet general needs regardless of which textbook is being utilized. Having such books already available for purchase certainly reduces the burden carried by braillists, who can now omit glossaries from the text being transcribed.

HOME ECONOMICS

The area of home economics has, perhaps, more relevance for visually handicapped girls and boys than for their seeing peers, because in home economics, visually handicapped students may be introduced for the first time to basic skills acquired by much younger seeing children. Such aspects of daily living as eating habits, care of one's clothing, housekeeping techniques, personal hygiene, and shopping for and preparation of foods are considered. Students may have been deprived of sharing routine chores in the home or dormitory. Not having been exposed incidentally earlier, these children are taught skills in a formal way in home economics.

Eating Etiquette

Eating correctly is difficult and stressful for blind children, even for adults who wish to be socially correct. Vision provides diners with helpful feedback information—the food itself, operation of implements, and need for specific action, such as cutting a big piece into small pieces. In short, seeing people eat with mouth, hand, implements, *and* eyes. Vision bestows certain abilities while eating:

1. Vision enables the diner to observe others and to imitate. How often has a seeing guest, confronted with a food that he is not certain how to attack correctly, surreptitiously watched and imitated his hostess's procedure.
2. Vision enables the diner to pace himself with the group; if he finds that he is eating rapidly, he can deliberately slow down or vice versa.

Children must be taught in a deliberate and structured way, since this may be their only avenue for learning correctness. A blind individual with poor table etiquette is an indictment of schools and rehabilitation centers. The tragedy of it is that the blind individual and not his teachers are penalized by society through isolation and rejection.

A few publications (Western Michigan University, undated; Pittman, 1964) deal exclusively with eating techniques, while others (Barraga, 1958; Bindt, 1952; Shults, 1957; Western Michigan University, 1966) include eating as only one topic treated. Some cookbooks (Tipps, 1957) contain sections on table etiquette as modified for the blind. More important than the quality of manuals is consistency on the part of everyone concerned with instruction and supervision of the child. It is of doubtful value to have the special education teacher devote time to instruction of eating techniques only to have the children hurried through their meals in the school's dining room or in their homes, thereby prevented from practicing what they have learned. Goals must be functional. Cooperation from dormitory staff and family is essential for achieving the desired goals.

These expressed goals should be written in a sequential fashion with stipulated objectives for each grade or age level. For instance, first grade might be concentrating on use of the fork but not on buttering of bread, a skill that will be treated in the second grade.

Familiarity with Household Machines

Many commonplace household machines may not be recognized or used by blind children, even though their siblings are familiar with them and use them often. Just because the automatic laundry washer is in the house is no assurance that the blind child knows how to operate it. His mother may use it while the children are in school, thus preventing any contact with it while it is in use. Or parents may warn him not to touch it or turn the knobs lest he cause something to go wrong, such as flooding the utility room. In brief, blind children of a given chronological age generally are likely to be more restricted in knowledge and use of these devices than their seeing peers.

Parents may feel that trained teachers should instruct their children in these matters. Teachers, feeling overworked already, may wish that parents would assume this kind of tutelage. Houseparents may claim that they are not teachers and, therefore, not qualified to do this. As a consequence, children may be neglected in this phase of development.

Home economics courses should begin earlier for visually handicapped children for two main reasons:

1. Early exposure may help remedy past gaps in experience.
2. Course work may move more slowly and require more than the usual amount of time assigned to it in curriculums for seeing students.

Teaching of home economics is probably easier to execute in a residential school where all pupils have a visual problem and classes are small. In an integrated program, when a junior or senior high school visually handicapped student enrolls, he or she may be at a disadvantage from the outset. To forestall failure and embarrassment, special education teachers should arrange to work with such students in the home economics room (prior to enrollment) and teach them how to use the appliances and gadgets found there as well as how to orient themselves generally to the room. Armed with this training, visually handicapped students have better preparation for the experiences to follow, and for success in an integrated setting.

Special education teachers should supply home economics teachers with appropriate manuals and cookbooks, as well as with counseling and demonstrations to convey the various approaches that, though different, enable the blind to achieve the same ends as the sighted.

Cookbooks

Cookbooks and recipes intended for the seeing are often inappropriate for the visually handicapped. Therefore, it is not so much a matter of copying such books as it is of editing them. Cookbooks for the seeing give directions based on color—"bake until brown" or "fry until redness is gone"—along with pictorial illustrations. Instead, directions must be stated in exact, measurable terms—"bake for 30 minutes at 350 degrees" or "place 4 inches below broiler."

Cookbooks prepared specifically for the blind or partially seeing are available from the American Printing House for the Blind and other agencies. Special education teachers refer their students to these books. A few such cookbooks are those by Tipps (1957); the American Association of Instructors of the Blind (1958); the Brooklyn Bureau of Social Service and Children's Aid Society (1964); Hooper and Langan (1948); Manners (1943); and the Campbell Soup Company (undated).

Adapted Aids

Having adapted tools, visually handicapped students and housewives can function adequately in matters of measuring ingredients, pouring hot water from a pan of vegetables, serving food at the table, turning hot food over in a pan, etc. Such tools include measuring spoons and measuring cups, slicing knives, egg separators, cake and pie cutters, thermometers, pancake turners, oven lighters, aids for frying bacon flat, etc. *Aids and Appliances* from the American Foundation for the Blind and other catalogs list useful aids for homemaking.

If enrolled in home economics with seeing peers, the visually handicapped students should be provided with adapted aids for use in class. These are as important in this course as a relief map is in social science. Schools should supply these along with other instructional equipment.

Two books (Manners, 1943; Tipps, 1957) are especially helpful in providing more than recipes, namely, techniques for executing certain tasks such as turning pancakes, peeling tomatoes, rolling out pie crust, and storing of foods.

Sewing

Special tools are available for sewing; these include self-threading needles and needle threaders, tape measures, hem gauges, sewing boxes for keeping colored threads organized, etc.

With easy access to ready-made clothing, it is more important for visually handicapped students to know how to mend and repair clothing than to make new garments. Mending involves knowing a variety of stitches, as well as how to attach buttons, snaps, hooks, and eyes; let down a hem or take it up; repair seams; darn socks; etc.

Knowing black thread from white is basic for many routine tasks. When other colors are needed, the blind sewer may need to have a visual check by a friend or relative to determine, for instance, if this pink thread is suitable for this pink dress. In certain situations, the stitching may not show from the outside of the garment, in which case matching colors is less crucial. Understanding color (Wheeler, 1969) for purposes of sewing, grooming, and interior decorating is essential for satisfactory effects. Knowing how to select, purchase, and care for clothing (Hildreth, 1959) stretches the clothing budget and prolongs the life of a wardrobe.

Available Periodicals

Periodicals available for students' use in home economics are *Our Special, Consumer Bulletin, Ladies' Home Journal, Madam, Seventeen, Today's Health,* and *Good Housekeeping.*

ARTS AND CRAFTS

Arts and crafts provide the same benefits to the visually handicapped as to the normally seeing: an outlet for creativity, satisfaction in the finished product, a sense of accomplishment, and release from tension as a kind of therapy (Anthony, 1969; Decker, 1960; Kurzhals, 1961; Lowenfeld, 1957). The type of activity must be selected carefully, because certain ones yield bigger dividends to the visually handicapped than others. A visually handicapped child's art work need not be like his seeing peer's in medium or theme; for instance, while seeing children are working with crayons, the visually handicapped child does not also have to be engaged with crayons just because he happens to be enrolled in an integrated setting (Freund, 1969). Similarly, if seeing children are concentrating on "clouds" or "houses" as their theme, a visually handicapped child can justifiably work on a different theme that is more meaningful to him. Another approach to selectivity is that seeing children might enjoy doing the kind of art work appropriate for the visually handicapped; perhaps the regular curriculum for art classes is too limited, prosaic, and stereotyped.

Process versus Product

The respective merits of process or product (Combs, 1962) are irrelevant except as either impedes or stimulates creativity in the visually handicapped child. If the teacher values product above process, his philosophical orientation will prevent him from accepting his role as art teacher of visually handicapped students in the class. If she maintains that the product must attain high conventional standards to be acceptable as art, he will insist that the product take on prescribed characteristics—usually those of his own art work, which children are expected to imitate precisely. In such a climate, the visually handicapped child cannot succeed, because his product obviously will not match the teacher's.

By contrast, when the teacher is more concerned with process than product, a visually handicapped child will fit into the class easily, because what happens to the child and how he feels about it and about himself will be of utmost significance (Lowenfeld, 1957). If the child enjoys art class, then this teacher has been successful. Enjoying, however, is more than merely feeling happy; it involves experiencing success or the freedom to be oneself and not in competition with seeing peers, and a realization that here one can have a true art episode without any apology. Such a teacher may have several types of activity occurring simultaneously, rather than forcing every child to do exactly the same thing. As Thanksgiving approaches, he gives children a choice of activities that relate to the Thanksgiving theme. With this elasticity, appropriate activities await the child who does not see but who can express himself through other channels than the visual.

Some art teachers distinguish between arts and crafts (Coombs, 1967) with the latter relegated to a subordinate role. To them, art means painting or sculpture but not the making of things such as trays, necklaces, or trivets. In spite of this differentiation, even crafts acquire individuality, reflecting the creator or craftsman. Despite the use of prepared pieces of material—leather, wood, beads, etc.—there is still much freedom to modify and project one's own personality. Combination of colors, textures, sizes, weights, designs, etc., reveals the imaginative powers of the worker. If "arts" and "crafts" must be separated, visually handicapped children, of course, will have more latitude and versatility in the areas of crafts, which are three dimensional and, therefore, comprehensible to them. McVay (1966) has discussed a crafts program for blind children in the Detroit public schools and stressed that many activities which seeing children enjoy can also be done by blind children. Skill in the use of certain tools "which sighted children learn by casual observation and practice, are major learning experiences for the blind" (p. 243). Through the media of crafts, it is possible to teach basic principles operative in art—form, balance, design, contrast, theme, background—if the teacher is of such a philosophical bent. If these elements were truly absent in crafts, designers of furniture, glassware, silver, clothing, jewelry, and carpeting would not enjoy such great reputations as individuals of creative talent.

Color, Texture, and Shape

In the making of things, the product made by the student will demonstrate the characteristics of color and color contrasts enjoyed by partially seeing children. True, the shades may have to be vivid and strongly contrasting rather than subtle. Blind children, on the other hand, work through texture and shape. Because the partially seeing can express themselves through color and the blind through texture and shape, activities for both groups (Jones, 1961) must be used to maximize the sensory avenues of each. Color may be present in the blind child's product, but it is related to differences in texture or shape. For example, a product may contain two textures and two colors or two different shapes and two colors. Contrasts in texture include smooth and rough, coarse and fine, or surface qualities of two different materials (wood and metal), whereas shape is represented by circle or rectangle, sphere or cylinder, plane and concave, etc. These elements are not contrary to good art form. The combination of eye appeal and tactual interest renders a product all the more pleasurable and satisfying with its multisensory stimulation.

Three-Dimensional Models and Sculpture

In the realm of sculpture (Kewell, 1955), especially by the blind, teachers must first determine the children's past experiences and draw from them an art activity. This practice is preferable to imposing an activity without foundation in the young sculptor's life. The child's past experience may include having had normal vision or at least more vision than he now has. If so, his visual imagery may influence his sculpture. Although blind children and clay modeling seem to be compatible, what the child attempts to sculpt must be something with which he is familiar. If he has never examined a cow in detail, his clay "cow" may not evoke happiness and satisfaction in him, because he feels inadequate about cow characteristics. His pet dog, whom he fondles and with whom he plays at home, is a much more appropriate subject. The child might capture in clay the dog in one of many characteristic poses so familiar to the child and beloved by him.

If three-dimensional models are brought to class, the goal should be discussing features of those models rather than copying them. There is little genuine creativity in having a certain vase on one's work table in order to examine it frequently so that the new product can be patterned after it. A richer experience might be examining a variety of different vases, discussing their differences and similarities, and then bringing together characteristics from several vases in the new product. With this approach, the product is not predetermined by the teacher but by the child's own imagination and versatility.

If the child is asked to select his favorite from among several products brought to the classroom, he might be led to verbalize on why he had chosen a certain one. However, the teacher should not argue about which is "best," his choice or the child's. Personal preference is a combination of emotion, intellect, past experience, ego strength, etc. As a child, he is perhaps reacting on the emotional level without really knowing why and because of insufficient sophistication and intellectualism, which may come in time with maturity and more education. Furthermore, the teacher may be responding primarily to visual characteristics of the product and the child to the tactual or motor-kinesthetic. Therefore, an art teacher must be able to understand the child's approach and, as far as possible, identify with it.

School Museum

Some residential schools have museums (Coon, 1953) of three-dimensional objects as educational aids. The children can visit the museum on the campus, and teachers can borrow selected items for use in the classroom. The collection should be dynamic and growing with new and interesting additions; the children should be led to sense a glow of excitement and appreciation at having access to such a museum that is alive with change and newness. Items on open shelves or in unlocked cabinets duly labeled in braille and large print should convey pride in the student's progressive and enriched educational center.

Acquisitions need not necessarily be expensive or even cost anything. Alert curators are attuned to situations in which they may contact merchants in the local community, company representatives, or civic-minded leaders for items that might otherwise be discarded in time. A sales campaign or a convention with the usual displays may have props that will be dismantled and discarded once the event has ended. Public museums may also donate artifacts considered inferior for display but excellent for blind children to examine tactually.

Such a museum for the visually handicapped has application in many curricular areas besides art—nature study, transportation and communication, architecture, conservation, etc.

Sharing Art Instruction

Where feasible, special education teachers must lead the way in creative art activities for visually handicapped children. Knowing which activities are appropriate or how activities might be modified, these teachers must share their expertise with classroom art teachers for the sake of successful integration. Special education teachers can, in communicating with art teachers: confer and share ideas; demonstrate a given activity; share books *about* art for the blind; send enough art material for the whole class to make the kind of product being made by the blind child; show appropriate films or slides at faculty meetings; share artifacts with her class; etc. The art teacher may be quite receptive to such support and cooperation. She may feel that she is now not struggling alone.

Creative Dramatics

Creative dramatics helps children to cast off their self and to assume the role of someone else (Martucci, 1959; Weckler, 1964). If the parts are not memorized, children can bring feelings that will inspire appropriate words. Understanding the part is far more important than learning the prescribed lines. Sharing roles adds flexibility and freshness to the experience; today Johnny might be the father, while tomorrow he will be the son.

Besides the values which all children gain from dramatic arts, they offer a unique opportunity to correct unobtrusively blind children's undesirable or faulty behavior patterns (Lowenfeld, 1971).

Playing with handpuppets often brings out the otherwise shy child; he can say something for the puppet that he could never say for himself. Furthermore, the audience is usually friendly classmates. All this removes anxiety and stress from the production and invites enjoyment and spontaneity. Too often children produce plays only for the audience and not for themselves.

Choric speaking is another means for drawing out the reticent child. A child who cannot speak aloud before a group can find anonymity in the group, speaking freely and relaxedly. Initially the teacher may do most of the talking, with the children saying an oft-repeated refrain. In more advanced numbers, the children are divided into parts based on tonal quality and personality.

Creative Writing

Creative writing is another channel for self-expression. The children's writings should not be graded or corrected except as teacher and child might work together doing it. If the child reveals his inmost feelings and secrets, he should not be betrayed or embarrassed by having his confidences divulged to the whole class without his permission to do so. Ideas are more important than grammar, spelling, and punctuation. Creative writing should be an ongoing process, with the child free to write when so inclined and to submit his piece whenever it is finished—rather than having creative writing for 30 minutes on

Thursday afternoon at 2:30. Some teachers have a box in the room so that children have a place to deposit their writing for the teacher without having to interrupt him or the class.

A child need not be proficient in writing mechanics before he can enjoy composing. Young visually handicapped children who have not yet mastered the Perkins Brailler may dictate to the teacher or into a tape recorder. The teacher can later rewrite the compositions and bind them between covers to make the child's very own book.

Older children can be given open-ended topics to which to respond with a composition. Such intriguing topics might be "My First Invention Would Be —" or "Suppose It Rained Up instead of Down" or "My Playmate Abe Lincoln."

Creative writing also includes original poetry. To inspire this medium, teachers must read aloud or recite poetry frequently in the classroom. Simple limericks can be read, with the children supplying the last line. The Japanese haiku can be introduced, with children trying their creative skill in writing this short form without rhyme or intricate design.

Creative dramatics, choir speaking, puppetry, essay writing, and poetry writing pose no real problem in integrating visually handicapped children with the normally seeing. Classroom teachers will experience less frustration and tension here than in crafts.

PHYSICAL EDUCATION AND RECREATION

Physical education and recreation can reasonably be considered together, because in actual living these two are not discretely separated or separable. Furthermore, one goal of the physical education program in schools is not only to promote health and bodily coordination but also to teach constructive and enjoyable ways in which to utilize leisure time through skills learned. Physical education and recreation run in a parallel line rather than lying end to end, with recreation not beginning until physical education in school has ended at the termination of school enrollment. Frequently physical education programs fail, not because there are too few organized sports at school or because the school teams are lowest in the league but rather because children and youth, when not in school under the direction of the teacher or coach, either do not know how to use leisure time profitably or have no desire to be so engaged.

Planning the physical education program is largely determined by placement of the visually handicapped child in a day program with seeing peers (Forman, 1969; Hatlen, 1967; Johnson, 1969; Kempter, 1969; Laufman, 1962) or in a residential program where all children have a visual problem (Buell, 1964, 1966; Pearson, 1965).

School Placement and Program Adjustment

In a residential program, classes are small, although a given group of children has its range of abilities and heterogeneity. Specialized equipment (goals or targets that sound like loud metronomes) and adapted conditions (saucer-shaped roller skating rinks) make physical activity natural and pleasant. Rules of games and techniques of play can be modified—using a large ball instead of the standard size, rolling the ball instead of throwing it, using a guide wire in track events, etc. Teachers may have had some special education training in the area of the physically handicapped and be less fearful about active play for these children. Emphases in the program are likely to be shifted away from ball games and directed toward calisthenics and gymnastics (Pearson, 1965; Lefkowitz, 1962), dancing (English, 1958; Morgan, 1956), skating, swimming (Belenky, 1955; Seamons, 1966), wrestling (Buell, 1958; English, 1957), bowling (Carter, 1959), bicycling, relays, etc. Many of these activities are not included in day-program curriculums, even for seeing children.

In day programs, because classes are large, physical education teachers may be hesitant to include a handicapped child lest he be injured. The resource room teacher—more than the itinerant teacher—can hope to work out a cooperative arrangement with physical education teachers and with regular classroom teachers. He might have use of the playground or gymnasium exclusively for visually handicapped children. Unfortunately, the children will probably range from kindergarten through eighth grade, which fact eliminates much in the way of group activities. He might divide his pupils into two or three homogeneous groups and then include normally seeing children to swell the numbers and provide healthy integration.

He might visit and observe the regular physical education class in which a visually handicapped child is a member to assist the child initially to become involved and to suggest and recommend to the teacher modifications that might be tried. This need not be done every day, but should be more frequent at the beginning of the school year or when a new activity is being introduced.

He might share his professional books and journal articles with physical education teachers and show appropriate films. The films might be shown after school hours even to a small group of interested teachers in an attempt to transmit ideas and to build confidence in the teachers' own ability to cope successfully with the situation.

Depending on how rigidly the curriculum must be followed and how flexible teachers are, some activities (ball games) might be minimized while others (relays and calisthenics) might be emphasized. Sometimes the root of the problem lies outside the individual school which visually handicapped children attend. If there is keen competition between several schools, the curriculum may be fixed in order not to penalize the one school for not having been involved in prescribed activities and hence suffering at highly valued meets and tournaments.

In order to provide physical education for the visually handicapped and yet not put the school at a disadvantage, a mobility teacher (many of whom have come from physical education programs) might serve here as physical education teacher. Thus he combines his training in physical education and special education.

If problems of transportation and scheduling can be solved, and if community resources are relatively close to the school, use might be made during the day or after school of the YMCA, YWCA, health club, or other community organizations. Parents and others might supply transportation and supervision; the staff at the Y or health club might be the teachers. Normally seeing children could be invited to participate, resulting in a number of dividends: good public relations, effective integration in active endeavors, encouragement of friendships outside the school itself, demonstration of what visually handicapped children can do, etc. The point in working out programs even outside the school, if necessary, is twofold:

1. Just because adapted physical education seems unworkable in the school with its physical education staff, there is no reason to dismiss the matter altogether and penalize visually handicapped children.
2. If recreation is a close ally of physical education, special education teachers have the obligation to demonstrate how community resources can be utilized and how an active, enjoyable life can be led outside the school— outside where children live the greater portions of their time anyway.

Corrective Exercises

Visually handicapped children can benefit from corrective work in posture, coordination, gait, etc. Blind children cannot see themselves in mirrors and cannot see others to imitate (Siegel, 1966). If preschool children have been too protected and sheltered, they have missed out on ordinary exercise and the active play experiences—walking, jumping, climbing, rolling, hopping, etc.— so common to young children. These children then come to kindergarten or first grade at a lower level of readiness for physical education than their seeing peers. They require very simple but necessary activities to strengthen muscles and produce tone.

These blind children may have to be engaged in such elementary activities as jumping from the bottom step of a flight, climbing stairs correctly, hopping, skipping, jumping upward and forward, throwing beanbags (not balls) and retrieving them, rolling, somersaulting, running, etc. Until blind children have mastered these activities, it is doubtful that they can participate vigorously with more experienced seeing children of the same chronological age.

Family Recreation

So far as family recreation is concerned, mention should be made here of some activities, such as table games, reading, membership in clubs, and spectator sports. Some of them are conducted singly, whereas others are best enjoyed in the company of friends, seeing or visually handicapped. Some pastimes are sedentary, while others are active and vigorous. Variety is the key to refreshing leisure-time pursuits.

Having experienced a variety of recreational activities with their visually handicapped child, inside the home as well as out in public, parents may be willing to enroll their children in day camps (Williams & Whitney, 1964) as well as in overnight camp settings exclusively for the visually handicapped (Edwards, 1965; Halliday, 1964; Huckins, 1963) and similar camp facilities for visually handicapped integrated with seeing campers (Kempter, 1969).

Only as parents witness success in their visually handicapped sons and daughters—not only in the academic realm but also in recreation—will they be less apprehensive about allowing their teenagers to broaden their worlds by leaving home to assume their first employment or to attend college or even to marry and establish homes of their own, often geographically distant from the parents.

REFERENCES

Aids and Appliances. New York: American Foundation for the Blind, latest edition.

American Association of Instructors of the Blind, Cookbook Committee of the Homemaking Section. *Food at your fingertips.* Louisville, Ky.: American Printing House for the Blind, 1958.

American Association of Instructors of the Blind. *Report of science workshop: Survey of materials of instruction.* Washington, D.C.: Author, undated.

Anthony, G. H. Creativity and the visually handicapped. *Education of the Visually Handicapped,* 1969, **1**, 122–123.

Auerbach, H. Teaching arithmetic to the partially seeing. *International Journal for the Education of the Blind,* 1959, **9**, 44–46.

Barraga, N.C. Social opportunities available to students in residential schools. *International Journal for the Education of the Blind,* 1958, **7**, 110–115.

Belenky, R. *A Swimming program for blind children.* New York: American Foundation for the Blind, 1955.

Bevans, J.E. Development of a recreational music program at Perkins School for the Blind. *International Journal for the Education of the Blind,* 1965, **14**, 72–76.

Bindt, J. *Handbook for the blind.* New York: Macmillan, 1952.

Boldt, W. The development of scientific thinking in blind children and adolescents. *Education of the Visually Handicapped,* 1969, **1**, 5–8.

Borgersen, R. Improving recording techniques. *New Outlook for the Blind,* 1965, **59**, 308–312.

Brooklyn Bureau of Social Service and Children's Aid Society. *The BBSS cookbook of convenience foods.* Brooklyn: Author, 1964.

Bryan, C. A. Secondary school sciences for the blind. *International Journal for the Education of the Blind,* 1965, **6**, 11–18.

Buell, C. E. Wrestling in the life of a blind boy. *International Journal for the Education of the Blind,* 1958, **7**, 93–96.

Buell, C. E. Developments in physical education for blind children. *New Outlook for the Blind,* 1964, **58**, 202–206.

Buell, C. E. *Physical education for blind children.* Springfield, Ill.: Charles C Thomas, 1966.

Campbell Soup Company. *Campbell cookbook.* Camden, N. J.: Author, undated.

Carpenter, R. H. *Special problems, special solutions: Handbook for teachers of the visually handicapped.* Atlanta: Georgia Department of Education, 1969.

Carter, V. R. Bowling into the spotlight. *International Journal for the Education of the Blind,* 1959, **8**, 100–101.

Code of braille textbook formats and techniques, 1965. Louisville, Ky.: American Printing House for the Blind, 1965.

Combs, A. W. (Chairman). *Perceiving, behaving, becoming.* Washington, D.C.: Association for Supervision and Curriculum Development Yearbook Committee, 1962, 141–163.

Coombs, V. H. Guidelines for teaching arts and crafts to blind children in the elementary grades. *International Journal for the Education of the Blind,* 1967, **16**, 79–83.

Coon, N. *Place of the museum in the education of the blind.* New York: American Foundation for the Blind, 1953.

Crescimbeni, J. *Arithmetic enrichment activities for elementary school children.* W. Nyack, N. Y.: Parker Publishing, 1965.

Crockett, M. C. The field trip. *International Journal for the Education of the Blind,* 1958, **7**, 136–137.

Davidow, M. E. *The abacus made easy: A simplified manual for teaching the Cranmer abacus.* Philadelphia: Overbrook School for the Blind, 1966.

Decker, R. J. Creative art experience for blind children. *International Journal for the Education of the Blind,* 1960, **9**, 104–106.

Dunkin, D. J. Educational TV. *International Journal for the Education of the Blind,* 1962, **12**, 55–57.

Educational Research Council of Greater Cleveland. *Greater Cleveland mathematics program.* Chicago: Science Research Associates, 1962.

Edwards, D. H. An adventure in learning. *International Journal for the Education of the Blind,* 1965, **14**, 76–77.

English, B. Wrestling in schools for the blind. *International Journal for the Education of the Blind,* 1957, **6**, 68–70.

English, B. A program of dance for visually handicapped young people. *International Journal for the Education of the Blind,* 1958, **7**, 85–89.

Feldzamen, A. N. *Numbers and such: A lively guide to the new math for parents and other perplexed adults.* Englewood Cliffs, N. J.: Prentice-Hall, 1968.

Forman, E. The inclusion of visually limited and blind children in a sighted physical education program. *Education of the Visually Handicapped,* 1969, **1**, 113–115.

Freund, C. Teaching art to the blind child integrated with sighted children. *New Outlook for the Blind,* 1969, **63,** 205–210.

Fulker, W. H., & Fulker, M. *Techniques with tangibles.* Springfield, Ill.: Charles C Thomas, 1968.

Gissoni, F. L. *Using the Cranmer abacus for the blind.* Louisville, Ky.: American Printing House for the Blind, 1964.

Halliday, C. School camping—A meaningful experience. *New Outlook for the Blind,* 1964, **58,** 81–82.

Hatlen, P. H. Physical education for the visually handicapped. *International Journal for the Education of the Blind,* 1967, **17,** 17–21.

Helms, A. *Recording science texts for the blind.* New York: American Foundation for the Blind, 1957.

Helms, A. *Tape recording books for the blind* (Rev. ed.). New York: American Foundation for the Blind, 1968.

Hildreth, G. J. Methods used in teaching clothing construction and selection. *International Journal for the Education of the Blind,* 1959, **9,** 18–20.

't 'Hooft, F., & Heslinga, K. Sex education of blind-born children. *New Outlook for the Blind,* 1968, **62,** 15–21.

Hooper, M. S., & Langan, P. J. *The braille cookbook.* Louisville, Ky.: American Printing House for the Blind, 1948.

Huckins, R. L. Camping for children who are blind. *New Outlook for the Blind,* 1963, **57,** 91–94.

Hussey, S. R., & Legge, L. The "Halifax Method" of arithmetical calculations. *International Journal for the Education of the Blind,* 1956, **6,** 36–40.

Johnson, P. R. Physical education for blind children in public elementary schools. *New Outlook for the Blind,* 1969, **63,** 264–271.

Jones, C. R. Art for the blind and partially seeing. *School Arts,* 1961, **60,** 21–22.

Kempter, R. R., Jr. Some effects of sighted teens in a camp for the blind. *Rehabilitation Teacher,* 1969, **1,** 25–29.

Kewell, J. *Sculpture by blind children.* New York: American Foundation for the Blind, 1955.

Kurzhals, I. W. Creating with materials can be of value for young blind children. *International Journal for the Education of the Blind,* 1961, **10,** 75–79.

Larsen, H. D. *Arithmetic for colleges* (Rev. ed.). New York: Macmillan, 1958.

Laufman, M. Blind children in integrated recreation. *New Outlook for the Blind,* 1962, **56,** 81–84.

Lefkowitz, L. J. Evaluating physical education programs. *New Outlook for the Blind,* 1962, **56,** 137–139.

Library of Congress. *Volunteers who produce braille books, large-type books, disc recordings, tape recordings for blind and visually impaired individuals.* Washington, D.C.: Division for the Blind and Physically Handicapped, 1967.

Lowenfeld, B. Psychological foundation of special methods in teaching blind children. In P. A. Zahl (Ed.), *Blindness.* Princeton: Princeton University Press, 1950. Pp. 89–108.

Lowenfeld, B. *Our blind children* (3rd ed.). Springfield, Ill.: Charles C Thomas, 1971.

Lowenfeld, V. *Creative and mental growth* (3rd ed.). New York: Macmillan, 1957.

Manners, M. (Ed). *Evelyn Lee's cook book.* Los Angeles: Braille Institute of America, 1943.

Martucci, E. A. Curtain going up. *International Journal for the Education of the Blind,* 1959, **8,** 77–83.

McVay, R. A. A crafts program for blind children. *New Outlook for the Blind,* 1966, **60,** 243–244.

Minnesota mathematics and science teaching project. Ann Arbor: University of Michigan Press, 1968.

Morgan, M. F. Square dancing in a school for the blind. *International Journal for the Education of the Blind,* 1956, **6,** 43–44.

Napier, G. D. Suggestions to facilitate mutual ease and adjustment. *The Construct,* 1966, **1,** 3–4; 1967, **2,** 3.

Napier, G. D., & Weishahn, M. W. *Handbook for teachers of the visually handicapped.* Louisville, Ky.: American Printing House for the Blind, 1970.

Nolan, C. Y., & Bruce, R. E. An experimental program in elementary mathematics for the blind. *International Journal for the Education of the Blind,* 1962, **11,** 71–74.

Olsen, M. Modern curriculum provisions for visually handicapped children—A conference summary. *International Journal for the Education of the Blind,* 1963, **12,** 80–83.

Pearson, K. Taking a new look at physical education. *New Outlook for the Blind,* 1965, **59,** 315–317.

Pittman, Y. H. An exploratory study of the eating problems of blind children. *New Outlook for the Blind,* 1964, **58,** 264–267.

Recording for the Blind, Inc. *The development of basic research materials and a manual on the use of recorded textbooks.* New York: Author, undated.

Seamons, G. R. *Swimming for the blind.* Provo, Utah: Brigham Young University, 1966.

Shuff, R. V. *School mathematics study group.* Ann Arbor: University of Michigan Press, 1962.

Shults, E. Social adjustment—The development of efficient living skills. *Proceedings, Institute for Houseparents of Visually Handicapped Children.* Louisville, Ky.: American Association of Instructors of the Blind and American Foundation for the Blind, 1957.

Siegel, I. M. *Posture in the blind.* New York: American Foundation for the Blind, 1966.

Smith, E. W., Krouse, S. W., & Atkinson, M. M. *Educators encyclopedia.* Englewood Cliffs, N. J.: Prentice-Hall, 1961.

Thompson, R. P. A music program for visually handicapped children. *New Outlook for the Blind,* 1957, **51,** 43–55.

Tipps, E. K. *Cooking without looking: Food preparation methods and techniques for blind homemakers.* Louisville, Ky.: American Printing House for the Blind, 1957. (In braille and large type.)

Waterhouse, E. J. Arithmetic aids for the blind. *International Journal for the Education of the Blind,* 1955, **5,** 25–29.

Weckler, J. L. A part to play. *International Journal for the Education of the Blind,* 1964, **14,** 13–19.

Western Michigan University, School of Graduate Studies. *Homemaking manual: A reference manual for home teachers working with the adult blind.* Kalamazoo, Mich.:

Community Services for the Visually Handicapped, Illinois Department of Children and Family Services, 1966.

Western Michigan University, School of Graduate Studies. *Techniques for eating: A guide for blind persons.* Kalamazoo, Mich.: Rehabilitation Service Administration, U. S. Department of Health, Education, & Welfare, undated.

Wexler, A. *Experimental science for the blind: An instruction manual.* New York: Pergamon Press, 1961.

Wheeler, J. G. A practical knowledge of color for the congenitally blind. *New Outlook for the Blind,* 1969, **63,** 225–231.

Williams, C., & Whitney, P. An experiment in day camping. *New Outlook for the Blind,* 1964, **58,** 83–84.

Wittich, W. A. *Educators guide to free tapes, scripts, and transcripts* (13th ed.). Randolph, Wisc.: Educators Progress Service, 1969.

CHAPTER 9

Life Adjustment

Stanley Suterko

School of Education, and Institute of Blind Rehabilitation
Western Michigan University
Kalamazoo, Michigan

ORIENTATION AND MOBILITY

It is generally recognized that a severe visual handicap imposes serious restrictions on an individual's ability to move about freely and confidently in his environment. Less apparent and not appreciated is the debilitating effect this forced restriction has on the total self of the individual. Finestone, Lukoff, and Whiteman (1960) stated that this competency plays a key role in the individual's performance of important social roles, has a profound effect on his relationships with sighted society, and contributes to his own self-image.

Irwin (1955) sums up its importance to the individual in the following statement.

> The inability to go forth alone at will without accommodating oneself to the convenience of one's associates is perhaps the greatest affliction resulting from blindness. To have to ask a friend or busy member of the family to go along on the simplest of errands is more humiliating than most seeing people realize and humiliation brings with it a deep resentment at one's lot [p. 169].

Some of the leading educators in the field, as well as mobility specialists, have come to the realization that teachers must assume responsibility for the development of orientation and mobility skills, just as they assume responsibility for the development of other skills. Alonso (1965) feels this recognition on the part of educators is the most significant development of this decade, in terms of lifetime needs of visually handicapped children and youth.

The Competency Committee for the U. S. Office of Education Study (Mackie & Dunn, 1955), dealing with the competencies needed by teachers of children who are blind, supports this role of the teacher in the following quotation.

> The blind child's physical orientation and ability to travel are basic to his independence, as well as to the respect which this competency inspires in others. Every teacher, recognizing the blind child's need for continued help in developing skills in physical orientation at each level of his growth, should also recognize that the child will need further instruction in this skill. The teacher should, therefore, be aware of the available facilities for training.
>
> The teacher should consider the varying degrees of ability of blind children in the interpretation of their physical environment, spatial orientation, and general physical mobility. With this in mind he should plan for activities to be carried on in an atmosphere of freedom and exploration which will continue to improve the skills basic to the children's physical orientation and travel [pp. 17–18].

It is inconceivable today that any educational program designed to meet the total needs of every visually handicapped child not include orientation and mobility. As Gockman and Costello (1966) stated, any program for visually handicapped children should emphasize training in orientation and mobility, or it is not a complete program.

The mobility methods available to the visually handicapped are five in number and may be categorized as (1) independent travel without the use of an aid or device for those having travel vision; (2) guide dog travel; (3) travel using the long cane (or more appropriately, prescription cane); (4) utilization of electronic mobility aids (one is presently on the market; however, in the opinion of many mobility instructors these devices have not yet been perfected); (5) travel with a constant companion or guide, a dependency means of achieving mobility.

The first serious and systematic effort to provide quality mobility services to the totally blind in this country was undertaken by The Seeing Eye in January 1929. Their achievements in the area of quality mobility services are recognized by everyone concerned with the visually handicapped. The next significant contribution to this specialty was made by the United States Army program at Valley Forge. In 1944 a large number of blinded servicemen were brought together for rehabilitation treatment. Among those concerned with this problem was First Lieutenant Richard Hoover, who had the courage to say: "Blind people in this country travel miserably." This inspired him and his colleagues to experiment with the cane and its use until they developed a longer cane to be employed in a specific manner. The cane that was ultimately developed was approximately 46 inches long, 0.5 of an inch in diameter, and weighed 6 ounces without tip (Hoover, 1950). In addition to the specialized cane, Hoover developed a systematic scanning system which was designed to be used with this travel tool; it has been referred to as the Hoover technique and is presently called the touch technique.

At the termination of the Valley Forge program in 1948, the Veterans Administration assumed responsibility for the rehabilitation of all blinded servicemen. The Veterans Administration Hospital at Hines, Illinois, was selected as the site for the program and the Central Blind Rehabilitation Section admitted its first patient in July 1948. In the establishment of this section a group of individuals carefully selected from such areas as teaching and corrective therapy, were given intensive training for a period of 6 months. They were given the title of Orientors and under the blindfold they validated each of the travel techniques before they were allowed to teach any of the blinded veterans.

The rehabilitated veterans returning to their home communities attracted the attention of those serving the civilian blind through their upright posture and graceful movement. It was not long before the Blind Section at Hines received recognition in the field as the center of progressive thought and action on the mobility of blind persons. The Hines personnel have been responsible for the development, refinement, and validation of formalized orientation and mobility techniques with the long cane (Ball, 1964).

These formalized travel skills which proved so effective with the blinded veterans were next tested and tried with blind children in several summer workshops. The results were rewarding since the mobility techniques proved to be adaptable and effective for the visually handicapped child. This efficacy, coupled with the demand by those serving the civilian blind for mobility instructors, resulted in graduate level training programs. To meet the ever-growing need for mobility specialists there are presently five graduate programs and one undergraduate program training these specialists. A recent step taken to ensure quality mobility instruction to the visually handicapped has been the certification of mobility instructors by the American Association of Workers for the Blind.

Definition of Orientation and Mobility

The terms orientation and mobility have assumed a special significance in the education of the visually handicapped. They have been used to describe that competency which enables the child to achieve safe, efficient, and graceful movement through his environment. As with the successful navigation of any individual through space, whether it be on earth or in outer space, one of the most important aspects is the individual's present position and his relationship to his ultimate destination. The individual needs to be effectively "oriented" before he can achieve purposeful mobility. Orientation is defined as the process of utilizing the remaining senses in establishing one's position and relationship to all other significant objects in the environment. This is an ongoing process, as indicated by Carroll (1961), in which the individual must not only perceive his present position but must also perceive it anew with each step taken.

The term mobility is used to refer to the actual locomotion of the individual from his present fixed position to his desired position in another part of the environment. This term then encompasses all of the motor skills involved in locomotion, such as footfalls for linear locomotion; proper heel and toe gait; facing movements; control of the body's center of gravity; detection of inclines and declines; etc. Perhaps the best way to remember the relationship of orientation to mobility is to recall Fuller's quotation: "The wise man travels while the fool wanders."

This orientation process is acquired by the visually handicapped through the use of their auditory, tactual, kinesthetic, vestibular, olfactory, and in a good percentage of the cases their visual, senses. Some writers feel the gustatory sense also contributes to the individual's orientation; perhaps it does, but not in relation to any physical objects in the environment. Because the senses play such an important part in orientation and mobility it behooves all teachers to acquire a better understanding and appreciation of their role.

Audition

Hearing, the prime long-distance sense, can be considered the "Queen" sense for the blind. It is the only means by which the child can perceive distance and depth in his environment.

Contrary to common belief, there is no automatic compensation in hearing acuteness because of the loss of vision. The greater sensory acuteness in hearing that is exhibited by the visually handicapped is a result of persistent efforts to use this sense to its fullest. Recognizing this fact, teachers should avail themselves of every opportunity to encourage the child to develop this sense to its maximum. One of the first uses of audition by the child is that it gives him an indication of a room. The acoustical qualities of a small room, such as a broom closet, are certainly quite different from those of a ballroom. The child should, therefore, be made aware of this fact and be prepared to make an estimate of the room size, such as a small or large room. If it is a large room, he should next be alert to making an appraisal of the quality of the room, that is, its makeup and furnishings. A room constructed of plaster walls and ceilings with bare wood floors has different acoustical qualities than a room constructed with a sound-absorbing ceiling and wall tiles. Furnishings of drapes and rugs will further change the sound quality of the room.

As he is seated in the room, he should also take cognizance of any unique sounds which will enable him to become oriented to the room. The opening and closing of the door should reveal its location and relation to him; sounds streaming in open windows during summer will indicate the relationship of the windows and outside wall to him; the teacher sitting at her desk and talking will tell him where the desk is located; the slight noise of the clock when the hands move will provide another landmark. As the child listens intently to the environment, he will discover there are a multitude of sounds which can be utilized as orientation cues.

The directions of school corridors can easily be determined by the footfalls of others in the hall. Open cross-corridors can also be readily detected by footfalls or echolocation. The application of these basic principles for utilizing sounds to acquire direction of travel are also applicable to mobility outdoors. As the child travels on the sidewalks outdoors, he will use the footfalls of others to indicate the direction of the sidewalk. Also available to him as an indicator of the direction of the sidewalk is the sound of parallel traffic.

Additional auditory cues or landmarks available in a school building are a constantly running drinking fountain; the widened area of a vestibule, such as is frequently located by offices; a narrowing of corridor width or height due to firedoor abutments or dropped ceilings; a change in the sounds of footsteps due to a change in floor surfaces. There are also the characteristic sounds from the kitchen and workshops, the ventilating fans, etc. Any audible sound has the potential of becoming an orientation aid, so the teacher should insist that the children become active listeners and learn to convert these cues to orientation aids.

There are numerous subskills of hearing that assist the visually handicapped in interpreting the environment and are indispensable in effective orientation. These aspects of hearing should be appreciated and understood by all teachers.

Echolocation

This term was coined by Griffin (1958) to explain the activity of emitting a sound and perceiving the qualities of the reflected echo. This activity was first discovered in bats in 1879 by Spallanzani. Most recently it has been recognized that porpoises do extremely well with echolocation in navigating about the ocean (Kellogg, 1961). In many of the popular magazines it is referred to as "sonar activity of the blind." The word sonar is taken from *so*und, *n*avigation, *a*nd, *r*anging, describing a device used aboard navy ships.

All visually handicapped employ echolocation in varying degrees, some especially young children being more overt about the emitted signal, while adults tend to be more subtle in generating a sound. Many times one will observe children employing echolocation as they enter a room or walk down the corridor. It may take any of the following forms: clicking of the tongue, snapping of the fingers, or even slapping the feet on the floor. Some adults use clickers on heels as they move about for this same purpose. This overt activity is always an indication of a desire or need to acquire additional information from the environment. Echolocation enables the visually handicapped person to acquire information concerning the dimensions of rooms, the presence of objects in the environment, and directions of hallways.

This echolocation activity is a tremendous asset in moving about, although it has also contributed to much misunderstanding by the sighted of special sensory endowments due to a loss of vision. This auditory object phenomenon has, over the years, been referred to as facial vision, obstacle perception, a special sixth sense, etc. A résumé of the research done on this phenomenon was written by Lowenfeld (1971). Of note is additional research by Kohler (1964) and Kellogg (1964) that substantiated that hearing is the prime requisite for detecting objects in the environment.

For lack of a better term, the author advocates the use of auditory object perception to describe this phenomenon. This term certainly more accurately describes the activity and is positive in its title. The term facial vision or facial sense is inaccurate and should not be used. "Obstacle perception" is a poor term, as it has a negative connotation, in addition to being erroneous: it suggests that the visually handicapped are threatened by every object in or alongside their path of travel. Whether an object is an obstacle or an aid ultimately depends on the individual's ability to cope with that object. With proper mobility skills the individual should be able to convert all objects in his environment to aids for travel. When a youngster perceives a tree adjacent to the sidewalk leading to his house, and utilizes this as a landmark to turn into his house, the tree is certainly not an obstacle. The detection of telephone poles, mail boxes, fences, etc., should indicate specific places along his route so that these all become travel aids.

Within the school building the child may use auditory object perception to perceive the walls at the end of the corridor or to detect open doorways and branching-off corridors. The reader may experience this by riding in a car with the window open and listening for the sound changes as the car passes a row of parked cars.

As indicated by the research of Worchel and Mauney (1951) and Kohler (1964), auditory object perception can be learned by anyone with normal hearing. However, to develop this ability requires practice and opportunities for learning. Teachers of visually handicapped children should be cognizant of this fact. It is believed that visually handicapped children develop this ability at about 1 year of age, so it is not unreasonable to expect children of school age to have this capability, provided they have normal hearing.

Sound Localization

This is the ability to determine precisely the location of a sound source. It is accomplished by comparing the time of arrival and the signal strengths of the sound at each ear. Hence, binaural hearing is important for sound localization. With a sound source directly to our right, the sound waves will reach the right ear a fraction of a second earlier, and with more intensity, than they will the left ear. Sounds coming from the right or left are more easily localized because there is a greater time lapse and intensity difference. Sounds directly in front or to the rear are more difficult to localize, and it is not unusual to see individuals turn their heads to determine if the sound is coming from the front or rear.

It is also possible to localize sounds with one good ear. However, the sound source must be of sufficient duration to enable the individual to scan with the good ear until he finds the direction of greatest loudness. In actual life situations this is not very practical, as sound sources generally do not remain in one place for an extended period of time.

Through sound localization the child is able to tell whether footsteps are coming toward him or going away and the precise direction of the corridor. He can also tell the precise location of doorways by localizing the sound of the door opening or closing. In some instances the visually handicapped leave a radio turned on as a constant sound source which enables them to locate the room or remain oriented in the room. Sound localization also enables the child to face the individual he is talking to and to ascertain his height.

In outdoor travel the visually handicapped utilize sound localization for maintaining their direction on the sidewalk and in crossing streets. This is accomplished by localizing the sounds of parallel traffic or the footsteps of others on the sidewalk or at a street crossing.

A teacher can evaluate this ability in a youngster by calling to him in the gym or on the playground and observing if the child comes directly toward the summoning voice. Another means of evaluating is to have the youngster locate dropped coins. This ability may be further improved by youngsters as they engage in games with auditory balls, or give attention to the voices of other players. A listing of activities for sound identification may be found in the *Curriculum Guide* published by the Michigan School for the Blind.

Selective Listening

This skill, the ability to select the one sound out of a group of many occurring at the same time, has been referred to as the cocktail party phenomenon (Gibson, 1966). It is important because it enables the visually handicapped individual to extract an auditory orientation cue from a maze of sounds. Many opportunities exist for the application of selective listening, most notably at street crossings, where among the maze of traffic sounds the individual is able to select the sound he needs to cross the street. Another application frequently seen is that the visually handicapped individual, while carrying on a conversation, occasionally samples footsteps down a corridor. Thus, when the conversation is ended he is immediately able to proceed confidently down the hallway.

Sound Shadow

The sound shadow is a region of relative silence behind an object which filters out the sound waves. This can be better understood if we liken it to a shadow produced by an object in the path of a flashlight beam. So it is with a sound shadow; if a large truck is parked at the curb beside a person standing on the sidewalk, the truck will filter out or mask the sound waves generated by a passing car. This ability may be used to detect large tree trunks in parks; telegraph poles, automobiles and trucks parked along the curb; and the corners of store buildings in shopping areas. The proficient user of the sound shadow will identify its leading edge (beginning) and its trailing edge (ending). This length or duration of the sound shadow will then reveal the size of the object. If we compare the sound shadows produced by a large truck with those of a compact car, we readily perceive that the truck produces a more defined shadow of longer duration than the compact car.

In business areas where the store buildings are located adjacent to the sidewalks this phenomenon is extremely useful in correcting a poor street crossing at intersecting streets. If a person wants to cross the street and veers away from the parallel street, he should, upon reaching the opposite sidewalk, note the cutting out or absence of the parallel traffic sounds. He should then realize that the building ahead must be producing the sound shadow, so he will have to alter his course of travel toward the street until he is able to hear the parallel traffic at some distance ahead of him. He should then realize that he is back on the sidewalk where he had planned to be.

It may be pertinent to point out that any one of several of the subskills of hearing may be applied in a specific situation. The conditions of a specific situation will determine which of the subskills will be employed. As an illustration, let us assume that a large tree is situated in the grass area between the sidewalk and the curb. There would be at least three different methods of detecting the tree. At one time as an individual approaches the tree, there may be fairly good wind rustling the leaves of the tree. In this instance his auditory awareness would indicate the tree's presence and his sound localization would reveal its precise location. As he negotiates this area a second time, there may be no wind present, which would preclude listening to the leaves rustling. This time he would probably use his echolocation ability to perceive the tree's presence. Still a third time as he approaches the tree, a passing car would go by and the tree's sound shadow would disclose its presence and location. There is also the possibility that he could employ any two of the foregoing subskills of hearing to confirm any doubts that he might have.

Tactual Senses

As is readily apparent, tactile information is an extremely important channel of information for the visually handicapped. For orientation and mobility this sense is second in importance only to hearing. The visually handicapped youngster obtains much orientation information through his hands, feet, and if properly used, the cane, which in reality is an extension of the hand. Also through the tactile sense additional environmental information is obtained by means of thermal cues and the tiny hairs in the skin.

A goodly portion of terrain information is obtained by the individual through his feet. Surface discriminations can be made of concrete, macadam, gravel, and grass. Also, the foot alighting on an expansion tar joint located at gasoline station driveways or at street crossings will aid the individual in maintaining his line of travel. Within the school building there may be sections of wood, tile, or cement floor which will become a landmark to the student. Other orientation aids that may be available are mats located at doors, or rugs in rooms which serve to signify specific locations in the room. The teacher should make note of these surface differences which are tactually perceptible and associate them with specific points in the environment. Once learned, these points can be excellent landmarks for the youngsters.

The extended tactual sense, namely, the cane, will provide the student with much of the same information obtained through the feet; however, it will provide this information at a minimum of one step in advance. The light sampling touch of the aluminum cane will conduct vibrations to the hand and finger of the user, so that he should discriminate differences between smooth and rough sidewalks, macadam, grass, or ground at the edges of the sidewalk, etc. It may be worthwhile to mention here that much more surface discrimination can be made through the cane with a light sensitive touch than with a heavy touch. Very little, if any, surface discrimination is possible through the tactual sense by bouncing or tapping the cane. The latter methods will only provide information through the auditory sense.

One of the prime reasons for extending the tactual sense by use of the long cane is to enable the visually handicapped walker detect objects and surface changes in his path in sufficient time to stop or alter his course. If properly used, the cane will detect tricycles, coaster wagons, parking meters, posts, and any other objects that might be in the path. It will also detect stepdowns, such as curbs, stairs, and holes, in sufficient time for the handicapped person to react.

The thermal receptors found in the skin are also important in providing orientation cues. Teachers of visually handicapped children should understand these receptors' importance and provide opportunities for the children to learn their use. Unfortunately, too many visually handicapped children in integrated classes sit next to the door, which is always on the inside wall. These children should have an opportunity to sit next to the outside wall during part of their school year. This certainly should not be done until the child has become familiar with his classroom. By moving the child to the outside wall the teacher can point out for example, that the warmth of the sun streaming in can be felt during the morning hours only. These windows must therefore be facing east. Perhaps the next school year the child would be in a classroom with the windows facing west. The teacher should then bring to his attention that the warmth of the sun is present only in the afternoon. So within the classroom the teacher would be developing basic orientation principles which are applicable to outside travel. From this classroom experience the child would learn that when he is traveling outdoors in the morning and the sun is striking him full in the face, he must be traveling in an easterly direction. If it were morning and he could feel the warmth of the sun on the back of his head and neck, he must be traveling west.

Another important use of the sun is as a rapid verification of a direction change in one's travel. Assume a person is walking west in the morning, he will feel the sun on his back and neck. When he gets to the corner and turns north, he can readily verify this direction by checking to ensure that the sun is on the right side of his face and body. This takes only a fraction of a second and could avoid a costly error.

Perception of warmth and coolness can also be of much help in assisting the child in going through the school cafeteria line. By trailing the backs of his fingers along the cafeteria counter he should be able to locate the warm section, which would indicate the hot food is there, and as he detects the cold of the refrigerated section, he can conclude that the milk would probably be there. A short study of most cafeteria lines will reveal sections of the counter that are warm and sections that are cold.

Air movement over the tiny hairs in the skin can also be of assistance to the child. Within the school building the child may detect the movement of air from a ventilating fan, open window, or an open door. In outdoor travel the movement of air may indicate the end of a building at the street corner, or it may indicate an alleyway.

Kinesthesis or Proprioception

For our purposes, kinesthesis can be defined as the sensitivity to muscular or joint motion. According to present usage, this sense makes us aware of our body's position and movement. When we raise our arm to shoulder height, the kinesthetic sense tells us the position of the arm. Many people are unaware of this sense, yet could not function if it were not present. A major use of this sense by the visually handicapped is in the detection of inclines or declines and lateral tilts in surfaces walked. The joints in the body are rich in proprioceptive receptors; for example, the ankle joint can provide one with valuable information. Many sidewalks have declines that should alert the traveler that the curb is only a short distance ahead. There are also many lateral tilts in walking surfaces caused by side drives and filling station aprons. These can be detected as the angle of the foot with the lower leg is changed from its normal position. Detection of this lateral tilt should indicate to the student that he needs to correct his direction away from the street.

Many streets have a distinct camber to them which should also assist in the crossing of streets. As a person departs from the curb, he tends to travel up an incline until he reaches the center of the street, at which point he should detect a leveling off. From this point on, the street has a decline to the opposite curb, with the last step or two before the curb having a pronounced dip. Thus, with sufficient practice the individual should expect to sense going uphill, leveling off, and then going downhill. Should this sequence of events not occur, it is most likely an indication that the individual has veered into the parallel street.

The visually handicapped are able to detect inclines and declines with much more sensitivity than most people realize. In studies carried on by Cratty (1965), it was revealed that the visually handicapped can detect declines of 1 degree, and inclines of 2 degrees. He further discovered that these slight vertical changes in surfaces go undetected through the visual sense. The implication of these findings is that most sighted people will not be aware of valuable orientation cues for the visually handicapped.

It may well be that there are slight inclines in the school corridors or the sidewalks adjacent to the school which will prove indicative to the students. Teachers should be alert to this fact.

Another aspect of the kinesthetic sense is muscle memory. Carroll (1961) defines this as the repetition of motor movements, often enough and in a fixed sequence, so that they become automatic. The tying of shoe laces is an illustration of this. For the visually handicapped this phenomenon can prove valuable in traveling short routes about his room. As he repeatedly travels from one piece of furniture to another, he should automatically know the distance without counting steps. Thereafter, he can proceed over the same route, but when he is one step short of his object he should reach out with his hand to make contact. As he becomes more proficient he will function as sighted people do when they approach tables, desks, kitchen counters, etc.

Vestibular or Labyrinthine Sense

The vestibular sense provides information concerning the vertical position of our body, plus linear and rotary components of movement. The information acquired through this sense is closely allied to the information obtained through kinesthesis. In referring back to the vertical declination and lateral tilts of sidewalks, it should be noted that this sense also plays a role in such instances. When the foot alights on a laterally tilted surface the first cue would be through kinesthesis as the angle of the ankle joint is changed. If this information is ignored, the individual's next step would cause a change in the vertical position of the body. This change would be registered by the vestibular sense.

Another aspect of the vestibular sense informs the individual when and how far he has turned. Thus, the right and left facing movements are registered through this sense.

Olfactory Sense

The sense of smell is important to the visually handicapped student in orientation and mobility since it conveys information concerning places, things, and people. Within the school building it will prove helpful in identifying wings or sections of corridors by their characteristic odors. The school kitchen, cafeteria, or chemistry labs will readily be identified by their odors. Stores in the community can be located by their characteristic smells: cakes and bread will reveal bakeries: odors of food, restaurants; the smell of oil or gasoline, service stations; etc.

Numerous cases have been observed where visually handicapped have identified individuals through their characteristic scent. In most of these cases it was the scent of tobacco or perfume that revealed their identity.

Taste

A number of authors feel the sense of taste contributes to the orientation of an individual to his surroundings. It is difficult to conceive how this sense will contribute information concerning the physical objects in one's environment. If a person is progressing through his environment and suddenly discovers his taste buds on a wall, tree, or lamppost, the chances are that other factors will not permit him to take cognizance of the taste sensation.

Residual Vision

As has been indicated in Chaper 2, many legally blind individuals have some remaining vision. In terms of orientation and mobility, these are some of the most difficult individuals to instruct. This is because in many cases the optimum conditions for the person's vision are continually changing. Individuals who have retinitis pigmentosa experience no difficulty in traveling in the daytime. Their vision enables them to detect stepdowns and objects in their path. At dusk this situation changes radically and they experience difficulties when stepping off curbs, often failing to detect holes and tripping over low objects in their path. The difficult question to answer is, should this individual use a travel aid, such as a cane? It certainly would be beneficial in the evening, though he would not need to use it in the daytime.

Students having light perception (they can only distinguish light from dark) have no useful vision for orientation purposes. Students with light projection (who can tell direction of the source of light) have some useful vision for orientation purposes. They should be able to utilize bright corridor lights or the window and door light for orientation purposes. Certainly those with measurable visual acuity should be able to acquire additional orientation information from their environment.

In terms of orientation and mobility, residual vision may be good or bad, depending on the use of the remaining vision and its effect on the acquisition of all other available sensory information. For example, if a student can see only at a distance of 3 feet, there is no point in attempting to use this vision to detect down curbs or stairs. It would be much better for him to use this vision to scan the area in front of the head and leave the detecting of the curb to the cane. In many cases, individuals with residual vision, upon completing a thorough mobility instruction course (which naturally includes a maximum training of the remaining senses), demonstrate that they are functioning with what appears to be more vision. The explanation for this is that they use their limited vision when it can do some good, while the other senses are allowed to gather information from sources where the limited vision is not able to obtain it.

All visually handicapped students should be encouraged to use their remaining vision to its fullest in moving about. However, they should not rely on it to the point where they exclude other sensory channels of information. In summary, it may be wise to remember that the most proficiently functioning visually handicapped individual is the one who acquires as much information from his environment as is available.

Basic Mobility Skills

Every teacher of visually handicapped children who desires to meet the competencies as spelled out by the Competency Committee for the U. S. Office of Education (Mackie & Dunn, 1955), will need to know the basic mobility skills. This will enable him to assist the student in becoming more proficient in his movements in the classroom and school building. These skills are sometimes referred to as precane skills, though they are employed even after an individual learns the formalized cane skills. The basic skills are designed to achieve safe, efficient, and graceful movement in a controlled, familiar environment. They are the fundamentals of movement for the visually handicapped and the advanced formalized cane travel skills are built upon these beginnings.

These basic skills should be taught to children at a very early age. They not only provide a means for safe mobility, but in addition impress upon the child that physical structures of buildings and stable furnishings can be employed as clues for mobility purposes. Many times it is this insight that permits a child to view his surroundings in a more positive manner.

Use of the Sighted Guide

This technique lends itself to being the first one taught to the student. It is one of the most efficient means of familiarizing the student with his school layout and classrooms. It is also a means of evaluating the student's perceptiveness to sensory information in the environment. In guiding the student about the school, the teacher should have the student verbalize any cues he notices in the environment. It will be helpful to know if he is able to detect cross-corridors, different floor textures, inclines, declines, etc.

The technique described here is rather universally accepted as the proper means of guiding a visually handicapped person. In teaching this technique, it is imperative to impress upon the student that he should assume an active role in this association and not a passive one. The amount of difficulty a guide experiences in negotiating doors or congested areas is directly related to the role assumed by the visually handicapped person. In addition, by assuming an active role, the visually handicapped student will be able to compensate for poor guides that he may meet in the community.

The Sighted Guide Technique

1. The student initiates the contact with his guide by placing his forearm in a horizontal plane and moving it laterally until he contacts the guide's arm. From this contact he can readily locate the guide's elbow. The student then takes the guide's left arm with his right hand, or vice versa, just above the elbow, so that the thumb is on the lateral side (outside) and the fingers on the medial (inside). This places the forearm parallel to the ground and the upper

arm parallel and close to his body. The student's arm and forearm and the guide's arm and forearm should be in the same lateral plane. This position places the student one half-step behind the guide for normal walking. The grip of the guide should be firm but not too tight. In this manner any movements of the guide's body and elbow will be communicated to the student.

2. In approaching narrow openings or congested areas in corridors, the guide should move his elbow toward the rear in the direction of the center of his back. This is a signal for the student to fully extend his arm and move somewhat behind the guide. The student's fully extended arm increases the distance from one half step to a full step, thus preventing the student from stepping on the heels of the guide. After passing the congested area, the guide returns his elbow to the side and the student resumes his normal position.

After some practice with this technique, the visually handicapped student should be encouraged to initiate this protective technique when he deems it necessary. Should he hear a crowd of voices in the corridor a short distance ahead and the guide fail to give him a cue for narrow places, there is no reason why he cannot implement it on his own. This policy should then carry over as he meets poor guides in the community.

In approaching rounded curbs or stairways the guide should always approach on a line perpendicular to the front surface.

3. In ascending or descending stairs, with this technique the guide normally mentions "stairs down" or "stairs up." As the guide pauses, the student should take half steps, and when the guide's elbow descends, this indicates one more half step and the next step is down for the student. He then proceeds down the stairs, preferably a full step behind, so that upon reaching the landing the guide's elbow will indicate this.

Going Through Doorways

Normally the guide will mention to the visually handicapped student that they are approaching a door and should indicate to the blind child to move in behind him, as mentioned earlier. The guide can be more helpful by mentioning whether the door opens to the right or left, and in or out.

In passing through the door the student should assist the guide by placing the palm of his free hand against the center of the door and holding it for himself. Neglecting to do this makes the door very cumbersome and awkward for the guide. Should the door open to the opposite side of the guide (i.e., when the student is on the right side of the guide and the door opens to the left), the student merely places his right hand on the guide's right elbow and employs the narrow opening technique. This permits his left hand to be free to hold the door open for himself. Once through the door, he returns to the normal position. It is also possible for the student to switch over to the other side of the guide, though it is much simpler and just as effective for the student to merely switch arms temporarily.

Seating in a Chair

In leading a visually handicapped student to the front of the chair, the guide should approach the chair until the student is approximately one half step from the chair. The guide should then tell him that he is at the front of the chair. If he fails to do this, the student should inquire if he is at the front or back of the chair. At that point the student should gently take another half step, until his leg makes contact with the chair. Or, if he prefers, he can make this initial contact by reaching out with his arm lowered to the approximate height of the chair. Remember, a word of information (front or back of chair) is important, but a contact is worth a thousand words. From this contact the student can check for height of the chair, armrests, and objects on the seat. In keeping with the philosophy of independence on his part, the student should initiate the movement to make contact with the chair rather than having the guide do it for him. In having the guide place the student's hand, we may be conveying through our actions that the student is not able to do this simple act for himself. After making the contact, the student can maintain his body relationship to the chair and gracefully sit down, avoiding the embarrassment of half sitting on the chair or sitting on the armrest.

In approaching a chair from the back, the same basic procedures just outlined are followed. This time, after the contact is made, the student should move around the front of the chair while checking its sides and seat. By maintaining this hand contact on the edge of the chair, he can gracefully sit down.

If for some reason he needs to arise from the chair, as in an introduction to someone, he should maintain his relationship and position relative to the chair by maintaining contact through his calfs. This can be done inconspicuously.

Seating at a Table

The procedure for guiding a visually handicapped student to a chair at a table in the lunchroom or a restaurant is much the same as just outlined with a few minor additions. If the setting is not obvious, the guide should be informed and the visually handicapped person guided to within one half step of the chair. After his free hand contacts the back of the chair, he moves to the left side of the chair. Maintaining this initial contact, he uses the other hand to contact the table in front of the chair. He then pulls his chair out the appropriate distance, which can be readily and inconspicuously checked with the right leg. After seating himself, he pulls his chair up to the table and "squares off" with the table edge. This is done by running the hands lightly over the table edge. In leaving the table, he should understand that he should place the chair back against the table as he found it.

Seating in an Auditorium or Theater

No doubt the setting will indicate this seating procedure. Upon being guided to the proper row, the guide should precede the student. If the seat is to the right and the student on the guide's left, they just move in, sidestepping. The guide then moves to the farthest seat, which will place the student in front of his seat. Inconspicuously he checks with the back of his legs to determine if the seat is down or up. Then he can turn and check with his hand for any objects on the seat.

If the seat is on the right of the aisle and the student on the guide's right, then as the guide stops at the row, the student remains there as the guide moves across and in front of him. By maintaining contact with his right hand across the guide's back he will find the left elbow and be ready to sidestep into the aisle.

Trailing

This is the act of using the backs of the fingertips to follow lightly over straight surfaces (i.e., walls, lockers, desks, tables, etc.) to determine one's place in space, to locate specific objects, and to get a parallel line of direction. This technique is especially applicable for the very beginning student and one who tends to get lost in space. It is also very effective in negotiating the corners of desks, walls, etc.

Procedure. The student stands parallel to the wall with his shoulder about 6 inches from it. He raises his arm forward, keeping the elbow straight, until the hand is waist level. After inwardly rotating the forearm he flexes his fingers, permitting the distal phalanges of the ring and little fingers to touch the wall. The hand and fingers are to be relaxed, permitting the trailing fingers to easily glide over small irregularities, such as door mouldings, bulletin-board edges, etc. In the initial stages many students attempt this technique with the hand in a horizontal plane and the fingers pointing directly ahead. This should be discouraged, as this method will invite slivers under the nails or jamming of fingers on irregularities.

Depending on the circumstances, this technique may be used alone or in conjunction with the arm and forearm across the body technique described next.

Arm and Forearm Across the Body

This technique is designed to protect the head region and upper body from half-open doors, outward corners of walls, walls, and pedestrians. It is used in familiar but uncontrolled areas, such as going down corridors where doors may be open, through doorways, and approaching the corners of walls.

Procedure. Either arm may be employed, although it is recommended that the arm away from the wall be used. The upper arm is flexed until it is in a horizontal plane with the shoulders, pointing directly ahead. The elbow is then flexed approximately 45 degrees and the forearm is inwardly rotated so that the palm of the hand faces away from the student. The fingertips are in line with the opposite shoulder and the fingers are slightly relaxed. Because many of the congenitally visually handicapped have a poor body image, it will be necessary, initially, to place the child's arm in the proper position.

Because half-open doors are most dangerous and are the most difficult to perceive, it is recommended that this technique be used at home or in the school whenever traversing doorways. It may also be used in conjunction with the trailing technique.

Lower Hand and Forearm

This is used to provide a measure of safety and protection of the student's lower body when traveling in a familiar and controlled environment. It is intended to locate such objects as desks, table tops, sinks, and chairs when walking toward them.

Procedure. The upper arm is flexed and adducted until the hand is in the centerline of the body and approximately 8 inches ahead of the body. The hand is placed below the level of the belt, with the back of the hand facing forward. In a totally familiar environment, such as the child's home where he has repeatedly walked from one object to another, he should gain sufficient proficiency so that he employs this technique for only the last step or two.

Squaring Off

In this procedure the student utilizes his body parts to establish a definite position in the environment in addition to the alignment of a body plane with a line of direction. This then enables the student to know his starting position and his line of direction to an object. It is recommended that this be used when entering a doorway, so the room and its furnishings will always have the same relationship to the individual. He may also use this procedure to travel from building parts to furnishings, or from furnishings to furnishings, providing they are stable. In a classroom he may square off from the door to the teacher's desk, or vice versa; from a radiator or window to a desk or bookcase; etc.

Procedure. In squaring off in a doorway, the student should place one hand on either side of the doorjamb and align his body accordingly. He may also square off against a wall by using the back of his shoulders and heels flush against the wall. Other means of squaring off are by placing the calves of the legs against a bedrail or the back of the thighs against a desk or table. The important thing to remember with squaring off is that when the individual gets his direction through body parts, he also aligns the body plane in that same direction.

Direction Taking

This technique is designed to get a line of direction, or course, from an object or sound to facilitate traveling in a straight line toward the desired objective. It is very similar to the trailing technique, though with this technique the surface lines of objects, such as desks, tables, chalkboards, etc., are projected into space. Therefore, it behooves the teacher of the visually handicapped to view the straight-surfaced objects just mentioned as potential orientation and mobility aids.

Procedure. Generally speaking, the student should use the back of his fingers along the edge of the desk. This gives him a direction in which to travel, and upon leaving the desk he should project the line obtained into space. By continuing along that line he should have no difficulty reaching his destination. He may also use parts of his legs laterally along a bedrail to obtain a direction. With practice, the direction-taking techniques should become inconspicuous to the average person.

Allied to direction taking are what the mobility instructors call "direction indicators." Direction indicators are straight-lined surfaces that provide direction to a destination. These may be desks, tables, chalkboards, etc.

Locating Dropped Objects

Procedure. When the object is dropped it is essential for the student to listen and turn toward the source of the sound. It is helpful to explain that the student should "point" his nose at precisely the sound source. When he turns immediately to the sound, he is able to correct for any overturning or underturning while the sound is still being made. In going down to retrieve the object he has two methods: (1) He can squat down, knowing the position his body occupies is free of obstructions. (2) He can bend down for the object, but in doing so he should employ a revision of the arm and forearm technique. The forearm is kept in an almost vertical plane, with the elbow close to the chest and toward the center of the body. The hand, with fingers extended, is placed 6 inches in front of the face. In bending down, the hand with outstretched fingers precedes the path the face and head will take. Should there be a shelf, back of a chair, or other obstruction, the hand will contact it before the face does.

After contacting the floor, he should place his palm with outstretched fingers flat on the floor and employ a systematic search pattern. A circular pattern, starting with a small circle and moving continuously to ever-widening circles, is very effective. The student should be cautioned against using a search pattern that does not contact every inch of the floor in a systematic manner.

Most failures in locating dropped objects stem from the failure to turn immediately and face the object when it is dropped. When this happens, the student has to approximate the turn in order to line up with the object. Should the dropped object roll, as a coin might, the student should continue listening to the sound and aligning his body accordingly. If the coin rolls to the wall, this can be determined from the sound the coin makes in striking the wall.

Familiarization

If the visually handicapped student is to feel comfortable and confident in his environment, he must have a good knowledge of the area. This knowledge of the environment will enable him to dispel fears of embarrassment and injury and provide him with confidence and security, which in turn will tend to minimize poor posture and gait. The teacher can and should expedite the student's acquisition of this knowledge by familiarizing him with the school building, classroom, lunchroom, and playground area. In familiarizing the student, the teacher should initially acquaint him with the general floor plan of the building. This includes the directions of main corridors and side corridors, and the type of geometrical pattern they make, if any. The floor plan may be in the shape of a square, rectangle, or T. The teacher should also evaluate the student's ability to detect landmarks and, where omissions are evident, point out the landmarks. This could mean detecting, by means of audition, cross-corridors or T corridors, kitchen noises, wide and narrow corridors, etc.; through the tactile sense, different floor textures, metal rails in floors for fire doors, etc.; through the kinesthetic sense, inclines or declines. Possible danger points should be pointed out to the student, including places such as open stairways, and doors opening into hallways, and projections from walls, such as fire extinguishers or water fountains.

After becoming familiar with the general layout of the school corridors, it is well for the student to go over the routes he will need to take upon entering school. Have him start at the door he will enter and learn the route to his first class or homeroom. Other routes he needs to know are to the washroom, drinking fountain, and office. The student should go over the location of every classroom on his schedule. This familiarization should preferably be done a few days before school starts, since it will eliminate the embarrassment of errors in front of others, and because that time is more conducive to detecting landmarks and sensory cues. With the influx of other students on the first day of school the conditions will change, some for the better and some for the worse. It would be well for the teacher to meet her pupil the first day and say to him: "I will follow you to see how much you remembered from our previous familiarization." After the general familiarization the student should be familiarized with his homeroom. The general procedure for room familiarization is as follows.

Have the student square off in the door and provide him with a verbal description of the significant objects and their direction. Have him point to the object as he understands its direction. He should next walk from the door to the teacher's desk and return to the door. As he successfully completes this route, he should move from the teacher's desk to his desk. It is suggested that these routes be planned out in their order of frequency in use. Ultimately, the student should know the routes to all significant objects in the room, such as the teacher's desk, his desk, the drawer for braille paper, the braillewriter, and braille reference books.

Geographical Directions

The importance of geographical directions to visually handicapped children cannot be overemphasized. It is important that teachers understand this and use the terms north, south, east, and west whenever appropriate. The acquisition of a thorough understanding of compass directions by the student enables him to mentally map travel routes and to understand the interrelatedness of rooms at opposite ends of the school building; it also develops a readiness to understand concepts of the outside world. How can the four corners located at an intersection be explained to the student without using compass directions? Or how can the relation of the two sides of the street, the west and east, be made clear without referring to compass directions?

The teacher can develop this readiness by using compass directions for the hallways in school buildings, the walls of the classroom, etc. The warmth of the sun can serve as a direction indicator, as already explained. The practical application of this technique is found in outside travel; if it is in the morning and the warmth of the sun is in the student's face, he must be traveling east.

Directions should also be employed for the hallways, so that the student learns that certain hallways lie in a north–south direction. The cross-corridors must then be in a west–east direction. As he travels north in the main corridor and turns right, he must be going to an easterly direction. In the north–south corridor the classrooms are located on the east and west side of the hall, much as houses are located on the east and west sides of a north–south street.

At an intersecting corridor the teacher could point out the four corners of the walls, the NE corner, the SE corner, etc. He could then have the student travel from the NE to the NW corner. This could be made more difficult by having him go from the NW corner to the SE corner, explaining the different routes available to him. The understanding of these principles could easily be transferred to a street intersection. Whenever the opportunity presents itself, the teacher should employ directions and evaluate the student's ability to understand them.

Howe (1932) has conducted a program of instruction in geographical orientation to children in the first grades of school. The children were instructed in such facts as that the sun rises in the east and sets in the west. Tests showed that this training improved the children's sense of direction.

In order to develop freedom of movement and speed, a physical education teacher had the children start from the entry door and asked them to go to the corner of the gym with the mats or stall bars. She had them run while she counted. I suggested that she should ask them to go to the NW corner, rather than to the stall bars, which had no carry-over value. Skeptical at first, she tried it. Some time later she heard the students relate their position in the classroom in terms of the compass.

Advanced Formal Mobility Training

Cane Skills

A thorough training in the basic skills at an early age provides the student with the foundation needed to succeed in advanced training of the formalized cane skills. The age at which a child should be introduced to the cane depends on his maturity level and the demands of his situation for independent travel. The decision to begin training a student with the cane should be made by the trained mobility instructor with the consent and approval of the child's parents and teacher. Some children have succeeded in learning the cane technique at 11 years of age, while others did not exhibit a readiness for the cane until they were 15 years of age.

Training in acquiring proficiency, confidence, and graceful movement with the cane involves an intensive and comprehensive course of instruction. Progressing from the basic skills, the course encompasses independent movement through a variety of situations and settings. It begins with travel in a quiet residential area, including independent street crossings, and progresses to more demanding residential areas which include more vehicular traffic. Following an outlined sequential lesson plan, the student progresses, at his assimilation rate, to business areas, which include traffic light crossings, stop signs, one-way streets, T intersections, and as many and varied traffic situations as the locality permits. Eventually he advances to the use of public transportation and downtown travel, which includes shopping expeditions into various stores. As the student's capabilities increase, the instructor provides him with experiences in "drop-off" lessons. In the drop-off lesson the student is taken to a previously traveled area where he has become familiar with certain landmarks, traffic patterns, stores, etc. Without informing him of his starting point, nor allowing him to ask passersby for information, the instructor directs the student to locate his exact position in the area. For the bright and capable student this is not as difficult a travel lesson as it appears. The positive value in this experience is that it tends to remove any fear the student might have of making a wrong turn or getting lost. Successful completion of this exercise is dependent on seeking out known cues and landmarks, and by deduction, establishing one's position in the area. As we mentioned when discussing the thermal sense, the sun will assist the student in determining which are the east–west streets. Adding to this a specific known characteristic, such as a one-way street or a heavily trafficked street, enables the student to complete this exercise successfully. Teaching the cane technique should be done by a fully trained and qualified instructor who is not only versed in the physical problems involved, but is also knowledgeable about the inherently stressful situations that may bring about emotional problems in the student.

Dog Guide

Another mode of independent mobility that has proved rewarding to adults is the dog guide. Contrary to a popular belief, the dog is not informed by the master that he wishes to go to the drugstore, whereupon the dog selects the route to the store. As with the cane, the dog guide user must have good orientation, and must instruct the dog regarding the route to follow and the turns to be made at the corners. Secondary school teachers should seek additional information from reputable dog guide schools in the event that one of the students desires to have a dog guide. The decision to use a cane or a dog guide is the inherent right of the individual and not the responsibility of the teacher or mobility instructor. However, it is the responsibility of the teacher and others to provide the student with accurate and complete information regarding each method of travel. It is assumed that prior to the time the visually handicapped youngster becomes a senior in high school, he will have been provided with proper long cane instruction.

Electronic Mobility Devices

Efforts to develop electronic mobility aids are not an innovation, but had their beginning in World War II. At that time the National Research Council was asked to direct research toward the development of an electronic device to assist the blind in travel. Since that time some 44 devices have been designed. Many of the devices never left the drawing boards; some progressed as far as the laboratory bench; and a relatively few advanced to the field testing stage. Initially it was intended to develop a mobility device that would solve all aspects of travel. At a later date this philosophy was changed and efforts were concentrated on developing devices that would do a specific function. A list of categories in which these devices can be placed follows.

1. Sensory Enhancement Devices. These devices were designed to enhance the sense of hearing.
2. Stepdown Detectors. These were designed to detect holes and stepdowns.

3. Object Detectors. These devices would detect objects in the walker's path; they were not designed to detect holes or stepdowns.
4. Linear Walking Devices. These were designed to enable the individual to walk a straight line; they were all either magnetic or gyroscopic compasses.
5. Sound Beacons. By emitting a periodic sound, they revealed a specific location in the environment.
6. Combination Mobility Device. This device was designed with three beams to detect drops and stepdowns, objects in the path, and overhead obstructions.

Of the 44 devices designed, only three show some promise. The Ultrasonic Torch or Kay Device has been in use for at least 3 years and is available for purchase. Some individuals view this device as a total mobility device, while others feel it should be used strictly as an environmental sensor, in conjunction with the cane.

The Russell Travelpath Sounder is being field tested; it is designed to detect objects in the walker's path from the waist up. The inventor states it is to be used in conjunction with the long cane.

The Laser Cane is one of the latest devices to emerge and is presently being field tested. As the name implies, it is built like a long cane; however, it contains three laser beams. The upper beam detects overhead objects and informs the user by a high-pitched tone. The horizontal beam detects objects in the user's path and informs him by a tactile stimulator. The lower beam functions to detect stepdowns and drops, and informs the user by a low-pitched sound. When, and if, this device will come on the market is difficult to predict.

With the several independent travel methods available to the visually handicapped, it is safe to say that no one method will meet the needs of every individual. The decision to select one method should be each individual's choice. Regardless of the method selected, the individual's functioning will be no more effective than his orientation abilities permit. Thus, it is the responsibility of every teacher to develop these orientation skills at an early age, so that the student will add a personal power that is indispensible to achieving his optimum as a human being.

LIFE ADJUSTMENT SKILLS

It has universally been recognized that the qualified teacher of the visually handicapped assumes responsibility for the development of each child's abilities and capacities so that he may achieve his rightful place in society. This means recognition of the vital need of every youngster to develop adequate life adjustment skills. In the past, when many of the visually handicapped were destined to work at menial tasks, often in dimly lit corners of workshops, a teacher could rationalize by saying there was no vital need for developing socially acceptable life adjustment skills. Today, however, when more and more of the visually handicapped are filling positions as typists and transcribers, and are becoming lawyers, teachers, college professors, and businessmen, there is an urgent need for this subject to be part of each school program.

The teaching of these skills needs to begin in the preschool years and should continue throughout the school years. All staff members concerned with the child's development should feel a responsibility to foster his growth in this area. This includes the resource or itinerant teacher, teachers' aides, and lunchroom supervisor, houseparents, and whoever else has opportunities to assist the child when the need arises. The school personnel should be knowledgeable in these skills and in the methods of teaching them to the visually handicapped child. Procedures for teaching life adjustment skills will vary from one individual to another and the time and setting will be varied. At times the teaching of these skills will consist of unobtrusive suggestions or corrections during the regular lunch period. At other times, when more intensive teaching is indicated, it is best done on a tutorial basis in the resource room.

Parents as well as school personnel should be involved in these activities. Parental involvement serves a twofold purpose. First, it ensures that the parents acquire the knowledge of how the skill may be performed without vision. Second, an understanding of how the skill can be learned will encourage them to provide opportunities at home for the child to practice these life adjustment skills in a realistic setting.

These life adjustment skills, which encompass several subject areas, have for convenience been grouped under three categories: daily living skills, home economics, and social skills.

Daily Living Skills

Posture and Gait

The early development of good posture and gait by the visually handicapped child should be a prime concern of every parent and teacher. A discussion of this topic in relation to the preschool child may be found in Lowenfeld's (1971) book. The lack of sight prevents the child from learning through imitative behavior the socially acceptable posture and gait behavior of his parents and peers. Thus, to acquire good posture in sitting, standing, and walking will require the concerted teaching efforts of the teacher and parents. It is important to remember that most of the functional postural abnormalities lend themselves to correction much more easily at an early age. Allowing these postural anomalies to persist over many years makes them extremely difficult, if not impossible, to correct. In correcting postural and gait anomalies it is important to understand and differentiate the causative factors. Uncertainty or fear in moving through an environment may produce or increase postural and gait anomalies. This can be seen in the child who extends both hands in front of him in a searching fashion or the child who slaps the soles of his shoes excessively. These behaviors can be minimized, if not eliminated, through good mobility techniques and a better understanding of the environment. Not all postural and gait anomalies are due to fear or uncertainty; some are developed simply because of a lack of understanding of what constitutes good posture and gait. The trained mobility specialist should be able to assist the parents and teachers in determining the causative factors and to provide suggestions for the amelioration of these anomalies.

Some of the postural anomalies commonly seen in visually handicapped children include head bobbing or twisting, rocking of the body, rubbing of the eyes, hanging of the head, and flailing of the arms. These habits or mannerisms are interpreted by many as the result of blindness and called blindisms. However, recent studies indicate that this overt behavior is also common with other groups of exceptional children.

Some gait abnormalities often seen in visually handicapped children include shuffling the feet, spreading the feet and rotating them outward, leading with the same foot when walking, and walking with the knees partially bent. Parents and teachers will need to understand that acquiring good posture and gait by children requires frequent reminders. Significant improvement will be slow and gradual, therefore consistent effort will need to be made over a long period of time.

Personal Grooming

The need for establishing good grooming habits is important for all children and becomes even more important for the visually handicapped child. With the lack of visual feedback a person can readily become lax about personal grooming. With boys, the teacher can stress the importance of periodic combing or brushing of the hair. In addition, he will need to alert them to the need for shampooing. With girls, the teacher will need to show them how to use rollers and bobby pins, as well as to explain styles of hair and the use of hair-setting agents. The teacher should take time to explain to and instruct adolescent girls in the techniques for applying makeup. Details regarding the application of these beauty aids may be found in Bindt's (1952) book.

Children should learn to use a handbrush frequently on the knuckles and nails. Cleaning beneath the nails with the point of a fingernail file or the point of an orange stick should also be stressed. The removal of hangnails can be easily accomplished through the use of an emery board. Fingernails and toenails can easily be trimmed with a fingernail or toenail clipper, coarse file, or emery board. A finishing luster on the nails can be achieved by buffing them.

Bathing of the body, followed by the use of deodorants and body powders, can easily be included in a discussion on health or hygiene. Students should be told that when drawing water for a bath, it is far safer to turn the cold water faucet on first, then the hot water. This may save some child from a scalding.

During one of the discussions on health, the teacher should make sure that the children know how to brush their teeth properly and how to use dental floss. At this time, he should discuss with them the two common methods employed by the visually handicapped in using toothpaste. One of the most common methods is to squeeze a small portion of the toothpaste directly from the tube onto the teeth. This method is not recommended for the family tube of toothpaste. The other method employed is to hold the bristles of the tooth-brush between the thumb and index finger while squeezing the paste directly on the bristles.

The visually handicapped child needs to develop at an early age good habits concerning his clothing. The teacher should, therefore, stress to the child the importance of cleanliness, neatness, and styling in his dress. To achieve these objectives, one of the most important principles for a visually handicapped child to learn is organization or orderliness. As soon as is practicable, the child should learn that when he takes his clothes off they should be neatly hung up or stored. In fact, much confusion, searching, and frustration can be eliminated if this principle is practiced with any supplies or equipment the child needs to find. The child should learn to hang up his outer garments on a specific hook in the classroom or at home so that he can return to this hook by himself and find his own clothes. During the adolescent years the visually handicapped child should establish the habit of brushing and examining his outer garments when he removes them. Any tears or loose buttons can be noticed and repaired before using the clothes again. It is also a good habit to have a sighted family member check for soiled spots on the clothing.

The importance of neatly folding and storing clothes in their proper place cannot be overemphasized. Life will be much simpler for the child when he learns that his handkerchiefs are stored in a certain drawer and perhaps on the right side. This same drawer may be used for socks or other clothing items, but they are placed on the left side of the drawer. Parents may be glad to learn that drawers with partitions will prove very helpful to the child.

The visually handicapped adolescent should be evaluated for his ability to identify the various suits he has and his knowledge of color combinations in dress. Garments are frequently identified through texture, weave of cloth, style, or ornamentation. Certainly there is no difficulty in readily distinguishing wool clothing from cotton or nylon clothing. The child would then need to remember which color his wool or cotton suit is. Assuming the texture of two suits is the same, a second identifying characteristic that can be used is the styling (e.g., men's suits may be single breasted or double breasted). Other styling characteristics that may be used are long sleeves versus short sleeves for dresses, blouses, or men's shirts. For identifying girls' dresses, the presence and placement of buttons (down the front, down the back, or none at all) and the type of neckline are useful characteristics. For men's shirts, additional distinguishing factors may be pockets, buttons or collars.

A third identifying characteristic for clothing is ornamentation on the garment (type or number of buttons, embroidery, or perhaps bows). The buttons may be large or small, cloth covered or leather covered; the embroidery design on dresses or men's sport shirts may also be used effectively. A close scrutiny of various items of wearing apparel will reveal many distinguishing ornamental characteristics on practically every piece of clothing.

The weave of the fabric may also be used as a means of identification. Some garments made from wool have a very close weave and, therefore, are thicker and heavier in weight than those made of fabric with a more open weave.

Assuming the student has several garments which are identical in every characteristic just mentioned, it is possible to add an inconspicuous identifying mark to distinguish them. This may take the form of a tag, French knots, cross stitches, or even beads sewn on the garment in a place not visible when it is worn (e.g., on the inside of a coat pocket, at the top of socks, on the back of a tie). In sewing these aids on clothing, it is recommended that the person adhere to some color code, always using one knot, stitch, or whatever to mean blue; two to mean grey; three to mean red; etc. Thus, when the visually handicapped child learns color combinations in dress, he will have no difficulty in selecting the proper accessories for the garment he wants to wear.

Any one of the foregoing characteristics may also lend itself to identifying shoes and shoe colors, especially for girls. In discussing shoes with children, the importance of a daily brushing and a periodic shining of shoes should be emphasized. In applying polish to shoes, the use of a cloth or the fingers is much more effective than a dauber. It may be helpful from the beginning to have the children spread a few newspapers on the floor before they apply the polish. After the polish is applied it should be followed by a good brushing and a final buffing with a shoecloth. The teacher can reinforce the importance of neat and stylish clothing throughout the year by letting the child know whenever he is dressed neatly and properly.

A female teacher should discuss the removal of unwanted hair with female students. A few helpful hints from a male teacher should enable adolescent boys to shave with no unusual problems. Either an electric shaver or a safety razor may be used, each having certain advantages and disadvantages. It is generally recognized that a safety razor gives a closer shave and, therefore, a cleaner looking shave for a longer period of time. Before the safety razor is used, the face should be washed free of dirt and grime. After this, lather has to be applied to the face; this can be done either with a brush or more conveniently from an aerosol can. When shaving, it helps to keep the skin on the face taut and to use an upward stroke with the razor. For the area over the top lip a sideward stroke should be used. To maintain an even length of the sideburns, some landmark on the face, such as the cheekbone or a part of the ear can be used. By placing the left arm over the head with fingers on the right cheekbone, the razor can be brought up to the fingers to shave the sideburns. This procedure is reversed for the left sideburn. Longer sideburns can be had by aligning the fingers with the earlobe instead of the cheekbone.

The electric razor, gaining in popularity for shaving, is more convenient to use and can be used in the morning and again in late afternoon without irritating the face. In using the electric razor the following hints will prove helpful. After washing the face free of dirt and grime, the student should be sure that it is thoroughly dried. Applying a preshave liquid will help the razor glide over the face more easily. Holding the cutting face of the razor flat against the face, short back-and-forth strokes should be used. Some individuals also employ short orbital or circular strokes in addition to the back-and-forth strokes. The progress and closeness of the shave is best determined by running the hand upward over a taut skin. The teacher or demonstrator should further stress that neglecting to clean the razor frequently and to keep it in good working order will result in its giving a poor shave and irritating the skin. The use of aftershave lotions should be discussed at the end of this presentation.

Eating Skills

The acquisition of socially acceptable eating skills by visually handicapped children is certainly one of the most important adjustment skills they should acquire. Proficiency in eating will enable the student to put others at the table at ease, and will not make his selection of foods dependent on the use of cutlery. A discussion of learning to eat for the preschool child may be found in Lowenfeld's (1971) book. The teaching of these skills should begin in the very early years and continue throughout the school years. Naturally, the degree of skill expected of each child will depend on his abilities, so that the degrees of competency acquired at any one age level will vary from one child to another. The following suggestions on eating will be restricted to some general eating hints that will enable the teacher to assist the youngsters. A more detailed and comprehensive discussion of eating skills for the visually handicapped may be found in the references listed at the end of the chapter.

As the visually handicapped youngster approaches his chair at the dining table, he should be encouraged to sit down from the left side of the chair. After being seated, he should "square off" with the table edge to sit properly. During the meal, the elbows should be kept close to the body and not on the table. While eating, the child should learn to lean his trunk slightly forward, bringing his mouth over the plate in the event that some food drops from the fork as he brings it up to his mouth. Some children will need to be reminded to bring the food up to the mouth, not the mouth down to the plate.

After being properly seated, he should proceed to identify the place setting. This is best done by keeping the fingers curled and low on the table, with the wrist and forearm in the path explored by the fingers. The most important landmark or reference point at the table setting will be the main plate, which should be situated directly in front of the individual. From this main landmark the child proceeds to ascertain the location and relationship of the silverware and napkin. The silverware will be found on either side of the plate, with the forks to the left and the knives and spoons on the right. If there are several forks and knives at the setting, a good general rule is to start with the fork, spoon, or knife that is on the outside. The salad plate will be found to the left of the main dish just above the forks. The water glass and/or coffee cup is to the right of the main plate above the knives. This tactual exploration of the place setting is done for the purpose of mentally and kinesthetically establishing the position and relationship of the dishes and cutlery. With practice, this exploration can be done unobtrusively. Encouraging parents to have their visually handicapped children set the table at mealtimes will facilitate learning the place settings.

The next important need is to establish the various food items on the main plate. The person serving the food should describe what food is being served and its location on the plate. If he fails to do this, the visually handicapped person should graciously ask the person serving the food or someone sitting at the table with him. The locations of food items on a main dish can best be described in analogy to the face of a clock. The meat at 6 o'clock; the potatoes at 10 o'clock; the vegetable at 3 o'clock; and so on. If a verbal description has not been given and no one is available to be asked, the location of the food items can be ascertained by systematically exploring the main plate. Using the fork in the right hand, the visually handicapped person inserts the tines of the fork into each food item as he goes around the plate counterclockwise. Many food items are identifiable by the resistance offered the tines; meat will offer more resistance than mashed potatoes, and carrots will offer a different resistance than the potatoes or meat. When the food items have been identified, a mental note of their positions should be made. It is recommended that the meat be positioned at 6 o'clock before the student starts to eat, as this makes it much more convenient to cut. This positioning can readily be done by turning the whole plate around.

One of the most difficult skills in eating is the cutting of meat. With much practice and patience this can be mastered. In the cutting of meat the fork should be held in the left hand with the index finger just above the base of the tines on the back of the fork. Considering the tines of the fork as an extension of the finger will aid in locating and determining the kinds of food items. Using the fork to locate the nearest edge of the meat, the fork is then placed into the meat about 1 inch from the edge. The knife is then placed along the back of the prongs and is used to cut on all three sides of the fork. The meat remaining on the fork should then be drawn slightly away from the main portion of the meat to ascertain that it is free. A check with the knife as a feeler and lifting the fork will indicate if the meat is bite size or larger. Meats containing bones, such as chops, steaks, and fowl, are among the most difficult foods to cut. In less formal circumstances, some meats, like chicken, can be picked up with the fingers. With the more tender meats, such as meat loaf or fish, the individual should be able to use the side of the fork (in the right hand) to cut through the meat.

The American convention of holding the fork in the left hand and the knife in the right hand to cut meat, and switching utensils after the meat is cut, is a very inefficient, cumbersome, and difficult procedure for the visually handicapped. A far superior method of eating is the "continental style," in which when it is necessary to use the knife, the fork is kept in the left hand and the knife in the right hand. This method eliminates the need to locate the same piece of meat twice, and does away with the needless manipulation of utensils. In this age of intercontinental travel, people everywhere are seen using the continental style of eating, and it should be demonstrated to visually handicapped children.

In the American style of eating some individuals use a piece of bread or roll in the left hand as a "pusher." This small piece of bread will help locate and place food on the fork. In seasoning foods with salt and pepper either of two methods may be used. In adding salt to food, the individual can spread the fingers over the plate while shaking the salt through the fingers. The amount of salt being added can be judged by the amount of salt striking the fingers. The other method often used is to shake the salt into the palm of the left hand, then with the thumb and finger of the right hand, take a pinch of this salt and spread it over the food. The preferred method of seasoning with pepper is to spread the fingers over the plate.

Pouring of liquids into a glass can be mastered after a short practice. The glass or cup to be filled should be grasped around the top and brought up to the pouring spout of the container. As the glass is being filled, it is important to be attentive to the sound the liquid makes as the glass is being filled. The weight of the filled glass is a secondary clue to the fullness of the glass. A third method used by some visually handicapped individuals in filling their own glass is to insert the index finger approximately 1 inch inside the glass.

The use of sugar at mealtimes should present no problems if the sugarbowl is held in the left hand and brought close to the cup. When spooning the sugar out of the bowl, the little finger of the right hand should be extended so that it makes contact with the cup. This will position the spoon directly over the cup. Individual packets or cubes of sugar present no problem.

In eating pie, the wide end of the pie can be held lightly between the thumb and finger of the left hand. The fork is held so that the prongs of the fork are sideways and the side of the fork is used to break through the crust, starting at the pointed end.

If the regular method of feeding the children in a school is cafeteria style, the visually handicapped students should be provided the opportunity to acquire experiences in negotiating a cafeteria line. The tray placed on the rails will make it simple to follow the counter line. Placing the leading hand on the tray with the fingers extended will reveal if there is another tray just ahead. Placing the trailing hand on the far side of the tray with the backs of the fingers along the cafeteria counter will reveal texture and temperature changes. These texture and temperature changes can be used as landmarks for locating the hot food section, the milk and dessert area, etc. In receiving the plate of food, the visually handicapped person should extend his hand so that the counter personnel will place the dish in his hand. In placing the dishes on the tray, it is advisable to have some system of placement. The tall glasses, desserts, and milk cartons should be placed on the tray farthest from the person. The main dish and salads should be placed on the near edge of the tray. If the way from the cafeteria counter to the dining table is direct and short, the blind youngster should be able to negotiate it by himself. If on the other hand the distance is great and circuitous, he should solicit assistance from a friend or the serving personnel.

The manner and place of teaching the eating skills will be dictated by the capabilities of the child. If considerable instruction and correction is needed, these skills should be taught on a tutorial basis in the privacy of a room. The youngster will feel much better knowing that others are not listening and watching. As the child gains proficiency and demonstrates his readiness, he should eat in the regular dining room, where occasional unobtrusive corrections can be offered.

Identification of Monies

Visually handicapped children should learn to identify and manage their own money as soon as possible. Handling money will present no problem once the characteristics of the various coins are learned and a system is adopted for keeping paper money. Coins may be identified by any one or more of these characteristics: size, weight, milling, and sound. The identifying characteristics of the coins are as follows.

1. Half-dollar. With the silver dollar out of circulation, the largest of the commonly seen coins is the half-dollar. It can readily be identified by its size and weight. It also has a milled edge and its sound is rather heavy.
2. Quarter. This coin is only slightly larger and thicker than the nickel, but unlike the nickel it has a milled edge. A person can avoid mistaking it for a nickel, therefore, by checking the coin's edge for milling and by dropping it on the counter.

3. Nickel. The nickel is slightly larger and thicker than the penny and like the penny has a smooth edge. It may be distinguished from the penny by its size and sound when dropped.
4. Penny. The penny is slightly smaller than the nickel and slightly larger than the dime. Sound and size recognition are most helpful in distinguishing this coin from the nickel.
5. Dime. The dime is the smallest of the coins and has a milled edge. These two characteristics will help distinguish it from the penny, to which it is closest in size. The sound the dime makes is quite distinct from that of the penny, which will assist in the recognition of this coin. Many of the dimes in circulation have their milling well worn, which makes it impossible to detect with the pad of the finger. This difficulty can be eliminated by using the thumbnail or fingernail along the edge of the coin. The nail of the finger is able to detect even the most worn milled edge.

Some visually handicapped individuals advocate the placement of different denominations of coins in separate pockets. This certainly is not necessary if the foregoing characteristics of coins are learned. For convenience, some individuals place the pennies in one pocket and all the other coins in another pocket. This minimizes the difficulty of distinguishing this coin from among the nickels and dimes.

The identification of paper currency can easily be done by employing some system of placing the bills in a wallet. It is impossible to identify paper currency through smell or touch, a power that is sometimes ascribed to individuals.

One of the most commonly used systems is folding of the paper currency within the wallet. The one-dollar bills can be inserted without any folds. The five-dollar bills are folded in half across the width of the bill. The ten-dollar bills are also folded in half, but across the length of the bill. All of the above-mentioned bills can then be contained in one compartment of the billfold. The twenty-dollars bills are folded over several times, across the width and length, and inserted into one of the smaller pockets of the wallet.

A second method employed is the addition of more dividers in the billfold. By adding two additional dividers in the wallet, a person can make three compartments for bills. The one-dollar bills then are inserted in the first compartment; the five-dollar bills in the middle compartment; and the ten-dollar bills in the last compartment. With this system, the twenty-dollar bills would be folded lengthwise and placed at the bottom of the ten-dollar bill compartment. In pulling out the ten-dollar bill, the individual would need to be cautious not to pull out one of the twenty-dollar bills as well.

The systems just described for the management of money are not the only systems used by the blind. These two systems have been described since they have been used by a large number of individuals and have proved very effective. On occasions, one hears stories of visually handicapped persons being able to "smell" the denomination of a bill. This can only be done by those having sufficient vision to see the denomination of the bill as it is brought close to the nose!

As soon as the visually handicapped child can manage his money and has the mobility competency to locate stores, he should be encouraged to handle his own financial transactions in making purchases.

Telephone Dialing

Proficiency in dialing a telephone can be achieved within a short period of time by the visually handicapped child if he is provided with certain basic knowledge concerning the telephone and if he employs a system for dialing.

The dial telephone contains a revolving dial, on the outer edge of which are located ten holes. The tip of the index finger inserted into any one of the holes and moved clockwise will come to a stop at the finger stop. The youngster must understand the numbers and letters assigned to each of the holes. (They are shown in the accompanying table.) The last hole is also used to dial the operator. It will be noted that two letters of the alphabet are missing, the Q and the Z.

Hole number	Number	Letters
1	1	None
2	2	ABC
3	3	DEF
4	4	GHI
5	5	JKL
6	6	MNO
7	7	PRS
8	8	TUV
9	9	WXY
10	0	None

In dialing a telephone number containing an exchange name and number, the individual has to convert the three letters of the exchange into numbers. Some visually handicapped individuals do this by putting the index finger in the second hole and reciting three letters for each hole, keeping in mind the two letters of the alphabet which are not used. Others who use the telephone frequently memorize the letters assigned to each number. With the modern trend of eliminating the exchange names, the need for this conversion is lessened.

The systems employed by the visually handicapped for dialing a telephone are many and varied. Some systems are more adaptable for certain individuals, while others prefer a different system. The important thing is that the visually handicapped individual master and become proficient in the system he employs. The following are a few of the dialing systems most frequently used.

One of the simplest methods employed, but perhaps the most time-consuming one, is the use of the index finger to dial each number. The individual starts from the finger stop and, going counterclockwise, counts every hole until he reaches the desired number. After dialing the number to the finger stop, he withdraws the finger, permitting the dial to return to its normal position. He then repeats the foregoing steps. To expedite this method somewhat, some individuals keep their finger in the hole while the dial returns to its normal position. So if they are dialing number 786, the finger need only be moved to the next hole, thus eliminating the counting of six additional holes.

A more proficient method in dialing a telephone is to insert all four fingers at the same time into four holes. For the first four numbers, the dialer would use his little finger for the first hole; the fourth finger of the hand in hole number 2; the middle finger in hole 3; etc. For hole number 5, he merely moves the index finger counterclockwise one hole. For the upper numbers of the dial, the little finger is inserted in hole number 0; the next finger in hole 9; etc. For hole number 6, the index finger is moved clockwise one hole. With this method of dialing, the finger selecting the number is kept in the hole at its normal position. This permits the fingers that were removed from the holes to be returned to their original position with ease.

Another proficient method for dialing involves putting the four fingers of the right hand into the odd-numbered holes. The little finger is inserted in hole number 1, the next finger in hole number 3, the middle finger in hole number 5, and the index finger in hole number 7. When the number 5 is dialed, the first two fingers are removed but the middle and index fingers remain in their holes throughout the dialing. When the dial of the telephone has returned to its normal position, the removed fingers return to their respective holes. To dial an even number, the finger adjacent to that number shifts over one hole. For holes number 9 and 0 the fingers are removed from the above-mentioned position and the index finger is used to locate these holes. This last-mentioned method requires a little more practice, but once skill is acquired it is one of the most proficient methods.

The dialing methods just described are merely intended to acquaint the reader with some systems that have proven to be effective for a number of visually handicapped individuals. The choice of a system to be used can best be determined by the individual concerned. The important thing is for the individual to master the system he uses.

In teaching visually handicapped children about the telephone, it is recommended that the teacher contact the local telephone company representative for a sample of different telephones. The children can then become acquainted with the common dial telephone, the pushbutton model, and the cradle phones with the dial in the hand receiver.

The visually handicapped student who is unable to master any type of dialing system, or is in an emergency, can always dial the 0 hole and get the operator.

Home Economics

Every visually handicapped high school girl, and possibly boy, should learn some basic fundamentals of home economics. In fact, the chances are that the resource or itinerant teacher will have to share her knowledge and encouragement with the regular home economics teacher if the students are to profit from her class. The first thing the visually handicapped girl will have to learn is the physical layout of the kitchen and the spatial relationship of the various kitchen appliances. Here the basic mobility skills mentioned previously will be helpful. She will have to learn to use the direction indicators of the kitchen, such as refrigerator, kitchen sink, or countertop stove.

The second need will be to learn the placement of objects and to return the various pieces of kitchen equipment to their proper places. Here again, as in clothing placement, organization is very important. A third item is a means of identification of foods and cleaning supplies. The following general principles can be used to identify the various kitchen supplies.

1. Identification by placement and location. If the same size cans contain fruits and vegetables, then placement is all important. The canned corn can be placed on one shelf and the canned carrots on another.
2. Identification by size, shape, weight, sound, and smell. Fruit juices generally come in the large economy-size cans. Fruits can be purchased in large cans, while vegetables may be purchased in small cans. Certain foods, such as tuna, are packaged in cans whose shape is quite different from that of any other can. The sound an applesauce can makes when shaken is quite different from that of a can of tomatoes, as is that of a bottle of vinegar from one of maple syrup.

If there are no natural means of distinguishing cans, braille labels and marks can be used. Some of the suppliers of aids and appliances for the visually handicapped have labels to put on cans.

Some orderly organization in clearing the table of dishes and washing them will prove beneficial. In clearing the table, working from the edge toward the center will be effective. In stacking the dishes for washing, the tall items should be placed at the rear of the counter.

The cleaning, polishing, and dusting of flat surfaces requires a systematic pattern, whether the surface be a table top or floor. The size and shape of the surface to be cleaned will dictate the pattern to be used. A small oval table lends itself best to a circular pattern of cleaning. A rectangular table may be polished with horizontal, followed by vertical, strokes. Floor surfaces should be cleaned in narrow sections with overlapping of the edges.

The use of the dials on the kitchen range, oven, or automatic washing machine should present no problems once the dials are marked in braille.

There are several ways of reading the dials on kitchen ranges, ovens, or automatic washing machines. Perhaps the simplest method is to braille the dials by using brads, or a buildup of fingernail polish. Some dials have a natural click at the various settings of the dial. Another means is to estimate in degrees the amount the dial has turned. As an illustration, a low setting may be 90 degrees to the right, a medium setting will be a 180-degree rotation, and a very high setting may be a 270-degree rotation. A more thorough discussion of the preparation of foods, ironing, cleaning, etc., may be found in the Western Michigan University's *Homemaking Manual* (1966).

Social Skills

Because social skills on the part of the visually handicapped tend to put the sighted at ease or to minimize a strained atmosphere, it is of utmost importance that these skills be presented to the adolescent visually handicapped person. One of the most important and first skills he should learn is to face people who are talking to him or to whom he is talking. This can be readily done by localizing the voice of the person. In fact, he can tell something of the individual's height by the height from which the voice comes. In being introduced to a sighted person, the visually handicapped male should initiate the handshake by putting his hand out toward the person. Many times a sighted person is alert for cues from the blind person for the handshake. With the visually handicapped girl, it is up to her if she wants to shake hands.

The boys should understand that they are to arise when being introduced to someone or if a woman enters the room. The cue for this can be gotten from the other males in the room.

The adolescent visually handicapped boy should also learn and practice some of the male courtesies extended to women. After some practice, he should be able to extend this courtesy to his girlfriend. Many adult visually handicapped males insist on being gentlemen when with their wives or girlfriends by opening doors and pulling out chairs for them when seating them. This can be accomplished readily providing the two people know one another's actions.

Another common courtesy which can be practiced is to keep track of time and when nightfall comes to turn on the light. All single light switches turn the light on when up and turn it off when down. It is also helpful for the visually handicapped always to be gracious in refusing sighted assistance when it is not needed and to be polite in soliciting aid.

There are many other social skills that should be learned by visually handicapped children, too numerous to mention here and too varied for different groups and strata of society. Also, the practicing of social skills depends to a large extent upon the basic social adjustment of the individual and is, therefore, also a sociopsychological problem.

REFERENCES

Alonso, L. The educator's vital role in mobility and orientation. *New Outlook for the Blind,* 1965, **59,** 249–251.

Ball, M. J. Mobility in perspective. *Blindness 1964.* Washington, D.C.: American Association of Workers for the Blind, 1964. p. 107–141.

Bindt, J. *A handbook for the blind.* New York: Macmillan, 1952.

Carroll, T. J. *Blindness: What it is, what it does, and how to live with it.* Boston: Little, Brown, 1961.

Cratty, B. J. Perceptual thresholds of non-visual locomotion, Part I. *National Institute of Neurological Diseases and Blindness Monograph.* Los Angeles: Department of Physical Education, University of California, 1965.

Curriculum guide, pre-cane mobility and orientation skills for the blind. Lansing: Michigan School for the Blind, undated.

Finestone, S., Lukoff, I. F., & Whiteman, M. *Aspects of the travel adjustment of blind persons.* New York: American Foundation for the Blind, 1960.

Gibson, J. *The senses considered as perceptual systems.* Boston: Houghton Mifflin, 1966.

Gockman, R., & Costello, J. H. *Mobility training for junior and senior high school students.* Project Summary delivered at the American Association of Instructors of the Blind Convention; Salt Lake City, Utah, 1966.

Griffin, D. R. *Listening in the dark.* New Haven: Yale University Press, 1958.

Hoover, R. E. The cane as a travel aid. In P. A. Zahl (Ed.), *Blindness.* Princeton: Princeton University Press, 1950. Pp. 353–365.

Howe, G. F. The teaching of directions in space. *Journal of Geography,* 1932, **31,** 207–210.

Irwin, R. B. *As I saw it.* New York: American Foundation for the Blind, 1955.

Kellogg, W. N. *Porpoises and sonar.* Chicago: University of Chicago Press, 1961.

Kellogg, W. N. Sonar system of the blind. *Research Bulletin No. 4.* New York: American Foundation for the Blind, 1964. Pp. 55–69.

Kohler, I. Orientation by aural cues. *Research Bulletin No. 4.* New York: American Foundation for the Blind, 1964. Pp. 14–53.

Lowenfeld, B. Psychological problems of children with impaired vision. In W. M. Cruickshank (Ed.), *Psychology of exceptional children and youth* (3rd ed.). Englewood Cliffs, N. J.: Prentice-Hall, 1971. Pp. 211–307.

Lowenfeld, B. *Our blind children* (3rd ed.). Springfield, Ill.: Charles C Thomas, 1971.

Mackie, R. P., & Dunn, L. M. *Teachers of children who are blind.* Office of Education, Bulletin No. 10. Washington, D.C.: Government Printing Office, 1955.

Western Michigan University, School of Graduate Studies. *Homemaking manual: A reference manual for home teachers working with the adult blind.* Kalamazoo, Mich.: Community Services for the Visually Handicapped, Illinois Department of Children and Family Services, 1966.

Worchel, P., & Mauney, J. The effect of practice on the perception of obstacles by the blind. *Journal of Experimental Psychology,* 1951, **41,** 170–176.

CHAPTER 10

Visually Handicapped Children with Additional Problems

Philip H. Hatlen

Department of Special Education
San Francisco State College
San Francisco, California

Within the past ten years no specific problem in the area of education of visually handicapped children has stimulated the field of services as much as that of the multihandicapped child. This is good and healthy, for a review of current educational programs reveals that visually handicapped children with additional problems in some instances may even outnumber those children who are only visually handicapped (Lowenfeld, 1969).

In order to simplify nomenclature, children discussed in this chapter will be denoted as "multihandicapped." This refers to the "multihandicapped visually handicapped," or "visually handicapped with additional problems."

Literature in this area falls within three general categories. First, much has been written dealing with the *incidence* of multiple handicaps within the population of visually handicapped children. These reports have served to emphasize in a dramatic way the need for services, and indeed, in some cases, have been the impetus for initiating special services for these children. Second, much of the literature is concerned with *descriptions* of multihandicapped children. Many articles and pamphlets present case studies of these children, and, though informative and interesting, they do little to suggest the manner in which these children would best be served educationally. The third area deals with recommendations for *educational approaches* to multihandicapped children. However, the material written on this subject tends to be, practically speaking, discouraging because it usually stresses the therapeutic clinical approach for successful educational and/or developmental intervention. A one-to-one pupil–teacher ratio is often recommended for best results, and, in fact, may be a necessity.

As the interest in, concern for, and stress on services for multihandicapped children has grown in recent years, so has the realization that few children who are sensorily handicapped are not multihandicapped. McCarthy (as reported in Abel & Hatlen, 1968) states

> Perhaps we need to think of all handicapped children as children with multiple handicaps. We talk about mentally retarded children as if mental retardation exists in isolation. And yet most of us have never been in a mentally retarded class that did not have some physically handicapped children in it—that did not have some emotionally disturbed children in it—or some culturally disadvantaged children—or some children with perceptual problems in it. We have never been in a class for the blind that did not have some brain injured children in it, some emotionally disturbed children, or some socially malajusted children [p. 88].

Many teachers who have within recent years served in educational programs for children visually handicapped by retrolental fibroplasia would undoubtedly concur with this statement. Congenitally visually handicapped children often are retarded developmentally. This retardation may be so severe that it interferes with normal educational progress. Given an understanding teacher, a flexible educational program, and experiential opportunites, this can be remedied, often in a short period of time. However, McCarthy's statement should result in some serious reflection on the provisions for educational services to all handicapped children.

DEFINITION

Definitions of visually handicapped children with additional problems tend to be descriptive, and as such, vary considerably. Wolf (1967) defines multiple disabilities as, "dysfunction or general loss of two or more body organ functions" (p. 5). This is an unusual definition. Most teachers would probably agree that in multihandicapped children there is most often not a dysfunction or loss of body organ functions. Mental retardation and emotional disturbance are examples which do not necessarily involve body organs. However, since Wolf's publication is most concerned with blind children who are mentally retarded, he is not dealing with the broad spectrum of multiple disabilities in children.

Moor (1965) defines multiply handicapped blind children as those who need special assistance in order to function in an educational program. She then describes a wide variety of blind children with multiple problems as being emotionally disturbed, as do Gruber and Moor (1963). Elonen, Polzien, and Zwarensteyn (1967) feel that multihandicapped blind children might more accurately be described as "deviant blind children" (p. 301) and for the sake of brevity they prefer this term.

Educators concerned with multihandicapped children are often confronted with medical descriptions used as definitions. Generally, the medical profession defines handicaps in two ways: by etiology, and by current functioning as determined by normal child growth and development scales. An etiological definition describes the physiological condition of the child. If, in addition to blindness, brain injury is medically determined, then the definition of multiple handicaps for that particular child would be brain-injured blind child. However, more often the educator will find terms such as mental retardation in medical reports, and it must be realized by the reader that doctors frequently will describe children and define the degree of handicap by comparing a child's chronological age to his growth and development. Therefore, a visually handicapped child who is 4 years of age and is seen by the pediatrician as functioning at a 2- or 3-year level may be classified as being mentally retarded. The pediatrician does not usually take into account the child's potential or whether or not the mental retardation is due to lack of developmental opportunities.

Since little is known about multiple handicaps in visually handicapped children, an educational definition should be presented in a functional, pragmatic way. It should describe the child's current functioning without limiting potential or prognosis. It is unfortunate both for the teacher and for those children so categorized that the terms mental retardation and emotional disturbance have been used so commonly in defining visually handicapped children with additional problems. To many educators and parents the term mental retardation denotes a permanent condition, and for young multihandicapped children about whose additional handicaps so little is known, such a label can be quite detrimental. With respect to the term emotional disturbance, Gruber and Moor (1963) have used it liberally because they felt that children who had gone through the experience of being multihandicapped could not possibly survive without severe emotional problems.

Definitions can be most helpful when they are utilized for initiating a service to a particular group of children. However, definitions can also be most harmful if they become narrow and create a labeling and categorizing from which children experience much difficulty escaping. The variations and degrees of additional problems in visually handicapped children are difficult if not impossible to describe or define. This is particularly true when such a definition or description is needed to isolate a particular group of children in order to provide a particular type of service. It is probably to the profession's advantage that definitions have been vague and varied, and that no one definition has met with general professional acceptance.

For the purpose of this chapter, the following descriptive definition will identify the group of children with whom we are concerned: the visually handicapped child whose additional problems are so severe that he cannot be adequately served by educational services provided for visually handicapped children.

One further definition must be added, that which described deaf–blind children. In general, the profession has accepted the definition that a deaf–blind child is one whose visual handicap exists to such a degree that he cannot be served by educational programs for sighted children and whose auditory impairment is so severe that he cannot be served by programs for hearing children. An interesting observation about this definition is that because criteria for admission to schools for the blind and schools for the deaf vary from state to state, definitions of deaf–blind children also vary. A child considered auditorily impaired to such an extent that he cannot be served by programs for hearing children might well be in a class for deaf children in one state and not be considered handicapped in a neighboring state.

Another group of children who might be considered specifically are those who are visually and orthopedically handicapped. Often an orthopedic handicap interferes little with learning, unless it is so severe that it prevents all mobility. This group of children does not create so serious educational placement and service problems as do children whose additional handicaps interfere with developmental progress and learning processes.

DIAGNOSIS

The usual diagnostic service for children is provided by the medical profession. An educator wishing to have a diagnostic evaluation on a particular child about whom he is concerned will more than likely refer the family to a medical center or a medical clinic. There the child might be seen by a pediatrician, a pediatric neurologist, an ophthalmologist, a psychiatrist, and other specialists within the medical profession. The resulting report might provide an educator, psychologist, or social worker with a good deal of physiological information about the child, which may explain certain behaviors. Also, a psychiatric evaluation might provide answers to many questions about the child's deviant behavior.

Clinical psychologists often work with the medical profession in diagnostic facilities. Social workers, too, are often utilized for family counseling, interviewing, etc., and participate as members of the diagnostic team. What is usually lacking in the traditional diagnostic evaluation is the educator as a member of the team.

Medical diagnoses provide information about etiology and prognosis of the medical or physiological disorder, but give little additional useful information to programs offering ongoing service for the child. Psychological diagnoses are an important part of a comprehensive work-up on the child, but alone they present only part of the picture. The same is true for the diagnostic contributions of social workers.

The potential capabilities of multihandicapped children are often best recognized and most effectively described by the educator. It is unfortunate that medically oriented diagnostic clinics have not recognized the potential contributions of educators to the total comprehensive diagnostic service. A real team approach to diagnostic evaluation which includes the teacher is sorely needed in order to provide the most comprehensive and meaningful information to those involved in long-term planning for multihandicapped children.

There are several diagnostic centers in the United States which have in recent years gained much experience in working with multihandicapped children. Reports of such efforts at the Center for the Development of Blind Children at Syracuse University (Donlon, 1964) and at the Johnston Training Center (Cicenia et al., 1965) may be found in the literature.

In other countries, the most notable work in diagnosis and treatment has been carried on at the Educational Unit of the Hampstead Child-Therapy Course and Clinic, as reported by Burlingham (1961, 1965) and others.

California has in recent years developed two outstanding diagnostic centers as an integral part of the State Department of Special Schools and Services. The primary role of these two centers is either short-term or long-term diagnosis of severely handicapped children.

Again, it should be stressed that diagnosis should be comprehensive and involve many professions. It should be an interdisciplinary activity with emphasis on medical, educational, psychological, and social aspects of the condition of individual children. Quite often an educational service will provide an informal diagnostic evaluation of a child which consists of a trial enrollment in an existing educational program with the teacher supplying the information which will help determine the ultimate placement of the child. Some educators have maintained that a fair diagnostic evaluation of any multihandicapped child should never be attempted in less than a year or possibly two. Lowenfeld (1969) has recommended a diagnostic service specifically for visually handicapped children, and certainly such a service could provide much information valuable to educational programs, and opportunities for much-needed research.

Of concern to the teacher, the therapist, and the clinician is the extent to which diagnostic information can be utilized in the day-to-day curriculum planning for visually handicapped children with additional problems. The medical, psychological, and social needs which may be discovered by diagnosis should be made known to the teachers so that they may provide appropriate experiences for each individual child. For example, medical conditions may preclude vigorous physical activity for one child, whereas such activity may be a necessity for the motor development of another child. In the area of psychological needs, it may be that one child can benefit from continuous individual attention from a flexible, permissive adult. Another child in the same program may require a more rigid, scheduled program in order to achieve optimum progress. Some children may benefit most from group experiences with peers, while for others such experiences may be detrimental to social and psychological growth.

It may be that diagnostic information could be utilized in curriculum planning to determine the remedial needs of children. A thorough, comprehensive diagnostic evaluation might well result in pinpointing strengths and weaknesses in the early growth and development of a child. Such information could lead to the identification of developmental needs on the infancy or early childhood level. A teacher could obviously put to good use information included in a good diagnostic work-up which would indicate, for example, that a child of age 7 is functioning developmentally at a level of only 12 or 18 months.

Better diagnostic services might also provide the means by which we can more accurately determine the differences between visually handicapped children who are physiologically mentally retarded and those who are developmentally retarded. If a diagnostic evaluation could determine, without question, that the current level of functioning for a particular child is all that can be expected due to brain injury or neurological impairment, then the teacher will find it possible to utilize this kind of information in planning an appropriate curriculum. Diagnostic evaluation should provide the teacher with information in these areas so that individual planning for children may be done with as little initial trial and error as possible.

Children who are severely multihandicapped as a result of maternal rubella present a formidable task for a diagnostic team. It is possible, in a very general way, to estimate the degree of visual loss due to cataracts, and a gross measurement of hearing loss may be determined. But many of these children are congenitally handicapped in the two sensory areas which are basic to a child's development. Among deaf–blind children who have been served during the past in educational programs, both handicaps have rarely been present at birth. The exceptions are children with an etiology of maternal rubella.

Until the 1960s, deaf–blind rubella children were not numerous and congenital deafness plus blindness did not present a severe problem. However, the 1964–1965 rubella epidemic resulted in a dramatic increase in numbers of deaf–blind children. As significant as the increase in numbers of deaf–blind children is the fact that these are congenitally deaf–blind children. They represent a population of multihandicapped children about whom little is known and no predictions can be made. Diagnostic approaches which are considered appropriate for children with other combinations of handicaps may not be useful when the two primary sensory modalities are congenitally involved.

DEVELOPMENT OF SERVICES
FOR MULTIHANDICAPPED CHILDREN

For many generations visually handicapped children with additional problems were usually categorized as feebleminded blind children. The exception to this was the visually handicapped child with additional physical handicaps, such as a crippling condition.

The attitude of residential schools and other early educational programs for visually handicapped children was that feebleminded blind children belong somewhere other than in schools with traditional academic curricula. It was recommended that these children be isolated, institutionalized, and in whatever other way possible kept separate from visually handicapped children who were academically capable.

For some time multihandicapped blind children were turned away from all educational services. This is not to say that such rejection was unique for visually handicapped children with additional handicaps; it was as true for children with other combinations of multihandicapping conditions which resulted in academic limitations. The alternative to full-time life-long care by parents was institutionalization in state mental hospitals or other facilities willing to accept such a child. Seldom did such placement result in any educational services to the children. Institutionalization meant defeat for the parents; for the educators, who felt a responsibility for all children; for many institutions, which were faced with more children than could possibly be served in any positive way; and, most important, for the child himself.

Visually handicapped children whose additional problems are not related to orthopedic handicaps have continued to be classified by many as mentally retarded, and from the standpoint of a functional classification this may be correct. However, as has been suggested earlier, such labels have a tendency to remain with children for a lifetime and can cause a good deal of harm by limiting professional efforts.

A customary technique for determining educational placement of multihandicapped children has been to establish a hierarchy of severity of handicaps and determine placement by admitting the child to the program geared to the most severe handicap. This often resulted in children with a wide variety of additional problems being enrolled in inappropriate services. It is difficult to justify admission of an emotionally disturbed blind child to an educational program for blind children. When the handicap most closely related to problems in learning is considered, it should be obvious that such a child would benefit most from admission to a program for emotionally disturbed children. Such may not be the case with visually handicapped children with cerebral palsy, for example, where the learning processes themselves may be virtually unaffected, and the additional handicap is primarily physical in nature.

When placing handicaps on a hierarchy of severity for the purpose of educational placement, attention should be given to problems which directly affect learning. In the case of multihandicapped children, this may not always be the obvious physical handicap.

It should be noted, however, that the educational, social, and psychological needs of multihandicapped children are not necessarily additive in nature. For example, the services necessary for an emotionally disturbed, orthopedically handicapped blind child may not necessarily be those of a psychologist, a teacher of the orthopedically handicapped, and a teacher of the visually handicapped. A child with multiple handicaps is unique. The effect of the combination of handicaps results in learning problems which may not be best treated by professionals in each separate area. Teacher preparation programs are only beginning to confront this problem.

As it became obvious to the professional educators of visually handicapped children that many children were being denied services, which often resulted in their early institutionalization, programs for multihandicapped children gradually began to develop.

Residential schools throughout the country began to establish special classes for multihandicapped children in addition to their normal academic program. Sometimes these were called classes for the mentally retarded blind, sometimes classes for slow-learning blind children; sometimes they were primarily classes for orthopedically handicapped blind children (Frampton, Kerney, & Schattner, 1969). Residential schools which had long stressed the academic proficiency of students and taken pride in selectively admitting visually handicapped children who indicated the highest intellectual capacities were now ready and willing to provide some type of service for those children who might never be considered academically talented. Such special classes were established in many residential schools.

It should also be noted that residential schools have long accepted the responsibility of educational programs for deaf–blind children, and until recent years there have seldom been any attempts to work with deaf–blind children outside the eight residential schools scattered throughout the United States which have been providing such service.

Public school programs, in attempting to meet the needs of multihandicapped children, were faced with serious problems. In the era of retrolental fibroplasia (RLF) many local school districts began educational programs for visually handicapped children based on the prevailing services of the day, those of resource or integrated programs. Often these programs were initiated and policies were formulated which limited enrollment to children who could gain from spending most of each day in a regular classroom. Therefore, many day-school programs for visually handicapped children which were initiated in the 1950s became as highly selective as those of residential schools. The visually handicapped child with additional problems was not served by either of them.

Parents of multihandicapped children often did not apply pressure or push for services because they thought that children as handicapped as theirs would not qualify for services in any educational setting. Services had been initiated and policies developed to define who would benefit from such services, and children were carefully and selectively screened to fit the mold as defined by policy. Many children who could be benefited greatly from educational services were being denied admission because they did not fit the definition established by the school district for inclusion in the program.

At long last, teachers, administrators, parents, and others began to realize (and are still in the process of this realization) that a service for *all* visually handicapped children was their responsibility. Educational services should be available to all of them within reasonable geographic proximity, and rather than expecting the child to fit the program, the program should be flexible enough to be adjusted to the needs of the individual children. It also took time to make the pressure of parents and educators felt by the legislators to provide the necessary legal-administrative changes and approve the needed financial support.

Local school districts and residential schools began to accept the responsibility of admitting visually handicapped children with additional problems, as did other services within the community. In many instances, it was a private agency serving a variety of children that led the way in providing services for multihandicapped children. Agencies specifically related to the needs of the blind and those more generally involved with the needs of all people provided family counseling to parents, home teaching to children, summer camp and day camp experiences, and other recreational opportunities.

Although many schools for the blind, school district programs, and other educational and therapeutic services have become actively involved in working with visually handicapped children with additional problems, a few should be particularly mentioned. The Michigan School for the Blind has provided intensive clinical services for severely handicapped children for a number of years (Elonen & Polzien, 1965). Under the direction of Dr. Anna Elonen, a psychiatrist, the Michigan School for the Blind has experienced a good deal of success by providing intensive therapeutic one-to-one service to severely multihandicapped children.

The Oregon School for the Blind initiated, with the help of Federal funds, a 3-year pilot project for visually handicapped children with additional problems (Graham, 1968). This program experimented with a variety of approaches. In addition to positive results with many children, this project produced an outstanding film, "Show Us The Way," and began developing a severity rating scale for assigning needed personnel in working with multi-handicapped children.

The Texas School for the Blind has also established services for multihandi-capped children and has kept very accurate records, particularly in the area of academic progress (Winn, 1968). The California School for the Blind has for many years provided classes for slow-learning blind children (Huffman, 1957), and in recent years has become a major center for developmental and educational services to multihandicapped children from throughout the state. A cooperative working relationship with local school programs within the state of California has resulted in an effective delineation of responsibility for children in California. The Edward R. Johnstone Training and Research Center provided services for severely handicapped visually impaired children in the state of New Jersey (Cicenia et al., 1965). Hope School for the Blind in Springfield, Illinois, represents one of the most positive developments in specialized services for visually handicapped children with additional prob-lems (Tretakoff & Farrell, 1958). According to its director, Maurice Tretakoff, pupil–teacher ratio is low, and the emphasis has been on the critical aspects of daily living as taught by both teachers and houseparents in the program. The Royer-Greaves School in Pennsylvania has long provided service for mentally retarded blind children.

CURRENT PROBLEMS

Despite the efforts of Gruber and Moor (1963), Lowenfeld (1969), and others, mental retardation continues to be used as a catchall for both diagnosis and placement of multihandicapped children. Visually handicapped children whose additional handicaps include problems in learning continue to baffle educators and defy accurate diagnosis. While mental retardation may be a convenient term to use when referring to visually handicapped children who are emotionally disturbed, developmentally deprived, brain injured, or neuro-logically impaired, there is a danger that the traditional definition of mental retardation will result in inappropriate services.

Educators in recent years have speculated that had adequate early identifica-tion and provision of services been available for the population of RLF chil-dren, we might not have the large numbers of additionally handicapped children in that group. This speculation may never be proven, since it must be hoped that we will never again have the size of population of congenitally handicapped children that we had with retrolental fibroplasia. However, we must wonder what might have been the fate of many severely multihandi-capped RLF children had early identification taken place and concentrated preschool services been provided to both child and family. What are, in some instances, drastic, last-ditch efforts to help young people at this time, might be unnecessary if concerted efforts to prevent developmental deprivation and environmental isolation had taken place during early childhood. Often parents interpreted deviant behavior in their infants and preschool children as being normal for blind children. Often an occasional visit from a preschool worker did little to alter the opinions and feelings of the family.

Lowenfeld (1969) has recommended that in California the number of pre-school counselors for blind children be drastically increased. This recommen-dation substantiates the need for many more comprehensive services for both the family and the child during preschool years. At present, parents in many areas must be content with infrequent visits by preschool workers whose training is usually in social welfare, and who may be unprepared to work with the family in terms of the developmental needs of blind children, particularly if additional handicaps are involved.

It must be stressed again that lack of comprehensive diagnostic services seriously impairs the ability of those responsible for the day-to-day educational program of multihandicapped children. Diagnostic facilities which truly con-cern themselves with the whole child, with his functioning not only in a psychologist's clinic or a pediatrician's office, but also with his functioning in the community, with his peers, in the home, with his family, in school, and with his teacher, need to be developed. Such facilities must include profession-als who understand the effects of visual handicaps on learning and concept development in children. Generalities must be avoided, and each child must be studied, observed, and examined individually. Services to each individual child should ideally be determined by the results of comprehensive diagnostic services.

Often programs most successful in working with visually handicapped chil-dren with additional problems have been unable to involve parents in the education or in the therapeutic treatment of their child. The necessity for establishing many of these programs in residential centers has made it incon-venient, if not impossible, for parents to become actively involved in their child's program. The extent to which this is a disadvantage for the child's progress could probably be debated, and indeed, some educators feel that this arrangement is ideal for some children. We must always question, though, the permanence or effectiveness of therapeutic treatment, away from home and not including parents, for a child who must ultimately return to the family situa-tion which is initially responsible for the development of some of the multiple handicaps.

Except for a few extremely expensive, highly experimental, clinically ori-ented efforts, much of what has been attempted with severely multihandicapped children has thus far been at best moderately successful. Elonen and her colleagues (1967) have reported success, but the services provided in their program could not be duplicated for economic reasons in most places.

It might be well for educators to admit candidly that many efforts to work with multihandicapped children within the framework of existing educational services have not been successful. Some programs developed without preplanning and without consideration for the type of staff needed. The urgency of the need for service to multihandicapped children has too often resulted in makeshift programs with ill-prepared teachers.

The recommendations of Ashcroft (1966), Elonen and Polzien (1965), and others, which stressed the need for a clinical approach in order to serve these children most effectively, should be viewed very seriously by those attempting services within some other framework. However, economic considerations cannot be divorced from any such planning.

Who will teach the multihandicapped child and what he will be taught are serious, critical, and as yet unanswered questions. Those responsible for teacher preparation facilities would like to believe that teachers now entering the field are at least more aware of their obligation toward multihandicapped children. What will be taught is a complex question that can be answered only after the teacher knows each child well, and must be answered entirely on an individual basis.

To what extent must services to such children be therapeutic and provided on an individual basis? What is the prognosis for children who may never be economically self-sufficient? These and other questions await answers.

CONSIDERATIONS FOR FUTURE PLANNING

Preschool Services

Education is being more and more broadly defined. It is no longer limited to what occurs within the space of the school day within the walls of the classroom. It no longer consists of what happens to a child between the ages of 6 and 18. The professional educator of visually handicapped children is beginning to recognize the necessity of providing services to visually handicapped children from infancy through school and into postschool years. A positive sign illustrating the trend toward recognition of the needs of preschool children is the concern of the U.S. Office of Education for preschool handicapped children, as evidenced by the Handicapped Children's Early Education Act, Public Law 90–538.

For many years preschool services in a variety of forms have been available to the families of visually handicapped children. Private agencies in some instances have met this need, and in other situations public agencies and education programs have provided preschool services. Regardless of the origin of such services, there is no question that they have helped in bringing about more normal growth and development in preschool blind children. Of concern to many educators, however, is that in some states where there is a high level of population, a single person provides this service to every family in which there is a preschool visually handicapped child. In many other areas the ratio is sometimes as high as 50 preschool children to one preschool worker, and even higher. The extent to which a visit from the preschool worker every month or two actually helps the family of a visually handicapped child is debatable, and an even greater concern might be how much help this system affords to the child himself.

A growing recognition of the developmental problems and needs of pre-school handicapped children will undoubtedly bring about a more comprehensive and intensive level of service to the family and to the child from early infancy to school age. If consideration is given to the fact that everything which a sighted child learns visually and in a casual way during his early years must be taught to blind children, sometimes very slowly and carefully, then there can be no question that professional services are vital and important for the visually handicapped child during his early years.

Diagnostic Facilities

Lowenfeld (1969) has recommended that consideration be given to initiating diagnostic services specifically for visually handicapped children. The multi-handicapped child who is blind clearly presents complex problems to a diagnostic facility. Blindness alone presents unique problems to such an extent that often a doctor or a psychologist without experience with blind children is reluctant to serve on an evaluation team.

Specialized diagnostic services should be arranged in an educational setting which is capable of providing long-term placement for a multihandicapped child. In the future many multihandicapped children, who might have been denied services a few short years ago, will be given one year or possibly longer in a practical diagnostic facility, the classroom. The classroom in such instances will be more clinical than academic, more therapeutic than disciplinary. The extent to which teachers in the future will be effective in this setting will depend on their preparation and the flexibility of the educational program.

Educational Facilities

Local day schools which are providing educational services for academically capable blind children often have found it difficult to include multihandicapped children in their programs. Such children may require intensive, undivided attention from a teacher for long periods during the school day. A resource teacher, attempting to provide the necessary services for eight or ten visually handicapped children who are integrated in regular classrooms, might find the additional responsibility of a self-contained unit for multihandicapped children beyond his strength and capability.

What are the alternatives? The obvious and, unhappily, most often employed alternative has been to deny admission to the multihandicapped child. Many parents will attest to the fact that local schools were not willing to provide service for their multihandicapped child.

Some school districts have found it possible to add a teacher and provide a realistic, usually self-contained program for multihandicapped children in addition to continuing a resource or itinerant program for other visually handicapped children.

Perhaps the most encouraging development in recent years has been the cooperative efforts of day schools and residential schools. Rather than competing for certain children—and this has happened in the past—all educational facilities for visually handicapped children are working together to determine how each child can best be served. Representatives of day schools and residential schools are sitting down together and are making mutually satisfactory decisions concerning services that are in the best interest of each visually handicapped child. The greatest beneficiaries of these cooperative efforts have been multihandicapped children, who are at last the recipients of as much concern as other children. It would be erroneous to infer that this close cooperation can be found in all states and in all programs. But the trend is obvious and encouraging.

No longer do we need to discuss the type of program which best educates visually handicapped children. There are many variations of excellent programs, and we need to work even harder to match services to the needs of children, rather than trying to mold children to fit services. This need for adjustable, flexible service is even more necessary for multihandicapped children than for the general population of visually handicapped children.

It must be remembered that appropriate placement at a given time in the life of a multihandicapped child may not remain appropriate for long. Placement must be continually evaluated, and enrollment in any program must remain fluid and flexible. Each child's *current* needs should be determined by a team of professional people and the child's parents. Then a program should be tailored to that child's needs.

In metropolitan areas, where a number of programs may exist, a multihandicapped child should be able to transfer easily from one program to another, based on an evaluation of his current needs. In more sparsely populated areas, a single teacher will have to be very flexible and constantly alert to the changing needs of the multihandicapped child. There should be available for the visually handicapped child with additional problems either short-term or long-term residential placement. A short-term residential placement might well be for no more than 3 or 4 months with a specific goal in mind. When that need is met (if that was the only reason for enrollment in a residential school) and a day-school program is available and more appropriate for the child, then he should be returned home.

For some multihandicapped children a long-term residential program is a necessity. This may be because of the child's needs or because of the situation within the family. Also, geographic factors may necessitate residential placement. The important factor is that the service should be provided if the need is apparent. It is encouraging to view the increasing involvement of residential schools in providing well-planned and well-developed programs for multihandicapped children.

There may also be a need in the future for combining residential and day-school programs for certain children. It may be that some multihandicapped children will be able to participate in a day-school program but will need the advantages provided by residential school living. This has been done with visually handicapped children with no additional problems, and if beneficial, should also be arranged for multihandicapped children. If a community in which a residential school is located has, for example, a particularly good program for children with learning disabilities, some children who need to live at the residential school could best be served by being enrolled in the learning disability program. Some school districts and residential schools have already proven that the legal and administrative problems encountered in such an arrangement can be resolved.

Some programs in both residential and day schools have found it possible to include multihandicapped children in work-study programs in the community along with other handicapped children. This may consist of a half-day program in the school, and include opportunities to learn independent living skills, grooming, social behavior, manual dexterity, and orientation and mobility. The rest of the day may be spent in a sheltered workshop in the community, learning the meaning of work, holding a job, and earning money.

There may be a necessity, too, for considering home teaching for some severely multihandicapped children. If a child is bedridden or otherwise so severely orthopedically handicapped that he cannot attend school, then the teacher must go to the child. If a child is not yet emotionally capable of handling himself in a setting with other children, he may need to be helped at home. Most larger school districts have home teaching programs, and these programs should serve multihandicapped children who cannot attend school. It may be that an effective home teaching program will ready a child for school placement more quickly than any other service.

It should also be noted that private agencies have become concerned with and involved in the problem of providing services to visually handicapped children with additional problems. In some instances private agencies have offered recreational programs after school hours and on weekends. For some multihandicapped children, these programs provide the only opportunities for physical and social activities. Other agencies have provided educational programs for children for whom nothing else was available. Multihandicapped children are certainly a community responsibility, as well as being the responsibility of the schools, the state, and nation.

Educational programs and vocational rehabilitation services have not yet faced the problem of what will happen to multihandicapped children when educational services are terminated. Some schools have found it possible to continue to offer appropriate services to youth beyond the normal high school graduation age. It is not uncommon to find multihandicapped youngsters in both residential schools and day schools who are older than 18 years.

Some schools are now cooperating with vocational rehabilitation services so that rehabilitation counselors may begin to work with visually handicapped youth before graduation or school termination. The mutual concerns and the combined efforts of teachers and rehabilitation counselors are important if the multihandicapped child is to live as full and satisfying a life as possible.

School Curriculum

As diagnostic services expand and become more available for multihandicapped children, the results of such services can help in determining educational approaches and a curriculum for the child. A number of developmental scales, both original and adapted from those for sighted children, are being utilized as a part of diagnostic evaluation. Developmental scales will not only help determine the level at which a multihandicapped child is currently functioning, but they may well provide the information the teacher is seeking for the next steps in the educational and developmental program for the child.

Also encouraging is the growing concern about educational placement and planning based upon individual needs of children. No longer is it possible to provide a service with a singular approach and expect visually handicapped children as a group to benefit from this service. As educational services for multihandicapped children have grown, so also has the recognition of the diversity of needs in children being served.

One result of providing for multihandicapped children within the structure of services to all visually handicapped children is that a single teacher may find himself planning for children with a very wide variety of needs. When extremes in the developmental level of a group of children are more spread out, the need for individual planning for children becomes greater. A teacher may help one child learn to factor fractions, and help another child learn to use a spoon in eating.

Early efforts to include multihandicapped children in programs for the visually handicapped often resulted in presenting a traditional academic curriculum. Expectations were adjusted downward, but in content the curriculum remained similar. In many of the early classes for slow-learning blind or mentally retarded blind children in residential schools, emphasis in learning stressed braille, sometimes resulting in a reading vocabulary of a few words after many frustrating years of teaching. Teachers must have wondered about the value of hours of instruction in braille in order to provide the child with a reading vocabulary which he cannot use either educationally or recreationally. Still the practice of a scaled-down academic curriculum for severely multihandicapped children continued for years. A reason for this procedure may be that teachers were prepared for dealing educationally with multihandicapped children in nonacademic areas. Now teachers are beginning to consider more broadly the needs of these children and are as concerned about the day-to-day independent living capabilities of the blind person as they are with his academic level.

Learning by listening has long been recognized as important in the education of blind children. Emphasis on the use of braille has tended to place auditory learning in a secondary role as a medium for obtaining information. In recent years, as the number of blind students at the high school and college level has increased significantly, educators have begun to realize that in many instances educational materials must be prepared and presented to blind students either by recorded means or by readers. Lack of availability of braille materials and the need for a more efficient reading system due to lengthening assignments necessitate a greater use of listening material (see Chapter 7).

Teachers of visually handicapped students at the secondary level are now also recognizing the need for the development of listening skills. Many blind students reach high school without adequate preparation in the use of auditory materials. It is not enough to simply hand a high school student a textbook recorded on tape and expect him to learn by listening if it is one of his first exposures to a recorded book. Preparation of students in how to selectively listen to materials and how to retain information obtained from auditory sources is the responsibility of teachers long before students reach high school age.

To whatever extent learning by listening is important to academically capable blind students, it is even a more critical academic skill for multihandicapped children. For those children who cannot utilize braille effectively for reading and/or writing, learning by listening becomes a primary source for gaining information about themselves and their environment. It is the responsibility of an education program for multihandicapped children to provide every opportunity for the student to reach his highest academic level possible. The higher the academic level reached, the more aware of the world and the more self-confident a multihandicapped child may become. If braille is not an adequate medium for a multihandicapped child, then learning to listen effectively becomes a necessity.

The availability of material prerecorded on tapes, on records, and more recently on cartridge tapes, provides the multihandicapped child with a generous supply of potential materials. Also, commercial publishers have in recent years prepared very effective programs on tape which have been developed to help children become better listeners. With little, if any, adaptation these programs can be very helpful in developing the listening skills of the multihandicapped children, particularly if they are geared to their level of understanding. The extent to which recent developments in speech compression and speech expansion will be applicable to the needs of multihandicapped children is yet to be explored. Early experiments tend to discourage the use of speech compression with them. However, it is possible that speech expansion will have some applicability for work with these children.

It should not be necessary to stress in this chapter the need for direct, concrete experiences for multihandicapped children. However, the continued existence of programs unduly stressing abstract learning suggests that there are teachers who fail to recognize that a child who does not have a good, varied background of concrete experiences cannot deal with subjects in an abstract manner. Tactual experiences with all physical objects which can have meaning for learning must be the foundation of any educational program for multihandicapped children.

When concrete experiences are not feasible in the classroom, then the child must be provided the opportunity to go to the experience. It is especially true for the multihandicapped child that his classroom cannot be limited to a room in a school building. He must have direct, physical experiences with such objects of daily life as trees, grass, vegetables, parking meters, grocery stores, and curbs. The need for concrete experiences has been stressed in past chapters so far as blind children are concerned. It is even more imperative for multihandicapped children, since they are more liable to be affected by early experiential deprivation.

The teaching of daily living skills to multihandicapped children must receive high priority in educational planning. The child who comes to school unable to dress himself, unable to feed himself, and still wearing diapers presents developmental problems to the teacher which are no less important than the normal school curriculum. Huffman (1957) and Lowenfeld (1971) include valuable suggestions in these areas of living competencies. Though the latter's book deals mainly with living skills of preschool blind children, much of it applies also to multihandicapped children with retarded capabilities.

In recent years, a number of curriculum guides dealing with the teaching of efficient living skills for visually handicapped children have been developed. Chapters 8 and 9 of this book contain additional information relating to the teaching of daily living skills. In applying curriculum guides and other courses of study designed for visually handicapped children, the teacher must make continuous adaptations and adjustments of expectations to the needs of the individual multihandicapped child at his specific stage of development.

School curricula for multihandicapped children should be carefully balanced. Opportunities for each child to attain his highest possible academic level must be offered, but consideration must also be given to the learning of a marketable skill. These two objectives must be considered along with the needs for these children to live as independent a life as possible, to engage in social activities, and to gain satisfaction and enjoyment from recreation. For multihandicapped children who seem unable to benefit from continued attempts at academic progress, teachers must consider an alternative or supplementary program which will enable these children to function as independently as possible in the community. The functioning alone, however, is not enough. These children should also have the necessary motivation and appreciation to live a satisfying, fulfilling life in the community. This would include the ability to live by oneself without the need of a responsible adult and to make use of opportunities, recreationally and socially, to interact with people in the community.

To some extent the area of education of visually handicapped children has been a "hardware-oriented" field. It has concerned itself with curriculum adaptation and the utilization of equipment. Unfortunately, very few structured programs have developed which are designed originally for visually handicapped children who are multihandicapped. Teachers of these children who may be searching for a structured approach in providing educational services might consider some of the models developed in recent years, including the engineered classroom of Frank Hewett (1968), the prescriptive teaching approaches of Lawrence Peter (1965), the perceptual motor program as devised by Newell Kephart (1960), the behavior modification techiniques of Norris Haring and Lakin Philips (1962), and many others. To state that no well-defined structured program has been developed for multihandicapped blind children is to overlook the possibilities which programs developed for other handicapped children offer.

During the late 1960s, a wide variety of services were initiated for deaf–blind children. When necessity dictates, education can move quickly and effectively. The 1964–1965 rubella epidemic, which has been over- and underestimated many times, resulted in a dramatic increase in the population of deaf–blind children in the United States. It does not matter whose statistics one reads regarding the actual numbers of handicapped children as a result of that epidemic. The fact remains that numbers of deaf–blind children have increased far beyond the capacity of services before and at the time of the epidemic.

Many preschool programs for deaf–blind children were conceived during the years immediately following the 1964–1965 rubella epidemic. Many of them were developed by medical centers and by speech and hearing clinics, and some were also initiated by educational services. It will be interesting and important to observe the extent to which preschool developmental services provided to this group of children will have affected their level of ability when they begin their formal education.

Plans as of 1969 call for ten regional centers for deaf–blind children funded by the U.S. Office of Education, which will be scattered geographically throughout the United States. Because of the extremely high cost involved in providing services to deaf–blind children, it is encouraging to note the involvement of the Federal government in providing these services. It is hoped that, as the regional centers develop and begin to provide direct service to children, every child who is visually and auditorily handicapped as a result of rubella will be provided with appropriate, meaningful services within a reasonable distance of his home community.

To reiterate, literature available on the subject of multihandicapped children provides information primarily in three areas: incidence, description, and curriculum. The latter is very limited, and this chapter does not add anything to the area of curricula for multihandicapped children. Reasons for the lack of literature in this area are obvious. Special services for visually handicapped children with additional problems have been provided only for a short period of time. Therefore, efforts to work with these children have been largely experimental and, in many instances, have not been as successful as was hoped.

Approaches to educational services for these children have varied from a traditional academic program to a "shoe tying" curriculum. Priorities have not been and may never be established because of the demand to emphasize the individual needs of multihandicapped children. It would appear, then, that most needed in terms of service is the economic and administrative support necessary so that each multihandicapped child can be provided the individual attention in a therapeutic setting of a good, understanding, well-prepared teacher-clinician. When problems of finance, of appropriate teacher preparation, of administrative support, and of priorities in education are brought to a reasonable solution, then better services to visually handicapped children with additional problems will be provided.

<h2 style="text-align:center">REFERENCES</h2>

Abel, G. L., & Hatlen, P. H. (Eds.). *Improved special education services for visually impaired children with multiple handicaps.* Proceedings of the Special Study Institute sponsored by the California State Department of Education, Division of Special Schools and Services, 1968.

Ashcroft, S. C. Delineating the possible for the multihandicapped child with visual impairment. *Sight-Saving Review,* Summer 1966, **36,** 90–94.

Burlingham, D. Some notes on the development of the blind. *Psychoanalytic Study of the Child,* 1961, **16,** 121–145.

Burlingham, D. Some problems of ego development in blind children. *Psychoanalytic Study of the Child,* 1965, **20,** 194–208.

Cicenia, E. F., Belton, J. A., Myers, J. J., & Mundy, F. The blind child with multiple handicaps: A Challenge. *International Journal for the Education of the Blind,* Part I, 1965, **14,** 65–71; Part II, 1965, **14,** 105–112.

Donlon, E. T. An evaluation center for the blind child with multiple handicaps. *International Journal for the Education of the Blind,* 1964, **13,** 75–78.

Elonen, A. S., & Polzien, M. Experimental program for deviant blind children. *New Outlook for the Blind,* 1965, **59,** 122–126.

Elonen, A. S., Polzien, M., & Zwarensteyn, S. B. The "uncommitted" blind child: Results of intensive training of children formerly committed to institutions for the retarded. *Exceptional Children,* 1967, **33,** 301–306.

Frampton, M. E., Kerney, E., & Schattner, R. *Forgotten children: A program for the multihandicapped.* Boston: Porter Sargent, 1969.

Graham, M. D. *Multiply-impaired blind children: A national problem.* New York: American Foundation for the Blind, 1968.

Gruber, K. F., & Moor, P. M. (Eds.). *No place to go.* New York: American Foundation for the Blind, 1963.

Haring, N., & Philips, L. *Educating emotionally disturbed children.* New York: McGraw-Hill, 1962.

Hewett, F. M. *The emotionally disturbed child in the classroom.* Boston: Allyn & Bacon, 1968.

Huffman, M. B. *Fun comes first for blind slow-learners.* Springfield, Ill.: Charles C Thomas, 1957.

Kephart, N. C. *The slow learner in the classroom.* Columbus, Ohio: Charles E. Merrill, 1960.

Lowenfeld, B. Multihandicapped blind and deaf-blind children in California. *Research Bulletin No. 19.* New York: American Foundation for the Blind, 1969. Pp. 1–72.

Lowenfeld, B. *Our blind children* (3rd. ed.). Springfield, Ill.: Charles C Thomas, 1971.

Moor, P. M. Who are the children and what are they like? *International Journal for the Education of the Blind,* 1965, **15,** 20–22.

Peter, L. J. *Prescriptive teaching.* New York: McGraw-Hill, 1965.

Tretakoff, M. I. *What they are all doing.* Washington, D.C.: American Association of Instructors of the Blind Convention Report, 1966. Pp. 42–44.

Tretakoff, M. I., & Farrell, M. J. Developing a curriculum for the blind retarded. *American Journal of Mental Deficiency,* 1958, **62,** 610–615.

Winn, R. J., Jr. Two-year progress analysis of project for multi-handicapped visually-impaired children at the Texas School for the Blind. *International Journal for the Education of the Blind,* 1968, **18,** 99–107.

Wolf, J. M. *The blind child with concomitant disabilities.* New York: American Foundation for the Blind, 1967.

CHAPTER 11

Preparation of Teachers

Ferne Root Roberts

Department of Special Education, Hunter College
City University of New York

The history and present status of university programs for the preparation of teachers of visually handicapped children naturally reflect the prevalent theories and practices of the total teacher education movement. There are, however, unique factors which have had a profound effect on professional training programs in this area of special education. These factors are related to a long history of residential school education for blind children; the use of medical diagnoses as bases for educational planning for partially seeing pupils; the limited educational research with visually handicapped children; a paucity of tests and scales for evaluation of both learning potential and academic achievement in visually handicapped children; and belated implementation of curricula in such crucial areas as daily living or orientation and mobility skills.

The administration and faculty in college and university teacher preparation centers are continually faced with a leadership dilemma, which arises from two not quite compatible public assumptions: On the one hand, it is assumed that the universities will prepare teachers to implement present local educational plans; on the other hand, it is also assumed that the universities will prepare teachers to resolve educational problems in new ways.

If the univeristy maintains a "following" role, it prepares teachers for the status quo in the schools. If it establishes a "leading" role, its teacher candidates encounter difficulty in finding and fulfilling local school assignments. The dilemma is intensified when the local schools or outside public and private agencies stimulate the growth of new types of programs for children, with the quite sudden result that neither teachers for the status quo nor, possibly, teachers for an anticipated innovation have adequate background for programs just off the drawing board. It is obvious that the university's goal would be a balance between fulfillment of present local educational demand and participation with schools and agencies to stimulate change in the educational establishment. Finding that balance has not been easy and the review of the history of preparation of teachers for the education of visually handicapped children is particularly interesting if this question of leadership for change is used as the focus.

EARLY HISTORY

The models for the preparation of teachers for the education of visually handicapped children were developed outside the United States during the nineteenth century, In the first schools for blind children founded by or under the influence of Valentin Haüy at the turn of the nineteenth century in Paris, Berlin, and St. Petersburg, teacher preparation took place within the school on an apprenticeship basis. The methods which Haüy, Pereire (education of the deaf), and Seguin (education of the mentally retarded) developed in their early schools in France would now be called diagnostic or clinical teaching. These men demonstrated their techniques to teachers who in turn trained apprentices.

A unique in-service training program was instituted by Dr. Francis Campbell, an American-born educator, when he founded the Royal Normal College for the Blind in London in 1872. The College was a model school for the education of blind children and youth. Since Dr. Campbell was acquainted with educators of blind children in the United States, he invited a number of them to London to assist in the training of British teachers for his school. Thus, while the apprenticeship type of training was perpetuated, teacher-trainers were "imported" to present their own points of view and impart their particular skills.

When residential schools for blind children were established in the United States beginning in 1832, they adopted the European model of apprenticeship training. Many superintendents preferred this pattern and later resisted the move toward university-based training because they wanted to introduce new teachers to their own techniques for educating blind children. As enrollments grew, however, residential schools turned to nearby universities for help with in-service training and eventually with recruiting and preservice preparation.

The first university-based teacher preparation course was offered by the University of California in 1918. Then in 1921 Dr. Edward E. Allen, superintendent of the Perkins Institution for the Blind and one of the educators who had assisted in the training of teachers at the Royal Normal College, sought the help of Harvard University to establish an extension course which eventually became a full time academic program. In this and subsequently established training centers, faculty from the residential schools often taught the college courses. Thus the distinguishing feature of these new university programs was not a change in philosophy or course content but a recognition of the trend toward more formal training and of the value of college degrees and teacher certification. A summary of the first 16 years of univeristy-based teacher preparation in this field in provided by Best (1934).

> Of later years there have been special training courses of more systematized order conducted, for a longer or shorter period of time, under the college or department of education in certain of the larger institutions of learning in the United States. The first efforts were at the University of California in 1918. Sometimes there is cooperation or supervision by some school for the blind. At the courses provided at Harvard University in conjunction with Perkins Institution there have been students from various countries. Training may be afforded for teachers of both blind and semi-sighted children. Universities or colleges having had this work are University of California, University of Pennsylvania, Columbia University (Teachers College), Harvard University, University of Southern California, Western Reserve University, Catholic University, Fordham University, University of Cincinnati, George Peabody College for Teachers, New York University and certain State normal colleges. In a few institutions, summer sessions for the training of teachers have been provided [p. 388].

Until the early years of the twentieth century very little attention was devoted to the special training of teachers of partially seeing children. Children who had useful residual vision either went to residential schools where they received the same education as blind children, attended regular school classes where they received limited special help, or remained at home. In 1907 the International Congress of School Hygiene met in London, where a statement was issued decrying education of partially seeing children in schools for blind children. In 1913 when Dr. Edward E. Allen in Boston and Dr. Robert B. Irwin in Cleveland spurred the opening of public day school programs, a virtually new teacher preparation problem arose. Hathaway (1959) says of this period:

> For some years after the first educational facilities were made available to partially seeing children in 1913, there was no established precedent for teachers to follow, and no opportunity for them to prepare for this very specialized work.

Each teacher had, therefore, to try to solve through the trial and error method the problems that were constantly arising, thus experimenting, to a certain extent, with children who had difficulties enough of their own to meet [p. 64].

Nine years after the first programs for partially seeing children were instituted, Dr. Irwin and some of his teachers from Cleveland staffed the first summer training program at Teachers College, Columbia University. Then in 1923, 1924, and 1925 George Peabody College for Teachers held summer sessions. At this time the National Society for the Prevention of Blindness was asked to draw up a minimum schedule of courses for the preparation of teachers of partially seeing children to be used for the first time by the University of Cincinnati in the summer of 1925. The schedule suggested six semester credits for 30 clock hours in each of these areas: methods and materials; observation and practice teaching; and anatomy and physiology of the eye (Hathaway, 1959).

The early experience of teachers of partially seeing children was soon paralleled by other teachers when the compulsory school attendance law was passed and the schools and handicapped children were forced into a reluctant mutual recognition of each other (Hollingworth, 1923). The sudden increase in numbers of handicapped children in the schools caught the universities in the twin traps of unanticipated demand for trained teachers and lack of theoretical structures for preparation sequences. The fact that many teachers floundered in their efforts to teach handicapped children is undoubtedly one of the contributing factors to the decline of special education programs and hence of teacher training programs in the decades between 1930 and 1950. Cruickshank and Johnson (1967) believe that the economic depression, the Second World War, and the "progressive education" movement also inhibited the growth of education for exceptional children.

TWO DECADES OF GROWTH

As the year 1950 approached, there was a new surge of interest in special education and a number of universities responded by establishing teacher preparation sequences in various exceptionalities. Four factors led several universities to expand or initiate training programs for teachers of visually handicapped children: First, physicians no longer believed that use of residual vision for reading and other close work would harm the eyes. On the contrary, they usually recommended use of vision as a means of increasing visual efficiency. This shift from "sight conservation" opened the door to education in the regular classrooms and ended the era in which protection of sight was the primary task of the teacher.

Second, the Veterans Administration developed a systematic program for teaching blinded veterans of the Second World War the skills of daily living and independent cane travel. Leading educators realized that this new curriculum could be adapted for use with children and that many of the techniques should be included in teacher training programs.

Third, evolving theories of child growth and development, some of which were based on studies of maternal deprivation, emphasized the overwhelming importance of each child's growing up within a family structure. Orphanages gave way to foster-homes, and many parents of handicapped children of all categories demanded local educational and training programs as alternatives to institutional or residential placement. The growth of local day-school education for blind children led to an increase in the number of teaching positions and to a differentiation of teaching roles for residential, resource room, or itinerant teachers.

Fourth, the unfortunate appearance of retrolental fibroplasia as a major cause of visual loss in infants forced rapid expansion of the school programs.

The two decades from 1950 to 1970 were characterized by change and growth in understanding of the educational needs of visually handicapped children, of the personal and teaching competencies of their teachers, and of standards for quality educational programs.

In 1952 seven university training programs were represented at a symposium at the annual convention of the Council for Exceptional Children: Harvard University (affiliated with the Perkins School for the Blind), Hunter College (affiliated with the New York Institute for the Education of the Blind), MacMurray College (affiliated with the Illinois Braille and Sight Saving School), Willamette University (affiliated with the Oregon School for the Blind), West Virginia State College (affiliated with Hampton Institute), Teachers College, and San Francisco State College (Abel, 1962). The deliberations of this symposium were published by the American Foundation for the Blind (1953). While the discussion was primarily focused on the status of teacher preparation in those centers, the meeting and publication marked the beginning of a period of remarkable activity directed toward improvement in preparation of teachers.

During the summers of 1953 and 1954, two national voluntary agencies, the American Foundation for the Blind and the National Society for the Prevention of Blindness, sponsored workshops with ten different colleges and universities: The American Foundation for the Blind was a cosponsor with George Peabody College for Teachers, Syracuse University, the University of Texas, and the University of Cincinnati. The National Society for the Prevention of Blindness participated with Michigan State Normal College, Wayne State University, Hunter College, Syracuse University, Illinois State Normal University, San Francisco State College and the University of New York College for Teachers at Buffalo (Mackie & Dunn, 1954). This type of joint sponsorship of summer workshops was not new to the National Society for the Prevention of Blindness but it was a new role for the American Foundation for the Blind, and for a number of years both agencies used this approach as a major means of increasing the number of qualified teachers, stimulating the growth of teacher preparation centers, and improving standards for teacher preparation. In addition to consultation on the content of workshops and course sequences, both agencies on occasion loaned staff and provided support funds to the universities or fellowships to teachers. Other agencies and organizations provided consultants and program specialists without charge to the universities for both the planning and active program phases of workshops. Among these were the American Printing House for the Blind, The Seeing Eye, Inc. and the Veterans Administration.

In 1954 the United States Office of Education published a status report, *College and University Programs for the Preparation of Teachers of Exceptional Children* (Mackie & Dunn, 1954). Subsequently the Office of Education published consensus studies on the competencies of teachers for the then existing categories of exceptionality, including *Teachers of Children Who are Blind* (Mackie & Dunn, 1955) and *Teachers of Children Who are Partially Seeing* (Mackie & Cohoe, 1956). In each of these studies, 100 teachers identified and evaluated the teacher competencies which seemed important in their work with handicapped children. Then supervisors of special education, specialists in state departments of education, and nationally recognized leaders in the field grouped and evaluated competencies and contributed further information for final publication.

At the completion of these massive studies of teacher competencies in ten areas of exceptionality, Mackie (1960) concluded that each area of exceptionality required distinctive competencies and that these competencies were different in kind or degree from those required of teachers of nonhandicapped children.

With regard to teacher preparation, the consensus of the two studies of competencies of teachers of visually handicapped children was that the optimum model should include an undergraduate major in elementary education, 2 or more years of successful teaching in the regular classroom, and graduate training in education of blind or partially seeing children, including 50 to 250 clock hours of practice teaching.

In yet another respect, 1954 was a significant year. The Southern Regional Education Board, George Peabody College for Teachers, and the American Foundation for the Blind participated in a cooperative study of the manpower needs in public and residential school programs for visually handicapped children in the southeast and projected a regional plan for the preparation of teachers. One recommendation of the study resulted in the establishment of a year-round teacher preparation program with a full-time doctoral level faculty member as director. For the first 5 years of this new program the

American Foundation for the Blind provided basic financial support (Dunn, 1960). One of the important aspects of this regional planning was an agreement on uniform teacher certification requirements on the part of the 16 states then included in the Southern Regional Education Board.

It was the conviction of many leaders in the field that regional planning was an essential aspect of the general effort to develop quality preparation centers. During this period, when financial assistance to colleges and to students was extremely limited and when there were only two or three people with doctorates in this area of exceptionality in the whole country, four full-time centers in the four major geographical sections of the United States were envisioned as the maximum feasible number. While this regional design was never fully implemented, it represented a radical departure from the earlier period when residential schools carried on their own apprenticeship training or relied on colleges in the immediate geographic area. In addition to their role of teacher preparation, the regional centers were envisioned as having responsibility for seminars and institutes for school personnel, for consultation to schools and agencies in their regions, for coordination of economic resources to be used for scholarships, and for educational research (American Foundation for the Blind, 1961).

In 1957 the American Foundation for the Blind appointed a Teacher Education Advisory Committee to work with its staff to formulate standards for universities or colleges that wished to include the preparation of teachers of blind children in their special education curriculum (American Foundation for the Blind, 1961). This Committee convened two national work sessions in 1958 and 1959 to develop program objectives for a functional teacher education sequence. The Committee described the educational needs of the legally blind school population and the teaching requirements of various school programs as the basis of a model for preparation of educational personnel. The resulting document, *A Teacher Education Program for Those Who Serve Blind Children and Youth* (American Foundation for the Blind, 1961), expressed the Committee's conviction that the schools and teachers should call upon many specialists within and outside of the school for help in meeting the personal, social, and learning needs of blind children and youth. This was a much broader view of the range of competencies required for adequate education for visually handicapped children than that reflected in earlier publications.

At about this time the National Society for the Prevention of Blindness appointed an advisory committee to assist in the fourth edition revision of Winifred Hathaway's book, *Education and Health of the Partially Seeing Child* (1959). This edition proposed a basic 120 clock hour program as minimum preparation for teachers of partially seeing children.

The American Association of Instructors of the Blind, now known as the Association for Education of the Visually Handicapped, published criteria for the certification of teachers and houseparents, sponsored regional workshops for in-service training, and awarded a limited number of scholarships for summer training.

At the end of the 1950s two types of special teacher preparation were envisioned and program plans were set in motion. Provisions for the training of industrial arts teachers of blind students and of orientation and mobility specialists represented important steps in the direction of curriculum development and preparation of personnel for differentiated roles in the schools.

In 1959 the American Foundation for the Blind convened a workshop to establish criteria for the selection of personnel for training in the special area of orientation and mobility, to outline a preparation sequence, and to seek suggestions for appropriate sponsorship of initial programs. The Vocational Rehabilitation Administration (now the Social and Rehabilitation Service) encouraged and partially supported the founding of the first two training programs in this specialty in graduate schools of education, at Boston College in 1960 and Western Michigan University in 1961 (Ryan, 1965).

In the summer of 1960 and for several summers thereafter, the American Foundation for the Blind, the American Association of Instructors of the Blind and the Vocational Rehabilitation Administration gave guidance and support to qualified staff at the State University of New York College for Teachers at Oswego to conduct workshops for industrial arts instructors in residential and public schools. These workshops were designed to increase the teachers' competence and to better their understanding of teaching procedures, materials, and industrial arts activities for blind students (Ryan, 1965).

Thus, while the decade of the 1950s was notable for progress in many directions, the focus of a major part of work and thought was the analysis of teacher competencies, and later the organization of these competencies into training categories.

The focus of the 1960s, professional standards and criteria for evaluation of programs, was the logical offspring of the competency studies. The development of standards was based upon the desire of leaders in the field to build a structure for teacher training which would reasonably assure at least a minimum level of professional education.

Early in the 1960s the Professional Standards Committee of the Council for Exceptional Children (CEC) channeled its concern for improvement of education for exceptional children into a recommendation for an intensive study of teacher preparation which was subsequently called the CEC Project on Professional Standards. This project, which received professional and financial support from many agencies for the handicapped, was active for over 2 years, and the deliberations enlisted the participation of approximately 700 special educators. The report of this project (Council for Exceptional Children, 1966) outlined standards for the preparation of personnel for administration and supervision, and for seven areas of exceptionality, including the visually handicapped.

Just as the competency studies of the U.S. Office of Education in the 1950s were status reports, the *Professional Standards* report was a "state of the art" study. Thus, the final draft of the document represented a consensus of the thinking of special educators which was, in effect, a compromise between those who wanted to recommend radical departures from traditional teacher preparation practices and those who preferred limited change. Accordingly, the foreword of the publication urges a continuous study of professional standards to avoid fixation on the insights of one brief period. From a historical point of view, the unquestioned importance of this project lay in the active participation of hundreds of educators in the *process* of the study. The philosophy and content of teacher preparation were discussed in committees, conferences, regional meetings, and writing sessions by teachers and other educators who do not ordinarily have an opportunity to influence university programs. Additionally, some of the meetings encouraged interchange of ideas among the various areas of exceptionality, a process which dramatized both the sameness and the uniqueness of problems in each area.

An example of the way in which the deliberations of the project affected change was the final decision to adopt the term visually handicapped as a replacement for the two older categories of blind and partially seeing. This issue was a subject of debate for seveal reasons, foremost of which was a fear that children with relatively minor visual losses would be ignored in the larger category. The ultimate adoption of "visually handicapped" was based on the desire to emphasize visual function rather than visual acuity as the chief concern of the educator.

The CEC standards for the preparation of personnel for the education of visually handicapped children included basic preparation in professional education, a general overview of all areas of exceptionality, and specific preparation in the area of the visually handicapped. This specific preparation included the following content (Council for Exceptional Children, 1966).

1. The influence upon children of various types and degrees of visual impairments.
2. The educational implications of eye conditions.
3. Identification and placement of visually handicapped children.
4. Educational procedures for children who are visually handicapped.
5. The teaching of communication skills.
6. Orientation, mobility, and daily living skills.
7. Educational appraisal and remedial techniques in the basic skill subjects.
8. Practicum experiences with visually handicapped children.
9. Information on local, state, and national resources for the education and assistance of children who are visually handicapped.

The report further stressed that the granting of certification be based upon completion of approved *sequential* programs rather than upon accumulation of scattered courses.

Another event which focused attention upon standards for teacher preparation programs was the amendment, in 1964, to Public Law 85–924, which extended funding to include training of teachers for all major categories of handicapped children. There was immediate necessity to establish criteria for the evaluation of applications for funds. Rotating review committees, composed of peers of the applicant agencies, were convened annually to review and rate applications. In the area of education of visually handicapped children, the committees were particularly alert to the following program provisions.

1. Supervised practicum in *various* types of educational settings.
2. At least one full-time faculty person, preferably one with a doctorate.
3. Qualified consultants and part-time specialists.
4. Administrative support for the long-term development of teacher preparation for the education of visually handicapped children.
5. Appropriate theoretical and practical training for leadership and research personnel at the post-master's level.
6. Integrated sequence of courses which ensures understanding of the teaching implications of theoretical concepts.
7. Admission and counseling procedures based upon teacher competencies required for optimum education of visually handicapped children.
8. Opportunity for special training for effective teaching in various programs including those for multiply handicapped children.

In a study of the professional preparation of educators of visually handicapped children 2 years after the initiation of the Federal grant program, Jones (1966) observed the following trends: (1) The number of full-time students increased 50% between 1964 and 1966. At the same time the number of universities offering summer sessions increased. (2) All of the 25 universities which offered training in 1966 had curricula in education of both blind and partially seeing children or had a combined curriculum in the area of the visually handicapped. (3) There was an increase in the number of educators who were enrolled in programs which were preparing them for leadership roles in universities, schools, state education agencies, or other agencies. (4) Some of the universities were initiating experimental curricula for the preparation of teachers of multiply handicapped children.

Aside from the fact that teacher candidates and the universities they attended were aided financially, the cumulative effects of program support influenced some major policy decisions. For example, as soon as Federal funds became available, one of the primary reasons for a regional plan with a limited number of teacher preparation centers was removed. The review committees which assisted in making decisions about applications for funds could not, even if they had wished to, recommend against approval of funds for a university which presented an excellent application with adequate evidence of ability to attract candidates.

Another of the far-reaching effects of the Federal funding related to the incentive to undertake full-time graduate study in preparation for leadership roles. Earlier, the urgent need for teachers had prompted universities to offer summer training to experienced classroom teachers who wished to complete special training in two or more summer sessions with no loss of teaching time. The importance of summer training cannot be overestimated for the exact purpose for which it was organized—teacher training for existing program vacancies. However, the leadership gap became apparent long before there was an incentive for promising candidates to enter full-time study or for universities to offer extensive graduate study. During that period the national agencies and organizations provided valuable leadership but no one was more acutely aware than they that the base of active leadership must be broad if a field is to experience healthy change and renewal.

It has been said that every reform breeds its own counterreform and the development of standards is no exception. In the late 1960s the disadvantages of listing minimum course requirements for the preparation of teachers of visually handicapped children prompted the field, and particularly several state departments of education, to revise certification and preparation requirements. Two serious problems had arisen as a result of the rigid use of standards. First, teachers were granted certification and given employment merely because they "collected" the right number of courses in the right areas of content. There was little concern for the integration of theory and practice and no way of monitoring coursework to assure grasp of basic knowledges and skills. Second, all teachers received virtually the same preparation, regardless of the types of programs in which they were to be employed. Furthermore, workshops or courses which might aid the teacher in his work with special groups of children were not usually accepted for certification.

Some state departments of education now base certification on the university's statement that a teacher candidate has satisfactorily completed a program of preparation. Where this is possible, the teacher candidate and the university have great flexibility in designing sequences of coursework which meet the needs of teachers in various settings who teach children of various ages, abilities, and levels of achievement.

PRESSURES FOR CHANGE

That both general and special education are experiencing radical change and undergoing intense scrutiny is obvious to even a casual observer. To our colleges and universities, many of which feel that they are barely out of the pioneer era in preparation of teachers for the education of handicapped children, the rate and extent of the current change pose extremely complicated questions. Numerous social and scientific events force the educational community to take a fresh look at how children learn and at what kind of teaching it takes to effect learning. It would be easy to say that the field of education of visually handicapped children, along with all of special education, has progressed in a cycle that has suddenly brought it back to a need for updating the competency studies of the 1950s. This would, however, be an over-simplified statement, even though many of the same factors exist. Now, as then, there is great urgency for understanding the needs of handicapped and multiply handicapped children in order to recruit and prepare teachers who are competent to help these children acquire an education. The major difference in the present situation is that the field is more concerned with understanding how children learn than with the precise nature of the handicap, and more concerned with analysis of teaching behaviors which produce learning than with special techniques. In other words, educators are now looking at the nature of *teaching* and *learning* as well as at the characteristics of teachers and learners.

There are many events and conditions which have contributed to the growing conviction that sequences for the preparation of teachers for visually handicapped children must be redrafted.

Research and experimentation have led to significant advances in the development of techniques and materials for *educational* diagnosis of children. These advances must be incorporated into the training sequences of educational personnel who can translate the findings into improved educational opportunities for children. There is an upsurge of interest in diagnostic teaching as having a crucial role in special education. This interest extends in two directions: First, there is hope that teachers will become better diagnosticians; second, there is a desire to explore the effectiveness of using diagnostic teachers as specialists in the constellation of special school services.

School organization patterns are shifting. Team teaching, nongraded programs, employment of paraprofessional or auxiliary personnel, and use of self-teaching equipment are four of the many factors which are altering the old pattern of one teacher in one classroom. All of these changes involve teachers in new roles and new relationships.

Curriculum development is recognized as an increasingly essential teaching activity. A number of factors, such as the advent of programmed instruction and advances in diagnostic techniques, have reinforced the conviction that teachers must be given time and opportunity for generating curricula for groups and for individual handicapped children. Educational planning for children who have specific learning disabilities, preschool children, multiply handicapped children, or children who respond to behavior-shaping techniques requires a high degree of skill. Additionally, educators of visually handicapped children are aware that the older concept of curriculum adaptation must be discarded in favor of a much broader involvement in curriculum development. Mere adaptation of methods and materials to allow visually handicapped children to participate in the general school curriculum is a concession to those professionals who promote the idea that visually handicapped children are essentially normal children who happen to have visual losses. Certainly many visually handicapped children can lead normal lives, but the skills which contribute to healthy, competent living are not acquired by chance—they must be systematically taught. They must be taught by teachers who recognize individual differences and the effects of handicaps, and who use these insights to build effective curricula. Skills relating to daily living, personal grooming, and orientation to environment have until recently been neglected as curriculum areas. There are other curricula which are still in the research and experimentation phase, some of which will soon require further development by teachers. These are related to the ways in which visually handicapped children apprehend concepts and ideas. For example, is adaptation of methods and materials the only way in which a blind student can be enabled to understand chemistry, or is there a new way of organizing and designing the lecture and laboratory curriculum which will be more effective?

New positions and new educational roles have been created in newly established or expanded programs. Federal, state, and local funds in unprecedented amounts have been allocated to schools to upgrade and innovate educational programs for handicapped children. Residential and local schools have developed special programs in orientation and mobility, skills of daily living, remedial and summer education, parent education, physical education, and education of multiply handicapped children. Regional Centers for Deaf–Blind Children and Early Childhood Education programs for handicapped children, both federally funded, have emphasized the need for education personnel in two relatively neglected areas. Amendments to the Vocational Education Act and funds for stimulation of physical education and recreation programs for the handicapped open many opportunities for special training for teacher candidates who do not wish to take a basic major in elementary education.

The availability of funds for the support of education of handicapped children, often coupled with the admonition to "innovate," has challenged educators to try ideas that only yesterday were dreams. Public and private funds have been used to launch pilot, model, and demonstration projects which have an immediate need for highly qualified and skilled staffs. Even those projects and programs which systematically describe roles and competencies for their various staff positions have difficulty in detailing the training requirements which should qualify candidates for their jobs. Furthermore, some schools do not make it a practice to write detailed job descriptions; instead, they specify a certain college major, a certain type of teaching certificate, and a specified

number of years of experience. Thus, teacher preparation centers are subject
to criticism because their graduates are not prepared to work in schools "as
they really are." One of the difficulties in this situation obviously relates to the
university instructor's lack of skill or failure to understand the importance of
analyzing teaching jobs and of describing personal and professional qualifications in detail. This results in a fundamental lack of communication, even in
those instances in which administrators of programs for visually handicapped
children are in touch with the teacher training center staff. Another of the
difficulties is a genuine and understandable uncertainty about the kinds of
training experiences which are required to assure certain teaching skills.

Many professional educators, including those who participated in the development of *Professional Standards for Personnel in the Education of Exceptional
Children* (Council for Exceptional Children, 1966), believe that practica offer
the training center and the teacher candidate opportunities to resolve some of
the difficulties just outlined. Practica, including observation, demonstration,
and practice teaching, do offer opportunities for greater understanding of
day-to-day education problems and for clearer assessment of teaching skills
which are essential in work with certain visually handicapped children. As
evidence of their conviction that practica offer training potential beyond that
generally exploited, several teacher preparation centers have expanded the
range of experiences by fostering or subsidizing demonstration programs
within their own or cooperating institutions. These model programs are
designed to provide student-teachers direct experience in educational decision
making, teaching, and evaluation with severely handicapped children who are
not usually found in schools. They are based upon the conviction that a teacher
cannot take courses in two or more areas of exceptionality and successfully
merge the various theories and methods when he encounters a multiply handicapped child. Two or more serious handicaps do not pose two separate sets
of educational problems—they pose complicated problems related to the combined effects of the handicaps.

It is possible, therefore, that the extension of practicum requirements will
offer a partial solution to the unmet need for larger numbers of educational
personnel to work in both traditional and innovative programs. This partial
solution will be effective only to the extent to which (1) there is a basis of
cooperation between the school system and the college; (2) competent cooperating teachers are enlisted; (3) good school systems are used for practica; (4)
there is continuous professional guidance for the cooperating teachers; (5)
there is adequate college supervision of the teacher candidates; (6) there are
comprehensive student-teaching experiences; and (7) there is continuing evaluation and modification of all aspects of the student teaching program (Council
for Exceptional Children, 1966).

Another approach to the problem of adequate preparation of personnel for
the growing numbers and varieties of school programs relies on systematic and
relevant communication between training centers and schools.

Close coordination and cooperation among school districts, colleges and universities, state departments of education, professional associations and learned societies are essential to the planning, financing, and conducting of sound programs . . . [National Education Association, 1963].

Conferences, position papers, exchange instructorships, and joint study sessions may be the modes for effective communication. A step in this direction was taken by a teacher preparation center which applied for and received funding from the U.S. Office of Education for a year-long study of the content of teacher preparation for teachers of visually handicapped children. The project enlisted the aid of teachers of visually handicapped children for a series of work sessions for which travel expenses were reimbursed.

The Bureau of Education for the Handicapped, U.S. Office of Education, has also taken steps to shorten the time between the initiation of certain new programs and the recruitment and training of personnel for adequate staffing. In some instances this is accomplished by including funds for staff development within the design of a project. In others it is accomplished by contracting with one or more universities to design and develop special units for the training of personnel for special programs or to design training modules which may be implemented at state or regional levels for short-term in-service training in a specific subject or skill area.

These are challenging times for all educators. Explosions in knowledge, population, and educational costs are creating unprecedented competition for talent and funds. This competition, coupled with the desire to prepare educational personnel for greater competency in working with children with visual disabilities, impels the teacher preparation centers to make a great many difficult decisions. The position paper of the National Committee on Teacher Education and Professional Standards identifies problems which are as crucial today as they were in the early sixties (National Education Association, 1963):

Innovation is essential to progress in teacher education. Some traditional approaches to solving the problems the profession faces will continue to be effective, but different conditions and the increased maturity of the teaching profession demand new approaches. A few examples will suffice:

The increased mobility of our population . . . requires teachers who are aware of many regional differences and sympathetic to the variegated strands of our culture.

The development of knowledge in many fields and the fundamental revisions in content and methodology in several fields . . . create new responsibilities for teachers, who must maintain and extend their competence.

The application of new technology to educational problems, current research into the behavior of teachers in the classroom, the accelerating trend toward school reorganization and new insights into the nature and structure of knowledge—all contribute to changing the functions of the teacher.

If these and other complex problems are to be dealt with, new social and professional concepts, procedures and relationships must be created. The times demand innovation [p. 4].

A glance at the past highlights the fact that a great many agencies and organizations have been involved in the process of change in the patterns of preparation of teachers of visually handicapped children. The agents of greatest pressure for change were the large national agencies which devoted significant amounts of money and staff time to the improvement of professional preparation. It will be remembered, however, that the ideas and plans which these agencies helped to implement came from many directions and that in all of the intensive studies, large numbers of educational personnel including teachers were participants.

In addition to the renewed emphasis on analysis of competencies for teachers of visually handicapped children, colleges and universities are sharing the concern of the total educational establishment for accountability. Along with concepts of client participation and relevance, this increased sense of responsibility for "outcomes" of the educational process is leading teacher preparation programs to be more attentive than ever before to self-study and self-renewal. Thus, in the current decade, the greatest pressure for change is the college or university itself. Program evaluation and analysis of outcomes as they occur in the public and private schools which educate visually handicapped children and youth cannot be undertaken without the willing assistance of the teachers who are alumni of the preparation programs. This, then, heralds a period of increasing professionalism among teachers and of greater participation in the vital process of problem identification and problem solving.

REFERENCES

Abel, G. L. Professional education for teachers of the visually handicapped in a teacher education center. *International Journal for the Education of the Blind,* 1962, **11,** 105–112.

American Foundation for the Blind. *A teacher education program for those who serve blind children and youth.* New York: Author, 1961.

American Foundation for the Blind. *Training facilities for the preparation of teachers of blind children in the United States.* New York: Author, 1953.

Best, H. *Blindness and the blind in the United States.* New York: Macmillan, 1934.

Council for Exceptional Children. *Professional standards for personnel in the education of exceptional children.* Washington, D.C.: Author, 1966.

Cruickshank, W. M., & Johnson, G. O. (Eds.). *Education of exceptional children and youth.* Englewood Cliffs, N. J.: Prentice-Hall, 1967.

Dunn, L. M. New directions in teacher education and certification. *Proceedings of the 45th Meeting of the American Association of Instructors of the Blind,* 1960. Pp. 14–17.

Hathaway, W. *Education and health of the partially seeing child* (4th ed.). New York: Columbia University Press, 1959.

Hollingworth, L. S. *The psychology of subnormal children.* New York: Macmillan, 1923.

Jones, J. W. The professional preparation of educators of visually handicapped children before and after the start of Federal grants. *International Journal for the Education of the Blind,* 1966, **16,** 16–18

Mackie, R. P. *Professional preparation for teachers of exceptional children: An overview.* Washington, D. C.: Government Printing Office, 1960.

Mackie, R. P., & Cohoe, E. *Teachers of children who are partially seeing.* Washington, D.C.: Government Printing Office, 1956.

Mackie, R. P., & Dunn, L. M. *College and university programs for the preparation of teachers of exceptional children.* Washington, D.C.: Government Printing Office, 1954.

Mackie, R. P., & Dunn, L. M. *Teachers of children who are blind.* Washington, D.C.: Government Printing Office, 1955.

National Education Association. *Teacher education and professional standards: A position paper.* Washington, D.C.: Author, 1963.

Ryan, M. M. United States government sponsored programs to train personnel in the rehabilitation of the blind. *Blindness 1965.* Washington, D.C.: American Association of Workers for the Blind. Pp. 130–138.

Recommended Readings

GENERAL*

Abel, G. L. (Ed.). *Concerning the education of blind children.* New York: American Foundation for the Blind, 1959.

American Foundation for the Blind. *Itinerant teaching service for blind children.* New York: Author, 1957.

American Foundation for the Blind. *The Pinebrook report. National work session on the education of the blind with the sighted.* New York: Author, 1954.

Bauman, M. K., & Yoder, N. M. *Adjustment to blindness—Re-viewed.* Springfield, Ill.: Charles C Thomas, 1966.

Bledsoe, C. W. The family of residential schools. *Blindness 1971.* Washington, D.C.: American Association of Workers for the Blind. Pp. 19–73.

Burlingham, D. Some notes on the development of the blind. *The Psychoanalytic Study of the Child,* 1961, **16,** 121–145.

Burlingham, D. Some problems of ego development in blind children. *The Psychoanalytic Study of the Child,* 1965, **20,** 194–208.

*Titles included were recommended by several chapter authors and are not repeated in the chapter listings.

Chevigny, H., & Braverman, S. *The adjustment of the blind.* New Haven: Yale University Press, 1950.

Cholden, L. S. *A psychiatrist works with blindness.* New York: American Foundation for the Blind, 1958.

Cowen, E. L., Underberg, R. P., Verillo, R. T., & Benham, F. G. *Adjustment to visual disability in adolescence.* New York: American Foundation for the Blind, 1961.

Cutsforth, T. D. *The blind in school and society.* New York: American Foundation for the Blind, 1951.

Farrell, G. *The story of blindness.* Cambridge, Mass.: Harvard University Press, 1956.

Fraiberg, S., & Freedman, D. A. Studies in the ego development of the congenitally blind child. *The Psychoanalytic Study of the Child,* 1964, **19,** 113–169.

Hathaway, W. *Education and health of the partially seeing child* (4th ed.). New York: Columbia University Press, 1959.

Hayes, S. P. *Contributions to a psychology of blindness.* New York: American Foundation for the Blind, 1941.

Lowenfeld, B. *Our blind children* (3rd ed.). Springfield, Ill.: Charles C Thomas, 1971.

Lowenfeld, B. Psychological problems of children with impaired vision. In W. M. Cruickshank (Ed.), *Psychology of exceptional children and youth* (3rd ed.). Englewood Cliffs, N. J.: Prentice-Hall, 1971. Pp. 211–307.

Lowenfeld, V. *Creative and mental growth* (3rd ed.). New York: Macmillan, 1957.

Norris, M., Spaulding, P. J., & Brodie, F. H. *Blindness in children.* Chicago: University of Chicago Press, 1957.

Scholl, G. T. *The principal works with the visually impaired.* Washington, D.C.: The Council for Exceptional Children, NEA, 1968.

Wright, B. A. *Physical disability—A psychological approach.* New York: Harper, 1960.

Zahl, P. A. (Ed.). *Blindness.* Princeton: Princeton University Press, 1950.

For current information about agencies and publications consult the latest editions of

Directory of agencies serving the visually handicapped in the United States. New York: American Foundation for the Blind.

Sources of reading materials for the visually handicapped. New York: American Foundation for the Blind.

I. History of the Education of Visually Handicapped Children.

Frampton, M. E., & Kerney, E. Appendix: History of the day-school movement. In *The residential school.* New York: New York Institute for the Education of the Blind, 1953. Pp. 97–149.

French, R. S. *From Homer to Helen Keller.* New York: American Foundation for the Blind, 1932.

Irwin, R. B. *As I saw it.* New York: American Foundation for the Blind, 1955.

Lowenfeld, B. Integration—The challenge of our time. In J. F. Magary, L. F. Buscaglia, & B. Light (Eds.), *Sixth annual distinguished lecture series in special education and rehabilitation.* Los Angeles: School of Education, University of Southern California, 1968. Pp. 12–23.

Roblin, J. *Louis Braille.* London: Royal National Institute for the Blind, n.d.

Ross, I. *Journey into light.* New York: Appleton, 1951.

II. Psychological Considerations

Ashcroft, S. C. Blind and partially seeing children. In L. M. Dunn (Ed.), *Exceptional children in the schools.* New York: Holt, 1963. Pp. 413–461.

Bateman, B. D. Visually handicapped children. In N. G. Haring & R. L. Schiefelbusch (Eds.), *Methods in special education.* New York: McGraw-Hill, 1967. Pp. 257–301.

Gowman, A. G. *The war blind in American social structure.* New York: American Foundation for the Blind, 1957.

Kirk, S. A. *Educating exceptional children.* Boston: Houghton Mifflin, 1962.

Lowenfeld, B. Psychological foundation of special methods in teaching blind children. In P. A. Zahl (Ed.), *Blindness.* Princeton: Princeton University Press, 1950. Pp. 89–108.

Patz, A., & Hoover, R. E. *Protection of vision in children.* Springfield, Ill.: Charles C Thomas, 1969.

Raskin, N. J. Visual disability. In J. F. Garrett & E. S. Levine (Eds.), *Psychological practices with the physically disabled.* New York: Columbia University Press, 1962. Pp. 341–375.

Scholl, G. T. The education of children with visual impairments. In W. M. Cruickshank & G. O. Johnson (Eds.), *Education of exceptional children and youth* (2nd ed.). Englewood Cliffs, N. J.: Prentice-Hall, 1967. Pp. 287–342.

III. Understanding and Meeting Developmental Needs

Burlingham, D. Hearing and its role in the development of the blind. *The Psychoanalytic Study of the Child,* 1964, **19,** 95–122.

Bloom, B. S. *Stability and change in human characteristics.* New York: Wiley, 1964.

Flavell, J. H. *The developmental psychology of Jean Piaget.* New York: Van Nostrand, 1963.

Fraiberg, S., Smith, M., & Adelson, E. An educational program for blind infants. *Journal of Special Education,* 1969, **3,** 121–139.

Ginsburg, H., & Opper, S. *Piaget's theory of intellectual development.* Englewood Cliffs, N. J.: Prentice-Hall, 1969.

Harley, R. K. *Verbalism among blind children.* New York: American Foundation for the Blind, 1963.

Ilg, F. L., & Ames, L. B. *Child behavior.* New York: Harper, 1955.

Josephson, E. *The social life of blind people.* New York: American Foundation for the Blind, 1968.

Kagan, J., & Moss, H. A. *Birth to maturity.* New York: Wiley, 1962.

Maier, H. W. *Three theories of child development.* New York: Harper, 1965.

Scott, R. A. *The making of blind men.* New York: Russell Sage Foundation, 1969.

Wylie, R. C. *The self-concept.* Lincoln, Nebr.: University of Nebraska Press, 1961.

IV. Psychological and Educational Assessment

Bauman, M. K. *Adjustment to blindness: A study as reported by the committee to study adjustment to blindness.* Harrisburg, Pa.: Pennsylvania State Council for the Blind, 1954.

Bauman, M. K., Gruber, A., Jones, W. R., Palacios, M. H., & Teare, R. J. *Correlates of adjustment to vision loss—A symposium.* Philadelphia, August 1963. Washington, D.C.: American Psychological Association, Dec., 1963.

Bauman, M. K., & Mullen S. C. Performance tests of intelligence for the adult blind: A comparison of three measures. *Blindness 1965.* Washington, D.C.: American Association of Workers for the Blind, 1965. Pp. 75–85.

Dauterman, W. L., Shapiro, B., & Suinn, R. M. Performance tests of intelligence for the blind reviewed. *International Journal for the Education of the Blind,* 1967, **17,** 8–16.

Davis, C. J., & Nolan, C. Y. A comparison of the oral and written methods of administering achievement tests. *International Journal for the Education of the Blind,* 1961, **10,** 80–82.

Dean, S. I. Some experimental findings about blind adjustments. *New Outlook for the Blind,* 1958, **52,** 182–184.

Lebo, D., & Bruce, R. S. Projective methods recommended for use with the blind. *Journal of Psychology,* 1960, **50,** 15–38.

V. Utilization of Sensory-Perceptual Abilities

Anderson, R. P. Physiologic considerations in learning: The tactual mode. In J. Hellmuth (Ed.), *Learning disorders,* Vol. II. Seattle: Special Child Publications, 1966. Pp. 97–112.

Barraga, N. Learning efficiency in low vision. *Journal of the American Optometric Association,* 1969, **40,** 807–810.

Bliss, J. C. *Tactual perception of visual information.* Menlo Park, Calif.: Stanford Research Institute, 1962.

Brain, R. Some reflections on brain and mind. In P. Tibbets (Ed.), *Perception.* Chicago: Quadrangle Books, 1969. Pp. 19–48.

Brod, N. Visual development and reading. *American Journal of Optometry,* 1969, **46,** 99–102.

Cohen, J. Effects of blindness on children's development. *Children,* 1966, **13,** 23–27.

Epstein, W. *Varieties of perceptual learning.* New York: McGraw-Hill, 1967.

Fields, J. E. Sensory training for blind persons. *New Outlook for the Blind,* 1964, **58,** 2–9.

Gibson, E. J. *Principles of perceptual learning and development.* New York: Appleton, 1969.

Goldish, L. H. *Teaching aids for the visually handicapped.* Boston: Perkins School for the Blind, 1968.

Gregory, R. L. *Eye and brain—The psychology of seeing.* New York: McGraw-Hill, 1966.

Lowenstein, O. *The senses.* Baltimore: Penguin Books, 1966.

Schiff, W., Kaufer, L., & Mosak, S. Informative tactile stimuli in the perception of direction. *Research Bulletin No. 14.* New York: American Foundation for the Blind, 1967. Pp. 65–94.

Schultz, D. T. *Sensory restruction—effects on behavior.* New York: Academic Press, 1965.

Smith, W. O. The visual system in reading and learning disabilities. *Journal of School Health,* 1969, **39,** 144–150.

Tibbets, P. *Perception.* Chicago: Quadrangle Books, 1969.

Vernon, M. D. *Experiments in visual perception.* Baltimore: Penguin Books, 1966.

Weiner, L. H. The performance of good and poor braille readers on certain tests involving tactual perception. *International Journal for the Education of the Blind,* 1965, **12,** 72–77.

Wiedel, J. W., & Groves, P. A. Designing and producing tactual maps for the visually handicapped. *New Outlook for the Blind,* 1969, **63,** 197–201.

Worchel, P. Space perception and orientation in the blind. *Psychological Monographs,* 1951, **65,** 1–27.

VI. Educational Programs

Abel, G. L. The blind adolescent and his needs. *Exceptional Children,* 1961, **27,** 309–310; 325–334.

Ashcroft, S. C. Blind and partially seeing children. In L. Dunn (Ed.), *Exceptional children in the schools.* New York: Holt, 1963. Pp. 413–461.

Bertram, F. M. The education of partially seeing children. In W. M. Cruickshank (Ed.), *Education of exceptional children and youth.* Englewood Cliffs, N. J.: Prentice-Hall, 1958.

Best, J. P. The need for the residential school. *Outlook for the Blind,* 1963, **57,** 127–130.

Cruickshank, W. M., & Trippe, M. J. *Services to blind children in New York state.* Syracuse: N. Y.: Syracuse University Press, 1959.

Johnson, Y. *A blind child becomes a member of your class.* New York: American Foundation for the Blind, 1961.

Jones, J. W. *The visually handicapped child at home and school.* Washington, D.C.: Department of Health, Education, & Welfare, U. S. Office of Education, 1969.

Kapela, E. L. Junior high readiness and the blind child. *Outlook for the Blind,* 1971, **65,** 12–17.

Moor, P. M. *A blind child, too, can go to nursery school.* New York: American Foundation for the Blind, 1952.

Pelone, A. J. *Helping the visually handicapped child in a regular class.* New York: Teachers College, Columbia University, 1957.

Scholl, G. T. The education of children with visual impairments. In W. M. Cruickshank & G. O. Johnson (Eds.), *Education of exceptional children.* Englewood Cliffs, N.J.: Prentice-Hall, 1967. Pp. 287–342.

VII. Communication Skills

Abel, G. L. The education of blind children. In W. M. Cruickshank & G. O. Johnson (Eds.), *Education of exceptional children and youth.* Englewood Cliffs, N.J.: Prentice-Hall, 1958. Pp. 295–334.

American Foundation for the Blind. *Research Bulletin No. 2.* New York: Division of Research & Statistics, 1962.

American Foundation for the Blind. *Report of proceedings of conference on research needs in braille.* New York: Author, 1961.

Ashcroft, S. C. Blind and partially seeing children. In L. M. Dunn (Ed.), *Exceptional children in the schools.* New York: Holt, 1963. Pp. 413–453.

Ashcroft, S. C., & Henderson, F. *Programmed instruction in braille.* Pittsburgh: Stanwix House, 1963.

Barraga, N. C. Mode of reading for low-vision students. *International Journal for the Education of the Blind,* 1963, **12,** 103–107.

Bateman, B. D. Visually handicapped children. In N. G. Haring & R. L. Schiefelbusch (Eds.), *Methods in special education.* New York: McGraw-Hill, 1967. Pp. 257–301.

Burklen, K. *Touch reading for the blind.* New York: American Foundation for the Blind, 1932.

Eakin, W. M., & McFarland, T. L. *Type, printing, and the partially seeing child.* Pittsburgh: Stanwix House, 1960.

Goldish, L. H. *Braille in the United States: Its production, distribution, and use.* New York: American Foundation for the Blind, 1967.

Jones, J. W. *Blind children: Degree of vision, mode of reading.* U.S. Department of Health, Education, & Welfare; Office of Education. Washington, D.C.: U.S. Government Printing Office, 1961.

Kenmore, J. R. Enrichment of the primary reading program in the resource room. *Outlook for the Blind,* 1957, **51,** 57–64.

Lowenfeld, B. Every teacher a teacher of reading. *Outlook for the Blind,* 1942, **36,** 104–106.

Lowenfeld, B., Abel, G. L., & Hatlen, P. H. *Blind children learn to read.* Springfield, Ill.: Charles C Thomas, 1969.

Meyers, E., Ethington, D., & Ashcroft, S. C. Readability of braille as a function of three spacing variables. *Journal of Applied Psychology,* 1958, **42,** 163–165.

Nolan, C. Y. Readability of large type: A study of type sizes and type styles. *International Journal for the Education of the Blind,* 1959, **9,** 41–44.

Nolan, C. Y. A 1966 reappraisal of the relationship between visual acuity and mode of reading for blind children. *Outlook for the Blind,* 1967, **61,** 255–261.

Nolan, C. Y., & Kederis, C. J. *Perceptual factors in braille word recognition.* New York: American Foundation for the Blind, 1969.

Roblin, J. *The reading fingers—Life of Louis Braille.* New York: American Foundation for the Blind, 1955.

VIII. Special Subject Adjustments and Skills

Bailey, J. L. Meaningful maps for the blind and seeing. *New Outlook for the Blind,* 1956, 50, 77–83.

Buell, C. E. *Recreation for the blind.* New York: American Foundation for the Blind, 1951.

Buell, C. E. *Physical education for blind children.* Springfield, Ill.: Charles C Thomas, 1966.

Carr, E. R. *The social studies.* New York: The Center for Applied Research, 1965.

Childers, J. W. *Foreign language teaching.* New York: The Center for Applied Research, 1964.

Coleman, M. E. *Primary arithmetic for the blind: A guide to the teaching of arithmetic in grades kindergarten–grade two.* Phiiadelphia: Overbrook School for the Blind, 1963.

Dorward, B., & Barraga, N. *Teaching aids for blind and visually limited children.* New York: American Foundation for the Blind, 1968.

Fulker, W. H., & Fulker, M. *Techniques with tangibles.* Springfield, Ill.: Charles C Thomas, 1968.

Howe Memorial Press. *List of geographical maps.* Watertown, Mass.: Author, undated.

Langan, P. J. *Handbook for school teachers of the blind.* Bristol, England: College of Teachers of the Blind, 1957.

Library of Congress. *Magazines: Braille and recorded.* Washington, D.C.: Division for the Blind and Physically Handicapped, 1968.

Neagley, R. L., & Evans, N. D. *Handbook for effective curriculum development.* Englewood Cliffs, N.J.: Prentice-Hall, 1967.

Nemeth, A. Teaching meaningful mathematics to blind and partially sighted children. *New Outlook for the Blind,* 1959, 53, 381–321.

Nolan, C. Y. Research in teaching mathematics to blind children. *International Journal for the Education of the Blind,* 1964, 13, 97–100.

Nolan, C. Y., & Morris, J. E. The Japanese abacus as a computational aid for blind children. *Exceptional Children,* 1964, 31, 15–17.

Ritter, C. G. *Hobbies of blind adults.* New York: American Foundation for the Blind, 1953.

Scouting for the visually handicapped. New Brunswick, N.J.: Boy Scouts of America, 1968.

Sherman, J. C. Needs and resources in maps. *New Outlook for the Blind,* 1965, 59, 130–134.

Syrocki, B. J. *Science activities for the elementary grades.* W. Nyack, N.Y.: Parker Publishing, 1968.

Wiedel, J. W. Tactual maps for the visually handicapped: Some developmental problems. *New Outlook for the Blind,* 1969, 63, 80–88.

IX. Life Adjustment

Alonso, L. The educator's vital role in mobility and orientation. *New Outlook for the Blind,* 1965, **59**, 249–251.

Ball, M. J. Mobility in perspective. *Blindness 1964.* Washington, D.C.: American Association of Workers for the Blind. Pp. 107–141.

Bindt, J. *A handbook for the blind.* New York: Macmillan, 1952.

Bledsoe, C. W. For parents looking ahead to future mobility needs of their blind children. *International Journal for the Education of the Blind,* 1963, **13**, 13–15.

Bluhm, D. *Teaching the retarded visually handicapped.* Philadelphia: W. B. Saunders, 1968.

Caring for the visually impaired older person. Minneapolis: Minneapolis Society for the Blind, 1970.

Carroll, T. J. *Blindness: What it is, what it does, and how to live with it.* Boston: Little, Brown, 1961.

Curriculum guide, pre-cane mobility and orientation skills for the blind. Lansing: Michigan School for the Blind, undated.

Dog guides and blind children—a joint statement. *New Outlook for the Blind,* 1963, **57**, 228–229.

Finestone, S., Lukoff, I. F., & Whiteman, M. *Aspects of the travel adjustment of blind persons.* New York: American Foundation for the Blind, 1960.

Griffin, D. R. *Echoes of bats and men.* Garden City, N. Y.: Doubleday, 1959.

Hoover, R. E. The cane as a travel aid. In P. A. Zahl (Ed.), *Blindness.* Princeton: Princeton University Press, 1950. Pp. 353–365.

Kenmore, J. R. Some aspects of mobility instruction for blind children. *45th Biennial Convention of American Association of Instructors for the Blind,* 1960. Pp. 26–32.

Mobility and orientation—A symposium. *New Outlook for the Blind,* 1960, **54**, 77–94.

Seeing Eye, Inc. *If blindness occurs.* Morristown, N.J.: Author, 1964.

Western Michigan University, School of Graduate Studies. *Homemaking manual: A reference manual for home teachers working with the adult blind.* Kalamazoo, Mich.: Community Services for the Visually Handicapped, Illinois Department of Children and Family Services, 1966.

Whitstock, R. H. A dog guide user speaks on mobility. *New Outlook for the Blind.* 1962, **56**, 19–23.

X. Visually Handicapped Children with Additional Problems

Abel, G. L., Birkholz, M., & Holm, R. (Eds.). *The counseling process and the teacher of children with multiple handicaps.* A summer institute report. San Francisco: San Francisco State College, 1968.

Ashcroft, S. C. Delineating the possible for the multi-handicapped child with visual impairment. *International Journal for the Education of the Blind,* 1966, **16**, 52–55.

Cooper, L. The child with rubella syndrome. *New Outlook for the Blind,* 1969, **63,** 290–298.

Cruickshank, W. M. The multiple-handicapped child and courageous action. *International Journal for the Education of the Blind,* 1964, **14,** 65–75.

Elonen, A. S., & Polzien, M. Experimental program for deviant blind children. *New Outlook for the Blind,* 1965, **59,** 122–126.

Elonen, A. S., & Zwarensteyn, S. B. Appraisal of developmental lag in certain blind children. *Journal of Pediatrics,* 1964, **65,** 599–610.

Elonen, A. S., Polzien, M., & Zwarensteyn, S. B. The "uncommitted" blind child: Results of intensive training of children formerly committed to institutions for the retarded. *Exceptional Children,* 1967, **33,** 301–306.

Graham, M. D. *Multiply-impaired blind children: A national problem.* New York: American Foundation for the Blind, 1968.

Gruber, K. F., & Moor, P. M. (Eds.). *No place to go.* New York: American Foundation for the Blind, 1963.

Lowenfeld, B. Multihandicapped blind and deaf–blind children in California. *Research Bulletin No. 19.* New York: American Foundation for the Blind, 1969. Pp. 1–72.

Robbins, N. *Educational beginnings with deaf–blind children.* Watertown, Mass.: Perkins School for the Blind, 1960.

Robbins, N., & Stenquist, G. *The Deaf–blind rubella child.* Watertown, Mass.: Perkins School for the Blind, 1967.

Wagner, E. M. Maternal rubella: A general orientation to the disease. *New Outlook for the Blind,* 1967, **61,** 95–105.

Winn, R. J., Jr. Two-year progress analysis of project for multi-handicapped visually-impaired children at the Texas School for the Blind. *International Journal for the Education of the Blind,* 1968, **18,** 99–107.

Wolf, J. M. *The blind child with concomitant disabilities.* New York: American Foundation for the Blind, 1967.

XI. Preparation of Teachers

Abel, G. L. Teacher training: Whence and wither bound? *Blindness 1967.* Washington, D.C.: American Association of Workers for the Blind. Pp. 105–125.

American Foundation for the Blind. *A teacher education program for those who serve blind children and youth.* New York: Author, 1961.

Bowers, R. A. Some considerations for future teacher preparation. *New Outlook for the Blind,* 1963, **10,** 384–388.

Council for Exceptional Children. *Professional standards for personnel in the education of exceptional children.* Washington, D.C.: Author, 1966.

Dunn, L. M. Teachers of exceptional children. *Education,* 1957, **77,** 483–490.

Heisler, W. T. Teacher training within a residential school program. *International Journal for the Education of the Blind,* 1962, **11,** 112–116.

Kenmore, J. R. Educating teachers for blind children. *New Outlook for the Blind,* 1960, **54,** 165–168.

Mackie, R. P. *Professional preparation for teachers of exceptional children: An overview.* Washington, D.C.: Government Printing Office, 1960.

Mackie, R. P., & Cohoe, E. *Teachers of children who are partially seeing.* Washington, D.C.: Government Printing Office, 1956.

Mackie, R. P., & Dunn, L. M. *Teachers of children who are blind.* Washington, D.C.: Government Printing Office, 1955.

National Education Association. *Teacher education and professional standards: A position paper.* Washington, D.C.: Author, 1963.

National Society for Crippled Children and Adults. *Opportunities for the preparation of teachers of exceptional children.* Chicago: Author, 1949.

National Society for the Prevention of Blindness. *Recommended basic course for preparation of teachers of partially seeing children.* Publication P304. New York: Author, 1956.

Schwartz, L. An integrated teacher education program for special education —A new approach. *Exceptional Children,* 1967, **33,** 411–418.

Schwartz, L. Preparation of the clinical teacher for special education: 1866– 1966. *Exceptional Children,* 1967, **34,** 117–124.

Author Index

Numbers in italics refer to the pages on which the complete references are listed.

A

Abel, G. L., 49, *57*, 159, 162, 170, 173, 174, *182, 183,* 192, 198, 203, 213, *218,* 320, *338,* 345, *356*
Adamshick, D.R., 146, *153*
Adelson, E., 49, *59,* 66, *91*
Allport, F., 121, *151*
Alonso, L., 280, *316*
Ames, L. B., 65, 66, 67, *91*
Amster, C. H., 203, 208, *218*
Anthony, G. H., 265, *273*
Arnheim, R., 147, *151*
Ashcroft, S. C., 130, 131, 132, *151,* 159, *182,* 198, *218,* 330, *338*
Atkinson, M. M., 222, *276*
Auerbach, H., 230, 273
Austin, G. A., 147, *151*
Axelrod, S., 36, *57,* 138, *151*

B

Ball, M. J., 281, *316*
Barg, C. F., 42, *60*
Barker, R. B., 53, 55, *57*
Barraga, N. C., 39, *57,* 125, 129, 130, 131, 132, 140, 150, *151,* 159, *182, 183,* 199, *218,* 247, 262, *273*
Bartley, S. H., 120, 124, *151*
Bateman, B., 48, *57,* 118, 131, 148, *151,* 175, *183,* 201, 206, *218*

Bauman, M. K., 53, *57,* 88, *92,* 99, 110, *115*
Belenky, R., 271, *273*
Belton, J. A., 323, 328, *339*
Benham, F. G., 51, 53, 55, *58,* 72, *91, 183*
Bereiter, C., 63, *92*
Best, H., 343, *356*
Bevans, J. E., 257, *273*
Bier, N., 131, *151*
Bindt, J., 247, 262, *273,* 304, *316*
Birch, J. W., 133, *151,* 158, 162, 172, 175, 176, *184*
Birnbaum, J., 36, *60,* 148, 149, *154*
Bixler, R. H., 203, 208, *218*
Blank, H. R., 32, 36, 47, *57*
Bledsoe, C. W., 17, *25*
Bloom, B. S., 64, 79, *91*
Bobgrove, P. H., 55, *58*
Boldt, W., 149, *151,* 253, *273*
Borgersen, R., 253, *273*
Bott, J. E., 164, *184*
Bourgeault, S. E., 213, *218*
Brazziel, W. F., 63, *92*
Bruce, R. E., 230, 234, *276*
Bruner, J. S., 125, 147, 148, *151*
Bryan, C. A., 253, *274*
Buddenbrock, W. Van., 118, *151*
Buell, C. E., 270, 271, *274*
Buktenica, N. A., 122, 123, 124, *151*

369

Subject Index

A

Abacus, 231
Adolescent blind
  adjustment of, 53
  self-concept, 53–54, 75–76
  socialization, 73
  sex role, learning of, 78, 87–88
  specific problems, 48–49
  struggle for independence, 78
Adolescent Emotional Factors Inventory
  (AEFI), 53, 110
Agencies for the blind, 3
  and the multihandicapped, 333–334
Aids and appliances
  adapted cooking tools, 264
  American Thermoform Duplicator, 233,
    237–238
  audio, 260–261
  cube slate, 230
  electric braille typewriter, 217
  electronic mobility devices, 280, 301–302
  glasses, 32, 134
  Hoover cane, 3–4
  Laser cane, 302
  magnification and projection devices, 133–
    135
  measurement instruments, 249
  microfiche viewer, 134
  overhead projector, 134–135
  Perkins Brailler, 12, 212, 230, 233

Aids and appliances *(continued)*
  Russell Travelpath Sounder, 302
  Sewell Raised Line Drawing Board, 233, 238
  slate and stylus, 12, 190, 212–213
  talking book machine, 195, 216
  Taylor Arithmetic Type Slate, 231
  telescopic lenses, 133–134
  televiewer projectors, 134
  Thermoform, 216
  travel device, 190
  Ultrasonic Touch or Kay Device, 302
  visual, 261
Aids and Appliances, 264
Allen, Edward E., 16–17, 343
Amblyopia, 129
American Association of Instructors for the
  Blind, 13, 347–348
American Association of Workers for the
  Blind, 281
American Braille, 10, 12
American Foundation for the Blind, 12, 22,
  114, 249, 345–348
  "Aids and Appliances," 264
  *Sources of Reading Material for the Visually
    Handicapped,* 13, 217, 244, 247
American Heritage, 246
American Medical Association, Section on
  Ophthalmology, 30
American Optometric Association, 134
American Printing House for the Blind, 12–13,